GENERATIONS

GENERATIONS

Academic Feminists in Dialogue

Devoney Looser and E. Ann Kaplan, editors

 University of Minnesota Press
Minneapolis
London

Published by the University of Minnesota Press
111 Third Avenue South, Suite 290
Minneapolis, MN 55401-2520

http://www.upress.umn.edu

Printed in the United States of America on acid-free paper

Library of Congress Cataloging-in-Publication Data

Generations : academic feminists in dialogue / Devoney Looser and E.
   Ann Kaplan, editors.
       p.   cm.
   Comprised of original essays presented at various conferences held
between 1993 and 1996.
   Includes index.
   ISBN 0-8166-2898-X (alk. paper). — ISBN 0-8166-2899-8 (alk.
paper)
   1. Feminism and education — United States.   2. Feminist theory —
United States.   3. Women college teachers — United States — Social
conditions.   4. Women college students — United States — Social
conditions.   5. Universities and colleges — United States —
Sociological aspects.   I. Looser, Devoney, 1967–   .   II. Kaplan,
E. Ann.
   LC197.G446   1997
   305.42 — dc21   97-20528

The University of Minnesota is an equal-opportunity educator and employer.

Contents

Contents

Preface

With the widespread use of the term *third wave,* anxiety has been registered about the current moment in feminism, who is included in it, and what it espouses. That those who identify themselves as "second wave" remain active in feminist circles hasn't made matters any clearer. Regardless of which label (if any) one embraces, it is apparent that feminist conflicts have been presented in generational terms inside and outside the academy. Most are quite familiar with the portraits that have been drawn of "young" and "old" feminists, although few of us seem to recognize ourselves in the caricatures. Younger feminists are sometimes said to be undutiful daughters, careerists, and theorists who are not political enough—not sufficiently grateful to the past generation for fighting the battles that made today's lives possible. Older feminists are often painted as bad mothers who long to see themselves in their offspring, who resent deviations from their second-wave plan, and who can't properly wield the power they have garnered. How are we to sort through all of these so-called conflicts, losses, and faults?

It hardly needs to be said that feminists in the academy are now having a difficult time, not just because of issues imposed from without in the form of backlash or budget cuts, but because of our own political differences, some of which have been attributed to age or generation. There are those among our ranks who see generational distinctions as false divisions. We suspect that for others, however, generational explanations have become more convincing and important. Regardless of one's take on these issues, the anxieties associated with feminist generations have been articulated widely. Despite wide articulation, we suspect that a majority of the discussions about feminisms and generations have been occurring intragenerationally—with one's academic peers—and perhaps behind closed doors. In order to open these doors, this collection engages in head-on cross-generational dialogue, within and across essays.

Some conversations on feminisms and generations have been staged public ones. We put together a panel on feminisms and generations at the Modern Language Association convention in 1993, sparking an interest that grew into this book. The mid-'90s have seen even more activity on this topic. The 1995 National Women's Studies Association conference featured Generations of Feminism as an organizing theme. Also that year, the City University of New York Graduate School hosted the conference Gender and Generations: Postmodernism and Its Discontents. A conference entirely devoted to feminist generations was held at Bowling Green State University in February 1996. Later that spring, two more conferences—the Fifth Annual Women's Studies Conference at Southern Connecticut State University and the University of Wisconsin, Milwaukee's Conference on Women and Aging: Bodies, Cultures, Generations—also took feminist generations as conference themes. A great deal of professional activity and interest continues to center on this topic; some of the papers given at these conferences have developed into the essays included in the following pages.

We suspect that many more important conversations on feminisms and generations have happened (and are happening) as innuendo, hearsay, and gossip. This book seeks to bring those conversations to the fore and to explore the terms *feminism* and *generation* in order to further conversation about these stereotypes and our supposed feminist divisions and impasses. *Generations: Academic Feminists in Dialogue* is more than simply a critical conversation. Comprising original essays from academic women at varying professional stages (from established scholar to beginning assistant professor to doctoral student), this book is also an enactment of feminist generations. In the spirit of dialogue, the essays collected here question the categories of old, middle-aged, and young in order to discuss feminisms—"proto," "post," and "present." We hope that this collection will productively engage how and why perceived feminist generational divisions circulate, what generational explanations reveal, occlude, or perpetuate, and what it might mean to speak to—if not "talk through"—our supposed differences.

Each of us has incurred personal and intellectual debts to people whom we'd like to thank.

Devoney Looser: I would like to begin by thanking Ann Kaplan for her enthusiasm in moving forward with this project, proposed to her while I was one of her graduate students. Ann's work on this book (and these issues in general) demonstrates her commitment to younger feminists.

Support from and conversations with many others made this project possible, including Nancy Armstrong, Paula Backscheider, Ann Bomberger, Antoinette Burton, Helen Cooper, Drucilla Cornell, Madelyn DeGaetano, Margaret Ezell, Pamela Gilbert, Janet Gray, Myrna Handley, Amy Hanson, Darlene Hantzis, Mike Hill, Catherine Ingrassia, Jake Jakaitis, Pamela Moore, Adrienne Munich, Ruth Perry, Sandy Redfield, Patti Sakurai, Clifford Siskin, Ann Snitow, Sandy Sprows, Susan Squier, Mary Sullivan, Alison Sulloway, Jan Thaddeus, Jeannie Thomas, Dutch Toenjes, Jeff Williams, and Rose Zimbardo. A special thanks to the graduate students at Indiana State University in my spring 1995 literary theory seminar and to those with whom I've had the privilege to work on feminist issues.

Thanks must also go to the women of my family—particularly my mother, Sharon Looser, and my grandmother, Virginia Sarslow, as well as Susan and Tiffany Bilotta and Colette, Kerry, and Dana Relph—for their personal and professional support within and across familial (if not feminist) generations.

E. Ann Kaplan: I want to thank Devoney, first, for approaching me about this project, second, for following through, pushing me, organizing the MLA session that provided the basis for our volume, and finally, for all the hard work she has put in on the volume. Her tough questions in our dialogue stimulated me to rethink my positions on feminism and the academy and to appreciate positions of younger women within and outside the academy. I have been challenged to situate myself therein to great benefit.

I first delivered my essay in this book at a conference organized by Diane Elam and Robyn Wiegman in 1995, in conjunction with their useful coedited volume *Feminism beside Itself*. Thanks to Diane, Robyn, and the conference participants for their stimulation regarding rethinking feminism in the 1990s.

I want to thank Marianne De Koven for helpful comments on early drafts of the manuscript and for inviting me to present the paper at the Institute for Research on Women at Rutgers University. Thanks also to the Humanities Institute at Stony Brook staff for their help with research for the paper and this volume.

Finally, both of us would like to thank Paula Haines, one of the Humanities Institute graduate assistants in 1995–1996, for her input on the collection's title; the anonymous readers of the manuscript; and Biodun Iginla, Robin Moir, Elizabeth Knoll Stomberg, and Lisa Freeman, our editors and their assistants at the University of Minnesota Press, for their expert assistance. This collection would not have made it to press in its present form but for the generous guidance that Freeman gave us through a more difficult than usual editorial process. We hope that the conflicts we encountered and worked through among ourselves and among our contributors as we put together this collection will prove worth the struggle.

Introduction 1: An Exchange

E. Ann Kaplan and Devoney Looser

From: ejlooser@root.indstate.edu
To: eakaplan@ccmail.sunysb.edu
Subject: introduction 7/31/95

Ann—

I'm excited about refining our ideas for a jointly authored introduction to *Generations: Academic Feminists in Dialogue* via e-mail. It's made me think of the collaborative feminist projects of the second wave that have influenced me and therefore this process. Do you remember the descriptions that the *Women's Ways of Knowing* authors gave of their collaborative process? That book was written in stolen pajama party weekends, which, I must admit, makes me wince a little; it's so cute. E-mail has changed collaborative projects, feminist and otherwise, in such important ways.

In fact, in all of the thinking about feminist generations that you and I have done over the past several years, together and separately, this is the first we've discussed the Internet as a difference for "third-wave" feminisms. Recently, I needed to get in touch with a senior feminist scholar, and in her faxed response she balked at my (snail mail) request for her to contact me via e-mail. She said, "My friends tell me that e-mail will add at least an hour of work to my day, and I just don't have it to spare." I wasn't sure whether I should admire that or not.

I know that some of my life as a feminist—among other academic feminists and nonacademic ones, too—is lived by e-mail. Participating on WMST-L is only the tip of the iceberg. I "sign" petitions on the Internet; I keep in contact with feminist colleagues and friends nationally and internationally; I send work-in-progress to generous readers at the flick of a wrist. Most important, when something upsetting occurs in my day-to-day work life, I know that I can hole myself up in my office and within minutes find a sympathetic "ear" and some advice, without worrying about who is listening outside my office door. This kind of instant connection with other feminists across the globe is certainly new.

I don't want this to turn into a message that only waxes rhapsodic about technology, however. I just wanted to begin by marking technology as it has enabled our cross-generational dialogue.

FROM: EAKAPLAN@ccmail.sunysb.edu
TO: EJLOOSER@root.indstate.edu
Subject: RE: introduction 7/31/95

Devoney: First, let me respond to your comments re e-mail and its generational implications for feminists. I, too, meet many second-wave feminists who don't want to go near e-mail and also cite the time it will take from their already packed lives. I think it's about growing up in a completely different technological environment, and simply finding the awkwardnesses of new computer technologies too much to struggle with. In other words, it doesn't come so naturally to people brought up in the era of typewriters and radio, for the most part! I know my own resistances, but for some reason, as soon as I got a computer in 1981, I was hooked on it.

And e-mail for me has been incredibly important, given my international framework and international scholarly projects. E-mail has made global contacts with feminists a reality: Yaori Taguchi at the Yokohama Women's Center was hired to be the networking person for women in Japan. Despite the great distance, I have been communicating with her for the past two years, and each year she organized my talk through e-mail to about 150 women from all over Japan! She worked via e-mail to contact other women's organizations in Japan to bring this event about. Now she's on her way to the Beijing meeting. Yaori will be chief networking person there, and she hopes to keep me in daily e-mail contact with what's going on at the China meetings.

I do think this opens a new era for American feminisms in linking us through technology to informal as well as formal personalized contact with women in faraway nations. And that some second-wave American feminists are not excited about this is a generational difference, I believe, that we might do more to address and understand.

As I try to say in my own introduction, time passes. We live in time. Those who have lived longer in time are different from those who have not lived so long in time. I know this is kind of a simple way to put it, but I don't know how else to. Generation for me is not about mothers and daughters, about passing on the torch, generativity, or anything (although I do think we should address those kinds of processes as well), but about living in time, accumulating a reservoir of experiences that then have an impact on how one sees the present. Time is another "reading formation" in itself.

My experiences in the 1960s were constitutive of who I am today. And mark me as different from people, like my daughter, who was born as feminism was coming into fruition for my age group (i.e., 1968) and being institutionalized. (By 1971, Rutgers had a women's studies certificate, for instance.) We did move from the streets into the academy because we could not get a footing in a political party that could ever hope to have any power; because we saw the limits of endless marches and demonstrations; and because we wanted to build in an institution we had been trained to be in, namely, the university. This did not mean abandoning activism or other communities, at least at first. But, rather, opening up a space for liaison with communities outside academia. That women's studies has become so professionalized tells more about how institutions work than about my generation's aims.

This rambling makes me think that we should address directly differing perspectives on the word *generation*. What does it evoke for different authors in our volume? Why has it become such a provocative term? What can we learn from Judith Roof, who objects to the implication of the term *generation*? Is the attack on the concept of generation also an attack on the concept of history? And what does that involve theoretically?

For me, *generation* connotes a kind of historical process. I agree that there's a danger of essentializing decades, like the '60s, the '70s, the '80s: that women working in the '60s (one "generation") don't at all share the same beliefs and attitudes, thus calling into doubt the idea of any meaning to a term like *'60s feminists*. Yet the matter of having been in time does apply to everyone coming into adulthood in the '60s.

Do we really want simply to talk about differences among women who call themselves feminists? Should our title be *Feminist Difference*?

One of the differences is feminist views of "generation," of course, and so our project comes in, in that way, albeit somewhat problematized. Were debates about generation first articulated in the university and not elsewhere? I think it's obvious that the university is one site where younger and older women come into close contact through the classroom and through mentoring in graduate school. Differences have emerged in that specific context. What form do such differences take in activist movements, like gay/lesbian organizations? AIDS organizing? What about the feminist difference in the public sphere, with the rightist women's attacks on feminisms, and its generational cast?

Feminists of all ages are obsessed with these differences because they hamper any kind of forward movement. Feminisms are at an impasse because we no longer understand clearly what the projects are, where we need to go next. Or perhaps each feminist community thinks it knows where it has to go or is debating where it wants to go. But there is no agreement among the parts.

Traveling to a nation like Japan makes me realize how much women here have achieved in terms of personal possibilities. Women in much of Asia still confront highly structured, powerful, and resistant patriarchal modes. The men simply do not want to shift or change. They are not even open to serious consideration of giving up any of their power or sharing it. American women are seen, rightly, in a way, as having far more possibilities and freedoms. Asian women are organizing, however, and they are making advances. Perhaps American feminists' debates are so extreme right now because we have achieved so much (relatively) that the stakes have gotten confused.

Must end. Sorry to give you this stream of consciousness. But that's all I am up for right now.

eak

From: ejlooser@root.indstate.edu
To: eakaplan@ccmail.sunysb.edu
Subject: Re: introduction 8/7/95

Ann—

There is so much that is worth addressing in your last message that I'm a bit overwhelmed. I'm not sure where to begin. You get at important issues that I don't feel I've worked through fully. Perhaps I never will feel that way.

I really liked your question, "Is the attack on the concept of generation also an attack on the concept of history?" It seems to me that for Roof a rejection of history-as-process is not the point. It's a certain kind of history—history as reproduction—that is rejected. But do we really want to reject in toto the reproductive metaphor for feminist knowledge? Is the rejection of feminist heritage in this mode always a positive moment?

Today's generational conflicts seem to me to be about what exactly the reproduction of feminist knowledge (and the reproduction of feminists) will look like. How many feminists have come to *expect* political allies in the form of would-be daughters or mothers? How are we failing or distorting each other's mirrors? How many of us seek clones or anticipate spontaneous regeneration? How many of us adhere to a naive expectation of linear history? Do we expect that feminism must have "a" history?

I'm thinking here of something else you wrote—that women's studies has become professionalized tells us "more about how institutions work than about [your] generation's aims." This brings up so much—the much-discussed academic-nonacademic split for one (also articulated as a supposed theory-practice split or a nonpolitical-political divide). This deserves much more space than I'm giving it here.

Your message also made me think about the belief that, as Gloria Steinem put it almost two decades ago, young women are more conservative.[1] Might her essay mark one beginning of second-/third-wave generational conflicts?

So much of what passes for generational conflict, or, as you put it, feminist differences, seems based on what we recognize to be stereotypes; at the same time, we must think these stereotypes contain at least a grain of truth. I suppose it would be worth trying to describe those stereotypes to each other. What are the "bad" stereotypes of a "young" feminist and an "old" feminist? I wonder, Ann, if you and I would have the same stereotypes in mind?

Pick up with this wherever you see fit...It does begin to feel like a jumbled series of thoughts.

Best, Devoney

FROM: EAKAPLAN@ccmail.sunysb.edu
TO: EJLOOSER@root.indstate.edu
Subject: RE: RE: introduction 8/7/95

Devoney: Your responses to my responses finally provoked me to think very personally about what feminism (one *s* deliberately because then there was only one in my mind) meant to me when I was your age, and what it means to me now. This might indirectly get at some of the issues in what you said.

Feminism between 1968 and 1978 was very personally related to my needs: as a single mother, I needed moderately priced day care; as a divorced woman I needed to challenge all kinds of assumptions about male-female sexual and dating traditions; and I was very concerned about abortion issues as someone liable to get pregnant anytime I lapsed care. As a young professor and intellectual, I saw the gap in attention to women's issues in my own fields — literary and film studies — and wanted to open up the academy and scholarship to approaches I wanted to pursue in my scholarship. As a '60s student and activist, I wanted to participate in liberation movements of all kinds, which I did outside the academy.

My situation is very different now. My needs are different. My lifestyle is different (no children at home being a major major difference; happily married being a major major difference; past child-bearing age, a major difference). My feminism(s) (now there are many!) turns to communities and topics not nearly so closely related to my own needs. I am now working on issues having to do with "women" and "nation" in specific contexts and texts; I am interested in non-European women and postcolonialism. Of course, these issues are linked to me personally (all our concerns, political and academic, usually are at bottom), but on different levels from those in my earlier feminist projects. The only similar level I am now pursuing has to do with aging and cosmetic surgery (and these may turn out to be major projects a bit later on). For instance, your generation is concerned about date rape, and about alternate sexualities; the question of abortion is uppermost because you can still bear children. These are concerns I no longer have on a daily basis. Of course, I am going to participate with younger women in fighting for issues that still concern them (especially abortion choice), but it's a different level of engagement. Of course, I am interested in alternate sexualities and freedom of choice there as well, and gay rights and issues of AIDS, but it has to be somewhat at a distance.

The point of all this is to emphasize two things perhaps usually not so openly discussed: first, how constructed our feminist and academic political goals are by larger political contexts and the surrounding discursive national/international, technological economic formations. You mention resources, for instance: I think this has a bearing on differences between your and my generations of feminists and determines a great deal regarding what we see is possible and what's not, in the current regrettable moment of university downsizing. Second, how constructed our feminist passions are by our personal needs, desires, and aims at different times in our lives. The end of socialisms has been underrated as it has affected feminist generations. The larger disinterested part of my feminist projects when I was your age came from a commitment to socialist ideals I had grown up with in England and saw somewhat enacted in Labourite post–World War II England. We've lost that kind of socialist idealism that '60s feminisms could still engage in and that did shape (in some ways, of course, negatively in that the "we" was unconsciously a white middle-class "we") feminism in those days.

Must fly! Sorry to end in a rush, but I just looked at the clock!

eak

From: ejlooser@root.indstate.edu
To: eakaplan@ccmail.sunysb.edu
Subject: Re: introduction 9/14/95

Ann —

Again, you've given me so much to think about, so many directions to go in. I agree that much of what interests us within feminisms has to do with issues that have touched our own lives. Though as you say, it is never only that . . . I have never experienced domestic violence, but I participate in the annual Take Back the Night march here — the only off-campus, staged political demonstration in Terre Haute that I can think of, unless you count the KKK rallies that have been held in the smaller surrounding towns. "Activism" for me more often takes the shape of a daily classroom activity rather than a "demonstration" — though I know some would consider that to be inadequate activism.

If it is true that I am more interested in feminist issues regarding young women because I am "younger" (will my age count as "younger" to most of our readers, I wonder?), then I fear for what will happen to many of the feminists with whom I went to graduate school and those young women who are in my classes. Issues of mentoring are so difficult. They deserve more discussion...The point is that — even now, when feminism has gained an institutional and perhaps a wider cultural, even global, foothold, however precarious — we still need feminists of all ages in order to be heard. We need older women to be not "at a distance," as you put it in a different context, when it comes to political and personal struggles for our well-being and advancement. Perhaps you would argue that older women need the same kind of support for "their" issues from younger women...Perhaps not. I wonder what your perception is of "our" support for "your" issues?

I am thinking of the article by Nancy K. Miller that was published several years ago, titled "Decades."² I keep coming back to it. Not because of any kind of philosophical difference with Miller's work in general...In fact, I'm using her wonderful essay on John Cleland's *Fanny Hill* in my graduate course next month. It's because I recognized in that "Decades" piece some attitudes and feelings that seemed to me to be pervasive among senior feminists, and I found these attitudes unsettling.

Miller talks in that essay about feminism's having reached "middle age" because it is in a moment of self-evaluation. Now, I am certain that feminism is not in its infancy. Few would argue that. But why "middle age"? Feminism may be in its youth; it may be in its old age. Who can tell? Perhaps Miller meant that with women's studies being a part of university structures for more than twenty years, feminism is therefore middle aged. I'm not sure. One thing she did go on to discuss, however, was her own middle age. She lamented the trajectory of feminism (moving out of the "community" of the '70s) and her personal trajectory, asking, "Is there life for a female academic after the feminist plot of tenure and promotion?"

I've never been sure how Miller meant that question to be asked. Is it ironic? Is it supposed to be funny? I can't ever get the tone "right" when I read that section. I'm sure it is in large part because I can't — even jokingly — feel sorry for the plight of the tenured academic feminist. Maybe this is narrow of me. I'm sure that senior feminists have many difficult hurdles in their daily lives, within the institution and without. But I can't help thinking about all of the brilliant feminist graduate students I know who can't find jobs, who end up splitting up with their partners to take across-the-country, part-time teaching positions, and who have a desire to teach and research that academia will not soon be able to accommodate, much less reward.

One exceptional recent feminist Ph.D. I know was just turned down for work in a bridal shop and ended up cleaning houses. I want Miller to talk about her. I want Miller to do all she can to make a place for my friend in the academy. And as I write this, I know that — as much anger and empathy as I have for my friend — there are women who are far, far worse off. I know my friend is not among the truly disenfranchised. So where does that leave us?

Fighting for more places for academic women and feminists can't be our only project, of course. There are surely many, many other ways and many other places to do the work of feminism/s. But then I think about all of the young students in this country and ways that they could be fired up to consider how gender issues impact their lives. There are very few lines of work in which about half of the country's young people parade before you every semester. We need to encourage more of them to grapple with the issues that interest us. We need more young professors — more young feminist professors — in academia. So many universities are reaching a breaking point in terms of being short staffed. I want "the next generation" of college students to have the opportunity to be educated by the first generation of professors who had access to *professional training* in feminism and women's studies.

We junior feminists expect that you senior feminists will help us, in any way you can, to stay in the game, to get tenure-track jobs. But surely there are times when those decisions are out of your control or times when those decisions, if you chose to intervene in their being made, would jeopardize your own jobs. I think, more than anything, what younger feminists need is for older feminists to have time for us, advice for us, and, finally, honesty with us about precisely what you can and can't do to "pass the torch" to us, now or at some time in the future.

Well, I've gone on and on here, and I need to run, too. I'm teaching Mary Hays's *Victim of Prejudice* (1799) in my Women Writers of Great Britain course. This novel has within the past year come back in print. It's exciting to have new resources available to pass on to students.

I hope you're doing well. Be sure to send updates as they come in.

Best, Devoney

FROM: EAKAPLAN@ccmail.sunysb.edu
TO: EJLOOSER@root.indstate.edu
Subject: Re: introduction 9/14/95

Devoney: I think we are finally coming down to the real issues of debate and tension. Your presentation of issues that face young feminists re getting jobs, which of course I know about, is clear, but your description makes it graphic and that's useful. . . . A great deal is about resources and about the way that this problem regarding jobs constitutes the younger generation in a way that we were not, did not have to be, constituted when there were more jobs. As you know (not that I'm getting defensive, I hope!), I do whatever I can for my own students. Maybe not enough . . .

One of the problems for senior women professors is getting pulled and pushed in numerous directions, and needing to prioritize better. I have to give all this much much more thought than I can now. Thanks for prompting so much. We must include these kinds of issues and tensions in the dialogue: I think both younger and older feminists need to hear them . . .

It's FINALLY raining raining raining down here. Too hard to even think about going out! We need it and it feels good . . .

eak

From: ejlooser@root.indstate.edu
To: eakaplan@ccmail.sunysb.edu
Subject: introduction 10/4/95

Ann —

I was reading over your comments from 9/14 (and realizing that that was a while ago). The one that struck me this time was the line "One of the problems for senior women professors is getting pulled and pushed in numerous directions, and needing to prioritize better."

I think this is a fruitful avenue to discuss. I, too, feel this push/pull at the junior level, though (I think) with different anxieties. And maybe this is what's worth articulating. What are the different directions and priorities for feminists of varying "generations" or academic locations? Obviously, economic issues may be differently felt, as may issues of job security in general. But I think issues of collegiality are differently configured, too. Successful senior feminists likely have the benefit of an already-in-place (one hopes) local, national, and perhaps international feminist community. We younger or junior feminists are still forging our communities — testing our peers (and our mentors) for their allegiances, prioritizing our own allegiances. Maybe, however, I'm not recognizing the extent to which one's allegiances are always in process.

Anyway, it is nearing midterm, and I am exhausted. It seems this is the time of the term when students start getting sick. All of my classes are filled with coughs and sneezes. I'm sure you are low energy at this point, too.

Best, Devoney

FROM: EAKAPLAN@ccmail.sunysb.edu
TO: EJLOOSER@root.indstate.edu
Subject: introduction 11/14/95

Devoney: I will try to take the manuscript to England with me over Thanksgiving and give it some attention on the plane. Had a great session at the Institute for Research for Women at Rutgers on my introductory essay for the volume. It's developed from the version you have, and I will add in a couple of things from the session. But I, of course, mentioned our book, and there was lots of interest!

eak

From: ejlooser@root.indstate.edu
To: eakaplan@ccmail.sunysb.edu
Subject: RE: introduction 11/14

Ann —

Hope the interest continues. Let's talk on the phone soon.

Best, Devoney

Notes

1. Gloria Steinem, "Why Young Women Are More Conservative," in *Outrageous Acts and Everyday Rebellions* (New York: Signet, 1983), 238–46.

2. Nancy Miller, "Decades," *South Atlantic Quarterly* 91.1 (1992): 65–86; reprinted in *Changing Subjects: The Making of Feminist Literary Criticism*, ed. Gayle Greene and Coppelia Kahn (New York: Routledge, 1993), 31–47.

Introduction 2

Feminism, Aging, and Changing Paradigms

E. Ann Kaplan

Part I. Performativity

All perspectives are limited, constrained by what one cannot see, and structured by context. One structuring context for the feminist standpoint I will outline is that of age. I use the word *age* rather than the more usual *generation* because it clarifies what is at stake and may avoid some of the problems that the word *generation* causes: *age* refers to the personal/longitudinal axis as against the loose cultural/historical subject-interpellation that *generation* connotes (see my "map" [table 1], following this essay). *Age* (on the longitudinal axis) means that one has been around for a while; that one has had certain experiences, participated in certain movements, perhaps helped produce certain social and intellectual changes within a specific historical span of time. The having-done-this-ness (by which I mean the having gone through such experiences) emerges as a special quality of aging.

While I would not claim that any of us are culturally fixed by any generational location, I would claim that such historical passings-through, which are named "aging," make a difference in the questions that different feminists think to ask, and in the conceptualizing of problems. For those who are aging, the series of experiences accumulates. One has memories, one has stories. One has narrativized the past (there is enough past to narrativize), which is far from saying that such narratives are "true." The stories have been made through the telling, which is why I have titled this section "Performativity," and the "map" that accompanies it "A Performance Piece." The stories are formed through the blindnesses and forgettings that characterize memory (as all the new psychological research tells us). Such narratives are limited and constrained by the specificities of the events one was part of—as against the plethora of other events that went on alongside the ones participated in. This means that generalization of the past, of what one experienced, is also impossible. As Judith Roof warns us in concluding her essay in *Feminism beside Itself*, we must "understand history as containing no truth, no knowledge, no enlightenment."[1] She asks that we narrate feminism not as a family affair (which Roof claims the term *generation* evokes) but "as a partial story with no beginning and no end and no structuring binaries."[2]

This theoretical position partly accords with my own. Indeed, it accounts for my naming my totalizing "map" a performance. Yet I allow my performance piece to include beginnings and binaries because intellectual understanding can only take place through positing and then debating, even discarding, such binaries. In order for Roof to make her claim, she has to express it by negating the binaries of beginning and ending, and by noting how binaries are structuring. Implicitly, then, Roof relies on prior binary thinking to locate her position, much as I do.

Performing Intellectual Feminist Paradigms

To provide a context for what follows, I will narrativize the broad intellectual paradigms that my stretch of feminism has involved—paradigms that do not rely on that of motherhood that Roof claims dominates feminist herstories, even though my story is teleological:

Feminism was originally a modernist movement: indeed, 1960s to 1980s feminisms arguably represented the last gasp of socialist modernity's challenges to the capitalist dominant. Feminist challenges probably succeeded because modernity was already becoming postmodernity—in terms of transnational capitalism, the insistence of the market, globalization, computerization, the end of colonialism, and an increase in diasporic communities. The start of the cyberage through imaging technologies, the Internet, the World Wide Web, and yet newer processes will bring to feminisms changes the extent of which are not yet known. Impacts of postmodernism on gender, race, and class—of what my feminist generation knew as liberal political traditions—are also not known. In a sense, second-wave feminists have moved from the social politics of modernism to experiencing a crisis in political activism itself. What can activism mean in a world where larger oppositional formations are not there to support the local levels of resistance? Second-wave feminists believe they must continue and/or support such local resistances—indeed, such resistances become more vital than ever. But such feminists must also seek ways of forging links across local actions.

Finally, the impact of global finance and the cyberage on the university (where many second-wave feminists find themselves, for reasons noted below) is as yet unclear: feminists know that the university is under severe attack (politically and economically), and that this institution will change dramatically in the near future. We urgently need to participate in those changes.

Performing Generations

None of the women at the Feminism beside Itself conference[3] who were of the same cultural or numerical generation necessarily thought alike or shared paradigms. But still, second-wave feminist use of postmodern or queer theory is different from its being used by a twenty-eight-year-old because, as noted above, the having-done-this-ness of women who have been involved in various phases and aspects of feminisms for thirty years is a different place from which to speak from that of a twenty-eight-year-old. The residue of the experiences remains and is never totally written over.

But why do some twenty-eight-year-olds (like Rene Denfield, discussed below) see the problem in terms of *generation*? What is at stake for them in using this word? Does the personal framing of the term *generation* in this case point to differences between a politics of the free individual subject and a politics of how institutions and historical periods construct certain subject-positions? How far is the debate really not so much about *generation per se* as between academic feminists and other career women who feel excluded from academic discourse and academic debates, whether they are in the academy or not? (For instance, both Camille Paglia and Katie Roiphe speak from academic positions.)

As a partial answer, the fact that first- and second-wave feminists have both the personal/longitudinal (age) axis and the generational one makes a difference (see my mapping). Young women are mainly just aware of the generational axis. It is less confusing for them since they have not had the experience of passing-through-ness that second-wave feminists have. Things appear to them as simply generational: second-wave feminists had the 1960s, they didn't; they have raced,

queered, scienced, and cyborged theory, second-wave feminists didn't.
The anxieties therefore have to be different.

Part II. Feminisms in the Public Sphere and in the Academy

There are two different main sites where generational feminist debates are taking place: there are, first, debates ongoing in the public
media sphere (popular books and book reviews; television news and
talk shows; journalism); and second, debates within the academy, where
I am.[4] These latter need to be further distinguished as dealing with
anxieties about feminist content or perspectives, and second, anxieties
about institutional structures. Many people are familiar with the main
lines of these debates, so I will be brief.

Feminist Generational Anxieties outside the Academy

There's no doubt that the United States is experiencing a continuing
backlash against "feminism" in the public cultural terrain. My quotes
around "feminism" indicate that what is being attacked from outside the academy is clearly a fantasy of a feminist monolith, a set of
myths and images that backlash discourse takes as "true." Witness
the review of yet another anti-"feminism" book in *The New York
Times Book Review* (Sunday, March 19, 1995), this time by Rene Denfield, who moves in on Katie Roiphe's coattails and calls feminists
the "new victorians."

What's interesting is that the reviewer, Michelle Green of *People
Magazine,* situates the book confidently within a generational discourse: her first line notes that Denfield is twenty-eight years old and
a "bold writer" who "fueled by good sense and righteous anger...
has taken on the feminist establishment in a book sure to provoke
her radical foremothers." Like others of her generation, the reviewer
continues, "[Denfield] is impatient with the women's movement and
appalled by *extremists who neglect real-life issues in favor of bashing men, worshipping the Goddess, battling porn-mongers and de-
nouncing heterosexuality*" (my emphasis). The reviewer concludes that
like Naomi Wolf, Denfield is weary of women being cast as "maid-
ens in distress." They want reforms and social change that will put
women on an equal footing with men, and, the reviewer says "*that*
will not happen until her generation reclaims feminism."

Something is seriously wrong when such stale views, such worn statements are taken as valid by the editors of *The New York Times Book Review*: the list of accusations describes no feminist communities I know today, if they ever existed (and if they did, it would have been between 1965 and 1970—something that gives this new discourse such a curiously archaic feel). I am appalled by an implicit ageist ideology that the term *foremothers* connotes: the term relegates first- and second-generation feminists to some fixed past place, where they are frozen in their texts. In reality, most first- and second-wave feminists are still growing, developing their ideas, and using their knowledge to understand changes taking place today.[5]

Further, what Denfield argues "her generation" wants sounds very like something most of my friends want. Certainly, women I know inside and outside the academy are actively pushing for abortion rights and child care. Denfield's kind of discourse has contributed to my current Stony Brook undergraduates' resisting association with the term *feminist*. As one of them noted recently, the term now means women who are against men, "radical," wild, and unrealistic. Students will say they want to work for women's issues but are definitely not *feminists*.

What does it mean that such stale fictions of generational splits continue to proliferate in the high-culture sphere that *The New York Times* represents? What are the anxieties underlying the construction of such generational polarities? What ends does this old discourse serve?

One end (and an anxiety) is an attack on lesbian feminism: the fact that lesbian women are finally getting some of their needs and rights articulated is making many women anxious. The backlash, then, seems to be primarily against lesbians, and lesbians, for some reason, are associated with "feminist foremothers," as if all "foremothers" were lesbians. This is strange, since while there certainly were activist feminist lesbian foremothers (e.g., Andrea Dworkin), many of the most public of early feminists (Gloria Steinem, Betty Friedan) were clearly heterosexual. And it is many of the younger women, like Catharine MacKinnon (perhaps the most public of legal activists) and Kimberly Crenshaw, who are dominant in the public sphere today. Why the creation of straw women against whom to rail? Why the assumption that foremother lesbian feminists have remained unchanged by all that has happened since 1960? Lesbianism is evidently still something that scares straight women, although I do not fully understand the deep underlying causes for this reaction. Many glib psychoanalytic answers come to mind, but these are not sufficient.

A second end is that railing against "foremothers" hides a difference I noted earlier, namely that between an ideology of free individuals who can bring about change for their personal fulfillment and an ideology that links women's oppressions to larger thought-systems and capitalist economic determinism. Second-wave feminists are dealing with an attack on socialist or oppositional feminists: Barbara Johnson was probably right when she noted that what women like Roiphe and Christina Hoff Sommers see as "feminist" is the liberation of the individual woman, subject of agency. Neither sees feminism as a systematic critique of institutions; indeed, they consider the critique of systems itself as limiting women's possibilities. That is, if you start out with a concept of the "free female subject," a theory of institutional (or, I would add, psychoanalytic) constraints seems like something that is limiting. The *critique* of patriarchy by some feminists appears to construct victims, passivity, instead of being seen as explaining and accounting for certain observable feminine constructs. Roiphe and Sommers do not see that claiming "victim" status can be empowering, as Johnson suggests it can be.[6]

This theoretical gulf seems unbridgeable. It's improbable that an understanding between the groups can be reached. What the debates highlight is how most generalizations about any monolithic "feminism" are bound to be made from a very specific location, cultural/ intellectual context, and historical moment—none of which is articulated in books by people like Roiphe, Sommers, Denfield, or reviewers like Michelle Green, who lack any awareness of what shapes their perspectives. Meanwhile, many second-wave feminists within the academy have painfully had to become aware of the blinders on our perspectives (for example, blindness to race and gay/lesbian issues), and to recognize that second-wave-feminist perspectives have performative aspects to them that need developing.

By the word *performative* here I mean both "making things happen" and recognizing the necessarily tentative aspects to structures and positions that second-wave feminists might advance. I have in mind something between adopting "strategic identities" (a term second-wave feminists developed a while ago) and "staging" actions/ changes where this concept carries with it a sense of the provisional, of another possible "staging" in the future. Second-wave feminists need to understand how difficult it is anymore to predict changes in the offing. Where before second-wave feminists felt confident about the necessity to build movements, protest government policies, and create a space in the university for women's studies, now it is important to be watchful about responses to what second-wave feminists are doing and have done, to think in terms of "performance" rather than fixed procedures.

A second painful example of backlash outside the academy was a November 1994 episode of William F. Buckley's *Firing Line* program. The thesis to be debated was "Has the women's movement gone too far? (Buckley's own side was to debate "that the women's movement has been disastrous.") Women from different generations and political positions were deliberately invited, in the usual manner of these programs. The women defending the thesis that the women's movement has been disastrous included the millionaire Ariana Huffington, Camille Paglia, and Elizabeth Fox-Genovese. Betty Friedan and other liberal women were on the other side, arguing, basically, that the women's movement had not gone far enough. Buckley intervened on the Huffington side, giving it the weight of the chair, interrupting, and making arguments against the liberal women. Buckley's side came across as glamorous (given prevailing norms and social codes), while those opposing it were less obviously so. And the ensuing debates provided one with the spectator sport of angry women throwing insults back and forth. Since little clarity emerged from the highly charged language, spectators may have been left to take sides on the flimsy ground of superficial televisual appearance.

Paglia's main point was that the women's movement has ignored the lives of women who love men (and she speaks as a lesbian), and the lives of religious women (and she speaks as an atheist). She complained about rampant anti-Catholicism because of the Pope's stand on abortion. And she concluded that "the Left" has a lot to atone for. Theories of the Left, she said, produced "this election" (presumably meaning Clinton's presidency). A lawyer from the liberal side objected to the feminist notion of "uncontrolled freedom" (I was not sure where this idea came from) and complained that "freedom" does not address the average working woman: "It's an individualism which hurts the person and lets the common good go to hell!" she said.

A liberal feminist claimed that the women's movement has not gone far enough and began to talk about the suffering that remains for many women, more of whom are out of work, 75 percent of whom earn less than men, and most of those in part-time work still have primary child care, getting no support from their husbands . . . But Buckley interrupted and stated that this was like complaining of biological injustices.

Fox-Genovese claimed that the group who is suffering the most is poor black males, who are dying of drugs, antiblack violence, and black-on-black violence. A voice was heard to say that "black women would have something to say about black men being the worst off!" Friedan commented that the women's movement has gone far enough and began to cite statistics regarding women's improved lives. But she argued that the threat to everyone is the growth of anxiety and impotent rage because of rapidly declining economic circumstances. Huffington entered: "If you think that people's anxiety is economic, you are so out of touch." She did not say, however, what the cause of people's anxiety is.

At this point, the discussion deteriorated (interestingly though) into personal comments. Someone said: "Well, I don't have $80 million . . ." Another: "I agree with Ariana here — she wrote two books before she met Mr. Huffington!" Huffington picked it up and said she wanted to know why there was such a level of anger directed at her. She claimed that it was because the liberals "hate her views; all you liberals hate me because I believe in less government."

They returned to the issue of freedom of choice when another panelist complained that feminists have been antireligious and have not reached out to women who believe. Paglia picked up the feminist refusal to let an antiabortion fanatic speak in Philadelphia. Fox-Genovese turned to the feminist demand for sex education in the schools, again arguing that this is an "intrusion into the prerogative of parents," taking over the parents' terrain: "It's not a reactionary backlash to say I don't want liberal sex values taught." Huffington came in to say that "poor women are the ones fighting against *Heather Has Two Mothers.*" A voice from the other side argued that sex education is needed so as to give girls the ability to say "no," and that people against sex education want to gag information. Paglia inserted that it was the white upper class who have imposed their values on the classroom; another voice on her side then said that feminists have devalued *good* choices like the Catholic Church.

I guess there are some bolts that hit their mark in these exchanges — such as many feminists' inability to reach out to religious women and to women who live lives devoted to men. Yet what was odd for me about such claims was that people did not understand that there are certain premises to being a "feminist," a certain "content" that goes with the term, surely. Were the panelists arguing that feminists should have reached and changed some women from being devoted to men and living lives devoted to God? I don't think so. They wanted feminists to support such women somehow. It's not clear to me how exactly. What they really wanted was for feminists not to be feminists — not to think as they think. The panelists seemed to want feminists to attend especially to men, at this point anyway, and not be focused on women's issues. Again, this seems to me fine, except doesn't that change the definition of *feminist?*

At any rate, it's clear that some "backlash" feminists have confused three different areas of feminism, namely, feminism as personal growth (gaining independence, sexual and intellectual self-fulfillment), feminism as political activism (changing laws and policies affecting women with a view to changing the world); and feminism as scholarship (developing new interdisciplinary insights through taking up female perspectives and topics). Backlash feminists tend to isolate academic feminist scholarship as overly "theoretical," "elitist," ignoring the "ordinary" (read: working-class) woman, not understanding that producing new knowledge, pushing at the limits of current knowledge boundaries is as important in academic feminisms as in any other academic field. Critics tar academic feminists with a brush that is not necessarily appropriate. And in any case, academic feminists usually are concerned also with the two other areas of feminism noted above: they may not speak as loudly about them, or be associated with them in public. Changing the world is a process that takes place across all three feminist areas: indeed, people need to be working actively in all three areas for the world to change.

It is true that first-generation feminists did have slogans like "the personal is political" and did strive to link activism and the classroom. Such linking made sense at the time (1960s-1970s), when many of the people engaged in activist movements were also dramatically altering their personal lives and were pioneering feminist scholarship and teaching. Because the same women were involved in all three feminist projects, it made sense to stress their intricate links.

Most of today's public feminists were not part of the political movements that shaped 1960s-1970s feminisms. They did not experience the ways in which institutions limited women's possibilities because first- and second-wave feminists have opened up society and created awareness of ways in which women were marginalized and debased. Feminist movements of the 1970s have produced a situation such that younger women no longer experience so strongly the constraints that gave rise to theories that emerged from activism. Here is where *age* matters: today's public feminists focus on personal growth and individual achievement, and this masks the larger forces that still oppress the lives of many less fortunate women. Young white middle-class women were not around when such oppressions were painfully in place for their group. They attack academic feminists because they do not understand how theory or scholarship works. They want a certain kind of activism—one that serves their personal, individual needs (abortion reform, child care). Often lacking a larger institutional or political theory, they are less able to see the need to think about, and do something for, less fortunate communities of women.

Summary of Generational Anxieties about the Content of Academic Feminisms

Anxieties of second-wave academic feminists

Worries include the idea of being left behind, of their day being over, of having had a central role and now being shelved as a "classic."[7] Many in this generation are located as "pioneers" by younger academic feminists but no longer seen as forging new terrain. The paradigms the second-wave used are being critiqued, but, as noted, younger feminists tend to freeze the women within these texts in an ageist move. In parallel fashion, second-wave feminists' concerns may be mixed unconsciously with anxieties about aging. Scholars may unconsciously succumb to the notion that it is time to "make room" for younger feminists in the academy. In this, they may participate in what Betty Friedan has called "the dominant view of age as decline."[8]

Anxiety on the part of older academic feminists takes the form of believing that new areas of study being opened up within feminism, like queer theory or ethnic studies, are not ones they can participate in. That theory is being "queered," and is increasingly replacing "French" literary feminism, was noted by Barbara Johnson.[9] Within film studies, debates have taken a distinctly generational form in the challenges to 1970s feminist paradigms developed around the journal *Screen* and the Paris Cinemathèque. New interdisciplinary feminist research on science, technology, and cyberspace represents another academic area that women in the earlier waves were not trained in.

Especially pertinent here is the impact of new theories of gender identity (like those of Donna Haraway or Judith Butler) because they appear to render dangerous the clinging to a specifically feminine category. More radical than the concept of "plural feminist histories" that some have advanced, Haraway's wake-up call to socialist feminists in her 1985 "Manifesto for Cyborgs" initiated new attention to a postulated "posthuman" body.[10] If past feminisms have relied on the category of "woman" as their main claim to methodological distinctiveness, we find ourselves at a new juncture—even at a crisis in our studies, when such a move is made.[11] What is often ignored is the close link between these apparently subjective anxieties and larger changes going on in the academy—an issue that I will return to shortly.

Anxieties of twenty-eight-year-olds-plus within the academy

For younger women, anxieties arise in competing with senior women scholars, as Jane Gallop and Elizabeth Francis affirm in their dialogue in this volume. While such women have learned from their feminist mentors, they need to go beyond them, which can provoke anxiety. Sometimes, there is anxiety on the part of both older and younger women because younger women's scholarship is not supported by an activist past, such as that which many of their mentors engaged in. Public critiques of academic feminists often ignore the role such second-wave feminists played earlier in their lives in activist movements for the social change that public feminists are now enjoying! Further, critics ignore how much prior activist experience grounded the personal/political changes they were pioneering. The professionalization of women's studies has meant that links with activism have slackened for second-wave-feminist white women. Minority group feminists may have anxieties through the opposite problem: they may have an oppositional group to identify with outside the academy (and be alarmed at the gap between this group and white feminists within the university), and they may lack an oppositional group within the academy. They may be alarmed also by the enduring whiteness of much feminist discourse they encounter within the university.

Anxieties about the Structures of Feminisms and about the Disciplines within Which Feminisms Grew in the 1960s and 1970s

As I noted earlier, the anxieties briefly outlined are closely linked with broad changes within the academy. For instance, at my institution, efforts to initiate a cultural studies Ph.D. program were viewed—not entirely wrongly—as endangering women's studies. While I would hope that any cultural studies program would be heavily committed to gender studies, the kind of concentrated research on women's issues clearly would not be viable within cultural studies. In the best of all worlds, with no limits on resources, cultural studies will work closely with other interdisciplinary programs, like women's studies. Then there is the question of whether lesbian/gay studies should be constituted as a separate entity from women's studies and of how much those studies compete with women's studies.

As the university itself comes under attack, and as political forces having little to do with feminisms directly are changing the university, demanding that it become economically self-sufficient in many cases, so faculty are being forced to rethink disciplinary organization not primarily from the point of view of what the best organization of knowledge would be, but of downsizing, efficiency. We face demands for cutting out administrators, course release, and graduate and other assistants. This could be turned to the benefit of women's studies, but it could also result in pressures to link women's studies with other new studies, like cultural studies, media studies, Latin American and Caribbean studies, to which, of course, women's studies is relevant.

There is the further issue of the degree to which specifically marked focus on women/gender is necessary. For example, in film studies, feminist perspectives were so powerful in the 1980s that they now permeate almost all the work, as does increasingly the category of race. Does this mean that flagging specifically feminist perspectives is no longer necessary? Or are such moves attempts at co-opting women's studies and "taming" feminisms into something else? Is there any validity to notions that feminism accomplished a paradigm shift such that from now on the category "woman" has entered all scholarly domains as an available topic for research? Is the paradigm shift over, as Thomas Kuhn would argue, precisely because administrations are beginning to question what the paradigm has yet to contribute?[12] Is the fantasy that feminism has achieved its main ends—integrating women into career worlds, acceptance of the two-career family by men, more provisions for child care, and so on—a defense against continuing to support feminist struggles? Few second-wave feminists have any doubt that there is a long way still to go, or that the backlash against feminisms is aimed at undoing much of what was done.

Part III. Changing Paradigms in the Academy, Widening Gaps between Civil Society and the Academy

The impact of the changes women brought about in all three feminist terrains noted above—politics and society, personal life, scholarship—has in turn altered the viability of all three being so intricately linked. This is because each terrain has expanded its specific area to include many more questions, demands, perspectives, and complexities than hitherto, so that any simple statement like "the personal is political is scholarship" could no longer manage to contain all that has gone on within the three terrains. It has been necessary to divide up the work that needs doing in light of the expansion of each area.

The widening gap between feminist activism and feminist scholarship, to which I now turn, is, then, partly a product of the expansion of what needs to be done in both of these areas. But the impact on feminism of the widening gap between civil society and the academy is a different kind of problem from that of age or generation. It has to do with what kind of feminist research one wants to, or can, undertake within the university: do women see their research as closer to activism and women's social oppressions? As closer to the level of abstract theory? Or do they see the distinction as invalid, and part of the problem? But this widening gap also has to do with the changing nature of the university in a period when both states and the federal government are increasingly reluctant to fund university research.

The question of what feminist research should be done is a different category of difference from that of age or generation, and it would be a mistake to try to align age with a specific sort of research interest, despite the fact that older women have come along the route from modernism to postmodernism to the cyberage. Some scholars keep on changing their paradigms as things change around them; others keep to paradigms they are familiar with and with which they have worked for many years; some try to integrate prior and newer paradigms.

Yet as I argued at the start, those of us who grew up inside modernist political, intellectual, and academic contours are situated in a way that is very different from those who grew up when postmodernism was already a transitional period in between modernism and the cyberage. Second-wave feminists' mental structures seem to require working through from earlier intellectual paradigms to new ones. While many second-wave feminists realize that we have to think everything through newly (particularly those of us engaged in cyber technologies), it is not clear to me that it is possible simply to ignore old philosophies, old binaries, old terminologies.

I wonder if there can be a real dialogue among what may amount to three different "generations," or feminist groups, with differing contexts: the questions and issues that interest scholars coming to their scholarship at different historical moments will vary. The very questions, that, for example, a scholar like Joan Scott asks arise out of moving from a modernist to a postmodernist feminism. They may not arise for the twenty-eight-year-old graduate student or young professor. Meanwhile, the queering of theory is likely to attract scholars who never grew up intellectually through psychoanalysis. It is perhaps in this strange sense that age *does* implicate research topics. Might collaborative projects be possible?

One of the challenges that faces all feminists is how to develop new resistance strategies along with new activist paradigms. Here, the strategies definitely have to be collaborative. And for that, feminists need to fully understand their political and theoretical differences. Must feminists find new language to describe themselves, given the disrepute that public women attacking us have managed to plunge feminism into "out there"? In this particular historical moment, facing (as do those of us in New York State) drastic budget cuts, feminists will need more collaboration and political alliances than ever before. Some university reorganization is being undertaken not for what is best for producing knowledge but for what is most cost-effective and efficient. With luck, cost-effectiveness *and* intellectually progressive, interdisciplinary reorganization will coincide.

The futures of feminisms — and feminisms in the future — will depend on three main challenges:

1. On how those of us inside the academy will be able increasingly to negotiate the gap between "inside" and "outside" the academy. How can academic feminists intervene in the right-wing attacks on a fiction of feminisms that women writing popular books outside the academy have invented? How can we insert our own competing discourse — not to convince the public feminists (they cannot be convinced!) — in order to reach teachers in high schools and in our classes so that feminism might have a future?

2. Futures of feminisms will depend on how much academic feminists are able to have a say in the demand for reorganization, downsizing, and efficiency that most state universities are already facing and will increasingly face. It will be important for us to articulate what our contributions to knowledge continue to be and what we need for our teaching and scholarship.

3. Last (but not finally — I am sure there are many more things), American feminists need to link up with feminists globally. Given postcolonialism, postmodernism, and the cyberage, women are all of course already linked economically through global corporations and market strategies that use our bodies in similar ways. The production and proliferation of cyberspace and computer technologies are rapid, and feminists (especially the more reluctant second-wave generation) need to keep on top of technologies. Philippine women processing an eighteenth-century novel so that we can have a machine-readable text is already a reality. Western feminists are implicated in this new form of colonialism and must plan strategies around our complicity.

Yet while the public sphere ridicules feminists who take cyberspace literally,[13] American feminists of all ages and in all disciplines need to develop cyberspace skills. As against the victim narratives about the Internet, my experience shows the tremendous tool it can be for crucial cross-national links among women situated at great geographical distances.[14] Meanwhile, research on the impacts of the cyberage on feminisms, on our understanding of the female body, and on our still heavily modernist theorizing is urgent. The relationship of women to cybertechnologies requires more analyses from feminist perspectives,[15] which should be able to avoid the resisting, demonizing, or idealizing of these technologies inevitable in the processes of their acceptance.

It is also not a matter of succumbing to Jean Baudrillard-style seductions vis-à-vis consumerism, the market, and commercialization, or of displacing activist politics with *cultural* politics (as Elizabeth Weed feared at the Feminism beside Itself conference). It is, rather, a matter of feminists including in our cultural work analyses of women's fascination with what the market produces or their fascination with cyberspace. The challenge is to understand the interaction among new technologies, economic pressures for constantly increased consumerism, women's oppressions, and feminist analyses. Feminists of all generations, and working in all the three main spheres outlined earlier, will need to be alert and in collaboration as we develop feminisms for the future.

Table 1
Mapping Feminism and the World Order: A Performance Piece

Personal/Longitudinal Axis *Age*		Cultural/Historical Grouping *Generation*
Social/ Technical/ Political	1. Capitalism vs. socialism	1. 60s–70s Feminism * *attention: white women*
	2. Postcoloniality/ the diaspora	2. 80s–90s Feminisms * *contesting first-wave feminisms* * *debates between white and black women* * *growth of nonwhite feminisms*
	3. Transnational finance corporations	3. Deconstructing gender * *queering theory* * *international feminisms*
Intellectual/ Cultural Movements	1. Modernism	1. Female identity politics * *"white woman" as category* * *politics of class*
	2. Postmodernism	2. Complex race/gender identities * *politics of ethnic authenticity*
	3. Cyberage	3. Destabilizing identities * *virtual realities* * *Internet subjectivities* * *new gender/race identities*

Notes

1. Judith Roof, "How to Satisfy a Woman *Every Time...,*" in *Feminism beside Itself,* ed. Diane Elam and Robyn Wiegman (New York: Routledge, 1995), 68.

2. Ibid., 68.

3. This conference, held at Indiana University by Diane Elam and Robyn Wiegman on March 23–25, 1995, featured many of the contributors to their anthology of the same title and coincided with that book's publication. See note 1.

4. This is not to deny other locations for these debates—such as within activist feminist spheres—but I can only address briefly the two sites of academic feminism and the public-sphere discourses in this essay.

5. See Betty Friedan's *The Fountain of Age* (New York: Simon and Schuster, 1993) for evidence both of ageist assumptions in American culture generally, and for an example of a first-wave feminist still growing and changing as she advocates our developing a new concept of aging.

6. Mentioned in a paper Johnson delivered on feminism at the Modern Language Association convention in San Diego, December 29, 1995.

7. See, for example, Nancy Miller's eloquent reflections on her coming into feminism in *Getting Personal: Feminist Occasions and Other Autobiographical Acts* (New York: Routledge, 1991).

8. Friedan, *Fountain,* 26.

9. See note 6 above.

10. Donna Haraway, "A Manifesto for Cyborgs: Science, Technology and Socialist Feminism in the 1980s," *Socialist Review* (March/April 1985): 65–107.

11. See Susan Stanford Friedman, "Making History: Reflections on Feminism, Narrative, and Desire," in *Feminism beside Itself,* 11–54.

12. Thomas Kuhn, *The Structure of Scientific Revolutions* (Chicago: University of Chicago Press, 1962).

13. Recently, a young professor at Birmingham University was ridiculed in the British *Times* for titling herself a "cyberfeminist." In Australia, there is evidently a group called the VNS Matrix: A Cyberfeminist Collective.

14. I am thinking of relationships I have developed and then been able to increase with both Australian and more recently Japanese women through the Internet. Geographical distance and time difference make even phone interaction difficult, even if one were to ignore the cost. E-mail is the perfect tool for communicating across the language and time/distance divide. Japanese women read and write English much better than speaking it, so that e-mail helps in that regard (my Japanese is not quite up to par yet!). The Yokohama Women's Forum both organized my lecture with me and then got the word out to women in Japan through e-mail. This same co-coordinator went to the NGO Beijing Women's Conference as the networking person and was supposed to have sent me daily bulletins! This did not happen, for some reason, but I am sure I will find an e-mail update in my inbox soon.

15. I just participated in my first virtual session at a conference on cyberspace. It was a quite remarkable experience, for the processes I found myself taken up in, for my reaction to the processes, and for the content of our panelists' discussions, which involved reflection on what we were doing. I tried to raise feminist-type questions from time to time; often they were ignored; sometimes I got the feeling (or was more or less told) that the language I was using, the categories I was working with were "old," and that we needed to be thinking in totally new terms. But the possibilities of such virtual conferences and of the hectic, often confusing but exciting kind of interchanges should be something that we are thinking about.

Introduction 2

Gen X Feminists? Youthism, Careerism, and the Third Wave

Devoney Looser

Widespread speculation about the everyday practices and intellectual commitments of feminism's next generation can hardly be called "new." For many years, I have read with great interest the writings of established feminists about those of us who are "following in their footsteps," and I have been enlightened—and sometimes angered—by these writings.[1] Many second-wave feminists have lamented what they see happening to the scholarly work they produced and the political projects they began a decade or more ago. These lamentations are not merely a result of backlash coming from outside the women's movement. Clearly, some second-wave feminist angst has fixed itself on what "younger feminists" are *doing* (or *not* doing) to and with the feminist achievements of the 1970s and 1980s.

At the same time that these writings by "older" feminists about "younger" feminists have proliferated, anthologies of second-wave feminist self-reflection have become de rigueur. Academic women have been in the vanguard of "personal criticism," and some of that work has focused specifically on individual histories of activity within the women's movement. This work includes *Changing Subjects: The Making of Feminist Literary Criticism* (which may be the most widely known book of its kind for those in the humanities) and *Gender and the Academic Experience* (which will likely ring a more familiar bell for social scientists).[2] In each of these volumes and others like them, second-wave feminists describe how they saw themselves in relation to the academy, how they struggled through graduate programs, and where they found support. Some use the occasion as a yardstick to measure how far we have (or haven't) come.

In the mid-1990s, younger academic feminists have begun to respond to these second-wave writings.[3] Nonacademic feminists have also made their voices heard. Published writings from these third-wave feminists fly in the face of those who have suggested that the next generation of feminists is simply nowhere to be found.[4] To date, two anthologies, Rebecca Walker's *To Be Real: Telling the Truth and Changing the Face of Feminism* and Barbara Findlen's *Listen Up! Voices from the Next Feminist Generation,* have published some of these newcomers' voices.[5] Those essays, largely confessional or anecdotal, show that younger feminists are not necessarily locked into the "personal conservatism of younger women" that Gloria Steinem once suggested we should expect to find in college-aged women.[6] On the other hand, as Findlen notes, this younger generation appears to be anything but cohesive:

> Generation X, thirteenth generation, twentysomething—whatever package you buy this age group in—one of the characteristics we're known for is our disunity. Maybe we're not as unified as the generation that preceded us. Maybe we're just not as categorizable. In any case, I wonder whether the famous unity of the baby boomers might not be a bit mythical.... So what may appear to be a splintering in this generation often comes from an honest assessment of our differences as each of us defines her place and role in feminism.[7]

Findlen's assessment of this (feminist) generation's lack of cohesion may be characteristic of us, but it is surely not unique to us. Second-wave feminists themselves have suggested that the perception that all feminists once got along is a nostalgic and largely mythical construction. The "disunity" in today's twentysomething feminists, however, has gained acceptance not as myth but as defining truth. For Walker, our generational disunity is made more difficult by the pressures that were handed down to us from the ideals of second-wave feminism. As Walker puts it, "Constantly measuring up to some cohesive fully down-for-the-feminist-cause without contradictions and messiness and lust for power and luxury items is not a fun or easy task."[8] Walker's "answer"—and that of most of her contributors—is both to revel in and trouble over these feminist contradictions. Implicitly, then, Findlen's and Walker's anthologies talk back to second-wave feminists and feminisms about their perceived expectations of the third wave.

If there is now a growing body of writing on second-wave and third-wave feminist experiences, beliefs, and platforms, little has been written on the traffic between each so-called camp. Very little indeed has been published on the caricatures of each generation and on the basis of these, if any, in fact. Furthermore, scant attention has been paid to the reasons that may lie behind the promulgation of generational stereotypes. We might ask why this is the case. Is it possible that there are not really any generational schisms to talk about in the first place—that there are not any feminist "generations" per se? Is talking about "generations" harmful to our feminist work? Judith Roof argues in her essay in this collection that reproductive metaphors like "generation" must be eschewed; their often unacknowledged heterosexism does not allow us to think outside of a familial model within the university. To my mind, however, we should continue to examine what are already quite entrenched and *perceived* feminist generational differences and alliances. These deserve to be further theorized now, even if they are ultimately cast out of our critical vocabulary.

As with the flurry of media attention to Generation X, it is likely that the outlining of feminist generations serves to caricature diverse feminist interests and practices. Should we discuss feminist generations knowing that we are walking on the thin ice of stereotypes? I think we must. Not to examine "feminist generation" out of a concern for its theoretical instability and violence as a category does little to address the effects of the category. This argument has, of course, been made about the deconstruction of "women"; we must sometimes retain the term in order to organize and to be comprehended. It is in this light that calls for a halt to all discussions about generations seem potentially harmful. Such claims seem to me to be easier to make from positions of relative professional stability and institutional power—easier to make as a feminist authority than as a feminist newcomer. Denying the force of generation as a category may in fact serve to prevent the questioning of its hold over us. Whether or not "generations" promote "false" divisions, feminist generational schisms are having and have had material effects—effects, I would argue, that can be more profoundly experienced by the "next" generation than by the previous one.

On the other hand, it is possible that those of us who perceive generational differences are merely repeating history and are not saying anything new about feminism—that we are going through roughly the same developmental processes that our feminist "foremothers" did. In her foreword to Walker's *To Be Real,* Steinem writes about her experience of reading that collection of third-wave voices. She confesses that "there are moments in these pages when I—and perhaps other readers older than thirty-five—feel like a sitting dog being told to sit."⁹ I like this image for its unlikely implications about feminist training. I like it for its suggestions about who is master, as well as who is active, in today's feminist communities. I am tempted to take Steinem too seriously here. At this point, can we twentysomethings really be mistaken for the ones responsible for setting the agenda or pulling the strings in the women's movement? Is history really so cyclical that we twenty-something feminists are, as Steinem also suggests, merely reinventing the wheel?¹⁰ Have younger feminists been guilty of barking hackneyed orders at the "old dogs"? Although I take Steinem's point that some feminist issues that third-wavers are now discovering have been around for decades, it is also the case that the new dogs are coming up with some new tricks. We face differently configured problems, issues, and ideologies—however subtly or radically changed. Second-wave feminists—like it or not—are destined to fail in their mission to "pass on" feminist knowledge. Passing on carries with it the idea of a linear movement, as well as a suppression of the inevitability of difference, as many of the contributors to this volume suggest. This transmission from second to third wave can never be fully achieved, regardless of how much Steinem and others might like to see themselves in us—see their issues echoed in our own.

Issues of feminist generational conflict have not been dealt with in print to a great degree, perhaps because of their status as political hot potatoes. For many of us—perhaps on both sides of the proverbial second- and third-wave fence—the current moment seems to be one in which we feminists had better "make nice" rather than enter into any more blame games with each other. Many have noted that we have too many external enemies to waste time working out conflicts among ourselves or that we have precious few resources and footholds as it is and therefore need to band together. I would not want to make light of such arguments and will admit that they have sometimes gnawed at me as we worked on this book. But downplaying differences has never served feminism well, and if there are indeed some feminist differences that can be theorized on the basis of age or of academic generation, ignoring them will not help us accomplish our shared (or our differing) political projects. As Susan Stanford Friedman has argued, "An effort to historicize the positions and perspectives of each generation could foster the multiplicity of generational voices rather than the silencing of one by another."[11] Friedman's point relates not only to second- and third-wave feminists but to earlier generations of feminists as well.[12] It is necessary that we continue to historicize "positions and perspectives," while retaining an awareness that such histories will also inevitably produce conflict and anger.[13]

As I write this, I am twenty-eight — the number that Ann Kaplan uses in her introduction to measure the differences between "having-done-this-ness" and, one would presume, having not. When I first heard Ann deliver that introduction as a talk, we did not know each other's ages. At that point, our collaboration on this collection was well under way, and we later talked about the coincidence of her choice. I was surprised to learn that I was, in fact, the same age as Ann's daughter. I didn't know what to do with this information, beyond remarking its curiosity. I remain unsure about it; I am troubled with the notion of imagining my feminist mentors as "mothers" for many reasons — among them, those dangers that Diane Elam lists in her essay in this collection. At the same time, attempting to gloss over the institutional hierarchies of feminist age and authority that remain entrenched in the academy and, perhaps, elsewhere (some of which seem based on patterns of parenting) has had pointed costs. At the very least — as Rebecca Dakin Quinn suggests in her open letter in this volume — it can prevent us from listening to each other.

Despite struggles over the kinds of distortion that the terms *generation* and *feminist generation* can cause, there are good reasons to retain the terms provisionally. Clearly, divisions among feminist "waves" or generations are named only to be broken down. If poststructuralist theories taught us anything, it was that categories are neither as seamless nor as innocent as they may pretend to be; categories are fraught with danger, are inevitably fragmented, and at the same time, offer the possibility for different configurations. Despite all of the difficulties involved in defining the beliefs (or even the members) of any given generation, we need more conversations about how we have come to perceive each other as feminists according to "age." Scrutinizing the pictures that have been painted of feminist generations and asking what kinds of ideologies inform these portraits should go some distance toward revising our inter- and intragenerational perceptions.

Ageism and Youthism

If Betty Friedan is right that the feminist movement has engaged in widespread practices of ageism,[14] I would counter that there have also been concomitant feminist practices of "youthism"—of dismissing the intellectual interests, contributions, and motivations of the next generation of feminists on the basis of our supposed naïveté and inexperience. This can take the form of "We know what is best for you." Madelon Sprengnether, for one, has gone into print with such couched assumptions, taking younger feminists to task for their "careerism" and "individualism":

> Whether or not older and younger feminists are friends matters less than that we be able to work together toward some agreed-upon aims. For this, we need to foster an atmosphere of mutual respect. Not only do we need to try to see each other as clearly as we can ... but we also need to acknowledge that some degree of cross-generational alliance is necessary for the continuing existence of our multiple feminisms. One painful contra-indication I see for this possibility is the phenomenon of what I will call "careerist feminism," the version of academic feminism that focuses on individual achievement as its primary goal, disavowing the very value of collectivity in its definition of feminism.
>
> Believing in the relative stability of academic feminism, some younger women, I think, are overly confident about its future and hence somewhat passive about sustaining the bonds among women that made it happen in the first place. In this sense, they not only benefit from the struggles of us older feminists, who created the fields and markets that allow their work to flourish, but they also underestimate the levels of resistance that remain and are actually on the rise. ... Yet today it is quite possible to make a tidy career in academic feminism without the labor of getting to know other women. If this is the career model that prevails, I do not see that we are much better off than we were when I started out. Increasingly, however, I find women graduate students pointing to just such a career pattern as the one they hold in awe, the one they seek to emulate. This feels to me like coming full circle—a reversion to the model of competitive individualism that seventies feminism (however limited in other ways) sought to transform. It was never our goal to challenge the patriarchal fathers, simply to take their place.[15]

Sprengnether's message is unquestionably important. Indeed, it is hard not to appreciate her passion for the continuation of feminist knowledge making and her "concern for our collective future." But the language in which this plea is made rankles. It perpetuates stereotypes of both older and younger feminists in ways that I find representative and ultimately damaging. For Sprengnether, '70s feminists are presented as the peacemakers. They are the ones who are like her, who are calling for clear sight, "alliance," continuity, and "collectivity." They are the ones who "made it happen," who "allowed" feminism to "flourish," whose "collaboration" and "mutual assistance" must serve as models for "long-term" strategies. They are the transformers, the challengers, the ones whom we should really seek to emulate and hold in awe. They had the "genuine," unpatriarchal career goals.

We younger feminists are not "agreeing," not "respecting," not "seeing clearly" (again to draw on Sprengnether's words). We are not "acknowledging" or making alliances, as we are "disavowing" second-wave models of community and collaboration. We are causing them "pain"; we are "overly confident" and "somewhat passive" in our "heady" approach to "short-term" benefits. We "neglect" the ways in which feminism is under fire in order to have "tidy" lives, without "labor," without "other women." In other words, we are a new breed of isolated faux-feminist academic worker bees, who merely want to "take [our] place" in the patriarchs' ivory towers. We, it seems, may bring the movement "full circle," may bring all of the second-wave achievements crashing down, may bring feminism back to a place that is not "much better off" than where we were when Sprengnether and others "started out." They are the purebred origin; we are the mangy strays.

In picking apart Sprengnether's language, I am perhaps doing the very things of which she would accuse my generation — concerning myself with deconstructing her words rather than with putting together collective resistance to the antifeminist powers that be, spending time "trashing" rather than "appreciating" her call for "our" feminist betterment. But I do not pick on Sprengnether to "trash" her. I take her point that feminisms are at a difficult moment in history and that we need long-term strategies. I am concerned, though, that the language for such strategies seems often to be framed in terms that put the second-wavers on pedestals and cast third-wavers as betrayers. Might Sprengnether's version of the young feminist (particularly the young academic feminist) as undutiful, careerist, apolitical, ungrateful, and ahistorical be an extension of media images circulated about young people in general? I want to entertain the possibility that some senior feminists' understandings of their junior colleagues (as well as of the students in their classes) tell us more about the ways in which our culture has stereotyped young people than about third-wave feminists per se.

This undertaking must begin with uncertainty about what *third wave* means. Like the term *postmodern, third wave* seems to have attached itself to the most unlikely collection of political issues, movements, and people, from Alvin Toffler to Katie Roiphe.[16] Even among feminists, these divisions are never neat ones. Catharine R. Stimpson recently remarked on the contradictions involved when "the waves wash over each other. Shannon Faulkner, for example, is chronologically a Third Waver using Second Wave legal theory to achieve a First Wave goal."[17] The only way in which I find the term *third wave* useful for feminism is (as many have argued of postmodernism) as a periodizing distinction. Walker's feminist and multicultural activist group, the Third Wave, was formed in 1992.[18] *The Third Wave: Feminist Perspectives on Racism* was published in the fall of 1993.[19] Most feminists use *third wave* to refer to the "new" feminisms and feminists emerging in the late 1980s and 1990s, many of whom purport to interrogate race, nation, and sexuality more thoroughly than did the second wave, and many of whom are skeptical about the unity of the category "women."

But is *third wave* the feminist equivalent of *Gen X*? The ways in which these labels are applied to historical periods have been (and could be) parceled out in any number of ways. Neil Howe and Bill Strauss suggest that the "13th Generation" includes those who were born between 1961 and 1981.[20] In their earlier work on generations, Howe and Strauss suggested that this thirteenth U.S. generation could be categorized as "reactive" and has been branded "dumb, greedy, and soulless."[21] Howe and Strauss tell us that older generations think of the thirteeners as

> frenetic, physical, and slippery . . . shocking on the outside, unknowable on the inside. . . . Elders find it hard to suppress feelings of disappointment over how they are turning out—dismissing them as a "lost," "ruined," even "wasted" generation in an unrelenting (and mostly unanswered) flurry. . . . The Boomer media often portray 13ers as driven more by appetites than by ideas.[22]

While Howe and Strauss's theory of a repeating cycle of generational characteristics deserves our skepticism, their rendering of the *stereotypes* of Generation X is accurate enough.

Academic feminist work on generations has further refined these divisions; Alice Jardine has suggested that academic feminist generations are best determined by the year in which one completed graduate school.[23] This marker might be able to predict the kinds of formative feminist training that a student would have had and, presumably, could suggest the feminist commitments that a scholar and teacher may still retain. Jardine's distinctions break down generations into smaller divisions than those of Howe and Strauss, and her academic feminist generations entail approximately ten years of Ph.D.'s. If Jardine's categories were each labeled separately, American feminism could be in the double digits in its naming of waves. Of course, there are important cultural reasons why Jardine's designations have not taken hold among feminists, even though they may much more accurately identify feminist intellectual trends. Although we feminists may like to think of ourselves as outside of the mainstream, our portraits of twentysomething feminists have sometimes been tied together with those of the larger cultural designation for "twentysomethings."

In their descriptions, some senior academic feminists draw on a hybrid formulation of Gen X slackers and their yuppie forerunners. One of the repeated complaints that can be heard at feminist conferences is that young feminists are not political enough — that they are into theory rather than practice, into showing rather than doing. Young feminists are implicitly and explicitly called on to prove their political and "practical" feminist credentials. As I have argued elsewhere (and as Sprengnether implied above), in the late 1980s and early 1990s many feminists lamented that their classrooms were populated by students who "used" feminism to further their careers.[24] Annette Kolodny complained that "the seminar in feminist theory [has become] solely a means to professional advancement."[25] Donna Landry claimed that she was "unnerved" by "young feminist critics whose introduction to feminism has been a course in graduate school, usually one in 'French Feminist Theory.'"[26] These do not rank among today's most pressing feminist concerns, yet they seem to be refrains in some recent feminist work. These issues have touched a feminist nerve, which might be summarized as follows: to come to feminism through participation in a rally is somehow more "real" than to come to it through a college course.

The Evaluation of Feminist Credentials

Do we feminists really want to be in the business of determining whose feminist coming-of-age stories are the most genuine? Furthermore, are not women like Landry and Kolodny (whose work I read and have admired, in graduate school and afterward) themselves part of the reason why some of their students desire feminist careers? Haven't senior academic women's lives to some small degree made such "careerist" feminist desires possible? The stereotyping of third-wave feminists as more "careerist" than their predecessors seems more than a little suspect for this reason alone. But there are certainly many historical reasons for these newer ("unsettling") ways of "doing" feminism. They would seem to arise from what Nancy Whittier has called the "postfeminist myth," which hinged on two assumptions:

> First, the conservative shift in the 1980s stemmed in part from former activists' abandonment of radical politics in favor of more mature and traditional goals and priorities. And, second, the 1980s drove a generational wedge between the women who had organized feminist groups and protests during the 1960s and 1970s and their younger counterparts, who came of age in an era that was simultaneously more hostile to feminism and less restrictive of women.[27]

Whittier claims that, like most myths, "this one contains a kernel of truth" (3). She notes that for some the 1980s brought new approaches to feminist activity:

> The 1980s did mark a turning point for individual feminists, who searched for new ways to be activists in the face of mounting opposition, financial difficulty, and their own aging. Yet women who had been activists in the 1960s and 1970s never abandoned their political commitments, and the radical women's movement not only survived the 1980s but began to grow again in the 1990s. Admittedly, as the social and political climate grew more conservative, the grassroots women's movement became smaller and smaller; but, as activists have known all along, neither the movement nor feminist individuals vanished. It is also true that a generational divide emerged between older and younger women, and even between older and younger feminists. But this divide was neither absolute nor based on the younger generation's wholesale rejection of feminist values. Many younger women were uninterested in feminist protest, just as many women of their mothers' generation sat out the feminist upheavals of the 1960s and 1970s. Other younger women, however, organized and agitated on behalf of women. Because women who came of age in the 1980s had sharply different experiences from those who came of age

ten or twenty years earlier, however, they redefined priorities and
reconceptualized the meaning of feminism. Generational politics, then,
are more relevant to the resulting debates and shifts within the
women's movement than to young women's decisions to become
feminists in the first place.[28]

Whittier's account is valuable in its attempt to trace who "we" have
been and are as feminist organizers of the past several decades. When
seen through this lens, however, so-called careerist feminists take on
a somewhat different hue. Perhaps what appears to be a lack of activism in third-wavers is a redefinition of priorities, a reconceptualiz-
ing of feminism; perhaps it is a lack of interest in feminist protest on
behalf of some or a refiguring of the forms that "protest" might take.
But it is foolish to think that young women today are choosing feminism *on any front* as an "easy" way out, or as a "simple" way to advance their professional goals, as Darlene Hantzis and I have argued.[29] Even in today's academy, declaring yourself a feminist hardly
guarantees you the key to the campus or the city.

Complaints about today's feminist graduate students, however, don't
stop with suspicions about their motives for gaining feminist knowledge. Such complaints often reflect on the *kind* of knowledge students
have been willing to digest and reproduce. In *Conflicts in Feminism* —
a book frequently cited in the essays that follow — Marianne Hirsch
claimed that feminists today have "somehow not been able to raise a
generation that builds on what came before" and lamented the passing of a feminist community in which it used to be a pleasure to work.[30]
Again, Hirsch is no lone voice, and these kinds of complaints have been
echoed in similar language elsewhere. As the 1995 National Women's
Studies Association conference call for papers on "Generations of
Women" put it, "How can we use, understand, and pass on the legacy
of previous generations"? It is usually assumed that this "passing on"
is, first, always a good thing and, second, that it is not happening to
a great enough degree — that those who should be receiving are dropping the ball.

Some younger feminists, too, have embraced this "passing on" of
the feminist legacy. For every younger feminist who engages in the
"trashing" of her elders (or, to reframe this through Whittier's words,
who chooses to redefine feminism or reconceptualize its priorities or
who refuses second-wave protocols for conflict and argumentation),
there is one who will not rock the boat. In fact, there are some younger

feminists who, in valorizing the efforts of their feminist "foremothers," see themselves as having little to contribute to today's women's movement. In February 1996, there was a thread of discussion about this on WMST-L, the international women's studies list on the Internet. In that thread, a faculty member at Virginia Tech wrote in to tell the list members that her students complained of being "born too late" for feminism. Others suggested how this professor could convince her students that feminism needed their "new life." One "older" woman explained that the "born-too-late" phenomenon was not in itself new. She suggested that, by the time she got into the women's movement at the end of the 1960s, all the leadership spots were taken; newcomers were welcome mostly as gophers and typists. She said that she, too, fretted then at being born too late for feminism. Feminist nostalgia may help to create or cement community, but it also seems to prevent some young women from seeing a place for themselves — prevents them from taking action. Inadvertently, then, second-wave feminists may perpetuate the very effects about which they complain, with their insistence on a certain level of nostalgia for and allegiance to previous feminist achievements and goals. If we see past feminist contributions as sacrosanct — if we long for former feminist communities rather than working with what we have at present or imagining alternative futures — what remains to be done but to retell rousing stories of the good (and simultaneously bad?) old days?

"Older" feminists' statements about the relative absence of "younger feminists" are not new to the '90s. Revisiting an April 1983 cover story in *Ms.* illustrates this well. This issue (curiously also featuring the "April Fools' Special" section on the "post-feminist woman") includes several articles under the heading "The Young Feminists: A New Generation Speaks for Itself." As one author, Diane Salvatore, writes:

> Where have all the feminists gone? Or, more precisely, where will all the new feminists be coming from? — a question that older feminists have been wondering aloud and in the pages of newspapers and magazines. As an active 22-year-old feminist, the wondering gives me a sensation of watching my own funeral — struck dumb — and unable to tell my mourners that I am still very much alive.[31]

More than a decade later, these words still ring a bit too true. Older feminists still wonder aloud. Some younger feminists, without access to forums such as *Ms.* or to university press book contracts, continue to read about their own funerals or see themselves derided for a lack of commitment to feminism. For proof that these blindnesses have endured, one need only look to the pages of *The Knowledge Explosion: Generations of Feminist Scholarship* (1992), in which Cheris Kramarae and Dale Spender suggest that their collection contains a virtual absence of young feminists because there are so few: "Another issue we would want to pursue now is, where are all the young women? They are virtually invisible in these pages."[32] For Kramarae and Spender, a so-called lack of young feminists is traced back to the possibilities of ageism and, again, to the difficulties facing established feminists who are trying to transmit information to the next generation.[33] Why have some second-wave feminists been so slow to see us? We are in their classrooms, their conferences. Haven't they also complained that we are occasionally too much in their faces?

Perhaps some second-wavers don't see many young feminists before them because they don't see us "doing it right."[34] I hope that relatively few feminist academics today would be willing to argue that there aren't *any* young feminists (though plenty could rightfully argue that there aren't *enough*). Although women—and feminists, male and female—are enrolled in graduate programs in great numbers, there are still plenty of reasons to worry about who will make up the next generation of feminist academics. These worries might be better expressed not just in terms of feminist "brand loyalty"[35] but alongside the crisis in higher education, discussed at length in the work of Cary Nelson and Michael Bérubé, among others.[36] Will new faculty lines replace those of the retiring (feminist and otherwise) professors of the late 1990s? How will these lines be defined? What kinds of teaching and scholarship will be rewarded? Will the feminist credentials allegedly sought in graduate school to increase marketability translate into viable, full-time academic work? Will those whose hands are now on the institutional purse strings desire a certain "kind" of feminist over another? Or will departments (and deans) decide that they have hired "enough" of us? Second-wave feminists may have had to fight tooth and nail for tenure, but some third-wavers may not even get a foot in the tenure-track door. Generational differences, put in these terms, are profound indeed. Our "coming of age" seems much less rosy than some would have it; we are not the spoiled feminist "offspring" who "had it easy" and never learned to show gratitude. The economic constraints our generation faces simply won't allow most of us to inhabit that role.

Foundations and Generations

It is important to acknowledge that the benefit of years—the perch from which one is a "successful" second-wave academic feminist—entails more than a relatively secure career (assuming one has survived the tenure process). It entails more than just "wisdom," or, as Steinem would have it, the likelihood of increasing feminist radicalism.[37] Those who are senior in the academy have the ability to claim foundational status for their ideas and practices. After all, they have already circulated and are still around, having stood the proverbial test of time. This easily relegates more recent developments to fad status. It hardly need be said that some of today's fads will become future (and just as tenuous) foundations.[38] Perhaps the tenor of these scholarly changes is not specific to feminisms—or even to the current moment. It's possible that some differences are intrinsic to disciplines, to intellectual movements, or to Thomas Kuhn's oft-cited "paradigm shifts."[39] But even if these explanations were used to make sense of recent feminist change, we would be hard pressed now to label one "wave" as genuinely revolutionary and another as merely reactionary.

Younger feminists are *not* counterfeits in the face of the older and more genuine article. We are not the badly manufactured copies of second-wave originals. To imply this seems sheer hubris. I don't mean to suggest that second-wave feminists have the monopoly on feminist policing or that third wavers are the hapless victims in intergenerational exchanges. As Jane Gallop and Elizabeth Francis show in their intergenerational dialogue in this volume, there is blame from both directions. Regardless of how we understand ourselves in relation to these feminist generational stereotypes, clearly second- and third-wave feminists must find ways to talk to each other and, when possible, to work together. Furthermore, third-wave feminists probably "need" second-wave feminists more than "they" need "us." In graduate school, we need you as mentors, as the authorities who will advise, critique, and pass our work—with any luck, landing us jobs and promotions.

Shirley Nelson Garner has written eloquently about the problems and possibilities of feminist mentoring:

> To be a mentor and to be mentored, as I see it, is to assent to an agreement. The agreement, as I understand it, is to listen to each other,

to take each other seriously, to treat each other with respect, to trust each other until there is reason not to, to speak about our differences and disagreements rather than to hide them in silence, and to honor the inherent limits in this professional relationship.[40]

Speaking about disagreements and differences, communicating limits, and listening well are often difficult to do in practice, of course — but they are even more difficult in a climate in which one party (particularly the "more powerful") is perceived as disappointed in the other. Ruth Perry has persuasively argued that the feminist movement is "inexperienced" with "generational transfers of power."[41] Feminists in the academy have simply not been faced with the *luxury* of such transfers in the past. These "transfers" present problems with which feminists of each generation must struggle; this book theorizes, practices, and historicizes such conflicts.

Generational investigations, if they are to be useful to us at all, require historical specificity, and many of the essays in this collection operate in this mode. Today, at the fin de siècle and the end of a millennium, we are living through a moment of looking back and taking stock, and it is not surprising that such reflection has found its way into our scholarship. As Peter Herman has argued about the next generation of literary critics, "We are better, it must be admitted, at diagnosing our situation than presenting a solution. Even so, if our generation (so far) lacks a blindingly original voice . . . our work elaborates, deepens and pushes into new directions the previous work of literary criticism. That is no small task."[42] I am less willing than Herman to see twenty- and thirtysomething *feminists* as lacking "blinding originality." We are starting from different places from where our second-wave counterparts started, and as a result we may end up in locations that are now unrecognizable — even unthinkable. This need not be seen as a failure of transmission or a tragedy of linear feminist history. The promise of feminisms yet to come can be found in the following pages, alongside some of the most resonant and important feminist voices of past decades. The juxtaposition of "second"- and "third"-wave is alternately jarring and reassuring, but the dialogue is crucial for our collective histories and our feminist futures.

The Essays

Diane Elam's essay, "Sisters Are Doing It to Themselves," considers what she calls "the specter of postfeminism." Arguing that the phenomenon of postfeminism is in some way related to problems within feminism itself, Elam's chief concern in her essay is feminists' handling of power, as it has played out among generations of contemporary North American academic feminists. In her essay within an essay "How Sisters Do It to Themselves: A User's Guide," Elam provides an outline of the kinds of struggles that have kept feminists of different generations at odds—and therefore have kept the specter of postfeminism in play.

"Generational Difficulties; or, The Fear of a Barren History" by Judith Roof argues for the need to eschew the term *generation* in our feminist critical imagination: "Thinking in generational terms contributes—and might even produce—the sometimes torturous relations among women in academe." Through consideration of the work of Betty Friedan, Elaine Showalter, and Julia Kristeva, Roof shows how "generation" and "wave" as categories obscure and avoid other kinds of politics and contests, as well as reinscribing a reproductive narrative that assumes a familial paradigm. Roof's essay challenges the notions of time and history that have grounded heterological ideas of feminist generations.

In her essay, "Black Female Spectatorship and the Dilemma of Tokenism," Michele Wallace considers second-wave arguments about the position of the "female spectator" in feminist film theory and the extent to which such positions have insufficiently considered race. Recounting her experiences at conferences in the past decade, Wallace argues for the need to see female spectatorship through more racially inflected psychoanalytic terms: "I would like to persist in arguing in favor of modernist readings and the continuing usefulness of master narratives such as history and psychoanalysis." She asks, "What if the black female subject is constructed much like the white female subject? Or what if the similarities in the psychoanalytic construction of the black female subject are greater than the dissimilarities?" Wallace discusses the history of black women in the film and music industries, as well as the positions into which white and black feminist academics have relegated themselves and others in regard to questions of race.

In their dialogue "Talking Across," Jane Gallop and Elizabeth Francis—distinguished professor and advanced graduate student—investigate the ways in which they have thought about feminisms in intra- and intergenerational terms. Beginning with a discussion of Francis's experiences at the prestigious Berkshire Conference on the History of Women, Francis and Gallop examine their assumptions about and expectations for feminist community (including experiences of feminist "trashing"), especially in generational terms. In their lively exchange, they discuss their stereotypes of senior feminists and of the "aggressive, snotty graduate student."

"Feminist Psychology at Thirtysomething: Feminism, Gender, and Psychology's Ways of Knowing" by Jeanne Marecek provides a bird's-eye view into academic feminist generations in that discipline. She argues that "in feminist psychology...complacency, even self-congratulation, remains the rule; skepticism is the exception," although she notes that this is changing. Marecek provides a gloss on the past thirty years of feminist psychology, exploring some of the primary axes of disagreement and difference among feminist psychologists, along with the conditions under which they arose. She argues that in writing a history of the field of feminist psychology the term *generation* simply does not hold water, as it suggests a "progression of ideas and personnel [that] is far less linear" than what has taken place in feminist psychology to date.

Mona Narain's "Shifting Locations: Third World Feminists and Institutional Aporias" argues for the urgent need to discuss the specific location and politics of third world feminists within the academy in the United States. Her essay uses personal experience and other strategies to come to terms with these theoretical and discursive concerns, contextualizing the intellectual genealogies of third world feminists. Narain's essay ends with a discussion of Cheryl West's play *Jar the Floor*, illustrating how that text enacts important questions now faced by different generations of women of color.

In her essay "Jason Dreams, Victoria Works Out, " Nancy K. Miller considers the situation of feminists and faux feminists bashing other feminists in print, of feminist enemies — or what she calls "frenemies." She considers, too, the extent to which individual experience can represent a category: "If I — a 'senior' academic feminist who began writing in the 1970s — am harshly criticized — by a 'younger,' or as my students bitterly refer to themselves, 'Generation X feminist,' does this mean that 'Feminism' is being 'trashed'?" Quoting at length from the papers of two of her graduate students on the subject of feminist trashing, Miller mulls over what happens when generations in feminism must coexist.

Rebecca Dakin Quinn's "An Open Letter to Institutional Mothers" is an apt follow-up to Miller's essay, as Quinn wrote her essay in Miller's graduate seminar at the City University of New York (CUNY). Quinn considers the metaphorical mother-daughter relationship that obtains within academic feminism, especially as she has experienced and interpreted it through the feminist colloquium series at CUNY. She argues that if feminists are unable to listen to each other transgenerationally, it won't be long before our short-lived success within the university is destroyed.

Lynda Zwinger's "Dancing through the Mother Field: On Aggression, Making Nice, and Reading Symptoms" engages directly with the institutional "mothers" she has encountered in her scholarly reading. Zwinger "works" mother in the form of a written confrontation with Nancy K. Miller's work, especially *Getting Personal*.[43] Speaking of and in "the personal" of feminist discourses, Zwinger theorizes her responses to reading the work of Miller and others—work with which she often disagrees but at the same time has found formative to her own feminist scholarship. Her essay is part of a larger project that investigates the stories we tell "and the ways in which those stories dramatize—and dictate—the process by which girls learn to be good daughters."

Ruthe Thompson's essay "*Working* Mother" also investigates the circulation of the trope of "mother" in feminist discourses, though in different forms. Thompson "works" mother first with an exploration of the periodical *Working Mother,* which (as she notes) "could hardly be considered a 'feminist' text." Thompson then argues that "feminists, academic and otherwise, have failed to deal adequately with the problem of motherhood in patriarchy despite a proliferation of published articles, books, talks, and conferences on the subject." She illustrates the ways in which much feminist scholarship has invested itself in trying to discuss motherhood without tarnishing the sanctity of the maternal position and examines this as an issue with generational ramifications.

Linda Frost's " 'Somewhere in Particular': Generations, Feminism, Class Conflict, and the Terms of Academic Success" considers the overlapping of the discourses of feminisms, generations, and class. She uses her own stories "in order to talk about how the generational influences—familial, feminist, and academic—that have done their work on me continue to play a part in my work as a feminist working in the academy." She argues that when many view intellectuals with suspicion, we "need to learn to use our personal narratives to forge and strengthen our connections with our students." Speaking as a first-generation college graduate and as a teacher of similarly positioned college students, Frost discusses the ways in which issues of class and regional background shape our sense of ourselves as academics, in and out of the classroom.

Angela M. S. Nelson investigates the positioning of women of color on television from a generation later, focusing on Diahann Carroll's series *Julia* (NBC, 1968–1971). In her essay, "The Objectification of *Julia*: Texts, Textures, and Contexts of Black Women in American Television Situation Comedies," Nelson argues that this series represented for the first time in television history a new type of black woman, and she compares the ways in which black women have been objectified on television since 1950. Her essay discusses *Julia* within its historical context by comparing its representations of African American women in television series of the 1940s and 1990s, measuring how far our culture has—and hasn't yet—come with its circulation of images of black females.

Jane Kalbfleisch's "When Feminism Met Postfeminism: The Rhetoric of a Relationship" considers feminism and postfeminism, suggesting the shortcomings of seeing these discourses as related antithetically or as escaping their binary logic through a tolerance of difference. Kalbfleisch proposes an alternative, one that is "better cloaked in the rhetoric of Jane Gallop, Jane Tompkins, and Jean-François Lyotard in their respective discussions of feminism and psychoanalysis, the personal and the critical, and modernism and postmodernism." Her discussion of feminist differences allows for new ways to theorize feminist survival.

Theresa Ann Sears's "Feminist Misogyny; or, What Kind of a Woman Are You?" discusses the problems of power and competition among academic feminists, concluding that relationships among women—among feminists even—are not as rosy as we might like to think:

> When the doctrine of universal support insists that we pass over individual qualifications and actions, it becomes psychologically naive, intellectually dishonest, and professionally unethical. Each of these charges must be dealt with in turn, as components of an academic

institutional feminism that is neoromantic at its core, and that confuses the goals and methods of three strands of feminism: the personal, the political, and the intellectual.

Sears argues that many issues of feminist conflict remain unexamined, obscured by the "myth of sisterhood."

Turning to the question of how feminism has historically dealt with the trope of feminist motherhood and knowledge transmission, Barbara A. White considers actual mother-daughter pairs of several generations ago to look at the configuration of feminism as it was (or was not) "passed down." White's essay, "Three Feminist Mother-Daughter Pairs in the Nineteenth- and Early-Twentieth-Century United States," focuses on the interactions of three mother-daughter pairs: Elizabeth Cady Stanton and Harriot Stanton Blatch, Lucy Stone and Alice Stone Blackwell, and Ida B. Wells-Barnett and Alfreda M. Duster. White shows that the daughters seem to have rejected anything but the most traditional mothering, which they received in full from their radical mothers.

Like Narain, Gita Rajan considers issues of feminist generations alongside those of postcoloniality. And like Roof, Rajan is interested in issues of temporality and spatialization for feminisms. In her "Fissuring Time, Suturing Space: Reading Bharati Mukherjee's *The Holder of the World*," Rajan uses Mukherjee's 1993 novel to make sense of the ways in which feminisms have understood themselves in terms of space and time; Mukherjee's novel, as Rajan argues, is a good focus for such an investigation as it "lays bare that moment when feminist scholarship began to shift from the second to the third wave." Rajan argues that the novel falls short in some of the ways we might like to see it succeed, suggesting that "space could have provided the map to embark on a new episteme, tell a different tale in feminist, generational terms."

In "The Anxiety of Affluence: Movements, Markets, and Lesbian Feminist Generation(s)," Dana Heller begins with a skepticism of the term *generation,* noting that it fails to carry the explanatory weight to make sense of her engagements with feminist, lesbian, and queer studies. She cites Katie King's work on the histories of feminisms to see generational anxieties as always interested anxieties. Her essay considers several generationally positioned texts, among them *The Beatles Anthology,* David Leavitt's novel *The Lost Language of Cranes,* and Rose Troche's film *Go Fish.*[44] Considering the interests that sparked the movement from "lesbian feminist" to "queer," Heller concludes that now is the time to "consider at what price uncritical images of queer commodity trafficking have ascended over abject images of lesbian feminist leftism, retiring critiques of consumer capitalism and commodity fetishism that will be necessary for our political survival in the uncertain years ahead."

Finally, Judith Newton, like Elam, describes the larger cultural forces that have led North American feminisms to our current historical moment in her essay, "Feminist Family Values; or, Growing Old—and Growing Up—with the Women's Movement." Beginning with an exploration of feminist "anniversaries" and of our internal struggles, Newton expands her scope to consider the new alliances that have begun to solidify, particularly in universities. Newton does not consider these alliances to be uncomplicated and merely celebrated. She argues that "old histories and antagonisms still lurk. If we are to pursue broader alliances in earnest, some of these histories and antagonisms may need to be encountered, revisited, and rethought." Her essay follows up on one such alliance, that between white feminists and white, progressive men. Newton concludes with a consideration of our metaphors of "community," arguing for the need to reform them in order to achieve feminist goals as we head into the twenty-first century.

Notes

1. A myriad of sources might be pointed to: Madelon Sprengnether, "Generational Differences—Reliving Mother-Daughter Conflicts," in *Changing Subjects: The Making of Feminist Literary Criticism*, ed. Gayle Greene and Coppelia Kahn (New York: Routledge, 1993), 201–10; Renate Klein, "Passion and Politics in Women's Studies in the Nineties," *Women's Studies International Forum* 14.3 (1991): 125–34; Nancy K. Miller, "Decades," *South Atlantic Quarterly* 91.1 (1992): 65–86; Jane Gallop, Marianne Hirsch, and Nancy K. Miller, "Criticizing Feminist Criticism," in *Conflicts in Feminism*, ed. Marianne Hirsch and Evelyn Fox Keller (New York: Routledge, 1990), 349–69; "Conference Call," *differences* 2.3 (1990): 52–97.

2. See Gayle Greene and Coppelia Kahn, eds., *Changing Subjects;* Kathryn P. Meadow Orlans and Ruth A. Wallace, eds., *Gender and the Academic Experience: Berkeley Women Sociologists* (Lincoln: University of Nebraska Press, 1994).

3. I use the term *younger* with some trepidation, knowing that it is a slippery category. For academic women, the term *younger* would perhaps most accurately designate feminist graduate students and junior faculty members. By lumping them together, I hope to discuss a group that is "less established" or often "less powerful" within institutions. I sympathize with those who, like Rosi Braidotti, are "reluctant to take 'youth' as a feminist political category *per se*" (55). However, I think the very hi-

erarchical distinctions that Braidotti goes on to describe within feminisms today can be explained, in large part, through the shorthand of age. See Rosi Braidotti, "Generations of Feminists; or, Is There Life after Post-Modernism?" *Found Object* 6 (1995): 55–62.

4. See Cheris Kramarae and Dale Spender, eds., *The Knowledge Explosion: Generations of Feminist Scholarship* (New York: Teacher's College, 1992), 15.

5. See Barbara Findlen, ed., *Listen Up! Voices from the Next Feminist Generation* (Seattle: Seal Press, 1995); and Rebecca Walker, *To Be Real: Telling the Truth and Changing the Face of Feminism* (New York: Anchor Books, 1995).

6. See Steinem's "Why Young Women Are More Conservative," in her *Outrageous Acts and Everyday Rebellions* (New York: Signet, 1983), 238–46.

7. Findlen, *Listen*, xiii.

8. Walker, *To Be Real*, xxxi.

9. Steinem, "Foreword," in Walker, *To Be Real*, xxii.

10. Steinem writes: "I want to remind readers who are younger or otherwise new to feminism that some tactical and theoretical wheels don't have to be reinvented. You may want to make them a different size or color, put them on a different wagon, use them to travel in a different direction, or otherwise make them your own—but many already exist" (xix). Steinem's point is an important one; history shouldn't be forgotten, and feminist work from centuries past needs to be noted. The implicit suggestion that third-wave feminists are unknowingly reinventing the wheel, however, is disturbing.

11. Susan Stanford Friedman, "Making History: Reflections on Feminism, Narrative, and Desire," in *Feminism beside Itself*, ed. Diane Elam and Robyn Wiegman (New York: Routledge, 1995), 50–51.

12. It is interesting to note that Betty Friedan's own generational position—and our understanding of second-wave feminism more generally—is being called into question by historians who have made claims for a tradition of feminist activity in the 1940s and 1950s. See Karen J. Winkler, "Relooking at the Roots of Feminism: Article on Betty Friedan Reflects New Scholarship on the Women's Movement," *The Chronicle of Higher Education* (April 12, 1996): A10.

13. On anger, see Audre Lorde, *Sister Outsider: Essays and Speeches* (Trumansburg, N.Y.: Crossing Press, 1984). On useful ways to conceive of feminist conflict, see Victoria Davion, "Do Good Feminists Compete?", *Hypatia* 2.2 (1987): 55–63.

14. See Betty Friedan, *The Fountain of Age* (New York: Simon and Schuster, 1993), 63.

15. Sprengnether, "Generational Differences," 206–7.

16. See Katie Roiphe, *The Morning After: Fear, Sex, and Feminism on Campus* (Boston: Little, Brown, 1993); Alvin Toffler, *The Third Wave* (New York: Morrow, 1980).

17. Catharine R. Stimpson, "Women's Studies and Its Discontents," *Dissent* 43 (1996): 67.

18. See Louise Bernikow, "Fearless, Funny, Fighting Mad," *Cosmopolitan* (April 1993): 163–65.

19. Jacqui Alexander et al., eds., *The Third Wave: Feminist Perspectives on Racism* (Latham, N.Y.: Kitchen Table Women of Color Press, 1993).

20. Neil Howe and Bill Strauss, *13th Gen: Abort, Retry, Ignore, Fail?* (New York: Vintage, 1993), 42. They also say that starting with those born in 1982, we will have a "Millennial" generation of baby boomlet-ers, who, as of now, have no media image to contend with. Some of these young people will enter college in the year 2000.

21. William Strauss and Neil Howe, *Generations: The History of America's Future, 1584 to 2069* (New York: Quill/William Morrow, 1991), 12.

22. Ibid., 319.

23. Alice Jardine suggests that there have been many generations of feminist scholars, including those who received a doctorate before 1968 and those who received it between 1968 and 1978, 1978 and 1988, and 1988 and 1998. Quoted in Donna Landry, "Commodity Feminism," in *The Profession of Eighteenth-Century Literature: Reflections on an Institution,* ed. Leo Damrosch (Madison: University of Wisconsin Press, 1992), 160.

24. See my article "This Feminism Which Is Not One," *minnesota review* 41–42 (1995): 108–17.

25. Annette Kolodny, "Dancing between Left and Right: Feminism and the Academic Minefield in the 1980s," in *Literature, Language, and Politics,* ed. Betty Jean Craige (Athens: University of Georgia Press, 1988), 30.

26. Landry, "Commodity Feminism," 160.

27. Nancy Whittier, *Feminist Generations: The Persistence of the Radical Women's Movement* (Philadelphia: Temple University Press, 1995), 3.

28. Ibid., 3–4. As Whittier concludes, "I think . . . that the women's movement community is a direct, and political, heir of the radical feminist movement. It has survived where externally oriented protest often could not. Cultural events sustain feminists' collective identity, recruit new women to the movement, and provide a base from which participants organize other forms of protest. More directly, cultural challenges undermine hegemonic ideology about gender by constructing new ways of being a woman that are visible to outsiders as well as insiders. Far from being nonpolitical, such efforts are central to the survival and impact of the women's movement" (250). Just as cultural events are seen as central and political here, so are theories and classrooms. It strikes me as odd that feminist professors would not be thrilled to find women who came to feminism through these channels.

29. See Darlene Hantzis and Devoney Looser, "Of Safe(r) Spaces and 'Right' Speech: Feminist Histories, Loyalties, Theories, and the Dangers of Critique," in *PC Wars: Politics and Theory in the Academy,* ed. Jeffrey Williams (New York: Routledge, 1994), 222–49.

30. Jane Gallop, Marianne Hirsch, and Nancy K. Miller, "Criticizing Feminist Criticism," 365.

31. Diane Salvatore, "Young Feminists Speak for Themselves: A Classic Case of Sensory Overload," *Ms.* 11.10 (1983): 43. Following this piece is a short essay by then feminist college student, Naomi Wolf.

32. Kramarae and Spender, *Knowledge Explosion,* 15.

33. *Ibid.*

34. See Hantzis and Looser, "Of Safe(r) Spaces."

35. On "brand loyalty," see Donna Landry, "Commodity Feminism," 154–74.

36. See Michael Bérubé and Cary Nelson, eds., *Higher Education under Fire: Politics, Economics, and the Crisis of the Humanities* (New York: Routledge, 1995).

37. See Steinem, *Outrageous Acts,* 239.

38. Sander L. Gilman recently noted, "Different generations not only ask different questions but have very different definitions of 'good' (that is, fashionable) scholarship. This diversity is a sign not of confusion but of strength, for the cumulative effect of such work is to show how each individual in each generation can add to the sum of insight." See his "What Should Scholarly Publication in the Humanities Be?" MLA *Newsletter* 27.3 (1995): 4.

39. See Thomas S. Kuhn, *The Structure of Scientific Revolutions* (Chicago: University of Chicago Press, 1962).

40. Shirley Nelson Garner, "Mentoring Lessons," *Women's Studies Quarterly* 22.1–2, (1994): 13.

41. Ruth Perry, "I Brake for Feminists: Debates and Divisions within Women's Studies," *Concerns* 25.2 (1995): 30.

42. Peter Herman, " '60s Theory and '90s Critics," *symplokē* 3.1 (1995): 53.

43. Nancy K. Miller, *Getting Personal: Feminist Occasions and Other Autobiographical Acts* (New York: Routledge, 1991).

44. Katie King, *Theory in Its Feminist Travels: Conversations in U.S. Women's Movements* (Bloomington: Indiana University Press, 1994); David Leavitt, *The Lost Language of Cranes* (Toronto: Bantam Books, 1986).

Sisters Are Doing It to Themselves

Diane Elam

A specter is haunting women's studies departments—the specter of postfeminism. In hallways, in meetings, in classrooms, this apparition keeps whispering that there is nothing more to be gained from feminism. It's time to get on with things, the voice says, time to stop worrying about women's oppression, equal rights, and the evils of patriarchy. However, given the continued attempts to make abortion illegal, the growing violence against women, and existing data on pay and conditions for working women, it would seem that postfeminism is more than a little out of touch, even for a specter. But postfeminism has thus far been surprisingly compelling, and efforts on the part of feminist exorcists have yet to prove effective. The specter persists.

This seems a remarkable failure for feminism, and it remains to be understood how postfeminism could be taken seriously either by feminists or anyone else. I am reluctant to conclude that the reason is that postfeminism is an opportunistic move on the part of the patriarchy, the introduction of a particularly vigorous and invasive weed into the otherwise healthy garden of feminism. Postfeminism is not merely the invention of sophisticated antifeminists, who hope to lull us into a false sense of security, a sense that nothing matters anymore. The very success of postfeminist arguments suggests that they are addressing some real problems within feminism itself.

While the backlash against feminism must certainly be taken seriously, as feminists like Susan Faludi have argued, merely instituting protective measures against threatening patriarchal intruders would be too simple a solution to the problem.[1] Rather, to understand the appeal of postfeminism I think it is important to ask some serious questions about what is happening *within* feminism: what claim does the notion that feminism might have come to the end of its trajectory hold on feminists? What fear leads a new generation of women, who want to keep their distance from feminism, to ignore their debts to their "mothers"? Are the mothers themselves wishing for the end of an era, a new day in which feminism is no longer part of the political and intellectual agenda? In short, what kind of malaise gives rise to the desire that feminism should have come to an end, either suffocated under the weight of its own successes or exhausted by a struggle that no longer seems worthwhile?

In order to address these questions, feminism needs to consider seriously its own internal struggles, internal struggles that often play themselves out along generational lines, as the formulation of my questions suggests. It needs to look at the ways in which feminist sisters may, in fact, be doing themselves in, be creating the very specter of postfeminism that has proven to have such a destructive and haunting presence. The possibility remains that feminism may not need patriarchy to bring about its downfall; it could self-destruct of its own accord.

This is a rather apocalyptic note. But the entire tune is not so prophetic, for several questions still remain unsung. To begin with, there is the question of what feminist success might mean: whether the success of feminism necessarily leads to the era of postfeminism. Does feminism have a trajectory, and if so, where is it headed? Can we happily contemplate the possibility that when all the battles have been won, feminism will no longer be necessary? In this regard, the historicization of feminism as a project installs a certain version of generational conflict and anxiety. Is feminism a *tradition* handed down by powerful ancestors, or is it a *progress* in which the latecomers, however dwarf-like, are always standing on the shoulders of those who came before, seeing farther, knowing more?

Along with the problem of success goes the question of handling power, which will be my chief concern in this essay. If feminists have achieved positions of power, and if feminist arguments have achieved a certain cultural weight, how is feminism to deal with this phenomenon? Two aspects seem important here. First, what would it mean for feminism to achieve cultural hegemony? What happens when feminism is no longer on the margins but at the cultural center? Second, how is power to be distributed among women (and men) in the feminist movement? Once feminism gains the power it has sought, how will it use that power? Could it be that postfeminism, rather than marking the success of feminism, is the indicator that feminism has not sufficiently come to terms with its own power?

It is clear that feminism has a hard time raising the question of power, be it internally or in relation to society at large. Power is not something women are supposed to have. It is what they lack, and their lack drives the struggle of feminism. In some sense, then, postfeminism is the by-product of this rather simplistic account of power. It arises precisely when the question of power becomes complicated: when feminists are seen by a younger generation as having power, as being like their parents who also try to make them behave in certain ways; when younger women feel themselves already to have power once they can vote, go to college, or fly combat aircraft. The relation of women to the traditional bastions of state power has definitely shifted. And the structure of women's oppression in the western industrial world is no longer simply a matter of exclusion, no longer simply a matter of being offered the role of wife, mother, or prostitute. The *marginalization of women* is perhaps the wrong term to use, then, because it implies an identifiable center of power, exclusion from which would constitute oppression.

One of the things that Michel Foucault was right about is that power is a matrix, a network of relations in which no one either holds absolute power or is absolutely powerless.[2] Postfeminism arises when this fact becomes harder to ignore, when claims of victimization seem overstated at best, hypocritical at worst. While there are millions of abused women in the world, the traditional discursive practices of feminism, focusing as they do on a trajectory of individual empowerment, are inadequate in the face of such a complex problem. Solutions are not merely a matter of individuals claiming power for themselves, or all women recognizing their common oppression together. In fact, recourse to "common oppression" as a political platform has done more to deny the social condition of various women than it has helped to redress any injustices. This is the point bell hooks makes clear when she argues that

> the idea of "common oppression" was a false and corrupt platform disguising and mystifying the true nature of woman's varied and complex social reality. Women are divided by sexist attitudes, racism, class privilege, and a host of other prejudices. Sustained woman bonding can occur only when these divisions are confronted and the

necessary steps are taken to eliminate them. Divisions will not be
eliminated by wishful thinking or romantic reverie about common
oppression despite the value of highlighting experiences all women
share.[3]

While there may still be some point for feminists to speak of sisterhood, a serious problem remains when that sisterhood is grounded
in an appeal to common oppression. In some sense, what is at stake
here is the need to rethink the feminist project in ways that do not
oversimplify either the nature of power in general, or questions of
power relations among women and among feminists.

In this essay, I want to begin thinking about such questions of power
in a very limited framework, by addressing the generational issue in
contemporary North American academic feminism. What makes generation such an important concern at the moment is the fact that feminism in general, and academic feminism especially, has often failed
to take generational conflict as a serious issue — as an issue internal
to feminism — with which it must contend. I would even go so far as
to suggest that it has been feminism's failure to address generational
problems that has caused the specter of postfeminism to begin making such frequent appearances lately.

For feminism to take the problem of generation seriously, then, it
is important to acknowledge that, in relation to the question of the
distribution of power among women, there is no single, essential, or
universal figure of woman. Generation stands alongside race, sexuality, and class as a form of difference among women. It would be a
mistake, I think, to believe that generational differences could always
be understood in isolation, without considering the ways in which
they are part of a complex matrix of differences among women. Furthermore, generation is not only a function of age but also of institutional position and position within the feminist movement itself. While
generation can be a difference predicated on age — and certainly there
are historical reasons for considering it in this way — age alone does
not account for where one is situated professionally or politically. It
is possible, for instance, for a feminist of forty to be a professionally
"junior woman" (an assistant professor or a graduate student within
the academy) while at the same time, in terms of age, belong to a different generation of women from that of many of her coworkers. In
this respect, generational lines are not always precisely drawn in response to the question "How old are you?"

It might be better to think of generation within the framework of *tradition.* That is to say, tradition is what is handed down from one generation to another, as the Latin root *traditio* reminds us. The split between generations is not established in terms of age alone or as part of a general history but by *the act of handing down.* Generations are thus structurally divided on either side of what is handed down between them. The younger generation receives the tradition as a *gift* (with all the structural ambivalence of this term that Sigmund Freud and Marcel Mauss have noted); the elder generation hands over the tradition as a gift yet must face the uncomfortable prospect, as with all gifts, of not being able to calculate what it may receive in return. The gift that brings the generations together also divides them from each other, as separate generational groups. This grouping thus does not so much occur among feminists themselves as it brings generations together in the face of a tradition that they either receive from others with whom they are in conflict or hand over to others over whom they have no control. For the elder generation handing down the tradition involves relinquishing a certain control over it, while to receive the tradition as gift places the younger generation in the position of being unable to control the actions of their ancestors, constrained only to interpret that tradition.

Within this framework it is easy to see that generational conflict is a *structural necessity.* Conflict and tension are the mode in which people face up to the fact that one does *not* control either one's predecessors or the generation that follows. One of the horrors of having children is the fact that despite all efforts to the contrary, they will come to view their parents as those parents themselves viewed their grandparents: as alien beings from another time zone, who just don't understand the present generation. All gifts come from nowhere, in the sense that the recipient can never absolutely determine what the giving of the gift meant to the giver. All gifts are thrown out into the void; the giver can never absolutely know what the gift means to the recipient.[4]

This structure of the gift distinguishes it from the commercial transaction—where a common standard of economic value is presumed that would allow such a calculation to be made—and radically affects the question of tradition in feminism. Generational conflict necessarily arises in the very act of defining one's relation to the tradition, to this gift that one hands on to succeeding generations, or that one receives from preceding generations of women.

It is by ignoring these conflicts, by failing to address the ways in which generational anxieties can also undermine feminism's political force, that feminists allow the specter of postfeminism to gain its power. Postfeminism counts on the fact that a younger generation will swing wildly between mother worship and disdain for past inadequacies, while the older generation will act out its nagging sense of the possibility of ingratitude by either accusing younger women of betrayal or seeking to control them in ways structurally parallel to patriarchy. This variation on a theme of Oedipal conflict, however, need not be the story that feminism must tell itself. And in order to strip away some of the power from the ghostly presence of postfeminism, I will risk being overly reductive and sketch out some of the basic generational conflicts that currently arise within academic feminism. This is by no means an exhaustive catalogue, and the problems facing feminists in the academy are not necessarily ones that translate into other feminist institutions. But even such a limited inquiry reveals a great deal about the potential attraction of postfeminism and explains the persistence of its ghostly presence in feminist circles.

How Sisters Do It to Themselves: A User's Guide

1. Feminist Misogyny: Why Isn't My Daughter More Like My Son?

While it is usual to associate misogyny with patriarchy, feminism proves to have its own long-standing tradition of misogyny.[5] Along generational lines, feminist misogyny tends to manifest itself when senior feminists, sometimes unconsciously, discriminate against juniors, treating them more harshly and with less respect than their male counterparts. "I had it rough and so should you" would be one of the battle cries here. More seriously, senior feminists who have always resented the fact that they themselves are women, who in short hate themselves because they are women, then displace these feelings onto the junior women who cross their paths. With these senior women, institutionally it proves a great advantage to be a male feminist. For while the work of misogynist seniors makes feminist claims, often their own institutional practices are far from feminist when it comes to their treatment of other women.

2. *Feminist Benign Neglect*

On the surface, this can appear to be a form of feminist misogyny, when in fact it is a less aggressive, although still serious, problem. In this instance, senior feminists simply fail to recognize any responsibility to help junior feminists. Whether out of a general state of tiredness from having fought too many battles themselves, or because it hasn't occurred to them that junior feminists would need any help, senior feminists lend little or no institutional support to their junior counterparts. The result: the old-boy network persists, while junior feminists are all too often simply left to fend for themselves.

3. *Feminist Misogyny Take Two: Why Can't Mom Be More Like Dad?*

Lest it seem that all generational conflicts within feminism are the fault of the more senior generation, it is necessary to recognize that feminist misogyny can also be a junior affliction. Admittedly, this scenario may seem less familiar, but that is only because it is such a recent development. It is now possible for junior women to produce feminist work but direct it entirely to please senior men, whom they position as the real judges and whose approval actually counts. The opinions of senior feminists seem not to matter, and their institutional power is viewed as second rate at best. So there is an odd hypocrisy at work here. To seek recognition within a patriarchal institution is a complex act for feminists, and many junior women seem to be blissfully ignorant of this fact. Feminism becomes a professional token with which the junior feminist buys recognition and the approval of a profession whose senior ranks are still male dominated.

4. *Great Expectations*

The case here is relatively straightforward. Junior feminists expect senior feminists to help them more than they actually can. The junior feminists then get angry when their unreasonable expectations are not met, and the senior feminists are left wondering what went wrong. The result can be merely some unnecessary bad feelings; at worst it resembles a version of feminist misogyny when the junior feminist sets out to exact revenge on her allegedly inadequate feminist senior.

5. *Dutiful Daughter Complex*

Also known as Blind Obedience Syndrome, this problem manifests itself when senior feminists insist that junior feminists be good daughters, defending the same kind of feminism as their mothers. Questions and criticism are allowed but only if they proceed from the approved brand of feminism. Daughters are not allowed to invent new ways of thinking and doing feminism for themselves; feminist politics should take the same shape that it always has. New agendas are regarded at best with suspicion on the part of the seniors, at worst with outright hostility. Daughters are regularly sacrificed if they step out of line.

6. *Nonpayment of Debt*

Ignoring any battles that older generations of feminists may have fought, junior feminists simply do not believe they owe anybody anything. They fail to acknowledge their debts to senior feminists and assume that, of course, they should share in the hard-won privileges they do not even realize were hard-won. The current state of women in the academy seems like a natural state of affairs to them; senior feminists are usually remembered when junior feminists need somebody to blame for feminism's problems. Here the tendency is for junior feminists consistently to view the work of their seniors as indifferently naive, boring, reductive, and outdated.

7. *Letting Go Is So Very Hard to Do*

Having established a tradition of feminism within the academy, these senior feminists then find it difficult to pass that tradition on to a new generation of feminists. This generational conflict is not so much one marked by the hostility of an older or younger generation toward the other, but more a problem with imagining what it might mean to construct and continue a changing tradition of feminist thought. The risk here is that by failing to make the necessary room for a younger generation of feminists, feminism merely withers away on the vine.

Do Feminists Just Want to Get Along?

These scenarios do not offer much by the way of a future for feminism, and I doubt that the solution to the problems I have outlined here is simply for the generations to hug one another and be friends.

While feminism has often stood for a kinder and gentler academy, many feminists can attest that quite the contrary is often the case. I am not suggesting, then, that feminists just need to be nicer to one another, although sometimes that might not hurt. If there is a solution here, it begins in being able to acknowledge that these and other generational conflicts exist and need to be addressed as such. This will not mean the end of conflict or argument—as I have indicated earlier, I understand generational conflict to be a structural necessity of traditions, including feminist ones. Rather, it will mean negotiating the Scylla and Charybdis of feminism: obedience and indebtedness on the one hand, misogyny and conservativism on the other. Postfeminism may seem to some like the powerful weapon that will keep them out of danger in such troubled feminist waters. And it will continue to be so if feminism itself does not come up with a better solution.

Before pursuing in more detail how I think feminism might arrive at possible solutions, it is worth looking more closely at the results of phrasing an argument about generational conflict in terms of "juniors" and "seniors." To begin with, if the more serious and widespread sins of generational conflict end up on the side of "seniors," that does not mean that the problem with feminism largely lies in the behavior or attitudes of the older generations of feminists. There is not a single group of seniors beating up on their junior sidekicks, and my intention is not simply to pit one group of women, "senior feminists," against another, "junior feminists," oversimplifying the power structure at work in the process. Significantly, most feminists find themselves to be both a senior and a junior at the same time. An assistant professor, for instance, will be a senior feminist to her students at the same time that she is positioned within her own department as a junior in relation to her more senior, tenured colleagues.

My argument is therefore not a matter of blaming one group of feminists while exonerating another, since the senior and junior feminist could, depending on the circumstances, be the same individual. That is to say, it is possible for any one feminist to participate in several of the scenarios I have described—sometimes as the junior, at others as the senior. So if generational conflict more often arises as the result of the behavior of senior feminists, this is not because older feminists are simply behaving badly. It points instead to a problem of power *within* feminism. The injustices committed by senior feminists are another indicator that feminism has yet to come to terms with what it would mean for it to have power and to put that power to good use. Feminism exists within institutions that perpetuate and encourage these sorts of unequal power relationships constructed along generational lines. This is not likely to go away on its own anytime in the near future. I would argue, then, that feminism needs to take account of the fact that it does not simply stand outside of institutional power structures at the same time that it tries to imagine new ways of standing together.

The problem with actually doing this seems to revolve around a lack of specifically feminist models of power and tradition. Patriarchal power structures of the family — imagining relationships between women as always those of mothers and daughters, for instance — stay in place by default. But no matter how difficult a rethinking of institutional power structures might be, feminism needs to do this if it's going to be anything more than patriarchy with a face-lift.

For a long time now the cosmetic surgery at feminism's disposal has been identity politics. But the easy answers that identity politics tend to offer are precisely what have created such a welcoming space for postfeminism. Postfeminism alleges that the gains made by feminist identity politics are now over and done with. Postfeminism, that is, tries to mark the success of feminist identity politics by posing as the specter that is, in fact, the logical conclusion of feminist politics. And feminist identity politics will have a difficult time explaining away the specter's argument; at best they can simply ward off the inevitable.

These may seem like harsh words leveled at political strategies that have brought feminism, and feminists, such a long way. However, if feminism is going to rethink the force of institutional power structures, it is going to have to begin by confronting the limitations, not the strengths, of identity politics. There comes a time when the solutions offered by identity politics prove worse than the problems they are intended to solve.

What, then, are the basic problems with identity politics that make them play into the hands of postfeminism? June Jordan offers a compelling answer to this question:

> I think that the reason I wanted to go beyond identity politics, and actually have opposed identity politics as certainly, ultimately, as a dead end, is because I'm a writer, I am a poet. Given identity, whether it's gender or race . . . is just too simple, it's not specific, it's not complete. . . . It's like saying somebody's *nice* — what do you *mean* by

that? Like saying somebody's Black, what do you *mean* by that, really in the consciousness of the United States, in the consciousness of the world, what does that mean?[6]

It is in the very fact of their simplicity that identity politics can be both effective and pernicious. By providing a forum in which to combat discrimination based on identity—be it that of race, gender, age, or sexual orientation—identity politics have proven to be a powerful rallying cry. But the battles that identity politics have won have not been without their casualties: uninterrogated politics that recognize individuals only insofar as they conform to particular identity categories; hierarchies of difference and identity that, practically speaking, serve to create contests in which the participants vie for the title of "most oppressed."[7] In these instances, identity politics promote the very stereotyping and tokenism that they allegedly fight against by trying to solve complex problems by merely invoking oversimplified labels.

The same holds true when generation is taken to be an issue of identity politics, when it is presumed that generations are grounded in identities. Each generation would thus have a group identity, and the politics of generational struggle would be a matter of deciding which generation was the most female, as it were. Here a generation functions as a historical parameter to establish an identity, so that identity becomes the *parole* in the *langue* of history, to borrow from Ferdinand de Saussure for a moment. In terms of identity politics (and explaining its problems by drawing the parallel to Saussure a bit further), the meaning of each generation is established differentially; identity is fixed in relation to the other, preceding and subsequent generations. The meaning of *Generation X* is determined in opposition to Generations W and Y. The important point (and problem) is that each generation has an identity, and the relation that establishes that identity is one of straightforward opposition. X is *not* Y, and so on. This wrongly fixes generations as units of meaning—meaning that can supposedly be calculated.

This account of generation in terms of opposed identities, however, misreads the function of tradition. Tradition situates generations in differential relationships, but those relationships are not simple oppositions. Generations are not identities between which the tradition is passed; rather, each generation must presume the other (be it the giver or recipient of the tradition) as an incalculable other. Hence, the difference of generations arises *within* each generation as the threatening recognition that there must be another generation that is finally inaccessible. Precisely because one cannot belong to two generations, one cannot *belong* to one generation either. For each generation is fissured by the thought that there must be, and must have been, other generations. Generation is therefore not a simple opposition in the terms of identity politics. While a straightforward opposition gives rise to identities on either side, the difference between generations does not allow an identity to coalesce or fix because the terms are always being negotiated.[8] The exchange is never made face to face; the gift always comes from nowhere and goes nowhere. That is to say, the gift always intervenes to make the relationship conflictual and incalculable.

Identity politics, however, desire to make the gift an economically calculable exchange between identifiable generations. They want to know the precise value of the gift, know in advance what the tradition will be worth to its heirs. What is more, identity politics seek to identify and name the heirs who will be the worthy recipients of such a gift. Thus, there is a terrible desire on the part of those who practice the most violent identity politics both to be the true heirs of their mothers and to designate their own true heirs in return. Of course, they can only attempt to realize this desire by ignoring the burden and conflicted nature of tradition because the gift (that is, tradition) disbars identity.

But given these desires on the part of some feminists, nonetheless, one of the curious things about feminism — one of the things that continually flies in the face of identity politics — is its inability to say who are its heirs, to locate with certainty the second generation of sisters-daughters. What I think feminism has at least implicitly understood is that tradition means there are no true heirs. That is to say, if for Freud paternity is a legal fiction, so is maternity for feminism. One of feminism's strengths is its resistance to founding mothers, its awkwardly handed-down gifts. For feminism recognizes that legal maternity is patriarchy once again.

In saying that inheritance proves problematic for feminism, some questions might still seem to have gone unanswered: how could feminism be handed down as a tradition without identity politics? How would it recognize who to hand itself down to and who was doing the handing? I would argue in response that these are actually the wrong questions. They are questions formulated on the side of identity politics, and feminism will not be able to think its way out of identity politics if it does not phrase its questions in different terms. While some days it may look as if feminism has never been anything but identity politics, that is really not the case. More accurately, feminism has never been an identity politics: rather, some feminists have done identity politics. That is why in this essay I have tried to argue that, first, generational conflict is a necessary problem and, second, that identity politics will always suppress this conflict because generational difference is what undermines the ground of identity politics.

My answer to the problem of identity politics and my reaction to generational conflict are not to institute a moral purity test. *There is no one feminist who can do justice to all other feminists of all generations.* There are no true heirs, no true mothers. Those who stand behind identity politics all want to be that one, morally pure feminist; that is the very lure of identity politics. But being a feminist is a messy business, and feminists can never pay off all of their debts or recognize all of their obligations. If, however, there is no pure justice to be had, that does not exempt feminists from their ethical responsibilities, including their obligations to and solidarity with other feminists. It would be pleasant to think that the expansion of the numbers of women in the academy could occur without disturbing the solidarity established by an oppressed minority. On closer inspection, however, that solidarity turns out never to have been as peaceful as all that. Being a feminist has always been a matter of taking a stand among women, as well as among men. In this sense, the development of generational conflict, of disrespectful daughters and oppressive mothers, is not a wholly new phenomenon. Sisters have been doing it to themselves for a long time now. What is perhaps new is how crucial the question of power *within* feminism has become. An appeal to mutual respect is certainly necessary, but it is not sufficient. Only when feminism develops an understanding of its own historicity, an account of its own temporality that does not simply mimic the modernist grand narrative of progress, will it be possible for feminists to form a critical community that is not predicated on its own disappearance, that is not haunted by the specter of postfeminism.

Notes

This essay was made possible with the financial support of the Social Sciences and Humanities Council of Canada and the Québec Fonds pour la Formation de Chercheurs et l'Aide à la Recherche.

1. Susan Faludi, *Backlash: The Undeclared War against American Women* (New York: Crown Publishers, 1991).

2. Foucault, of course, addresses this topic frequently throughout his work. In *The History of Sexuality: Volume I: An Introduction,* trans. Robert Hurley (New York: Vintage Books, 1980), Foucault makes it clear that "power must be understood in the first instance as the multiplicity of force relations immanent in the sphere in which they operate and which constitute their own organization; as the process which, through ceaseless struggles and confrontations, transforms, strengthens, or reverses them; as the support which these force relations find in one another, thus forming a chain or a system, or on the contrary, the disjunctions and contradictions which isolate them from one another.... Power's condition of possibility... must not be sought in the primary existence of a central point, in a unique source of sovereignty from which secondary and descendent forms would emanate; it is the moving substrate of force relations which, by virtue of their inequality, constantly engender states of power, but the latter are always local and unstable.... Power is everywhere; not because it embraces everything, but because it comes from everywhere" (92–93).

3. bell hooks, *Feminist Theory: From Margin to Center* (Boston: South End Press, 1984), 44. June Jordan confronts this same problem when she points out that "if I, a black woman poet and writer, a professor of English at a State University, if I am oppressed then we need another word to describe a woman in a refugee camp in Palestine or the mother of six in a rural village in Nicaragua or any counterpart inside South Africa" (interview with Pratibha Parmar, "Black Feminism: The Politics of Articulation," in *Identity: Community, Culture, and Difference,* ed. Jonathan Rutherford [London: Lawrence and Wishart, 1990], 112).

4. It would also be possible to phrase these complex issues of inheritance (which the gift necessitates) in terms of *genealogy,* using the word as Friedrich Nietzsche and then Foucault would understand it. Karin Cope makes this case, insightfully arguing that the advantage of genealogical critique is that it "is not invested in the construction or preservation of particular lineages, rather its strength is that it opens up the procedures of claims to inheritance, and makes their mechanisms, racist and otherwise, visible" ("'Moral Deviancy' and Contemporary Feminism: The Judgment of Gertrude Stein," in *Feminism beside Itself,* ed. Diane Elam and Robyn Wiegman [New York: Routledge, 1995], 172).

5. For an excellent analysis of this issue, see Susan Gubar, "Feminist Misogyny: Mary Wollstonecraft and the Paradox of 'It Takes One to Know One,'" in *Feminism beside Itself,* 133–54.

6. June Jordan, "The Craft That the Politics Requires," *Fireweed* 36 (Summer 1992): 34.

7. I discuss the problems with identity politics in more detail in *Feminism and Deconstruction: Ms. en Abyme* (New York: Routledge, 1994).

8. It would be possible to put this in Jean-François Lyotard's terms and say that generation is a *différend.* See *The Différend,* trans. Georges Van Den Abbeele (Minneapolis: University of Minnesota Press, 1988).

Generational Difficulties; or,
The Fear of a Barren History

Judith Roof

"It was the need for a new identity that started women, a century ago, on that passionate journey, that vilified, misinterpreted journey away from home," recounts Betty Friedan in *The Feminine Mystique*, her 1963 "bestseller that ignited women's liberation."[1] Offering this feminist prehistory in chapter 4, Friedan suggests that the feminist journey halted after women won the right to vote. The movement's 1920s inertia transformed the "passionate journey" into an apparently barren history that seemed to end with a brood of unhappy daughters "who could not go back to that old image of genteel nothingness" (*FM*, 93). Employing an idea of extended generational role modeling, Friedan situates the daughters of these unhappy daughters—a granddaughterly third generation—as women who must generate anew the fervor of their grandmothers' trip to women's freedom and self-realization.

In her brief history, Friedan inscribes the two somewhat contradictory metaphors of progress through time that will come to characterize feminist accounts of feminist literary criticism. On the one hand, feminist movements generate themselves from women's recognition of oppressive conditions; Friedan's nineteenth-century suffragettes and feminist daughters of the 1940s are both spurred to action by the passionate need to redefine women's identity. On the other hand, generations produce a feminist history. Mothers influence daughters and daughters look to mothers for identity, reproducing what they see. Change comes from a generation's initiative in relation to cultural oppression. Once a consciousness has been raised, however, a generational history materializes to provide the comforting retrospective matrix assuring feminist pioneers that they are indeed part of a tra-

jectory—a passionate journey—that has always been leading somewhere.

Friedan's version of this two-paradigm history is aimed at explaining
how and why a feminist consciousness seems to arise spontaneously
in the late 1950s and early 1960s. But her appeal to generations as a
kind of empty/full repository of feminist possibility suggests two different generational dynamics. The more felicitous, cooperative dynamic
is that through generational legacy, women make strides in consciousness and actual rights. Each generation builds on the work of the previous one, and through time women realize substantial change. The
more problematic possibility is a spontaneous generation where succeeding generations will in some way ignore their forebears and either
pay no attention to the previous generation's fecundating matrix, letting progress lapse, or will effect an Oedipal rebellion, rejecting their
mothers' model and commencing a new and different battle.

Apparent in other feminist accounts of the development of feminist thought, these two paradigms—generational legacy and spontaneous generation—shape the assumptions by which feminist critics
define feminist movements. As time goes on, feminist accounts become
increasingly informed by generational paradigms of history. While Betty
Friedan's *The Feminine Mystique* inscribes a sense of motherlessness
and self-generated consciousness, approximately half of Kate Millett's
Sexual Politics (1970) is devoted to "Historical Background."[2] More
than a list of foremothers, Millett's history indicates that sexist oppression is longer-lived than women might realize. Robin Morgan's 1970
Sisterhood Is Powerful anthology is fully aware of a feminist prehistory,
though, like Friedan it also locates a groundswell of activism generated from within women's lives.[3] *The Feminist Papers* (1973), however,
is fully devoted to the project of inscribing a feminist history, and by
1975 Jane Rule's *Lesbian Images* is primarily about foremothers.[4]
Generating their own consciousness of oppression, the groups of
women thinking about feminism in the 1960s and early 1970s also
generate a family history. Or in recognizing their circumstances in an
oppressive patriarchy, feminists begin to seek historical precedents.

In the late 1970s and early 1980s academic feminist critics embark
on their own developmental accounts, which pick up the same para-
digmatic tensions present in feminist histories, but which employ the
difference between spontaneous generation and generational legacy
in a more artful (the good reading) or insidious (the dubious reading)

way. In most cases, the Oedipal form of the generational model dominates, and the reiteration of Friedan's model of alternating spontaneous generation and generational legacy bespeaks an anxiety about the same kind of barren history or interrupted "passionate journey" that Friedan traces. This most recent deployment of a familiar—even comforting—generational metaphor assumes a reproductive narrative that produces as many problems as its paradigm might resolve. Importing the full force of Oedipal rivalry, recrimination, and debt, generation is neither an innocent empirical model nor an accurate assessment of a historical reality. Rather, generation reflects and exacerbates Oedipal relations and rivalries among women, relies on a patriarchal understanding of history and a linear, cause-effect narrative, and imports ideologies of property. The more open presence of this Oedipal model does less to enlighten the trajectory of feminist intellectual history than it does to superimpose assumptions about property, propriety, and precedence that attempt to ensure that feminism's offspring remember their mothers and in so remembering reproduce their mothers' gains, while honoring their mothers appropriately. Thinking in generational terms contributes—and might even produce—the sometimes torturous relations among women in academe.

Generation's reproductive familial narrative assumes a linear, chronological time where the elements that come first appear to cause elements that come later. This results in a very reproductive (and almost automatically familial) understanding of change through time; the past produces the future as parents produce children. Conceived as unidirectional, the linear logic of a temporally bound cause-effect narrative creates a perpetual debt to the past. While this seems logical and obliged by the physics of human existence, it also prevents us from understanding the movement of cause in any other direction (the present or future producing the past, for example, or a multidirectional causality), sustaining the supply of debt as well as the illusion of a progress ever dependent on the past's temporal preeminence.

The past's causal primacy in turn fosters an understanding of the past's products as both legacy and property. Those things produced through time become the property of those who produced them and are not shared but are endowed on the next generation. The reproductive narrative thus imports a complex (and fairly noncooperative) parent-child model to describe the relations of working critics who might otherwise be regarded as equals. History becomes a series of pitched battles between one generation and the next that forces too clear a demarcation of opponent generations (one that is impossible to make), envisions change as oppositional and reactive, and denies the possibility of sustained, cooperative relations through time.

The generational model is invoked even as women in academe or in feminist movements do not arrange themselves into tidy generations or waves. Not only is there no clear notion of what constitutes a generation in academe, adopting a generational metaphor means espousing more than a convenient way of organizing the relations among women of different ages, experience, class, position, and accomplishment. It means privileging a kind of family history that organizes generations where they don't exist, ignores intragenerational differences and intergenerational commonalities, and thrives on a paradigm of oppositional change.

It may seem that these dynamics are in fact already present for the generational metaphor to describe. There is no question that feminist academics of any age sometimes reproduce familial behaviors in their collegial encounters. That is not, however, because this behavior is necessarily either programmed or natural, but because individuals already employ the familial narrative as a way of understanding their relations to the institution and to one another. My question is whether it is necessary to think of relations through a familial paradigm at all. Can we possibly conceive of them in any other way? What damage is wrought when we deploy the generational metaphor in histories of feminist criticism? It may be that the reproductive narrative that underlies the familial and the Oedipal can only transform feminism's "passionate journey" into an Oedipal tourney.

Generating Histories

The generational model is omnipresent in feminist accounts of feminist critical history, especially as a way of defining meaningful ways of understanding historical change. Jane Gallop's painstaking analysis of Shari Benstock's *Feminist Issues in Literary Scholarship* (1987) in the "History Is a Like Mother" chapter of *Around 1981* illustrates the extent to which critical relations are conceived by feminist critics as generational and familial.[5] Linking some of feminist criticism's generational anxiety to the ingress of "theory," Gallop demonstrates the critics' ambivalence about family and generation at the moment where a "third" generation of feminists is contemplated—at the moment when bad feminist children threaten to become wayward. This Oedipal generational paradigm does not just creep into feminist discourse in the face of the sudden presence of grandchildren (to use the generational metaphor) but, rather, has already persisted in evocations of greatgoddesses and foremothers that are in fact generated retrospectively by an anxious first generation.

But why should historical change be at all linked to generations, especially when the notion of discrete generations is itself already the product of a familial narrative rather than an observable phenomenon? The presence of a generational model may already attempt to neutralize a perceived threat of nonreproductivity or nonattribution in renderings of historical development. It also translates tensions into familiar terms; by substituting an Oedipal dynamic for other, perhaps more dangerous conflicts that might mar the field, a generational paradigm also tends to account for and absorb conflicts rather than encouraging the exploration or exploitation of the causes and potential benefits of differences and anxieties.

A most enlightening essay in this regard is Elaine Showalter's "Women's Time, Women's Space" included in Benstock's anthology.[6] In her discussion of two "different emphases and perceptions of the role of feminist inquiry," Showalter borrows part of a sentence from Julia Kristeva's famous "Women's Time": " 'When evoking the name and destiny of women,' Kristeva writes, 'one thinks more of the *space* generating and forming the human species than of *time*, becoming, or history' " ("WTWS," 37). Reading *le temps des femmes* as a pretext for her idea of "gynesis," Showalter uses Kristeva's description of the woman's perceived place in the symbolic contract to emphasize the key terms of her own critical differentiation. Employing Kristeva's observation as authority for a "problematic of women's space," ("WTWS," 37), Showalter contrasts space with time as the figures governing the "two theoretical directions" that feminist criticism takes after 1975. One time — the gynocritical — remains within linear generational history, while the other — gynesis — evades linearity through a primarily spatial configuration. "Gynesis," as Showalter defines it, "rejects...the temporal dimension of women's experience...and seeks instead to understand the space granted to the feminine in the symbolic contract" ("WTWS," 37).

Showalter is not only attempting to describe a critical history; she is also trying to define that history in terms of conceptions of time reconceived in feminist terms. Splitting space from time, Showalter displaces space from the diachronic logic of history, finding in the spatial metaphor an alternative, "Other," perhaps more purely feminine configuration than that provided by time's linearity or history's necessarily motley contexts.

Showalter's time/space, gynocritics/gynesis distinction, which as she carefully points out, is neither "oppositional [n]or exclusive," is complexly redistributive, cleverly organizing the Anglo-American and the French, empiricist and poststructuralist, into the nonopposing camps of time and space. By characterizing time and space as co-equal emphases, Showalter avoids any problem of influence, historical priority, or debt; time and space become alternatives that broaden the affective range of a diachronic feminist criticism to include the synchronic. Insofar as generational metaphors might apply to the populist terrain of academic feminism's first wave, Showalter avoids any overt appeal to the familial model even though the incipient rivalries and differences of the generational model are all present.

Both canny and politic in her evasion of openly generational terms, Showalter begins her essay with Grant Webster's model of the history of literary criticism. This characteristically generational Oedipal model sets the stage for what Showalter sees as feminist criticism's difference from the patriarchal norm. Conceding that "feminist criticism fits this [Grant Webster's] model reasonably well in most respects," ("WTWS," 30), Showalter is interested in the ways in which feminist criticism is an "anomaly," not only because of its gender but because there is no "Mother of Feminist Criticism," no *Totem and Taboo* figure or parental authority to moor generational history. Like Friedan, Showalter believes in spontaneous generation, at least for what she envisions as the first generation of feminist critical activity. This first generation derives its impetus from context instead of parentage, from the vague, primordial mix of communities, theories, methods, interdisciplinarities, literatures, and women that seem to have parthenogenically produced their fertile challenge to the academic status quo.

Seeming to put aside the familial model, Showalter initially prefers the figure of "women's time" as a way of sequestering and foregrounding the development of a specifically feminist practice. But, she concedes, women's time cannot in itself host an accurate history. A part of larger critical movements, feminist criticism "operates at the juncture of two traditions," having "both a Mother and a Father Time" ("WTWS," 33). Women's time turns out to be the entrée for a veiled generational model especially since Mother Time, as we find out later in the essay, is really space. Mother and father cooperate in a covertly nuclear time-space continuum, a hidden familial matrix that insistently, stubbornly pushes its way back into even the most carefully constructed histories. And while Showalter circumvents the term *generation* in her description of the first and second "waves," she does not always avoid evoking the familial model ("Mother time"). Finally, the notion of generation appears openly—as it does with Friedan—when it comes to speaking of a new (third?) generation of feminist critics, one that will inherit the "feminist canon" as established by Sandra Gilbert and Susan Gubar's *Norton Anthology of Literature by Women* ("WTWS," 40).

But what is wrong with generational metaphors as long as they aren't Oedipal? Why should Showalter avoid them as they sneak insistently back into the most carefully wrought accounts of feminist critical history? One reason, as Showalter's careful deployment of the generational paradigm illustrates, is that generations represent an overdetermined figure of control and order that prevents unruly "Others" from escaping the law (of legacy and debt) that combats mortality. Generations in accounts of historical development are about staking a claim and not being forgotten. Another reason is that the overwhelming obviousness of generations obscures and avoids other kinds of politics and contests, such as the clash of theory with empirical methodologies, which in turn translate into disciplinary tensions.

Evidence of generation's additional obscurations exists in the evasions, pretexts, and ambivalent uses of generational metaphors (including the wave) in Showalter's account of feminist critical history. In her apparent rejection of parentage ("there is no Mother of feminist criticism"), Showalter simultaneously installs and rejects the familial model. Seeing no parents for feminist criticism within the academy, Showalter locates the inception of feminist criticism outside, in "the polemical force, activist commitment, powerful analysis, and sense of mutual endeavor that came out of the women's movement" ("WTWS," 34). A spontaneously generated product of women's "mutual endeavor" and "commitment," feminist criticism might look a little sapphic if it weren't for the immediately sobering fact of history and ensconced academic tradition that constitutes feminist criticism's initially hostile academic context. There is no generational narrative organizing the relations between feminist critics and feminist activists because in large part they are the same; academic feminist critics were also engaged in the women's movement. Although, as Showalter implies, feminist activism owes academic feminism nothing while academic feminist criticism owes activism everything, there isn't enough difference (read: heterogeneity or heterosexuality) in the field until a "second wave" introduces foreign, poststructuralist theory, activism's Other, influenced (fertilized?) with the theoretical seed of male theorists.

As the second wave crashes ashore, Kristeva appears. While academic feminism's first wave is a heterogeneous mass of women activists, the second-wave encounter of activism and theory threatens to be too familial, too full of sibling rivalries, too Oedipal (the first wave is decidedly *not* Oedipal; it was not "an Oedipal rebellion against Cleanth Brooks," Showalter says ["WTWS," 34]). No longer pure (i.e., spontaneously generated from the women's movement), the second wave is nonetheless still epic — larger than life. To avoid the Oedipal rivalry that might spring from this arrivist difference, Showalter situates American and French feminists as alternatives rather than competitors, using the model of the wave rather than openly evoking generations. In other words, Showalter's undulant evasion of the generational metaphor at this point in her history suggests that on some level the generational Oedipal is too dangerous a way to inscribe an encounter with a difference that threatens to disestablish the fledgling family altogether. French theory washes ashore, commingling with American feminism, producing a variety with a different, more paternal pedigree (Showalter mentions Jacques Derrida, Louis Althusser, and Jacques Lacan ["WTWS," 36]). Kristeva and Showalter are parallel and covalent, representatives of a new, more heterogeneous terrain, even though the sibling battle is fought anyway, as Showalter appropriates Kristeva's words to erect a gynetic category not really contemplated in Kristeva's essay.

The tensions Showalter attributes to the arrival of theory (as if it were foreign, as if it weren't already present, as she anxiously points out ["WTWS," 36]) bespeak a tension described as arising with the second wave's advent. Figuring theory as a secondary phenomenon is itself a way of establishing the generational precedence of experience over a set of theoretical questions that are suspiciously far too male-derived. It may well be that theoretical ideas associated with the French were not translated until after the beginning of an American feminist critical tradition, but conceiving of the relation between feminist criticism and theory as covertly generational is a way of putting "French" theory in its place while maintaining one's priority.

Showalter's deployment of the wave metaphor is, however, a diplomatic way of both continuing the essay's illustration of feminist criticism's breadth and dispersing the antagonisms between poststructuralist and empiricist (already characterized as generational) that apparently broil beneath the surface of Showalter's stouthearted ploy to provide them with equal turf and envision them as "dialectical possibilities" ("WTWS," 37). But Showalter does not really situate the second-wave-inspiring Kristeva as a peer but, rather, as an interloper who represents the "psychoanalytic, post-structuralist or deconstructionist theory" ("WTWS," 36) that disrupts the domestic image of American feminist consciousness that Showalter has carefully drawn in her autobiographical appeal to the nuclear family. Self-generated from within women's lives, but propelling itself outside of the Oedipal politics of academic criticism, American feminist criticism itself becomes the foremother that feminist criticism lacks. In other words, Showalter is one of the foremothers who hosts the landing of this wave of unruly Oedipal (they bring the father's ideas) immigrants.

Although the term *wave* is a common idiom for describing intellectual movements through time, it also obscures and repeats the generational metaphor that organizes the relation between Showalter and Kristeva. Showalter employs the wave as the figure through which she registers shifts in ideas and praxis at the same relative points where Kristeva employs the term *generation* in "Women's Time." A metaphor of generation, the wave also adds its own connotations. According to the *Oxford English Dictionary,* the wave is either "a forward movement of a large body of persons (chiefly invaders or immigrants overrunning a country, or soldiers advancing to an attack), who either recede and return after an interval, or are followed after a time by another body of persons repeating the same movement" or "a swelling onward movement and subsidence (of feeling, thought, opinion, a custom, condition, etc); also a movement (of common sentiment, opinion, excitement) sweeping over a community, and not easily resisted." These two figurative meanings convey both a pattern of movement and a threat; not easily resisted, invaders take over but are temporary. The difference between referring to changes in thought over time as a wave or a generation is a difference in connotation. Generation comports the entire familial apparatus; the seemingly benign and neutral wave evades but still implies the familial apparatus and at the same time figures change as aggressive, foreign, and superficial—both more and less frighteningly Oedipal than the family might be.

While the second wave's appearance may suggest aggression, it is Showalter who aggressively commandeers Kristeva's ideas on time, wrenching them from their psychophilosophical rumination on reproduction and the symbolic contract—exactly the issues that Showalter's feminist critical categories avoid. Amputating Kristeva's line from its temporal meditation and displacing time into a spatial model for unisex sequestration ushers the "French" challenge into a gynetic chamber that represents space as a dimension that "repossesses as a field of inquiry all the space of the Other, the gaps, silences, and absences of discourse and representation, to which the feminine has traditionally been relegated" ("WTWS," 37). Showalter's gesture making Kristeva an authority is a generous one, but it also serves to dislocate both alterity and reproductive politics in the maintenance of a still virginal feminist criticism that absorbs Otherness by appearing to split itself.

I would not be so momentarily critical of Showalter if it weren't for the openly reproductive regime her transformation of Kristeva's time into space erases, a regime that seems central to the project Showalter so puritanically delineates and to which Showalter openly (but unknowingly?) gestures in her quick passage over the phrase "symbolic contract." The line Showalter cites from Kristeva's essay is in fact about the symbolic contract and reproduction itself as figured through a maternal space instead of a paternal time. Kristeva's entire passage goes as follows: " 'Father's time, mother's species,' as Joyce put it; and indeed, when evoking the name and destiny of women, one thinks more of the *space* generating and forming the human species than of *time*, becoming, or history."[7] Showalter omits Kristeva's nod to James Joyce, a nod that would superficially aid the case that Showalter is trying to make for categories of feminist criticism. Kristeva's passage focuses on a time-space distinction as a way of understanding women as the space "generating and forming the human species" instead of as a dimension devoted to the feminine Other. While Kristeva delineates the association between women and space in psychoanalysis and uses the spatial dimension as a way of introducing an alternative concept of time, the passage makes it clear that women's association with the spatial is also a maternal dimension. Showalter picks up the spatial and omits both the maternal and the intrinsic relation of space and time.

That Showalter ignores the reproductive in favor of the spatial is a symptom both of the suppressed generational paradigm that informs her history and of her suppression of the impossibility of separating time and space, since space serves as the primary figuration for a time. Kristeva's essay is, in fact, about time rather than space, or about both time and space as they combine in various ways to express the historical permutations that define the phases of women's activism and lead ultimately to "a viable stance for a European — or at least a European woman — within a domain which is henceforth worldwide in scope" (*KR*, 190). Openly evoking the concept of generation, Kristeva analyzes time as a way to predict the future. Using different time frames as ways of typifying the characteristics of a generational notion of feminist progress, Kristeva recommends a future where the differences that Showalter bundles into a joyous mass are recalibrated to individual intrapsychic space that operates within the register of sacrifice and *jouissance*.

Kristeva begins her analysis of the dynamics of "supra-national socio-cultural ensembles" (*KR*, 189) where history, the symbolic, and reproduction coincide. Political organization aligned with a capitalist production narrative creates, according to Kristeva, a specific history, but she does not premise her analysis of feminist thought on either history or the spatial dynamics of what she identifies as the recent gradual erasure of ever-enlarging frames of geographical and national reference. Instead, Kristeva views this history as a narrative of the simultaneous constitution and loss of identity whose relation to the history of production corresponds to specific understandings of time.

Kristeva's temporal project is twofold: first, to "situate the problematic of women in Europe within an inquiry on time...which the feminist movement both inherits and modifies," and second, to correlate different generations of feminists to different geographic and symbolic fields of action in a time-space continuum. In thus stating her topics, Kristeva already intimates what appear to be two different problematics of time, the first philosophical and epistemological in its attempt to locate the temporal place of seeing or theory, and the second, biological, historical, curiously traditional: a vision dependent on the metaphorical production of generations that returns to literal reproduction as a part of an ethical salvation. She hopes, as a result of the examination of these differing histories, to "propose... a viable stance for a European—or at least a European woman—within a domain which is henceforth worldwide in scope" (*KR*, 190).

She locates her two questions—what time is theory? and how is feminist change engendered?—within an additional temporal schema provided by Friedrich Nietzsche: a "cursive" or linear time—the time of narrative, objectivity, and the particular—and a "monumental" time—the time of the global, the eternal, and the recurrent. Kristeva links two aspects of monumental time—"repetition" and "eternity"—to female subjectivity by way of biology and maternity, claiming and reifying a foggy gender essentialism. In "repetition," according to Kristeva, "there are cycles, gestation, the eternal recurrence of a biological rhythm which conforms to that of nature and imposes a temporality whose stereotyping may shock, but whose regularity and unison with... cosmic time occasion vertiginous visions and unnameable jouissance" (*KR*, 191). As she describes it, this kind of time, supposedly out of linear time, is still comprehended by the prototypical productive narrative, the cosmic version of reproduction, a stereotype of the joyful harmonies of universal reverberation. Repetition is opposed but also linked to monumental time in a circular causal relation that is finally a matter of perspective rather than of the quality or narrative of monumental time itself. Monumental time, a time so "all-encompassing and infinite" that it cannot be perceived as passing, is also recurrent, but recurrent on a vaster level, its reach so immense that it seems to cover all. But Kristeva also links monumental time to the maternal, to myths of resurrection and the Virgin Mary as monumental events depicting the sacrificial character of what becomes a monumental temporal ethics.

Although Kristeva's essay might be characterized as an attempt to account for the relation among feminist thought and practice, reproduction, and political history, it is also the formulation of an ethical possibility in response to Benedict de Spinoza's question about the relation of women and ethics. To respond to this question Kristeva looks toward reproduction as both a temporal and a practical, experiential model for feminist thought. Her use of reproduction as one of the foundations for a feminist theoretical resolution would seem simply to reiterate (or reproduce) the narrative position of reproduction as the ideologically positive culmination of a historical narrative of progress generated from the perspective of a symbolic economy shaped around universalized, potentially conjunctive opposites. But maybe not.

Although her connection of the two aspects of monumental time to female subjectivity seems rightly metaphorical and challenging in its suggestion of a different temporal matrix, time's reconnection to reproduction is required by Kristeva's real argument about woman's place in the symbolic. The gesture of locating a history of women while challenging the temporal bases of history is a false counter, a decoy to her other, more "monumental" argument about women's coming to and changing the symbolic from a productive to a reproductive economy. The generational history that both challenges and inscribes linear time provides a matrix for a parallel history of the symbolic as it weathers spatiotemporal warps manifested by the change from nationalism to globalism. But Kristeva's point, finally, is that women must embrace the symbolic, and it is here that reproduction makes a different kind of sense.

While Showalter uses spatiality as a way of avoiding the symbolic, Kristeva argues for an intersection with the symbolic, conceived through spatial metaphors that lead back to the mother. Even if Kristeva would like to shift the capitalist productive narrative to an openly reproductive one that enables women access to the symbolic, the introduction of the maternal marks the reinscription of the productive narrative and its concomitant ideology of linear time *as a necessary counter to the symbolic,* which in ignoring reproduction in favor of production has located women outside of the symbolic. Kristeva thus employs an insistent figuration of maternal reproduction and its apparent links to both repetitive and monumental time to pervert the symbolic in its own terms. The duplicity of Kristeva's appeal to time functions to turn the symbolic away from itself even as it returns to the time of the productive narrative it reproduces, revivifies, relives. The purpose of this turning away is a recapture and relocation of the symbolic, not within patriarchy but among women whom Kristeva sees as dangerously eschewing the symbolic, courting psychoses in their separatism and reification of difference—in fact, in precisely the formulation of gynesis that Showalter proffers.

Kristeva actually proposes two interrelated alternatives as a way of combating this feminist embrace of the imaginary, the embrace that Showalter uses Kristeva's language to introduce and authorize. The first is literally theoretical, "how women, starting with this theoretical apparatus [of language and castration—that is, the symbolic], might try to understand their sexual and symbolic difference in the framework of social, cultural, and professional realization, in order to try, by seeing their position therein, either to fulfil their own experience to a maximum or—but always starting from this point—to go further and call into question the very apparatus itself" (KR, 198). The other alternative she proposes is a multilevel embrace of the symbolic undertaken through the experiential, beginning with an exploration of "the constitution and functioning" of the social contract "from the very personal affect experienced when facing it as subject and as woman" (KR, 200), to maternity, which makes concrete the experience of split subjectivity, to religion, to the hope of a third generation, which Kristeva sees undertaking the intrapsychic problems of difference within instead of without, in what she calls "an interiorization of the founding separation of the socio-symbolic contract" (KR, 210).

In her generational narrative Kristeva seems to ratify Friedan's vision of intergenerational cooperation, the utopian version of what might happen through history. Kristeva paints an image of development through time as generational players take over where others leave off. But what has happened to time? The complex and potentially radical interplay of the suggestion of "other" times engaging with the symbolic has a way finally of disappearing as a rhetorical strategy, replaced by the double whammy of generational prediction and a call to aesthetics as that which can combat technology, embody interiorization, and enact the simultaneous burden and joy of sacrifice. Given that Kristeva has perhaps unwittingly returned to a linear production narrative, her generational prediction becomes itself predictable as a manifestation of that same symbolic she urges women to consider.

In other words, the story of generations is the same story all over again. Kristeva defines the first generation of feminists as tied to linear time, as national, political, rational, existential, privileging power and equality over essence and aesthetics (the political version of Showalter's gynocritics). Her second generation, the post-May-of-'68 group, in an interesting Oedipal logic rejects linear time, politics, and rationality in favor of aesthetics, language, psychology, and an identificatory separatism that refuses both the previous generation of women and patriarchy in general (Showalter's gynesis). First-generation linear time spawns second-generation monumental time. Both defined by their times, both become dangerous in time. These opposites can do nothing other, in the ideology of the production narrative, than, in a curious hetero-lesbian metaphor, together spawn a third generation of feminists, one that is an admixture of the first two, evidence of the operation of the oppositional, reproductive narrative. It is with this final filial product of the ironic union of two generations of feminists that Kristeva ends her generational history.

The Revelations of History; or, The Problem of the Third Generation

Both Showalter and Kristeva land the force of their nongenerational generational histories on the "third" generation, those who, at the publication of these essays (1979–1984), are still sitting at their foremothers' feet, those who would, as students or activists, be reading these essays to discern the past and future of feminism itself. The underlying familial narrative in both of these essays is fairly clear. Both Showalter and Kristeva address a third generation, one whose direction and dreams they try to define. For both, the third generation should combine the best of the previous two: for Showalter that means thankfully receiving the canonical gifts proffered by mother, but also successfully managing the relation between theory, empiricism, and experience. For Kristeva, the third generation combines the linear and the monumental, the local and the global, the symbolic and the imaginary aesthetic. The third generation is imagined as a chip off the old blocks.

But imaging the third generation as both the same as and better than the second (but not the first, whose pioneering courage makes it unapproachably heroic) masks a fear that the third generation—and the fourth—will do no such thing. Both Showalter's and Kristeva's histories inscribe a past and a pattern of generational change as a way of trying to control the future, a future that will be sufficiently attentive to the past to go in the direction imagined by the past, fulfilling the past through precisely the reproductive dream that generations import in the first place. This generational fantasy locates responsibility and credit for the future in the past; children who do not follow the program become wayward and disrespectful and threaten to erase the past's meaning and accomplishments as well as thwart feminism's future. Influenced by too much television and too many commodities, parading too much style, the third and fourth generations already seem to be too superficial and apolitical, too uninterested in history's lessons, too entranced with theory and posturing.

Insofar as history provides a lesson, feminist scholars who have participated in academic battles might have a point. But the lessons learned from history depend on the version of history that is offered. If history is inscribed as a generational caveat, then history invites an Oedipal response. No matter what we might wish to retain from the collected experience and wisdom of those who have participated in feminist critical debates, what is forgotten is that after a lifelong investment, new ideas may become a threat. Such a threat and challenge may be exciting, not as an Oedipal rebellion but as a way to keep things moving, to keep the experienced from becoming ossified in confident wisdom, to keep from returning quite so quickly to the patterns that feminist criticism has always tried to escape. While the hope for a third generation might be that it will be a gaggle of dutiful daughters, the hope for feminist critical practice could be that those beginning their work will not follow that narrative at all, since the narrative of family and mother is already too much an institutional part of feminist criticism itself. Instead, this problematic third generation will probably question the first two and perhaps even the idea of generation itself.

The Foremother's Angst

The search for a feminist critical history seems laudable, but its familial reinscription seems more anxious and Oedipal. The irruptions of feminist consciousness seem to require a history, a set of precedents, a feeling of context. But insofar as the familial paradigm also imports other habits of mind — debt, legacy, rivalry, property — it may be time to think of the development of criticism differently. The family, especially this devolved and Oedipal version of the family, is a particular historical patriarchal formation linked to both ideology and the exigencies of capitalism. Why, then, employ this model as the seeming truth of relations among women scholars in an academic setting, whose Oedipal reverberations make it already one of the most childish of institutions? Are we doomed to relive familial politics throughout our lives? Must we understand and respond to colleagues as mothers, fathers, sisters, or brothers? Must we perpetuate among ourselves what we already recognize as an oppressive paradigm, even if we, in our more perverse moments, try to extract from it some hopeful germ of mother-daughter utopia? While the frightening spontaneity with which these roles are replayed seems to suggest the ineluctable force of a natural predisposition or an inherent situational proclivity, such importunate spontaneity bespeaks ideology rather than necessity, the kind of ideology that obscures other, perhaps more perfidious interests in maintaining what is really an illogical, destructive, and not at all "natural" relation among professional colleagues.

Seeing academic endeavor as a matter of generations means acknowledging accomplishment and conferring recognition according to a model of intellectual property that inherits property's correlative linear narrative of entailment, blood, and debt. Seeing relations among feminists as generational means adopting the metaphor of the patriarchal family in the throes of its illusory battle against mortality. Our enticement by this model with its chimera of order and all-too-real Oedipal drama focuses blame, energies, and even the dilemma of women's relationships in the wrong place: among women themselves. Instead of looking to larger institutional and cultural forces that perpetuate sexism, foster rivalry, and undervalue women's contributions, we look to ourselves and to what we see as a family drama as the cause of our dysphoria while thinking that a correct and orderly disposition of generational history and appropriate recognition would solve the problem. Of course, this model isn't a fitting model at all but, rather, contributes to the production of a tension that might otherwise not be so prominent, while preventing the emergence of other, less hostile, more charitable models.

While the Oedipal is the child's trauma and remains viable insofar as we all repeat childhood patterns, generation is the parent's angst. Representing insecurities about continuity and mortality, generation connotes a certain fear about a failure of cohesion, the dissolution of heritage, and the loss or defection of heirs that might dispel the myths of impossible continuity that mark in their most literal manifestations academic buildings, distinguished chairs, and endowments and fellowships. What is at stake here is death combated through frantic ploys at individual perpetuation again through the symbolic system of the name; contribution and legacy beget memory. The real may depart dearly, but the symbolic lives on, carved in stone.

The narrative ideology that underwrites concepts of academic generation accounts for the bad fit between the generational metaphor
and experience, and the pain of intergenerational feminist politics that
openly assumes the virtues of sharing, community, and commonality
figured by a mother/daughter or sister model and actually operates
on another, far more patriarchal postulate. While the kinds of Oedipal recrimination and accusations of ignoring history that occur among
feminist scholars of different "generations" seem shocking and disappointing on one level (and in a perverse repetition of Oedipal logic,
attributed to intergenerational competition), they make perfect sense
if we understand the patriarchal, linear nature of our expectations of
scholarly production, its history, and our place in it. In a paradigm
where history, governed by linear time, becomes the cause of ensuing
events, the concepts of originality, pioneer, tradition, and precedent
make sense. But if we challenge the very notions of time and history
that ground these ideas, *generation* becomes an insignificant term in the
creation, re-creation, sharing, and proliferation of feminist knowledges.

Postscript

In a certain way this essay is an exercise in Oedipality performed by
a third generation (am I third?) in relation to the exclusions, presumptions, and blindnesses of those whose body of work I can lay before
me (the advantage of those who come after). In a way history always
resists its telling; there are always exceptions, contrary trends, and
cases that defy the norm. It may be that the history Friedan and
Showalter inscribe is more accurate than it looks, since it may be
that many women, regardless of when they were born, undergo the
same trajectory from recognition to interest, from activism to academic criticism. But it might also be that we understand this history
this way because we understand it through the lens of a reproductive
narrative that assumes a familial paradigm from the start. Is it possible for me to be neither a daughter nor one who spontaneously generates? What paradigms exist outside of the familial and the reproductive? Can we conceive of time as multidirectional instead of
linear? Can we conceive of cause and effect going both ways? Can
we let go of the myth of intellectual property or at least be wary of
all claims to ownership of ideas generated in a community? Can we
at least begin to question these kinds of assumptions?

When I presented this paper publicly, it met with a certain resistance.[8] On some level it seemed inconceivable to think of academic relations outside of a familial model, since the institution itself thrives on the taboos normally associated with family. But universities are not families, and if we stop thinking of them that way, we might be able to begin to imagine power relations in a much different configuration. This is in a sense what both Showalter and Kristeva try to do, but, restrained by generational thinking, they cannot go far enough. What if we perceived time not as linear or monumental (monumental is generational), but as multidirectional? What if we understood narrative as repetition, alternation, oscillation—anything but the heterological and productive intersection of differences? What if cause and effect can go both ways? What if action and thought are a gift that expect no return and create no debt? What if we cease to insure ourselves against the certain effects of mortality?

Notes

1. Betty Friedan, *The Feminine Mystique* (New York: Dell, 1963), 73. Subsequent references are cited in the text as *FM*.

2. Kate Millett, *Sexual Politics* (New York: Ballantine, 1970).

3. Robin Morgan, ed., *Sisterhood Is Powerful* (New York: Vintage, 1970).

4. Alice S. Rossi, ed., *The Feminist Papers* (New York: Bantam, 1973); and Jane Rule, *Lesbian Images* (Trumansburg, N.Y.: Crossing Press, 1975).

5. Jane Gallop, *Around 1981: Academic Feminist Literary Theory* (New York: Routledge, 1992).

6. Elaine Showalter, "Women's Time, Women's Space," in *Feminist Issues in Literary Scholarship*, ed. Shari Benstock (Bloomington: Indiana University Press, 1987), 30–44. Subsequent references are cited in the text as "WTWS."

7. Julia Kristeva, "Women's Time," in *The Kristeva Reader*, ed. Toril Moi (Oxford: Blackwell, 1986), 191. Subsequent references are cited in the text as *KR*.

8. After my presentation, a prominent feminist scholar asked me privately if I were not afraid to make this kind of critique while working in the same department as another quite prominent feminist critical scholar from the "first generation." Habits of mind are difficult to change.

Black Female Spectatorship and the Dilemma of Tokenism

Michele Wallace

Preface

When I wrote this essay, I was struggling with something crucial in my knowledge of myself as a writer, intellectual, and perhaps even as an "artist" (although I don't usually think of what I do as art), but, as usual, I had no idea where it all would lead. As such, this essay was not written with the intention of sharing conclusions already arrived at but, rather, it was a sketching out of ideas in formulation, more or less, at the moment of composition. There has been considerable editing after the fact in an attempt to make things fit in a coherent fashion, but I have felt in the end as though a real revision of the piece would completely destroy it. I would not write such a piece now about how I felt at feminist academic conferences. I can hardly remember exactly what I was going through at those conferences then, although I continue to be faintly surprised at myself as someone who is black in a largely white profession. Although it still can be creepy (any kind of privilege is creepy), I am not nearly as afraid as I used to be. After all, it wasn't the white people I was afraid of but myself.

Nevertheless, I thought the essay deserved publication (1) because I don't like to suppress things I've written merely because I now find them embarrassing, and (2) because I think the question of spectatorship—whether there could be said to be such a thing as a black female spectator in a psychoanalytic sense, and where that left me so far as being somebody who was interested in spectatorship, black and otherwise—is still important.

At that time, I was beginning to think seriously about the idea that everything in one's life wasn't simply black or white, or, indeed, even related to race in any way. Lots of people who are not black take this kind of thinking for granted, but for me it was something new. Also, all of my concerns had to do with feminist generations of one kind or another: the generation of feminists who had embraced psychoanalytic feminism as a significant advance over materialist feminism; the generation of black feminists, and other feminists of color, who had elevated the differences of race and sexuality to paramount importance, over and above gender, and who had subsequently discounted the validity of psychoanalysis to feminism because it was thought to be inherently too white and bourgeois; and then the generation of black feminists that I myself had helped to create in which feminism was presumably "theorized"—that is, depersonalized, abstracted, and distanced—from the lived experience of the theorizer. In the midst of these questions, I was going through some knotty identity thing, and it centered on the problems I had with any kind of public speaking. I felt invisible. How could anybody who was invisible speak before an audience and be heard?

In any case, I stand slightly verified by a film I've just seen by Cheryl Dunye called *The Watermelon Woman*. A film by a black lesbian filmmaker, it deals with many of the issues of identity that have troubled me in the particular context in which I raise them, in the context of stereotypical images of black women in film. Plus, it is also a delightful and joyous film about the link between black feminist and lesbian generations. It lifted my spirits. I hope this piece will lift yours.

Despite being concerned with the *visual* arts, however, the discipline of art history can never be exclusively defined by visuality. The making of art objects, monuments, buildings, sculptures, prints, and all range of materials which are the topic of art histories involves a complex of historical, institutional, sociological, economic, as well as aesthetic factors. Feminists working in and against this field need deal as much with issues of training, patronage, access to exhibiting facilities, languages of art criticism, and mechanisms of the market, as with the semiotic and ideological productivity of the "image" itself. Cinema, we might argue, has distilled the visuality of visual culture to create an apparatus which interpellates its consumers above all as spectators— a condensation which is not true of the domain of the visual arts.
GRISELDA POLLOCK, "Trouble in the Archives: Introduction"

I know that what replaces invisibility is a kind of carefully regulated, segregated visibility.
STUART HALL, "What Is This 'Black' in Black Popular Culture?"

In a special issue of *Camera Obscura* in 1989 on the "female spectator," the editors posed a series of questions to contributors, one of
which was:

> The very term "female spectator" has been subject to some dispute
> insofar as it seems to suggest a monolithic position ascribed to the
> woman. In your opinion, is the term most productive as a reference to
> empirical spectators (individual women who enter the movie theatre),
> as the hypothetical point of address of the film as a discourse or as a
> form of mediation between these two concepts? Or as something else
> entirely?[1]

The array of responses was fascinating and informative, but what
attracted my attention even more was that, although quite a number
of the fifty-nine contributors mentioned "race" as an unsettling factor to previous conceptions of "spectatorship," there was only one
black writer, Jacqueline Bobo, the prominent black feminist communications theorist, among them.[2]

"Unfortunately," Bobo writes, "when the female spectator is usually spoken of and spoken for, the female in question is white and
middle class. As a black woman working within the discipline of cultural studies, my goal is to expand the scholarship on the female spectator beyond this."[3] In the process, Bobo, whose work on film and
spectatorship I admire immensely, was inadvertently responding to
the question posed by the editors of *Camera Obscura* by saying that
she saw "female spectatorship" as a "reference to empirical spectators,"
not as a "hypothetical point of address of the film as a discourse."[4]

I concur with Bobo's interest in the historical realities of black female spectatorship, but I am not as willing as she to cede the
psychoanalytic framing of spectatorship. I feel that a psychological approach, even a specifically psychoanalytic approach to black forms of
spectatorship is much needed, but I would add that we need not use
psychoanalysis as we have found it. In fact, the range of acceptable
interpretations of what psychoanalysis is and what it can do is already quite vast. Yet all the approaches I've found, from the use of
feminist psychoanalysis in cultural criticism to the theorization of
feminist psychologies, continue the pretense of color blindness. In theories of psychoanalysis in general, as well as in the practice of psychoanalysis, race has no reality. This is an unacceptable state of affairs. Even if it turns out to be impossible to theorize "race" as a
fundamentally psychological phenomenon, it seems to me that "race"

should always be viewed as a present and relevant (social, historical, material, ideological) context for psychological phenomena and psychoanalytic interpretation.

Feminist film criticism generally employs psychoanalysis in a rigorous and precise manner. Either to a lesser or greater extent, it uses Jacques Lacan's rereading of Sigmund Freud in order to analyze "textual" or filmic issues, or issues of discourse, with little reference to possibly relevant social and historical contexts. When one reads it, it appears as though such interpreters are coming up with timeless and universal psychological criteria. At the same time, the disclaimer that feminist film critics have begun adding lately that their observations about spectatorship have no application or interest for people of color and only apply to a narrow bourgeois realm of a white Euro-American middle class goes too far, I think. The white Euro-American middle class of the past century is not yet some obsolete aboriginal tribe on the verge of extinction. Its values have been for some time, and continue to be, ideologically dominant.

On the other hand, I am willing to agree with Griselda Pollack and other critical perspectives in art history that the historical and material specificity of the multiple visual realms of the past and the present have not been adequately articulated or described by feminist film criticism's use of "the gaze" or "spectatorship." Because my concerns are related to a discussion of society and culture in the present, it seems important to keep in mind the historical context of film (especially films that include references to race), as well as the impact of other cultural forms and intellectual discourses on film. I would like to examine how issues of "race" might be relevant to multiple concepts of spectatorship (the historical/social and the textual/psychological), first, by telling a story.

In the fall of 1990, I participated in a feminist art history conference at Barnard at which I was to lead a workshop on race, gender, and modernism along with the white art historian Ann Gibson. Immediately prior to my own session, I attended the session of a white female friend that was on popular culture with a focus on music. My friend, whose training is in art history and critical theory, did her presentation on Sinead O'Connor, and her copresenter talked about Madonna. My own recollection is that the session was packed and that I was the only person of color present. After brief presentations by my friend and the other white woman presenter (much more of an expert in music than my friend), a general discussion took place that handled popular culture and rock and roll with a kind of reverence and awe that I can now see, in retrospect, had much to do with the rarity of popular culture discourse at an art history conference.

At the time, however, what annoyed me as somebody who was inadvertently representing "race" through my body in the room, as well as choosing to represent "race" at my session that would follow, was that everybody in that room was talking about rock and roll in particular, and popular culture in general, as though black people had never existed and never made any contribution to it. What stands out in my mind is their wondering aloud where the rhythm that was apparent in Elvis Presley and in Madonna had come from? One particularly astute art critic (who just happened to be male) suggested that we refer to Rosalind Krauss's work on rhythm in Picasso.

By this time, I was absolutely steaming but I was also afraid to speak, afraid to say that the rhythm that Elvis exhibited (not to mention the rhythm in Picasso) had come from the same place, from Africa, that rock and roll was largely the invention of African Americans, that it was impossible to talk sanely about popular music in the United States without dealing with "race."

Now, I am not altogether sure why I was so afraid to speak then. I know that I am now beginning to lose that fear, but at that time I was very much in the grip of it. I also know that I was often successful in hiding my fear, and as a consequence no one ever knew or believed (especially white people) that I was afraid.[5] I can remember, however, telling myself that I should save my energy and my anger for my own session, although I didn't recognize at the time that the critical space of my session (high modernism/primitivism) was qualitatively different from the critical space of this session (the only session at the art history conference on popular culture).

Both women followed me into my session, whereupon I immediately began the calculated time release of my barely suppressed rage. I was still afraid to speak, by the way, which made my fury, no doubt, all the more difficult to bear for my listeners. The thing that I can best remember saying, which seems to me still instructive for my remarks here, was: "You [white women] are interested in Madonna because she is white. You are not interested in Tina Turner, not because she's less interesting but because she is black." Of course, my friend felt completely betrayed, attacked, and confused by the way in which her session had resurfaced in my session. Matters were not helped by the fact that my session, as was hers, was well attended by feminist art historian high-muckety-mucks (as Zora Neale Hurston might have called them). So the whole antagonism took on the aura of a professional challenge.

Meanwhile, the other white woman, the copresenter, engaged me in lengthy and not unfriendly conversation afterward. Obviously baffled, she insisted, again and again: "Of course, I am well aware of the contribution blacks have made to rock and roll. I don't know why I didn't mention it."

At a more recent meeting of the Society of Cinema Studies in New Orleans, on a panel on "multicultural feminist theories" chaired by Ella Shohat, I tried to spell out what I saw as the analogous relationship of this narrative to the situation then at hand in regard to explaining the problem of black female spectatorship. The idea that every story, every narrative cloaks a deep structure, a simpler and more logical narrative that will then reveal the hidden meaning and order of the less astute and self-conscious narrative, is not only a foundational idea in high modernisms but also an idea I am highly drawn to. On the other hand, I am well aware that from a postmodern perspective, or a multicultural perspective (these two dissimilar discourses have this in common), master narratives may not necessarily unlock the meaning of lesser narratives, and, instead, knowledge is seen as an endless series of narratives, great and small, linear and fragmented, stretching on into an alternately meaningful and meaningless, heterogeneous infinity. After all, when you think about the appeal of textuality as the very thing you can never get rid of, or live without, you can't help but wonder whether the meaning of the story (or the novel, the film, or the song) was ever the point at all.

Nevertheless, I would like to persist in arguing in favor of modernist readings and the continuing usefulness of master narratives such as history and psychoanalysis. During the Society of Cinema Studies panel, I tried to suggest one partial modernist reading. First, as we all know, I said, in established practices of feminist film criticism (as in the field of feminist art history) "race" is generally ignored or trivialized in the form of the "race/gender/class mantra." But even more disturbing, I said, is that—both before the past few years when "race" wasn't being mentioned in feminist film discourse and now that it is being mentioned in the work of Mary Ann Doane, E. Ann Kaplan,

Sandy Flitterman-Lewis, Judith Butler, Jane Gaines, and Lucy Fischer—I still continue to have the feeling that "I" (the "I" of my subjectivity as an individual black woman who is too dark to "pass for white") am still being ignored or erased or silenced.

Moreover, I continued, I suspect that as in the construction of the famous Freudian reference to "a child is being beaten," it might be a good idea to acknowledge that this effect may have many points of origin, some of them internal to individual/collective black female psychology. It is also important to remember that the process of being silenced or erased or ignored is not some analytical abstraction. After all, I said, it makes "me" angry, so angry that "I" usually can't speak rationally or honestly about it, especially at those moments when it is occurring. And if you remember that in this case the "I" is probably not just I alone, then you begin to realize that this blockage may represent a massive obstacle to black women and white women's becoming reconciled to one another's positions.

In this construction, I pointed out that I was well aware that I was leaving out everybody else except white and black women. Questions arising from interactions among white women and other kinds of women of color, other kinds of women of color with black women, and women of color from different places among themselves were all the more complicated. Differences of sexuality and class also wouldn't make it any easier.

But what I neglected to do was to provide the problem of being silenced, erased, or ignored with a historical context because, of course, I no longer view myself as silenced, erased, or ignored. I was speaking then, at the Society of Cinema Studies, about being silenced in the past, about coming to understand how my own rage had silenced me to such a degree that even when I was speaking the loudest, I was not really saying what I needed to say.

Moreover, to dichotomize visibility and invisibility, or voice and silence, in such a way as to suggest that the former inevitably leads to power and the latter inevitably leads to disempowerment is perhaps misleading. While I think that visibility and voice are important strategies for emergent discourses, invisibility and silence (as in, for instance, working behind the scenes or foregrounding the talents of others) can be useful strategies, too. I hardly need to add that structures of domination can be both invisible and silent and yet quite as powerful.[6] The key thing is not to forget that voice and visibility are being employed as metaphors for empowerment, and that invisibility and silence are metaphors for lack, repression, and powerlessness.

So here "I" was, then, at the feminist art history conference in 1990, or on the feminist film criticism panel in New Orleans in 1993, and "I" was in possession of one legitimately rational argument, concerning the importance of "race" as a historical and material reality, and one illegitimately irrational argument, concerning the importance of my own individual subjectivity as a black woman, without which neither I nor any other black woman could function as an intellectual in either the fields of art history or film criticism. The rational voice spoke while the irrational voice twisted the knife in the wound. By virtue of entering either profession, I was immediately faced with the adult job of defining both "race" and my own black female subjectivity. Did it matter then that I was not especially well equipped to do either? Moreover, was there some way that I hadn't yet recognized how to avoid personalizing these issues?

Nevertheless, at the art history conference (in 1990), I began confidently with the statement, "You're interested in Madonna," or as I might have said at the cinema studies conference in New Orleans, "Rita Hayworth and Lana Turner" (in 1993) "because they are white, not because they are interesting. You're not interested in Tina Turner" (in 1990) or "Hattie McDaniels and Butterfly McQueen" (in 1993), "not because they aren't interesting but because they are black." In either context, the feminist art history conference in 1990 or the cinema studies conference in 1993, what manner of statement is this? Is it true? How is it true? Moreover, what did I hope to gain by saying it, besides isolation and ridicule?

I think that both statements were true, and that they start to take us to the root of the problem—specifically, that white women are often interested not in black women but, quite naturally, in themselves. Moreover, that preoccupation, as opposed to the possibility of being interested in black women, has been as much a structural aspect of a so-called female spectatorship as either the "gaze" or the objectified "image."

Granted, it is easy enough to observe that black female intellectuals aren't usually interested in Madonna, Rita Hayworth, or Lana Turner, but they usually aren't any more interested in Tina Turner, Hattie McDaniels, or Butterfly McQueen than white female intellectuals. I suspect that for black women, at least as adults, the possibility of identification, at any level, is much more problematic than it is for white women. On the other hand, "I" (the "I" who is interested in the problem of black female subjectivity) am interested in Tina Turner, Hattie McDaniels, and Butterfly McQueen because I want to understand how the hate/love feelings for them are constructed in film discourse and, by so doing, how black female self-hatred (or perhaps *self-hatred* is too strong a word here and I really mean something like ambivalent self-esteem) is constructed by the videos and films in which they appear.

Most important of all, I don't see the recent preoccupation in critical circles with "passing," or the construction of the nearly white or actually white actress playing the black female—as in the two versions of *Imitation of Life*—as a problematization of "race" that necessarily brings us anywhere near the questions I am trying to pose about black female subjectivity. Most black women are not passing and never have been able to pass or look nearly white. Hasn't the precise nature of the problem of "race" all these years been the impossibility of "passing" for most of us? After all, the question of black women who look white, or nearly white, or as "good" as white (for example, Lena Horne, Dorothy Dandridge, Fredi Washington) seems to pose virtually the same question in terms of spectatorship as the white woman herself. In such a context, "race" becomes an abstract concept that makes as little visual or linguistic difference as possible.

I am well aware, however, that "passing," miscegenation, and lightness have been privileged in African American discourse as well. In novels by African Americans such as *Iola Leroy* (1890) by Frances Harper, *Contending Forces* (1900) by Pauline Hopkins, *The Autobiography of an Ex-Colored Man* (1921) by James Weldon Johnson, and *Passing* (1929) by Nella Larsen, as well as in the film *The Veiled Aristocrats* (1932) by the black filmmaker Oscar Michaux, "passing" becomes a key issue in African American culture. Nor do I mean to suggest that the problems associated with "passing" and being light enough to pass don't constitute a valid black experience. In an essay called "Passing for White, Passing for Black," conceptual artist and philosopher Adrian Piper recounts such problems in fascinating detail.[7] A recent documentary called *A Question of Color* by black filmmaker Kathe Sandler and a book called *The Color Complex: The Politics of Skin Color among African Americans* by Kathy Russell explore these issues as well.[8]

Also, as I have become more familiar with the lives and careers of the actresses who were forced to play the mulatto roles, such as Fredi Washington, Lena Horne, Nina Mae McKinney, and Dorothy Dandridge, I come to realize the courage, fortitude, and political acumen of these women. Light versus dark was never a seamless and carefree operation in the black world, however it was read in the white world.

What I do mean to suggest is that it is harder still to focus on the black woman who is in the majority but who, nevertheless, remains in the margins of discourse and representation, who is invariably viewed by many as desexualized and trapped in a maternal role.[9] In *Imitation of Life*, the woman in the margins, the so-called mammy figure played by Louise Beavers in the earlier version (directed by John Stahl) and Juanita Moore in the Douglas Sirk version, seems to resist explication and examination. On the one hand, you may say there really is nobody there, as Sandy Flitterman-Lewis said in a recent talk about Mahalia Jackson at the end of *Imitation of Life* (1959). On the other hand, Jackson's position as a coda figure precisely mirrors the plight of black women in the dominant discourse.

On closer examination, the so-called mammy stereotype inevitably gives way to the frequent textual complexities of particular black female performers and their collaborators. In *Imitation* (1934), Louise Beavers rubs Claudette Colbert's feet and speaks warmly of the pleasures of sexual satisfaction. Cloaked in such scenes, in the guise of servitude and ignorance, is the experience and worldliness of the black woman as well as the privilege and innocence of the white woman.

In regard to the work of Ethel Waters in *Cabin in the Sky* (1943) and in *Pinky* (1949), I would challenge the description by both Donald Bogle and Thomas Cripps of her as a stereotypical mammy. In *Cabin*, Waters is clearly still a hot momma, although not as thin or as young as Lena Horne, her competition. In *Pinky*, she plays an old woman, but her spiritual wisdom and beauty and her quick-witted intelligence give her as much dignity as the white character played by Ethel Barrymore, who is ostensibly her employer but has become more of a friend.

While *Imitation of Life*, *Cabin*, and *Pinky* are not black films in the sense of having been produced under total black control, neither are they really films about black people. These films, nevertheless, incorporate significant traces of a potentially subversive black talent, dance, and musical performance. These landmark performances by black women also indicate a slowly shifting terrain for visual representations of black women. The proof of the pudding, it seems to me, is that such films were the exceptions rather than the rule, and that despite their financial success, production of "problem" films and black musicals never progressed to the next logical step but were somehow squelched during the McCarthy era.

Such films as *Imitation* are still films about conventional and tradition-bound stereotypes of black life, about how white people feel about black people. *Imitation of Life* only engages with black female subjectivity, in any real sense, at the level at which Louise Beavers or Juanita Moore (much less successfully in the 1959 version) manage to assert themselves as actors, or at the level of Mahalia Jackson's brilliant solo at the end. Needless to say, *Cabin,* cast in the classic Hollywood musical mold, does not get much closer to the realities of black life.

One may argue that classic Hollywood is not about real white people either. I would argue that there is an additional dimension to the unreality and reification of Hollywood representations of "race." As Stuart Hall explained at the Black Popular Culture conference in 1991, "what replaces invisibility is a kind of carefully regulated, segregated visibility." That statement applies especially well to black women in popular culture, even as it also applies to the configuration of images of white women, black men, and everybody else in the dominant discourse.

In this regard, I would like to pose a further question: what if the black female subject is constructed much like the white female subject? Or what if the similarities between the psychoanalytic construction of the black female subject and that of the white female subject are greater than the dissimilarities? Moreover, if you accept the thesis that psychoanalytic film criticism proposes of a closed Eurocentric circuit in Hollywood cinema in which a white male–dominated "gaze" is on one end and the white female "image" is on the other end, what happens to the so-called black female subject? Does she even exist? And if she does, how does she come into existence?

Helpful to me in thinking about the problems suggested here has been the writing of black female conceptual artist and theorist Lorraine O'Grady in "Olympia's Maid: Reclaiming Black Female Subjectivity" and in her unpublished "Postscript," and the writing of black feminist art historian Judith Wilson in "Getting Down to Get Over:

Romare Bearden's Use of Pornography and the Problem of the Black Female Body in Afro-U.S. Art."[10] In looking at the status of the black female nude in art history, which is handled very differently from the white female nude, O'Grady insists that the only constant in Euro-American theoretical analysis has been "the black body's location at the extreme," whereas Wilson remarks on how black fine artists have also avoided the black female nude because of its negative associations, perhaps with the sexual exploitation of slavery.

O'Grady, who says her goal is to "deal with what Gayatri Spivak has called the 'winning back of the position of the questioning subject' " is thus prompted to suggest that "the black female's body needed less to be rescued from the masculine gaze than it had to be sprung from an historic script surrounding her with signification while at the same time, and not paradoxically, erasing her completely."[11] While I think that O'Grady is onto something here when she suggests that the issue for black women is one of establishing subjectivity, I haven't always been able to see the notion of a black female subject as separate from the notion of a white female subject. Would this mean, after all, that there were Asian, Indian, and African female subjects as well? Is subjectivity really divided by race, nationality, ethnicity? I don't think so. I'm not saying that subjectivity isn't divided. I think it probably is divided in some manner, but I'm not sure that it can therefore be viewed as historically and materially specific, and that it divides easily by ethnicity, nationality, or any other constructed or natural rubric. Certainly, "spectatorship" as it is constructed by the dominant discourse does not.

On the other hand, things like class allegiances and identity, sexuality, and experience seem to make a profound difference in how the female subject is constituted visually and how those images circulate. Even more significant here is O'Grady's suggestion that the status of the white female "image," or the objectification of the white female body, is part of the circuit of subjectivity for women. In other words, although the white male "gaze" (or the gaze of the dominant culture) objectifies and, therefore, dehumanizes the white woman, in fact, that objectification also implicitly verifies the crucial role white women play in the process or circuit of spectatorship. In other words, the process of objectification also inadvertently humanizes as well a built-in advantage that is then denied to women of color in general, but to the despised (or desired) black woman in particular.

So the problem of white female subjectivity is one of reversing the terms somehow, or reversing the connection or the hierarchy between male and female, whereas in the case of the black female body, or the body of the other, the connection is to a third, much less explored level in the hierarchy, the sphere of the abject, which includes, as Sander Gilman and Michel Foucault have pointed out, the pathological.[12]

As such, reversal is no cure and cannot take place. Black female subjectivity remains unimaginable in the realm of the symbolic. O'Grady's approach as an artist seems to be to attempt to upgrade the status of the black female nude, or at least to get us to think about how and why the black female nude is devalued. Can you imagine Louise Beavers in a sexy dress in *Imitation of Life*? And yet Bessie Smith played just such a role in *Saint Louis Blues,* not to mention in life.

Lately, I have been working on my mother Faith Ringgold's series of story quilts, *The French Collection,* in which she illustrates the adventures of a protagonist named Willa Marie, born in 1903, who goes to Paris to become an artist and who alternates working as an artist's model with her own painting (true of many female artists). In the process, the subsequent images toy with this circuit of subjectivity that O'Grady proposes as so crucial, for Willa Marie is configured as both subject and object by the text and the images.

In a multicultural context, the response of many is to historicize the question of subjectivity (which I believe is crucial as well) and, in the process, dispense with the synchronic explanations of psychoanalytic complexity and abstraction. But, then, how do we account for the play of the unconscious in black cultural production and in the everyday lives of black people? The play of the unconscious roughly refers to the highly ambivalent relation of plans to practice, and stated intentions to unconscious motivations, in African American cultural and social life.

I ask the question about the unconscious precisely because of the problem of interpreting the sexual and gender politics of recent mainstream black cinema. Clearly, the construction of spectatorship in *Malcolm X* cannot be wholly explained by relying on empirical data. We can guess that the construction of gender and sexuality in Spike Lee's *Malcolm X* has more to do with Lee's own issues around gender as well as cinematic traditions in the specularization of women's bodies, and black women's bodies, in Hollywood cinema than it has to do with Malcolm X's life. Moreover, there is apparently the mediation of how Malcolm X also fictionalized his own life in his *Autobiography*, which provides the documentary basis for the film.[13] Gender and sexuality were also very problematic in Malcolm X's self-conceptualization.

On the one hand, regardless of the specific problem of interpreting *Malcolm X*, it is no longer surprising that Spike Lee, as well as other black male filmmakers, succumbed to reinscribing precisely the same hegemonic fantasies about the nature of sexual difference as other filmmakers in the dominant discourse of Hollywood cinema. From the perspective of the question of what is happening to the real, historically determined black female spectator, there is little here to interfere with her conventional construction. But from the perspective of the question of what is happening in terms of the construction of the subject both internal to the discourse of the film and internal to her unconscious psychological processes as a viewer, I suspect that a complicated series of changes is occurring. On the theory that the Eurocentric circuit of white male "gaze" and white female "object" has a psychic cost, variations in that system surely make a difference, but what difference?

Meanwhile, *Daughters of the Dust*, a film by independent black filmmaker Julie Dash, attempts to provide a corrective to the boyz. The film deliberately sets out to tackle the problem of upgrading the black female image and gets bogged down in excessive visuality. Yet again, something crucial has to be occurring on the level of "the hypothetical point of address of the film as a discourse." After all, if it makes no difference how a film deploys its black bodies, why have they been so relentlessly excluded in the past?

Of course, the important thing about all of this is that some of the rules regarding the conventional Hollywood characterization of the black female are finding their way into recently released black films. Black film theorist Ed Guerrero, at a recent Society of Cinema Studies panel on blaxploitation film, referred to the most recent crop as following a credo of ghettocentricity.

And yet the opportunity still exists in the examination of the work of these or any other black filmmaker for thinking about the black women's bodies in the margins, for reformulating notions of spectatorship to encompass the impact of "race" on subjectivity.

Notes

1. *Camera Obscura* 20–21 (1989): 17–18. The above epigraphs are take from Griselda Pollack, "Trouble in the Archives: An Introduction," *differences: A Journal of Feminist Cultural Studies* 4:3 (1992): iii–iv; and Stuart Hall, "What is This 'Black' in Black Popular Culture?" in *Black Popular Culture: A Project by Michele Wallace,* ed. Gina Dent (Seattle: Bay Press, 1992), 21–33.

2. I am not accusing *Camera Obscura* of racism. Cinema and communications studies are still largely white fields, and the reasons for this (racism is only one of many) originate at a much deeper level in the structure of our cultural arrangements than the particular racial views of any set of academic editors. Forced to make a selection of black feminist intellectuals engaged in debates around female spectatorship in 1989, there weren't a lot of possible candidates, although I might have asked Valerie Smith, Judith Wilson, Coco Fusco, Hortense Spillers, Mae Henderson, Lorraine O'Grady, and myself, as well as other black feminists already engaged in visual studies of one kind or another, or in psychoanalysis.

3. Bobo, *Camera Obscura* 20–21 (1989).

4. Ibid.

5. Years of therapy have been crucial in helping to finally dispel, or at least hold at bay in critical academic situations, the paralyzing stage fright I used to experience. I think that stage fright had to do with many things. Race was only one of them.

6. See Peggy Phelan, *Unmarked: The Politics of Performance* (New York: Routledge, 1993).

7. Adrian Piper, "Passing for White, Passing for Black," *Transition* 58 (1993): 4–32.

8. Kathe Sandler, director, *A Question of Color* (California Newsreel, 1993); Kathy Russell, *The Color Complex: The Politics of Skin Color among African Americans* (New York: Harcourt Brace Jovanovich, 1992).

9. In a talk at the CUNY Graduate School in 1993, E. Ann Kaplan greatly contributed to my understanding of how the maternal melodrama serves to construct the black female in film.

10. Lorraine O'Grady, "Olympia's Maid: Reclaiming Black Female Subjectivity," *AfterImage* 20 (1992); O'Grady, "Postscript to 'Olympia's Maid: Reclaiming Black Female Subjectivity,'" unpublished manuscript; and Judith Wilson, "Getting Down to Get Over: Romare Bearden's Use of Pornography and the Problem of the Black Female Body in Afro-U.S. Art," in Dent, *Black Popular Culture.*

11. O'Grady, "Postscript."

12. Sander Gilman, *Difference and Pathology: Stereotypes of Sexuality, Race, and Madness* (Ithaca, N.Y.: Cornell University Press, 1985); Michel Foucault, *Discipline and Punish: The Birth of the Prison,* trans. Alan Sheridan (New York: Vintage, 1979); and Michel Foucault, *The Order of Things: An Archaeology of the Human Sciences* (New York: Vintage, 1970).

13. Malcolm X, *The Autobiography of Malcolm X* (New York: Ballantine, 1992).

Talking Across

Jane Gallop and Elizabeth Francis

JANE GALLOP: Let's decide who is going to talk first. How are we going to decide that?

ELIZABETH FRANCIS: I think we should just start.

JG: Well, we shouldn't both talk at the same time.

EF: Okay, so we are going to explain who we are. Well, there's two of us having a conversation. I'm Elizabeth Francis.

JG: And I'm Jane Gallop, I say looking at the tape recorder.

EF: And how do we know each other? ... I am the wife of one of Jane's graduate students at the University of Wisconsin, Milwaukee.

JG: I want you to talk about me in the second person because we're supposed to be talking to each other.

EF: Right. It's weird. [Laughter.] Let's see, I know Jane, or I know you, because of Chris, and also because of your work. I am a graduate student, just finishing my dissertation in American civilization at Brown, so I am a little bit distant from my institution.

JG: Geographically.

EF: And temporally somewhat.

JG: And I teach in the modern studies program at the University of Wisconsin, Milwaukee, where I mainly teach graduate students. I got to know you because I'm your husband's adviser — through getting to know him I got to know you. I perceived us as being of different academic generations and as feminists, but it seemed possible to talk across generations because we don't have a direct institutional relation to each other.

EF: So we're in a generational situation but not a direct institutional one; we could talk about generations without necessarily talking about each other.

JG: Maybe some of that has to do with the difference between the narrow meaning of generations (people in the same family) and the broader meaning of generations (people belonging to a generation even if they don't know each other and have no direct relation). What we mean—well, I don't know—what *I* mean when I see us in different feminist generations is our academic positions, first of all, maybe only. You're just finishing graduate school and I'm twenty years out of graduate school, ten years past tenure, teaching graduate students. And I feel very established in the profession and very involved in teaching and advising and mentoring (although I hate the word) what I think of as another generation of graduate students—people who are your peers but who aren't you because you're not a student at this university.

EF: But that's not necessarily a feminist generation—in that your students aren't necessarily feminists—or maybe they all are.

JG: No, all my students aren't feminists, but because what I teach is feminist theory the majority of students I have are doing work that they think of as feminist. I thought maybe we could talk about things more freely because we don't have any literal institutional relation to each other—you're not my student, I'm not your mentor, we're not connected to the same school or in the same field. But also because we know each other.

EF: But also we have both been thinking about these things, in various ways, in our work, and about the institutional politics of feminism. Our fields do overlap to a certain extent—the fact that we're both feminists, both interdisciplinary, both . . . I don't know.

JG: Yes, well, we're both interested in feminist theory and the history of feminism. When we first started talking about doing this conversation, I certainly didn't realize that both of us, or even either of us, had been thinking about feminism and generations. But it turns out we both had.

EF: I hadn't realized that I was thinking about it, but it was definitely an aspect of my dissertation, which is on women and modernism and their relation to feminism. There is a generational aspect to that having to do with the history of feminism. Maybe we should talk about when we first started talking about this conversation.

JG: Yes, I think so. I got the idea of doing this conversation with you because of a phone call we had in June or July this past year. It must have been when I got back from Australia in June. I was probably calling to talk to Chris and you answered the phone, and I knew that you had been at the Berks while I was gone, and I asked you, "So how was the Berks?" I mean it was really just a chatty "How are you?"

EF: Yes, a "How did it go?" And I launched into this, I don't know if *tirade* is the right word, but I was excited and troubled at the same time, I guess.

JG: You must have just come back because you were really...

EF: Still in the thick of it. Still sorting through it all. But the Berkshire Conference really offers a model—right?—for thinking about feminist generations because the goal of the Berkshire Conference is to produce feminist women's history and to create an institutional place where that can be both nurtured and reproduced. By creating an institutional structure in which women can talk about their work in women's history, that work will keep going.

JG: Well, there's also a sense of the Berks as an important place because of its tradition. I mean, it's old.

EF: It's old but it only started out, I think, in the '30s.

JG: Oh, it's that old? I had no idea; I assumed it started in the '60s.

EF: It actually wasn't a conference before 1970-something. But it was a place where women in the historical profession got together. The reason why it's called the Berkshire Conference is that women historians got together every year to talk and discuss each other's work, and, you know, they had prizes and things like that. I can't remember exactly the year when it started as a conference, but they took the model of women getting together every summer and made it into a conference presenting work on women's history. It was part of the emergence of the New Scholarship in women's history. It became much more than that, though, and I think that's where my relation to it becomes a little more interesting. The Berks was not only a public demonstration of the growth of women's history, but it was a place where issues were worked out and also a place where women's history and a sort of feminist community intersected. To go to the Berks was to participate in women's culture in a grand way— it was like a festival, kind of, and that's why it was never held at a hotel, always at a women's college.

JG: So it's related—a kind of heritage from that whole separate spheres, separate culture thing.

EF: Absolutely.

JG: I didn't know that. One of the things that I wanted to say before — because what we're doing is deferring starting, but we're also setting it up in a really good way — is that the reason why, when I was actually calling to talk to Chris, I didn't just say, "Hi, how are you?", which is my usual way of being polite on the phone, is that I knew that going to the Berks had been really important to you. A year and a half earlier, when we were out with a bunch of people, you sat down and said to me with some excitement, "I just found out that I'm going to be giving a paper at the Berks." I remembered that it was very important to you to speak in that scene, which is why it felt appropriate for me to make sure that I asked you how that went.

EF: So it wasn't just chitchat; this significant thing had happened, and you wanted to keep track and all that. The Berks only happens once every three years, so great anticipation and planning go into it. It's gotten enormous and very competitive, which I think is interesting. The Berks, for people who do the history of women, has become more important as a forum in which to talk about your work than practically any other academic conference.

JG: So it's a site not just of a women's community — it's also prestigious.

EF: Well, yes.

JG: That's important to think about because it has to do with the growth of the discipline, the place where it becomes a professional site. What once might have been fantasized as an alternative space is also now a place where . . . When you told me that you were going to give a paper at the Berks, as you talked about other people who would be on the panel and all of that, I read your pleasure not as marking going to some women's retreat (which was not actually a fantasy that I thought you had anyway) but rather having made it into the big leagues professionally.

EF: Yes, absolutely. And not just. I thought of it as not just prestigious, but also as a place where I would really get a strong response to my work. There would be a dialogue, or enough common ground that I would actually feel like I was participating in something; it would be an exchange as well, and that was something that I both looked forward to but was also really nervous about.

JG: Can I ask you one more question? Because I think you are about to tell what happened at the Berks—and I'm deferring it more, but I already know what happened. Up until the time you went to the Berks, did you retain a sense that this was something you were really excited about? What was the Berks for you as you went there?

EF: I guess the meaning of it has changed throughout my graduate career. It started out as the pilgrimage kind of thing. The first year I went as a feminist, participating in a feminist culture. And the second time it was much more professional. And then the third time, I *really* thought of it as professional, I guess.

JG: The third time was the only time you went to give a paper?

EF: That's right. And you know, I thought about it as a professional conference, but I still also thought of it as a community. But that's where the trouble came in, I guess, and that's where the connection to this sort of generational conversation comes in. The Berks, for me, is no longer a place for feminist celebration but a place of professional development or professional display, really, or performance.

JG: Yes, probably more display than development. So it's actually more like the AHA (American Historical Association), which I assume is like the MLA (Modern Language Association). The whole thing sounds like the MLA to me.

EF: It is. In some ways it's more prestigious now than the AHA.

JG: Because it's more exclusive.

EF: It's more exclusive but it's also bigger.

JG: Literally bigger?

EF: I think so, yes. There were something like three thousand people there.

JG: That's fascinating. Does that mean there are actually three thousand people who are scholars of women's history?

EF: There were more people at the conference at Vassar than Vassar could actually hold.[1]

JG: Oh, I had no idea it was so big. Like literally, so big. I knew it was big symbolically, but I didn't know it was physically so big.

EF: It is literally big and cramped.

JG: But there weren't three thousand people in the audience for your talk?

EF: No.

JG: That's too bad. [Laughter.]

EF: It's not too bad. Anyway, so what happened at the Berks: I went alone; Chris dropped me off, literally at the gates. I knew I was going to see people that I knew, see friends, but I was staying by myself, I didn't go in a group, which is how I'd done it before. I didn't have my own generation around me both to commiserate and have fun with. So I felt like I was both participating in it but also observing. I'd been so focused on my dissertation that I really wasn't involved in a community; I definitely had a participant-observer feeling about it, and that feeling stayed with me throughout. I had it when I gave my paper, so that was, I think, significant. Because I was on a panel with two really prestigious feminist scholars and two others who are going to be, my paper was really well attended. It was not held in a big ballroom or something, the way it would be at the AHA; it was held in the chapel. So there was again this sense of pilgrimage.

JG: So the assumption of the organizers, given some of the other people who were on your panel, was that this was going to be one of the biggest sessions during that time period, so you got the biggest room. And that biggest room happened to be the chapel.

EF: Happened to be the chapel. And the panelists were all up on the...

JG: Pulpit, isn't that what it's called?

EF: And there was a big pipe organ and huge ferns; so there was really this sense that a stage had been set. But beyond that, the performance itself wasn't, I don't think, that dramatic, except that a lot of people went—there were like 250 people in the audience, which is big.

JG: Which is more people than you've ever talked in front of.

EF: Well, I'd given a lecture before to students in a big course.

JG: But not a paper.

EF: I didn't have the sense of people listening or participating or whatever. I felt like I was just up there by myself with the big spotlight on and not really able to see anyone. I didn't get the thing that I wanted, which was dialogue and exchange and a sense of where I fit—and if I fit. The feeling of not fitting continued.

JG: So what you wanted was not to be heard or even to be seen.

EF: Sure, I wanted that.

JG: But there was something else you wanted that involved more exchange.

EF: Yes, and I realize that I did and also didn't feel equipped for the occasion. I couldn't quite rise to the occasion and felt drained by the experience of standing up in front of a big audience I imagined filled with people whose work I respected and admired. I was so drained and scared that I felt empty afterward—like even if I had gotten a question I wouldn't have been able to answer it.

JG: Forget for the moment your literal audience. Either before or during, did you imagine your audience as basically established feminist historians?

EF: Yes. In fact I imagined that some of the people that I talked about in my paper were there.

JG: Were they?

EF: I don't know; they could have been. I know that they both were at the conference.

JG: For you the scene somehow was not speaking to peers, to other graduate students (even though that's what the bulk of any audience usually is). What was important about the scene—what was difficult about it or scary or exciting, all those things—was that you were being listened to by people senior to you in the profession.

EF: Definitely. I also felt a kind of anxiety about that because the opening talk by the president of the Berks was all about the idea of the Berks as a celebratory space. She specifically talked about that in terms of where we reproduce women's history. I talked about generational stuff in my paper but not as something that is easy. I was critical of work that preceded mine and of the way that generations had been played out in feminist history as a narrative. I wasn't *playing* at celebration. I was being much more critical, and that made me feel anxious, too.

JG: I'm wondering how the person transcribing the tape is going to mark the way you just pronounced *playing*. Hopefully by italicizing it. I can't imitate your tone but . . .

EF: They could put scare quotes around it.

JG: You're saying two things that sound contradictory to me, and I'm sure they're both true. You're saying you felt like an outsider who didn't get what you wanted, which was to be part of the community. At the same time you're saying that you felt like people were demanding you be part of the community, but you didn't want to be.

EF: Yes.

JG: Right, then you see why this sounds contradictory.

EF: Right, it is contradictory. But I also felt like it was a sham. I think that what I want (and maybe this is where it's not contradictory) is a real community, and I thought the Berks offered that. Lip service was paid to that—it was part of the official discourse of the Berkshire Conference. But I didn't see that being enacted in a significant way. I saw it as institutionalized, about prestige and competition—both of which I don't necessarily think are wrong.

JG: As I listen to you talk, when "prestige and competition" come out of your mouth, I hear them as "Oh, those terrible things, prestige and competition." Yet simultaneously I thought, "But you were excited about going there because it was prestigious."

EF: And because it was competitive to get on the program. I think that those contradictions are operating. That's part of what it means to be a feminist in the academy. You want both things, right?

JG: Right.

EF: Especially as a graduate student. You go to graduate school and remain a feminist and do feminist things and teach feminism and help your students think about feminism—not necessarily to make them feminists but certainly to give them that perspective as part of a critical relation to the world. But graduate school is also about professional development, and you want to go to a conference like the Berks because it represents both things. It provides the nexus of both professional development and feminist community as a place outside of mere prestige and competition.

JG: I believe you honestly want both of those things or all three of them—I'm going to call "prestige and competition" the same thing since they came out of your mouth the same way. I think you do want that and community, but they're nonetheless contradictory. I think that we (now I'm including myself) experience them as contradictory. I'm not saying they have to be contradictory, but there is no utopia where they won't be. I think they're structured to produce something—at least you produced it in me—which is that, at the moment I mentioned your contradictory relation to community, you started taking on the positive discourse of community. You spoke your desire to be part of a community so that when you said the words *prestige and competition* it sounded like they were the spoilers of community. I don't think it's you; that's the way it's configured, and maybe not just in feminist discourse, but in discourses about community.

EF: But acknowledging that those things are operating and that they are contradictory is important. There is this idea that feminism is contaminated by the structures of competition and the process of institutionalization, that feminism is destroyed when those processes begin.

JG: Those ideas really circulate. In fact, I heard those ideas in what you were saying.

EF: So when I say it was a sham (even as I say it I feel bad for saying it) . . . When I say that the discourse of feminist community was a sham because in fact there was competition and desire for prestige and alienation and all going on at the conference, I'm also saying that the Berkshire Conference ought to acknowledge itself as an institution. It was a sham because it was talking about celebration and community when in fact it was fully institutionalized and wasn't acknowledging that. That, I think, is what made me start to get angry.

JG: Do you think that community and institution necessarily have to be different things? Can an institution be a community?

EF: Yes, I think so, but you have to be pretty conscious about how you do that.

JG: The fantasy of community has been so centrally empowering for a lot of feminism. It's a fantasy of undifferentiated community, just a mass of people who are in some way together, whereas institutions are also masses of people, but they have differentiated functions and there's a hierarchy. In fact, real communities also involve hierarchies and differentiation. But there is this idea of community around which makes it hard to imagine "prestige" in a community. Not because there are any communities in the world that don't have prestige, but . . .

EF: But community is often opposed to other ways of thinking about social organization.

JG: Community has a special meaning that sets it in opposition to institution and institutionalization . . . What happened at the Berks, Elizabeth, when you went there?

EF: That's what happened.

JG: No, you haven't yet said what you told me on the telephone.

EF: I don't remember. What did I tell you?

JG: You really don't remember? The thing you have not yet said is the thing that made me want to have this conversation.

EF: Give me a hint.

JG: I'll *tell* you; it doesn't have to be a guessing game. I'm just surprised. You talked about something much more specifically generational. You didn't use the word *cohort,* but you said that you and your friends—some of them assistant professors now and some late graduate students, dissertators—were all talking and were horrified at the way senior scholars at the Berks were attacking junior scholars and were being like . . . were being like dismissive and aggressive and were trashing. That's what you told me.

EF: Okay. M-hm. I definitely feared that, but it didn't happen to me. I did see it a lot, and I know people had exactly that experience—of senior scholars, not trashing their work but failing to engage in a productive exchange (I realize these words have a sort of utopian meaning, but I still want to hold on to them as something that scholarship can and should be about). They decided what was good and what was bad. These are basically the structures of scholarship—this is rigorous scholarship, this isn't—cloaking a critique from their point of view in the guise of "I'm a senior scholar; I know what's good scholarship, and you're not doing good scholarship." In fact there was politics going on in the sense that there were different kinds of scholarship being done, which weren't the same as they had done. Using the mantle of being senior to attack new scholarship seemed to happen frequently, and I thought that was disturbing.

JG: On the phone, when I asked, "How was the Berks?" I was first of all struck by how you chose to answer the question. It was clear to me that not only were you upset, but this was something you hadn't expected, something you thought was bad, if not scandalous. You very much put it in generational terms: you saw a senior generation of feminist historians basically disallowing, dismissing, refusing, or attacking a junior generation of feminist historians. I had never heard anyone say what you were saying. I had never heard anyone who was junior or new in the profession talk about senior people attacking junior people. I just never had heard it.

EF: In the context of feminism?

JG: Well, I'm not sure I had ever heard it, period.

EF: Really? Because it seems what the whole structure of professional development is all about.

JG: It was totally unfamiliar to me. It was both unfamiliar and uncannily familiar, which is why I wanted to have this conversation. I was surprised by this formulation, which you made clear was not yours but was formulated with other people. This thing was obviously going on in some wide way; it didn't involve individual personalities so much as structures and positions. It sounded to me exactly like a mirror image of the discourse I produce and that I hear all the time from my peers, from my friends and colleagues. We always talk about how graduate students will just attack whatever we say. I was so surprised to hear the other side of this—to hear it so clearly and coherently. I wanted to have this conversation because I was fascinated by what seemed like two parallel discourses or parallel perceptions going on. I think of them as parallel because you didn't think you were saying something new and unusual, and yet I had never heard it. They seem parallel because people talk about this with their own generation but never with people of another generation, which is why I wanted to talk about it with you. I thought we might be able to talk because I didn't think either of us would attack the other. I don't think of you as one of those . . . You don't fit my stereotype (what you pointed out was my stereotype) of the graduate student, of the aggressive, snotty graduate student.

EF: What's this stereotype? And maybe I can tell you my stereotype.

JG: Yeah, let's exchange stereotypes. I'll tell you mine in a second. I felt that through the chance of this social relation—which was just asking you a polite question on the telephone because I wanted to talk to your husband, who's my research assistant—when I asked you about the Berks, suddenly I'd gained access to this other world, to how the other side looks. It was like going through the looking glass. I recognized what you were saying: I mean, I recognized the structure; I don't know if I recognized it as true. I had never heard anyone say it, yet it sounded exactly like what my friends say about . . .

EF: Graduate students.

JG: I thought that, maybe, if we could sit and talk about it, we could understand more than when we talk in our parallel worlds.

EF: So that we can stop having the worlds be parallel and have them intersect in some way. Even as you lay out the scene of your going through the looking glass, I think that if I had thought of you as "Jane Gallop, Senior Scholar, Chris's adviser, generational relationship," I would never have said those things to you.

JG: So what do you think of me as? [Laughter.]

EF: As someone who was interrupting me while I was working on some chapter. I wanted to be distracted, and you were a likely candidate to get me out of my malaise behind the computer.

JG: A couple of days ago you brought up the idea of the construction of the graduate student as part of your response to the dialogue I had with Nancy Miller and Marianne Hirsch.[2] I felt defensive because I recognized the construction you were talking about as one I share — but it's so deep that I don't think of it as a construction. I think of it as literally true.

EF: Even though you have graduate students who violate it every day?

JG: Right. Which is a really bad sign, isn't it?

EF: When you think about it in these contexts, it's intransigent even though your daily life belies it.

JG: All the time.

EF: That's why we have to talk about it in terms of feminism because even though this isn't necessarily our "experience," it's something that's certainly going on. I think it has all sorts of historical resonances and registers as well.

JG: I'm going to tell it to you, but since it comes from the conversation we had three days ago, some of this is stuff *you* actually said. You helped produce my understanding of it, so I want to give you credit. After we talked, I came to see something about the way that I keep talking about the graduate student in that dialogue. Like the way I say that I wrote *Around 1981* for graduate students, to correct their misunderstandings about the history of feminism.

EF: I don't think the book reads that way, but...

JG: Well, I may not have succeeded. Or maybe I'm really lucky.

EF: The acknowledgments aside. [Laughter.]

JG: I guess *that's* the only part... It's like the difference between the fantasy version I have of something and its practice in my teaching and my writing. But the fantasy version involves graduate students as stubborn, resistant, likely to be misled—unless they have a good teacher... As you made me aware of it, it seems quite horrible.

JG: One possible difference between the way our academic generations think of each other is that every one of us was once a graduate student and none of you were ever senior scholars. I was thinking about that because I was wondering, "What is the relation between my construction of the graduate student and the graduate student I remember being?" It may be twenty years ago, but I still remember being a graduate student. Not only are the students who I like and work with not like the graduate student I construct, but I would have been horrified for anybody to think that I was like that when I was a graduate student. I also was remembering something about peer competitiveness, remembering my investment in being superior to other graduate students. I'm wondering if that's part of where the construction comes from. I was supposed to be different, separate from the commonality of the graduate student. The rest of them were both resistant and sheepish, some weird combination. This construction involves someone who's both easily misled *and* resists learning.

EF: Both are not good learners.

JG: And both are not good, just in general. They err in two different directions.

EF: You'd think both wouldn't apply to graduate students, or else why would they be in graduate school?

JG: Well, I won't go into that. I feel I actually know people who are like this construction.

EF: But it's beyond either your peers when you were a graduate student or those students you teach when you are actually in a classroom. When you talk about it with Marianne Hirsch and Nancy Miller, it's not graduate students you teach. It's graduate students who appear like a disease at a conference and stand...

JG: And ask aggressive questions.

EF: I guess they don't even ask questions. They just get up and launch a tirade, an attack, that's very destructive and disheartening.

JG: Right, the graduate student as terrorist. I'm trying to figure out why this is so strong for me.

EF: And I think I know why that happens.

JG: You do?

EF: Yes.

JG: Well, tell me.

EF: This particular thing happens not in the context of a classroom or within the confines of your own institution; you come in as a scholar from elsewhere and give a talk that attracts a bunch of people. It's about graduate students defending what they do in the confines of their own department or institution.

JG: But I've actually encountered this graduate student in my classes. Repeatedly. I don't see this as someone who isn't at my institution. This is the relation I have to graduate students who don't want to work with me, who don't like me, who don't like the way I teach, or whatever. I've taught numerous feminist seminars in which people who fit the stereotype for me are mouthing some line, some fashionable position, and refusing to listen to what I'm saying and attacking me for my power and authority.

EF: So it's both intellectual and personal. You don't think what they are saying is particularly interesting or useful.

JG: I respond to it as aggression for the sake of aggression. That is probably an exaggeration: I'm generating a kind of composite experience from specific examples that have this sort of thing in common. Although it is contradictory that these people are both too easily influenced and resistant, that's the profile I have: people with some kind of fashionable, politically correct line who use it to attack whatever it is that I'm saying. And it's true, I think, of that graduate student. I know that I have this discourse all the time. I've heard myself using this stereotype in talking with some of my graduate students and becoming self-conscious because I'm talking to someone who is not only a graduate student but *my* graduate student, someone who wants me to think well of graduate students . . . So, maybe that's the way I locate what I'm struggling against, in my pedagogy. Graduate students are struggling against that same thing, but they don't locate it as a graduate student problem. In fact, maybe they locate it in what *you're* talking about. It's rigidity, it's stubbornness, it's defending one's position rather than listening to what somebody else is saying. So maybe it's actually related to the position you were dismayed to see senior people take, except that I locate it as the graduate student.

EF: I don't hear you talking about feminists; I hear you talking about graduate students. You say that because you teach feminist theory they are one and the same. My assumption was similar. I thought because scholars of women's history were feminists, they would treat younger scholars as both feminists and as scholars, and I didn't see that. I saw them treating us as "graduate students," not as "feminist graduate students." So I see a political distinction there that isn't getting articulated somehow.

JG: I'm having trouble following what you're saying, and I think it's because our categories are different.

EF: I think that when feminists go to graduate school they see themselves as different.

JG: From other graduate students. And I don't see feminist graduate students as different from other graduate students.

EF: I do. And I think that a lot of people that I know—and I include myself, although I feel like that's changing a little bit now—wouldn't go to graduate school if they weren't feminists and couldn't do feminist work. It's a personal, intellectual, professional knot. And I don't see what you're saying—that feminist graduate students aren't somehow special—as responding to that, I guess. I'm not saying that they are; I'm saying that's how it's construed.

JG: That doesn't correspond to anything that I'm talking about. I don't even know how to think about it in relation to what I'm talking about...

EF: But you're talking about it as if it's any student; there's no feminist component to it—any student can be resistant, stubborn.

JG: Well, in fact, that's my perception. I see feminist graduate students doing to senior feminist thinkers—both people they meet in lectures and people they write about in their work—the exact same thing that I remember my cohort of graduate students (who were largely not feminists) doing. It just looks identical to me, so it doesn't seem to make any difference. I was surrounded by graduate students who were trying to find what was wrong with Derrida, trying to find the holes in his reasoning, the places where he contradicts himself, and my graduate students are now doing that with Donna Haraway in the exact same way. So, yes, I don't see that difference.

EF: So you're still special, right? You're still in the scenario of being different from the other graduate students.

JG: No, because I too did that as a graduate student.

EF: But you were also a feminist, and you went on to become a feminist author. So there are still all of these graduate students who are like your peers who are just being graduate students. I'd like to know where feminism was for you as this place that both defined you professionally and set you apart.

JG: There's an interesting answer to that, but I want to say one more thing first. Because the field that I'm in is called "feminist theory," all the senior and junior scholars in it think of themselves as feminists — and this is complicated, whether that's a political identity at that point or a disciplinary identity. When I imagine or when I experience this terrorist graduate student, she's always a feminist. And she's always a she. In fact, the worst attacks that I have suffered have all been by feminist graduate students. Being feminist in some ways doesn't make a difference and in some ways makes it much worse.

EF: I'd like to know how it makes it worse.

JG: I don't get attacked by nonfeminist graduate students. I think that's because I'm marked as a feminist, so graduate students who aren't feminists don't consider me an authority figure. They might take a class of mine or go to a lecture, but they are unlikely to be invested in...

EF: Or they might think of themselves as having something to learn from you, which is feminism. But I don't think that feminist graduate students come in and think they are going to learn "feminism."

JG: From me. Or from anyone.

EF: Right.

JG: Which may be part of the problem. They go into a class thinking that they have nothing to learn.

EF: Yes...

JG: Which is maybe why I have such trouble teaching.

EF: Well... [Laughter.]

JG: You've just answered a question I've had for years: "Why are feminist theory classes the ones that never work?" Because I always go into the class assuming that I have something to teach and that students have something to learn. But if the subject matter of the course is "feminist theory" and if people are there because they already think of themselves as "feminist"...

EF: Then it's already an identity, or an experience, or a worldview.

JG: I want to say for the record that it's not because I don't think my students are feminist that I think I have something to teach them.

EF: No, it's because they're not good students.

JG: No, it's because I think they can learn to read and write and think better.

EF: Well, that's the thing. That you're not there to teach them feminism. You're there to teach them.

JG: Right, but they think I'm there to teach them feminism. It's in the title of the course.

EF: Okay, they think it's going to be — well, I don't know who the "they" is . . .

JG: I don't think that they're going to learn feminism from me, but they think that. If the issue of my teaching them or their learning something comes up, they imagine it has something to do with feminism, which they think they have nothing to learn about because they already are feminists. And therefore, we're in some kind of contradiction: they believe (and we're talking about a subset of students that I run into, not all of them . . .

EF: Yes, I think we need these qualifiers.

JG: The "they" for whom I never establish any kind of productive pedagogical relation) "they" believe that what you learn from courses is the subject matter of the course.

EF: Which makes sense.

JG: Right, that's a widely held belief, but it's not mine.

EF: But I also think it's something that one learns as a graduate student. That's what constitutes the process in graduate school. I went into graduate school thinking that I didn't know enough and that I needed to know more, and that if I knew more, then I would be able to do this interesting work — that I would be able to take my point of view and apply it to much more stuff. And that the more I knew, the better off I would be. It would ground my scholarship. That was my idea — that I was going to be grounded. And I think that's how I thought about history, too.

JG: You didn't think of yourself as learning feminism; you thought of yourself as learning history. But you took feminist courses.

EF: Yes, I did, but I felt conflict about that. It ended up not really mattering because, as you said, it's about method, it's about ways of thinking, it's about rigor, that kind of thing. I think that's the point that a lot of graduate students arrive at—realizing that it's not about gaining more knowledge. It's about learning a way of thinking. And that the politics are located in that more than anything else. I did take feminist courses, but I have to say that my feminism, as an experiential, political worldview, became more distant. I think of myself as a feminist and I think of my scholarship as doing something feminist. That's what happened when I took feminist theory courses. That cohesive moment of the knowledge as feminist and the mode of thinking as feminist broke apart to a certain extent. Even though I was reading exactly the same things that I had read as an undergraduate, or as someone out in the world, I read them completely differently. I was forced to read them completely differently.

JG: Forced by your teachers.

EF: And I found it quite difficult at first.

JG: Because you were actually being deprived of texts that you already had a relation to.

EF: That effect, I guess, is what it is. These were texts I had actually learned from, but I stopped learning the things that they had to teach me and started thinking about them as things that I had to critique.

JG: And the graduate student I struggle with has not yet given that up—or doesn't want to give that up.

EF: I don't want to position myself as the "good" graduate student because in some ways I think I was a really "bad" graduate student.

JG: And who would want to be positioned as the good graduate student, anyway? [Laughter.] Yuck.

EF: I mean, everyone hates the good graduate student.

JG: The brownnoser.

EF: But everybody is locked into that anyway. Feminist graduate students want to be thought of as special by their feminist teachers. But that's exactly the kind of thing that *you* don't think happens.

JG: That doesn't happen to me. What makes graduate students special to me is not their feminism, but their ability and willingness to learn, which doesn't necessarily mean being good.

EF: That's how you define *good*.

JG: What makes graduate students special to me is participating in pedagogical dialogue where I feel like I can do what it's my job to do. People who are good partners in that for me are what I think of as good graduate students. And some are feminists — most of them are feminists in some vague way.

EF: Certainly most would take feminist positions on major issues.

JG: Let me get back to your earlier question. You asked me about being a feminist graduate student myself. And I said I thought of something interesting. It is different for feminists who went to graduate school when I did or earlier than it is for feminists who went to graduate school ten, fifteen, twenty years later. I was the kind of graduate student who was very involved in trying to find places to critique the thinkers who had the most authority in the field I was learning. Feminism for me was the tool of that critique. It was the way that I could critique Lacan and Derrida, and so feminism was what made that possible. The thinkers who had authority when I was in graduate school — both the texts we were reading and the teachers who were in my program — were not feminist and in fact were not really great on issues of gender, so you could start paying attention to gender and feel like you had some power in relation to them. That's what's not there for the generation after feminism became a discipline.

EF: I think it's still there. The dynamic is still there: desiring to find critical tools that are also political and revolutionary, that will change the shape of both the discipline and the paradigm. But it's within feminism, and feminism itself has split apart in so many ways and into so many disciplines that there's no one feminist tool. Feminism has become both the agent and the object of your critique. That's the moment in which things get really difficult. What I don't understand is why that leads to attacks by feminist graduate students on feminist scholars, you know, beyond the classroom situation. Or in reverse, why feminist scholars wouldn't see the power of what younger scholars are doing but instead would feel the need to attack it or use the mantle of scholarly authority to dismiss it.

JG: I would assume that it's not about *not seeing* the power of something but in fact seeing something as a threat.

EF: If you see it as a threat, then you can't see the power of it.

JG: No! What do you mean? Anything you see as a threat you see as powerful, but you see it as power to be used against you.

EF: Well, you see it as personal.

JG: But I assume that you don't attack anything that you don't see as powerful.

EF: You say that feminist graduate students stand up and attack you, your position, your work? What is it they're attacking?

JG: It seems like it's not me, my position, or my work. It seems like they're looking for something to attack. It often takes the form of "You didn't talk about this in your talk," which to me is not about attacking anything I said; it's just having some category by which to dismiss what I did. I'm stereotyping a little. No one actually ever asks that question, but there are a lot of questions that resemble it, in which someone dismisses the entire talk for what it doesn't say, rather than engaging with what it does say.

EF: Doing that doesn't seem very interesting to me.

JG: No, but it's very widespread. I mean, just because it's not interesting to you doesn't seem to stop it from existing. [Laughter.]

EF: I know it happens a lot.

JG: I mean, you must have heard such questions before.

EF: Ad nauseam.

JG: I mean, they're really common. They're like your basic academic questions. And, in my scenarios, they are more likely to come from graduate students than from anyone else. Do you think that's true, or am I just making that up?

EF: I guess I don't see it coming primarily from feminists. I definitely see what you're saying as a structure of what graduate students do. They attack because that's what they're taught to do.

JG: Which is to say, you blame the parents, whereas I think they do it because they're such ornery cusses—they're just bad seeds. [Laughter.] I want to pose a question. You don't have to answer it now. You said that after I described my construction of the graduate student you would attempt to imagine your construction of the senior scholar that corresponds in some way. So I wanted just to put that on the agenda so that it doesn't get forgotten.

EF: I'm not saying that they're doing it because that's what their scholarly parents . . .

JG: You did say they were taught to do it.

EF: They are taught to do it because that's the structure. There was no one who said, "You must do this because I tell you to do it," like a parent would say, "You have to make your bed."

JG: You are talking about teaching by example, I assume.

EF: Teaching by example, but also that in order to be a scholar in the academy, we have to do these things. Either the professor or the student can sit there and say, "We don't like this structure, but we have to do it, we have to jump through these hoops. We have to critique these books; we have to consume this scholarship and find a critical relationship to it."

JG: I don't believe that. Not only do I not believe you should do that—which you probably don't believe either—but I don't believe that the academy is just like . . .

EF: This autonomous machine . . .

JG: But also I don't believe that system is privileged by the academy. I know that system is privileged by some. I actually don't believe that you are rewarded particularly for these dismissive kinds of attacks. I think that's a kind of misinterpretation of what the academy wants you to do. People who ask those questions are generally understood to be kind of dumb because they are not very interesting questions. People start their own work by showing what's wrong with the work that came before them, but it's usually understood that it has to be careful and attentive and all of that sort of stuff. I think that the idea that the academy teaches trashing is actually a rationalization.

EF: But I think you're collapsing the bad attack with a good critique. The critique is supposed to be good.

JG: Right, you're supposed to show that you understand what you're critiquing and not dismissing it.

EF: And everybody hates an agenda that's just ideological and propagandistic.

JG: And everybody does it, too. [Laughter.]

EF: I don't want to defend the whole idea that "This is what the academy wants you to do" and feminists participate in it because they just want to have a place in the academy. But I do think that has played a role in feminist inquiry in relation to the academy. Feminist critique was a wholesale attack on entire epistemologies.

JG: And they were—and these are the things that I value—they were in fact dismissive. They were saying, "We don't have to read this stuff anymore because this stuff is so sexist it's just fucked." So it actually is a tradition. It is *the* tradition. The beginning of feminist scholarship was saying, "Wait a minute. This stuff is sexist, so I'm just going to stop reading it. I'm not going to engage with it and get into its arguments and show where it's wrong on its own terms. I'm going to dismiss it because in my terms it's fucked." And that's the kind of person I hate. [Laughter.] So I do think it's a problem that has to do with feminism because it's our tradition. But as a feminist, I can't stand when somebody does this to me.

EF: There are problems with that because in feminism, like other "avant garde" positions, part of its charm (if you can call it that) is its gusto, the sort of explosiveness of it and its ability to say, "Let's just not play anymore. Let's just not participate in this. Let's just do something else." There's a role for that, and major things have been accomplished through that. So the question then becomes what you do when, by flouting the conventions, you have gained a foothold. Feminism, as a mode of inquiry within disciplines as well as a discipline in itself, became a part of intellectual culture.

JG: I find the figure of the feminist (or otherwise) radical naysayer very charming (the word you used) and very attractive. But part of the attraction of that is associated with something like youthful exuberance. I think there is a connection to age. Which is why I also think of it as the graduate student. For me the construction of the graduate student as terrorist is very close to another construction I have, which is the graduate student as totally attractive figure, full of energy, youth, and vitality, who is going to do something new.

EF: So that is threatening.

JG: Yes. And although it's annoying, there's a kind of romanticization possible of the graduate student who stands up and asks the dismissive question, a romanticization very hard to feel toward the senior scholar who is equally dismissive because that just looks like oppression. It doesn't look like radical questioning; it looks like the voice of the law coming down and saying "No."

EF: And I think that's how it feels.

JG: And that's how you hear it... So tell me your vision of the senior scholar.

EF: It's not located in any single person or personal experience. Let's take the example of a conference. A panel is composed of either graduate students or assistant professors. This happens in women's history particularly with people who are doing a sort of poststructuralist analysis. The respondent is someone very eminent in the subject matter. That seems so pervasive at conferences. And that's why it's so depressing at the Berks.

JG: That's not something I know from English; I think it may be different.

EF: It's not that way at the MLA?

JG: No. It varies, but I don't recognize that structure. That structure sets up the respondent to be the teacher.

EF: Yes, the respondent is the teacher. The respondent is an expert, in the position not only of knowing the field but also of upholding the method because the two are so one and the same in history. People give their papers, and some are extraordinarily good and some less so, you know, like any panel. And the respondent evaluates them — what's better, what's worse, what's been left out, what needs to be grappled with further.

JG: So it's like the remarks that the teacher writes at the bottom of the paper. That's a different kind of response from what I'm used to at conferences.

EF: To me, the model response to a paper says what the paper accomplishes, then says what the paper can do. At a conference, there is a general gesture to the significance of the work as a whole, and then each paper is evaluated on its merits or its lack of merit. It's always about grading.

JG: Did your voice just crack? Is it from cigarettes?

EF: No, I think it's from talking a lot.

JG: Because I actually heard your voice crack, and it sounded like you were talking about something that was difficult for you.

EF: I don't think so.

JG: No, you're losing your voice.

EF: Yes, a little bit. I am getting a little hoarse. It could be a sign of talking about things that make me nervous. It does make me nervous to talk about this stuff.

JG: All of this or this particular stuff?

EF: This particular stuff because I feel like it's going to keep on happening to me, that it's something I have to look forward to. And I really don't like it much at all. I find it so unuseful, so terribly unuseful.

JG: And it's unuseful because it doesn't help you make your work better?

EF: It just tells you what's wrong.

JG: And it makes you feel...bad.

EF: It makes you feel like there's some magic entrance that you haven't found yet. And that's where feminism comes in. And part of this is also disappointment; you thought you were going to get something. Because they are feminists, you think they will appreciate the achievement, the work it takes to do this kind of scholarship.

JG: What you're saying reminds me that when I run into feminist graduate students who ask me those kinds of questions, I think, "Because they're feminists, they should realize I've been doing this work for them." There's something about expecting to be appreciated and instead being criticized that is very, very painful. I found myself identifying with what you were saying, even though it was an opposite sort of thing. It seems to me that there is some connection. What I heard you describing on the telephone, which I hadn't heard before but which also sounded very familiar, was this description of something very painful, very painful and very disappointing. This goes back to something that you said in describing the context of the Berks: the assumption that it should be different among feminists. I think I have that assumption, too, although I feel like I should be not naive but more jaded. And therefore I take the position, "I know it's not different among feminists." I think my sense of it as painful comes from the teacher's fantasy that this work I've been doing (which I believe I've been doing for feminism and for feminists) should be appreciated. Not that it shouldn't be criticized; it's not about that. But I was trying to do it for graduate students who are also trying to make feminism. I hear you describing a painful refusal of commonality that I also experience.

EF: The alliances seem to be not with feminism but with your cohort. You used that word—you know, that weird sociological word. Senior scholars appreciate, sustain, promote, and defer to the work of their own peers.

JG: Although you know that it's much more complicated than that. You do know that. [Laughter.]

EF: Absolutely. I do know that. What isn't often articulated is that a lot of feminists—at least feminist historians—feel they're the only one in their department. They feel marginalized, that they had to fight really hard just to carve out a place for themselves. They feel that their feminist graduate students are going to have to struggle, too. That's my stereotype, right? It's always going to be about struggle, about trying to find a place where you can do this work, about uneasy alliances in the institution. You'll always have to be a trailblazer; to be a feminist means to be a trailblazer. It's never going to be easier, and you have to teach your students to be the same way, to accept that it's going to be a struggle. You don't make it easier by nurturing and creating an artificial community. This is of course my fantasy...

JG: It's the discourse of raising one's daughters to struggle against oppression...I want to ask you a question that is not directly related to this. When you were describing the panels with three junior speakers and the senior respondent, you said at some point, "Aren't we ever going to be able to enter?" You used the image of entry. These panels were, after all, public panels. They were meetings, not classes, but in some way they reproduced a classroom structure. At the very moment you were giving a talk at a conference, which is one of the marks of entering the profession, you felt you hadn't entered, that you were still in the wings.

EF: It's like getting me back in the box or something. I think a lot of people feel that way.

JG: As I was listening to that, I thought, when you're senior and you have a respondent, it continues to be true that the thing the respondent is most likely to do is to say what's wrong with your paper.

EF: I think that's the structure of response.

JG: It's at least the most prevalent one. But it always drives me crazy—I hate it. The respondent does take up the ideas in the paper but says, "This is wrong." Like that's the response. No matter how much I'm retacked...(Retacked? By a spondent?)...although I'm horrified and I feel like this person's not listening to me, etc., I never feel like I can't be in. Because I am in. So I wonder if the position you're in shapes the interpretation in a certain way. The same things might be said to a senior person.

EF: It has very real effects. Right? If your work isn't received well, you don't get the same...

JG: I'm not sure about those effects because although there's a lot of correlation between never having your work accepted to give at a conference and not getting jobs and not getting published, there's not much correlation between giving a paper at a conference and having a negative response to it (which most papers get) and not getting jobs and not getting published. I wish dismissive responses didn't exist, but I don't think that they hurt people professionally.

EF: I disagree. I'm not sure I have real examples to bring up, but I do know that if a paper is well received it gets a certain buzz. Key respondents are often people who are on editorial boards of journals or job search committees who say, "This is a good candidate."

JG: I think you're mixing two things. Yes, a paper that is received well gets a buzz, but that reception is produced in the audience, not by the respondents.

EF: All right, all right.

JG: I mean, you've been to talks where you loved the paper and hated the respondent's response. You were not influenced by the negative response. It's true that the responder may be the editor of a journal, but someone sitting in the audience could be also. If the respondent is the editor of the journal and doesn't like the paper whatever they say, they're not going to publish it. I hear two different realms condensed in what you're saying: the critical response that not only makes you feel bad but also makes you feel like you'll never get a job. That's a central issue for anybody writing their dissertation and trying to get a job; every negative response feeds into "I won't get a job." Even though they don't feel separable, it's important to separate them.

EF: M-hm. Well, they don't feel separable. I was going to say something else about the structure of feminism as intervention. Several other people at the Berks and I responded, "Well, okay, the Berks has to be dismantled. The Berks has become just like any other conference, and now we have to do it over. Let's make something new." It was this destructive impulse, "Let's just raze it"—not that we wanted to destroy the Berks itself but we had to create something entirely different. We just couldn't participate. I'm not sure if that's part of feminism or if it's part of being "the dissatisfied younger generation." And I'm sure the other side of it is that a lot of people feel that it's the new work getting published— not that I think the older generation is doing old work.

JG: You're right that older work and older people are not necessarily the same. But it is also true that the people most recently coming out of graduate school are more likely to be doing whatever is the fashion at this moment, and people who have been out of school for a while move much more slowly because they're involved in projects that take years, and you kind of half keep up and you kind of half don't. So that's another thing that I think that people of my generation feel: we've devoted all this time and effort, and people come along and tell us that's not what you should be doing anymore. I spent a lot of effort trying to figure out psychoanalysis and feminism, poststructuralism and feminism, French feminism, that whole realm, and one day I turned around and it was not in fashion anymore. And I had to retool myself; I've been trying to retool myself ever since because I felt pushed by what people coming out of graduate school or in graduate school are interested in doing. I felt like I was scrambling not to fall further and further behind. I felt like, "Boy, at this point in my life I thought I could work less hard," and I was working harder. I had to do the equivalent of putting myself through grad school, intellectually, by trying to catch up on what people were writing and thinking about. The feeling is that if we keep doing the same work we've been doing, we won't get published or we won't get read. In fact, it sometimes feels to me like the agenda is being determined by younger people.

EF: But I still don't understand how this fits. We're just not getting at this question of feminism. All of these structures that we're talking about are the structures of being scholars. But what does it have to do with feminism? Where is feminism? Aside from the fact that the work we do is feminist. Does feminism change this at all? A lot of people who aren't feminists feel that way about retooling.

JG: Every time you ask this, I feel like it's a showstopper; it has this rhetorical force: "Where is feminism?" I feel I should be able to answer it, and if I can't, then I'm bad or wrong or I've failed. It makes me anxious. We have to stop talking soon, so this question is probably as far as we can get before we turn off the tape. I keep thinking feminism makes it worse. What a terrible thing to say. I don't mean that if we give up feminism these problems would be less bad. But feminism produces the expectation that it should be different, and so when it isn't different it's much more painful—and therefore worse. That's the only place I can see where feminism is. That's the way it seems to keep coming up in these stories, in the expectation and desire for community, which I have, too. I know I have it, but it's harder for me to talk about because to feel it directly rather than sarcastically is to experience disappointment. Feminism makes all of these things that weren't supposed to be seem much worse, more like betrayal.

EF: But to me feminism isn't just about community. In fact, it never was really about community. That whole notion was always in question as soon as I became a feminist.

JG: There's no causal relation. [Laughter.]

EF: Yeah, I became a feminist and then community was impossible. Feminism has always had this individualistic impulse, so it wasn't just about community. I think community was always an impossibility. But feminism was also a critique of the structures of how we reproduce knowledge. So where is that? I'm posing it to you, but I'm also posing it to myself because I don't hear myself articulating that any more than you.

JG: But when you pose the question, even though it sounds like a rhetorical question, I feel like I'm supposed to answer it because I'm in a position of responsibility and therefore it's my fault or the fault of those like me that we haven't changed things.

EF: I never expected you or anybody else to change things just by the force of your own, you know, will.

JG: But I don't mean as an individual, I mean as feminists within the academy. I hear it this way regardless of how you intended. I feel responsible for the way things are in the academy. I can't blame the academy since I am an active participant. If it is this way, then I'm responsible for it. I don't feel individually responsible for it, but I feel responsible. I hear this and feel like we failed, we didn't do what we were supposed to.

EF: I feel responsibility, too — it's not like I can just be a career-minded scholar; there has to be something more. And feminism is that more. It's like what you were saying about a sense of disappointment and betrayal. You have to be more than just a good academic. Nobody wants to be a good academic either, right? But it seems to me that there has to be more of an alliance. Not that it's unproblematic, but is it impossible to change this? People went into this for a reason, right? Feminism has made incredible progress in knowledge and criticism, but not in how that gets reproduced. Feminist work is thriving. And so feminist scholars have reproduced yourselves. That's been enormously successful.

JG: Feminist work is really good; it's really very profitable. You're saying, "Is there no way to change this?" Of course, there must be a way to change it, first of all, because I'm not going to say, "There's no way to change it," and just give up and be unhappy forever. That doesn't seem right. I always think that one of the reasons why it hasn't changed is that feminists were too optimistic about how quickly we could change it and too dishonest with ourselves about the investments we had in things like "competition and prestige," to go back to those terms. And if we're going to change the relation between prestige, competition, and community (just to take those three words we were talking about at the beginning of the conversation), we can only change them by recognizing we want all three. I feel like there's been an official discourse about how feminists or women (or somebody) are different, and at the same time there's all this behavior that contradicts the official discourse. This goes back to what you were saying about not being able to stand the lip service. There's all this behavior, but because there is no discourse about the behavior, the behavior is basically disavowed or denied. "There's no way to change it" as long as there's this discrepancy between ideology and behavior. The only thing I can figure out to do is to try to start talking honestly about what we're feeling and why we're doing what we're doing, even though it includes things that we're not supposed to want. I don't know.

EF: Let's stop.

JG: Let's play tennis.

Notes

1. These figures and comparisons are overstated a bit. According to Barbara Harris, the president of the Berkshire Conference, the June 1993 conference at Vassar College drew just under twenty-four hundred scholars. According to an article published on June 16, 1993, in the *New York Times*, the Berks is larger than any other regular meeting of historians *except* that of the American Historical Association. See "History, They Insist, Isn't All His," *New York Times*, June 16, 1993, B7.

2. A few days before we taped our conversation, we discussed another taped conversation Jane Gallop had participated in with two of her colleagues and friends. Among the issues they take up is the problem of graduate students "trashing" their work. See Jane Gallop, Marianne Hirsch, and Nancy K. Miller, "Criticizing Feminist Criticism," in *Conflicts in Feminism,* ed. Marianne Hirsch and Evelyn Fox Keller (New York: Routledge, 1990), 349–69.

Feminist Psychology at Thirtysomething: Feminism, Gender, and Psychology's Ways of Knowing

Jeanne Marecek

Viewed from the outside, feminist psychology in the United States appears to be a burgeoning success. The field boasts four journals, a vast library of books, and two flourishing professional organizations — the Division of the Psychology of Women of the American Psychological Association and the Association for Women in Psychology. But as the number of workers in the field has grown and the scope of its projects widened, the contours of feminist psychology have shifted, opening up fault lines and fractures. These rifts reflect differing epistemological commitments and different feminist politics. Moreover, it once seemed unproblematic to locate a praxis at the conjunction of women's studies and psychology; with the turn to theory in women's studies, however, the points of intersection have dwindled. For many feminist psychologists today, the dual allegiance has become burdensome or even impossible. Some are alienated from the mainstream of psychology. They refuse to speak its mechanistic language and they cannot subscribe to its methodological dicta. Others feel out of step with women's studies — pushed to the fringes, insufficiently appreciated by feminist colleagues in other disciplines, baffled by the cloud of jargon raised in the rush to theory.

The field of psychology has traditionally taken its task to be the production of scientific facts about human behavior, preferably through laboratory experimentation. In setting their own tasks, many feminist psychologists have been dutiful daughters of the parent discipline. They viewed themselves as using the tools of empirical science to produce new knowledge about the lives of women and girls, an agenda that many subscribe to, even to this day. Moreover, American psychology throughout its one-hundred-year history has disdained theory in favor of empirical pursuits. In this regard, too, feminist psychologists have been loyal offspring. Indeed, the latest editorial policy of the *Psychology of Women Quarterly* (the official journal of the Division of the Psychology of Women) describes it as "a research journal with an empirical, scientific tradition" whose mission is "provid[ing] a voice for a side of feminist psychology that we want to preserve in this age of Postmodernism."[1] Furthermore, in the United States at least, the discipline of psychology has thus far sidestepped the skepticism about knowledge, truth, and power that has swept other areas of intellectual life. In feminist psychology, too, complacency, even self-congratulation, remains the rule; skepticism is the exception.

Yet signs of unease have appeared in some quarters of feminist psychology. For instance, two workers recently confessed to contradictory desires for reflexive, critical theory on the one hand and the reassuring certainties of conventional empiricism on the other.[2] For others, the contradiction lies between their intellectual sympathy for social constructionism and their desire for recognition and respect among their fellow psychologists. Young scholars ask, "How can I do the kind of work I believe in and still earn tenure?" One senior feminist psychologist, Sandra Bem, has described herself publicly as having abandoned her disciplinary commitment to psychology in order to do meaningful work on gender and sexuality;[3] others have privately voiced similar sentiments. In a recent book addressed to lesbian readers, Celia Kitzinger and Rachel Perkins declared that psychology has been bad for lesbians and feminists, substituting a vacuous, amoral, and apolitical discourse of personal growth and inner transformation in place of crucial moral debate and political work.[4] Strains of dissent such as these are like the seismic tremors signaling mounting subterranean pressures. Until recently, they have been largely imperceptible and thus ignored. I hope to cast attention on them in this essay. My aim is not to repair rifts or to dissolve differences but, rather, to subject them to closer scrutiny.

Among psychologists, it is customary to regard all disagreements as matters of scientific controversy, as signals of methodological weaknesses or deficiencies in the scientific data. Psychologists defer to the impersonal and automatic forces of research as the sure means to intellectual progress, recasting philosophical, political, and even ethical questions as no more than hypotheses for empirical investigation. In psychology articles, the tired admonition "Further research is needed" serves to foreclose further conversation and sustained argument. I disavow such rhetorical moves: further research will *not* dissolve the disagreements that are the focus of this essay. They are not matters of scientific controversy; rather, they are controversies about the nature of science itself.

My own stance regarding these controversies is neither neutral nor dispassionate. In my view, psychology's project of uncovering universal laws of human behavior is moribund. Its research technologies are not neutral tools for assessing human behavior; they deform in characteristic ways that which they measure. Psychology has focused obsessively on individual psyche, with the result that the cultural, historical, social, and political context is pushed out of sight. Moreover, the field's pronouncements about social life and human action too often have furthered the interests of privileged sectors of society. Finally, exaggerated claims of expertise by psychologists serve to mystify everyday experiences, disempower ordinary people, and buttress psychologists' own positions of power in society.

Feminist Psychology: Little Women and How They Grew

The endeavors of feminist workers in psychology have yielded a widely dispersed collection of pursuits, interests, and commitments. There are self-identified feminists in virtually every area of academic psychology and in every professional specialty. The breadth and variety of accomplishment defy easy summary and work against a common conceptual vocabulary.

At the onset of the second wave of feminism in the United States, feminists' encounters with psychology challenged the sexist and discriminatory treatment of women as psychotherapy patients, professionals, and students. The low status of women in the profession and their absence from decision-making and leadership roles in professional associations were also targets of activism. Clinical theories, psychotherapy practices, and ethical malpractice came under sustained scrutiny and activism.[5]

The knowledge base of psychology, too, came under feminist scrutiny. Since the earliest days of the discipline in the late nineteenth century, psychologists have weighed in on debates on the "woman question," providing theories about female nature and empirical evidence of sex differences. Such theories and data have always been contested. Indeed, in criticizing psychology's knowledge about women, feminists of the second wave followed in the footsteps of those of the first wave such as Helen Thompson Woolley, Mary Calkins, and Leta Hollingsworth. Following Sandra Harding's usage, we might term their project *feminist empiricism*, a self-conscious program of corrective scholarship aimed at debunking sexist assertions.[6] Feminist empiricists endeavor to gain accurate knowledge about women through the use of research methods purified of sexist biases. Indeed, feminist empiricism has yielded a substantial corpus of knowledge about women, gender, and sex differences. In addition, feminist empiricists have developed intricate refinements of the techniques for researching gender, along with elaborate guidelines for such research.[7] Standing back, however, we can see a paradox: although such efforts stem from dissatisfaction with orthodox methods of inquiry, they nonetheless simultaneously reaffirm a fundamental faith in them.

Women's studies scholars have devoted sustained critical attention to the methods of inquiry and objects of knowledge of many disciplines, resulting in a rich body of theory and acute intellectual interchange. In psychology, however, critical attention to epistemology is comparatively new and relatively fragmentary. Instead, in keeping with psychology's fixation on research technology, critiques are usually limited to technical aspects of research design, such as selection of comparison groups, questionnaire design, and scale construction. Only recently has debate opened on larger questions of how knowledge is produced and warranted. This should not surprise us. The original psychologists were dissident philosophers who repudiated armchair speculation about the mind in favor of active investigation. Even now, data collection is the valued activity; theory building and critical reflection are widely regarded as frivolous, diversionary, and self-indulgent. Among feminist psychologists, too, the taste for theory is an acquired one, and the tools for theory building must be imported from other disciplines or from traditions of psychology outside the United States. In this regard, the recent inauguration of *Feminism and Psychology*, published in England, promises to be a major impetus to theory development.

What's Wrong with This Picture? Psychology in the 1990s

Developments in feminist psychology must be read against the backdrop of current trends in psychology itself. Most important is the resurgence of biological foundationalism. Both in psychology and in the culture at large, biologism goes hand in hand with political and social conservatism. Thus, there is heightened interest in the neural bases of homosexuality, sex differences, intelligence, personality, and criminal violence, lines of work that would have been considered far-fetched a decade ago. Similarly, there is renewed interest in the hereditary basis of mental illnesses, suicide, alcoholism, crime, and various forms of social pathology. The national associations of psychologists in the United States have been enthusiastic proponents of the federal government's proclaimed Decade of the Brain, and individual researchers have refashioned their investigative programs in response to new funding opportunities.

The emergence of a new field called evolutionary psychology is another sign of psychology's ready enthusiasm for biological foundationalism. Evolutionary psychologists draw on the constructs of Darwinism and sociobiology to explain human personality development, interpersonal relations, and social organization. Evolutionary psychologists have focused special attention on sex and gender, including such topics as heterosexual attraction, mate selection, marital fidelity, and mother-infant attachment. In offering functionalist accounts for such behaviors as rape and male infidelity, evolutionary psychologists have seemed to offer an apologia for male supremacy. Nonetheless, they have dismissed feminist critiques of their work out of hand as nothing more than political harangues. Evolutionary psychology has rapidly risen to prominence in American psychology, and the American Psychological Association has honored several evolutionary psychologists with national awards. Some claim that it will become the major unifying paradigm of the discipline.

The social conservatism of the 1980s and 1990s is reflected as well in the remedicalization of the mental health professions, including clinical psychology. This can be seen in the increasing reliance on medication for treating psychological disorders. It is also apparent in the increasingly widespread use of the *Diagnostic and Statistical Manual of Mental Disorders,* the official classification system of the American Psychiatric Association.[8] The medical framework of the the *DSM-IV* implies that psychological disorders are closely akin to physical disorders. Its language locates the causes of psychological problems largely within the individual, implying that such problems exist apart from the life situations and cultural backgrounds of those who experience them. This works to foreclose consideration of interpersonal relations and societal context as sources of unhappiness or dysfunction, disguising the way that psychological disorders are products of their time and place.

Meanwhile, tensions between academic and applied psychology brought the field of psychology in the United States to a crossroads. Relations between academic psychologists and professional practitioners (primarily therapists and counselors, but also school psychologists, forensic experts, media psychologists, and a variety of other applied workers) reached the breaking point. Historically, academic psychologists have always regarded themselves as the superior members of the discipline. As the number of professional practitioners swelled in recent decades, however, their control over the financial resources and leadership of the American Psychological Association increased, as did their public visibility as the spokespersons for the field. Rancor over these developments and continued struggles over resources eventually splintered the association.

The long-term consequences of this split remain to be seen. Meanwhile, academic psychologists, in a rhetorical move seemingly intended to distance themselves from applied workers and to secure their prestige, have firmly reinscribed their identity as scientists. Indeed, some have renamed the field "psychological science" instead of "psychology." This appellation, like other efforts to cloak psychology in the mantle of science, not only allies psychology with the physical sciences but also lays claim to the prestige and status that our culture accords to science.

Such rhetorical maneuvers are problematic for feminist psychologists, among others. The science-practice dichotomy is a gross oversimplification, reducing a complex reality to a single dimension. It elides other identities and stances of psychologists, including some that are crucial to feminist praxis. Opposing science and practice, moreover, implies that they are mutually exclusive. Yet a sizable number of psychologists are both academicians and practitioners. Also, it is presumptuous to label all academic psychologists "scientists," a label that asserts a commitment to laboratory experimentalism and quantification that some, though researchers, do not share. In particular, it denies the very methodological pluralism and innovation that feminist psychology has encouraged, as well as the critical stance toward the discipline that feminists, along with other dissidents, have tried to promote. Furthermore, feminists' many contributions to the public interest and to policy formation and analysis do not fit the rubric of either science or practice.

What options are available for feminist psychologists in a milieu of increased biologism, scientism, social conservatism, and retrenchment? How has the changing milieu reshaped the mandates and proclivities of the present generation of feminist psychologists? Will workers bend to accommodate disciplinary pressures, or will such pressures energize resistance and opposition? Some of the fault lines in feminist psychology reflect our divided responses to the pressures exerted by the parent discipline.

Feminist Fault Lines

Modernism, Postmodernisms, and the Construction of Gender

One such fault line is the modern-postmodern divide. Psychology is a modernist institution: its goals are the prediction of human behavior; it relies on technology and rational analysis as means of solving social problems; and it upholds the myth of progress through the accumulation of knowledge. In North America, at least, most psychologists were taught to swim in the waters of logical positivism, abstracted empiricism, and biological foundationalism, but we were never taught that we were wet. Postmodern thought thus constitutes a drastic upheaval in psychology, and a radical departure from business as usual.

The modern-postmodern divide is an important line of demarcation and difference among feminists in psychology. Consider how modernist and postmodern feminists approach the study of gender. Gender—whether roles, stereotypes, self-concepts, or attitudes—has been the central subject matter of feminist psychology. In modernist thinking, gender is "out there," waiting to be observed and measured. It is construed as masculinity and femininity, attributes resident within an individual and readily amenable to quantification. Drawing on the conventions of psychological research, gender has been measured by scales, inventories, and other instruments designed to yield standardized, replicable, numerical indices. Moreover, the modernist framework construes gender as a locus of agency, a force that impels people to act in sex-differentiated ways. In the mechanistic language of the field, it is customary to speak of "gender effects" and to speak as if research participants "contain" greater or lesser amounts of gender (masculinity or femininity) that cause them to act in certain ways.

Postmodern psychologists take gender as a construct of a different order. The postmodern project focuses on gender as a category of knowledge, one that is both profoundly important and profoundly indeterminate. Gender and gender-related constructs are local, time bound, and subject to negotiation. One line of inquiry into gender examines how people enact gender through language and social interaction.[9] Gender can be thought of as both an ongoing performance and a social achievement. For postmodernists, to say that gender is a social construct rather than a reality "out there" is not to say that it is imaginary or unimportant.[10] Rather, it is to demand sensitivity to the construct itself.

More generally, postmodern feminist psychologists train their sights on the conceptual scaffolding of psychology, and the categories of knowledge that it uses. They inquire into the way that categories of knowledge are gendered. For example, Stephanie Shields's work on gender and emotion asks such questions as "What does it mean to say that someone is emotional?", "Who decides?", and "What counts as emotion in our everyday understanding and in our psychological theories?" "How do discourses about emotion shape personal identities and serve to distribute power across different social categories?"[11] These questions are not posed as mere exercises in armchair theorizing but, rather, as a program for systematic inquiry. That inquiry likely will take forms that depart from the canonical methods of psychology. It may involve, for example, close work with words and texts, or investigation into the history of the meanings and uses of a psychological construct.

Postmodern psychologists have also turned their sights on the discipline of psychology itself. How, they ask, did psychology come to be the way it is?[12] How do the cultural, social, and material conditions of the time give shape to the discipline? By emphasizing the cultural and social history of psychology (as opposed to its intellectual and institutional history), such investigations uncover the situatedness of the discipline. Other work emphasizes the backstage operations of the discipline, raising questions about the choice of research agenda, the quotidian work practices and social relations of the field, and its gate-keeping mechanisms. Taken together, these efforts yield an enlarged understanding of the discipline, one that serves as a humbling antidote to the self-aggrandizing proclamations of psychology's "scientific" basis.

Roaming the Methodological Frontier

The methodological canons of psychology pose a sharp dichotomy between quantitative and qualitative work, that is, between numbers and words. The dichotomy is aligned with other dichotomies: scientific/artistic, fixed/slippery, precise/sloppy, and even male/female. These alignments make clear the high esteem that psychology attaches to numerical data. Indeed, psychology's fascination with numbers is so intense that for many workers in the field, what is not numbers is ipso facto not psychology. Psychology has long been a discipline whose method took precedence over its subject matter, and its adherence to a single method of inquiry has been little short of dogmatic. Some feminist workers have objected to this narrowing of investigative options. They have challenged disciplinary orthodoxy by crossing to the qualitative side of the quantitative-qualitative divide. Needless to say, such crossings are risky ventures.

For most psychologists in the United States, research technologies that involve quantification and statistical analyses are the premier means of producing and warranting knowledge. Quantification seems to promise precision and conciseness. Moreover, it allows researchers to amalgamate the data from large numbers of research subjects into a simple numerical shorthand; the ability to manage large samples may seem to address the thorny problem of generalizability. Also, statistical methods such as meta-analysis appear to rely on impersonal and automatic processing, and thus they may foster an illusion of protection against subjectivity, bias, and human error. For many psychologists, the unquestioned route to intellectual progress lies in increasingly complex computational procedures, more elaborate mathematical modeling, and innovative statistical procedures.

A minority of psychologists, including some feminists, have registered doubts about psychology's unquestioned and complete reliance on quantitative methods. In their view, such methods treat research participants as mute specimens to be assessed, labeled, and explained. Imposing a numerical shorthand on human experiences seems to yield only a crude and distorted approximation of them. Moreover, research technologies such as scales and inventories compress ambivalent and multifaceted experiences into a single number, imposing a false uniformity and homogeneity on respondents. Although precision may have been gained in the analysis (or output) stage of a study, it may come at the expense of precision in the data-gathering (or input) stage. When we see words and numbers as opposites, we ignore a crucial and fundamental similarity between them: whether we use verbal or numerical symbols to represent others' experiences, interpretation is still involved. We cannot avoid the question of who is to have authority over the meaning of others' experiences.

For some psychologists, feminist principles dictate that they take women at their word. Understanding "from the natives' point of view" is thus a political and ethical imperative as well as a scientific one. They insist on approaching research participants as articulate beings whose words are conscious expressions of lived experience, loaded with ambivalence, self-critique, and awareness of contradiction.[13] This requires new ways of working with words and texts, and so such workers have ventured beyond the boundaries of what is conventionally mapped as psychology, roaming into such disciplines as cultural studies, literary criticism, and sociolinguistics.

Psychology's traditional goal is the discovery of universal principles of behavior that transcend time, place, and circumstance. Its focus has been on the individual in isolation from culture and history, and its research methods privilege the study of matters internal to the self. Moreover, laboratory experiments, the epitome of investigatory methods, are designed to examine behavior in highly controlled situations that are contrived to eliminate the contaminating influences of respondents' lives outside the laboratory. One could say that laboratory experiments are specifically designed for context-stripping, that is, to decontextualize the processes under study. Yet, for studying gender, historical, social, and cultural circumstances do not constitute mere "nuisance variance" but, rather, the crucial objects of investigation.[14] This is why some have turned to alternative forms of inquiry that reposition research participants in real-life contexts. These include ethnography, participant observation, participatory action research, biography, and discourse analysis.

Centrists and Boundary Dwellers

Some feminist psychologists face squarely toward the center of the discipline. They make use of the standard tools of psychology to produce empirical information about women and gender. This information can make an important contribution to policy debates. Examples include research on the incidence of intimate violence against women and its consequences; studies of adolescents' abilities to make reasoned decisions about unwanted pregnancies; studies of the impact of maternity leaves on the health and well-being of women and their babies. Apart from its real-world significance, such canonical work seems necessary if feminist psychology is to gain legitimacy and recognition in the discipline as a whole.

Other workers choose to dwell on the boundaries of the discipline, turning their sights toward other disciplines and toward venues outside the United States. Standing at the edge of the field offers different vantage points and new vistas, and for some, intellectual traditions that are more congenial and scholarly debates that are more compelling. Conventional psychology emphasizes lawful regularities of behavior—generalizations, average responses, and normative tendencies. The exceptions, contradictions, and inconsistencies are lost from view. Workers on the margins are free to explore the full range of behavior and to ponder the exceptional, complex, and paradoxical. Such work may point toward cracks in the edifice of societal norms and thus to new possibilities for escape or rebellion.

Philosophically and pragmatically, centrists and boundary dwellers are at odds; temperamentally, they may be at odds as well. At times their approaches may seem to undermine one another. Yet it is important to acknowledge that they are also mutually interdependent. Each enables and complements the other, and both enrich feminist psychology.

Psychology of Which Women?

At this moment in the history of feminist psychology, there is no demand felt more urgently or endorsed more widely than the demand to overturn the largely white and middle-class character of feminist psychology. Developments on college campuses, in feminism, and in the nation at large have propelled issues of race, ethnicity, class, and culture to the center of attention. Most, if not all, feminist psychologists embrace the hope that new generations in feminist psychology will be more inclusive, diverse, and multiethnic, and that the knowledge base can be rendered more multicultural and pluralist. Yet, although moral commitment and political will are genuine, interrupting psychology's "whiteness" is not an easy task. The whiteness of psychology is not an accident. The reasons for it are tied up with psychology's epistemological commitments, as well as its historical social relations and work conditions. What psychology takes as the objects of knowledge, what it takes as the proper research questions, and what it defines as the proper forms of knowledge all produce its whiteness.[15]

Knowledge in psychology is couched in terms of universal principles of behavior. Its theories are presumed to pertain to everyone, irrespective of social group membership, cultural background, and life history. Much social psychology research has been conducted using convenience samples of college students, whose participation is a course requirement. Social psychology thus largely comprises a body of knowledge about the experiences of white, middle-class, educated, young North Americans, most of whom are eighteen or nineteen years old. This knowledge has been generalized to humankind. When individuals from other backgrounds have been studied, such studies are automatically regarded as studies of "special populations," and wider generalizations are not attempted. Moreover, studies of the latter type are held in low esteem because they are seen as mere "applied" research, that is, efforts to address a specific problem, and not as "basic" research addressed at eliciting universal principles of behavior.[16] At the same time, demands for productivity — measured in terms of quantity of publications — force researchers to seek research participants who are ready at hand and inexpensive to recruit. Psychologists have avoided studying people who are difficult to locate, who are presumed to be unreliable informants, or who are deemed unlikely to be cooperative. Such choices have contributed to the whiteness of psychology's knowledge.

There are other obstacles to creating a body of psychological knowledge that is inclusive of all women. One is that psychology has typically framed the study of culture and ethnicity as a question of sameness versus difference. This approach focuses on group comparisons to study social categories such as race, ethnicity, class, and sexuality. That is, researchers divide women into categories (e.g., African American and white) and search for attributes that distinguish normative members of one category from the other. Some women of color[17] and others[18] have taken exception to this approach. It is flawed by its essentialism and categoricalism. Moreover, by centering attention on supposed personal attributes, it suggests that the plight of disadvantaged groups results from their personal deficiencies. At its worst, this view supports a politics of blame. Even at its best, it is aimed only at personal transformation rather than social change.

As cohorts of feminist psychologists moved through the life course, they turned their scholarly attention to issues and experiences that emerged in their personal lives, such as mothering, chronic or incurable illness, or menopause. As a source of inspiration, personal experience is deemed not only legitimate but highly valued. But when researchers draw on their own lives to define issues of relevance, we must ask which issues will rise to the fore and which will be inadvertently overlooked.[19] Precious few feminist psychologists are nonwhite; few live in impoverished circumstances; and only a handful are from third world backgrounds. The task of making feminist psychology inclusive of *all* women cannot be relegated to the tiny group of workers who are drawn from such backgrounds. Moreover, at least in the case of African Americans, psychology's efforts to recruit nonwhite workers thus far have not been sufficient to produce the desired outcomes. Moreover, studies of African American populations represent only a minuscule proportion of published research, and that proportion has diminished since the early 1970s.[20]

How Psychology Disciplines: Resistance and Exclusion

The fault lines within feminist psychology are minimal in comparison to the gulf between feminist psychology and the mainstream of the discipline. Indeed, a constancy throughout the thirty-year history of feminism in psychology is the resistance of the parent discipline to feminist scholarship. In what follows, I describe some of the maneuvers that psychology has employed to keep feminist work in its place and to contain its challenges. These maneuvers are part of the intellectual apparatus of the discipline. They come into play not only in regard to feminist thought, but also in efforts to contain other kinds of innovation.

Exclusion and Assimilation

Over the past thirty-odd years, very little work in feminist psychology has leaked into the mainstream. Textbooks in abnormal psychology, for example, rarely incorporate feminist research on eating disorders, violence against women, or depression. Nor do they mention feminist critiques of diagnosis and treatment, even in order to refute them.[21] Similar patterns of exclusion have been documented in textbooks in introductory psychology, developmental psychology, social psychology, and research methods.[22]

What has edged its way into the mainstream of psychology neither threatens disciplinary orthodoxy nor upsets conventional gender politics. Consider, for example, Sandra Bem's early work on psychological androgyny, arguably the only line of feminist work that has crossed the semipermeable membrane between feminist psychology and conventional social psychology.[23] The Bem Sex-Role Inventory, a widely used paper-and-pencil measure of masculinity, femininity, and androgyny, was devised as part of this research. Although the concept of psychological androgyny and its associated research program was criticized and abandoned by feminists more than fifteen years ago, it lives on in mainstream psychology to this day. Perhaps we should not be surprised. The theory of androgyny can be used to assert that conventional gender roles pose equal and symmetrical difficulties for men and women. Moreover, the notion of a so-called sex-role self-concept lends itself to assertions that personal psychological transformation is all that is needed to solve the problem of gender inequality.

We can see a similar pattern of containment by assimilation emerging as psychologists confront the challenge of postmodern thought. For instance, the "social construction of gender" has become a commonplace slogan, but its meaning has been altered to fit into a positivist framework. For many, it means nothing more than the unexceptional—even banal—idea that gendered behavior is learned, not biological. Thus, the epistemological challenge of constructionism and related postmodern ideas is dissolved altogether.

Boundary Definition

Deeming certain issues to be outside psychology is another way that psychology has resisted change. One hears statements from colleagues in the field like the following: "It's too bad that so many smart women graduate students get interested in gender. Psychology can't afford to lose them"; "All the candidates for the joint position in women's studies and psychology were completely hopeless, of course"; and "Haven't we had enough of that gender stuff yet?" The number of women seeking careers in psychology increased dramatically over the past few decades. By the late 1980s, this trend was registered as a problem and given the loaded label the "feminization" of psychology. By 1991, the American Psychological Association commissioned an official task force to investigate the problems that "too many" women would create for the field. This backlash against women, along with the backlash against feminism, may mean that women—especially those with scholarly interests in gender—face exclusion from the field.

Psychology has also evaded feminist challenges by drawing a sharp boundary between psychology and politics. Feminists have repeatedly been accused of engaging in politics, not psychology. For many feminists, however, psychology, as an endeavor concerned with the conditions of human life, is always political. It is impossible to separate facts from values, whether in the selection of research questions, the choice of methods, the decision rules for interpreting data, or the applications to which psychological knowledge is put. Moreover, work that serves to support the status quo is no less political than work that challenges it.

Recently, a prominent feminist psychologist has invoked the science-politics dichotomy to draw a boundary between herself and other feminist workers. In a prolonged series of public lectures and professional articles, Alice Eagly repeatedly has contrasted the "science" of gender with the "politics" of gender.[24] She has accused feminist psychologists of "politics," that is, of distorting the scientific record and suppressing (her?) data in order to support an outmoded political agenda of denying male-female differences. Like the trick question "Who stole feminism?", such accusations attempt to pit feminists against one another. They purport to identify some as responsible, serious, and genuine feminists, and the others as bogus and dangerous.

Setting Conditions for Relevance

From the perspective of mainstream psychology, the subfield of psychology of women remains largely irrelevant, a special interest with a dubious and unscientific character. In a recent survey of members of the American Psychological Association, the Division of the Psychology of Women was rated in the lowest third of all the divisions of the association in terms of interest and in the lowest quarter in terms of importance.[25] Moreover, psychology, with its feet firmly planted in logical positivism and with the physical sciences as its ideal, has deemed irrelevant the critiques emerging from philosophy of science, feminist theory, critical theory, and postmodern thought. Such critiques, even when carried out by psychologists, are often dismissed out of hand as nihilism or "antiscience," and the critics are tarred with epithets like "number-phobic" and "jargon-monger." Even when such work addresses psychology in a specific and detailed way, it is often characterized as no more than a frivolous distraction from the serious business of producing data.

Feminist Generations: In Search of Other Metaphors

In this essay, I have explored some of the primary axes of disagreement and difference among feminist psychologists, along with the background conditions under which they have arisen. As I reflect on what I have written, it is apparent that the metaphor of generations is not an apt one for feminist psychology. In some women's studies disciplines, lines of conflict may be drawn between senior and junior scholars, or between old and new forms of scholarship. But in feminist psychology, neither sense of the term *generation* seems to apply; the progression of ideas and personnel is far less linear. The field of psychology of women has been pluralist since its inception, stemming, as Mary Crawford and I have said, "from various specialty areas of psychology, grounded in several intellectual frameworks, and reflecting a spectrum of feminist perspectives."[26] With a profusion of coexisting theoretical frameworks, lines of work, and projects, feminist psychology features few orderly lines of development and succession that can be readily discerned. There has been little reflection on how or why particular lines of work have emerged and been abandoned, or on what is at stake in pursuing or relinquishing particular questions.

In the scientific rhetoric of psychology, the binary opposition of old/ new is a powerful device. To claim to do what is new is to claim the intellectual high ground. Theories and data that are new are assumed to improve on all earlier ones, so claiming that one's ideas are the newest ones is tantamount to claiming they are the best. The myth of presumptive progress reigns unchallenged, and thus claims of newness and innovation arise from all sides.

The metaphor of generations of feminist thought may wrongly imply that the field is developing in accord with a self-contained and inevitable process of maturation and renewal. But change is not necessarily growth, nor is all development necessarily positive. Moreover, the metaphor of generational change may focus too narrowly on developments internal to the field. As I have tried to show, developments in feminist psychology must be situated in the context of the discipline of psychology, which in turn takes its shape from developments in society and culture. As one anonymous pundit noted, "Psychology follows culture, but at a respectable distance." In particular, feminist scholars must reckon with the potent swing to conservatism in present-day academic and political culture, and the backlash against women in the discipline of psychology.

Among academic feminist psychologists, there is little sign that age, experience, or seniority (or any other demographic characteristic) maps the lines of disagreement. If any pattern can be discerned, the emergent fault lines seem to have some relation to locale: as the saying goes, where you stand depends on where you sit. There are strong differences between North American psychology and British psychology, with the former grounded in biology and the latter in social theory. Institutional setting seems to be another locale that makes a difference: By and large, feminist psychologists situated in liberal-arts institutions seem more conversant with theory, more open to interdisciplinary work, and more able to resist the pull of the discipline. On the other hand, departments that are large, situated in public institutions, and oriented toward graduate training seem to exert more centripetal force on their feminist members. Moreover, psychologists who work in settings other than traditional psychology departments (such as women's studies programs, education departments, schools of communication, and freestanding professional schools) seem to be more free to "work the hyphens," in Michelle Fine's apt phrase.[27]

Conclusion: Fault Lines or Footholds?

At thirtysomething, feminist psychology in the United States stands in an ambiguous position, simultaneously strong and precarious. On the one hand, its record of accomplishment is a source of pride and a cause for celebration; its roots are deep; the pace of scholarly and political activity remains brisk. On the other hand, feminist psychology, as a subfield of psychology, mirrors many of the unfortunate traits of the discipline, such as its white ethnocentrism and the invisibility of white and middle-class privilege. Moreover, even though many feminist psychologists have played strictly by the rules, the field has garnered relatively little acknowledgment from the mainstream discipline. Early goals of transforming psychology seem grandiose in today's climate of intellectual conservatism.

Developments in women's studies leave little room for the kind of unreflective empiricism that is normative in psychology. In the words of Jane Roland Martin, essentialism, ahistoricalism, and false generalization are "three traps . . . already well marked by feminist theorists and researchers."[28] Unfortunately, all of these practices are thoroughly entrenched in psychology. As women's studies and psychology drift farther apart, common ground is harder to find. Emerging divisions among feminist psychologists may appear to threaten the field's integrity. But that is not the only way of looking at them. Such divisions also represent explorations into new terrain, efforts to find and stake out new footholds for feminist psychology in a shifting intellectual landscape.

Notes

1. Nancy Felipe Russo, "Editorial. *PWQ:* A Scientific Voice in Feminist Psychology," *Psychology of Women Quarterly* 19 (1995): 1–3.

2. Stephanie A. Shields and Jill Crowley, "Practicing Social Constructionism: Confessions of a Feminist Empiricist," paper presented at the annual convention of the American Psychological Association, Los Angeles, 1994.

3. Sandra Bem, "Is There a Place in Psychology for a Feminist Analysis of Social Context?", *Feminism and Psychology* 3, no. 2 (1993): 230–34.

4. Celia Kitzinger and Rachel Perkins, *Changing Our Minds* (New York: New York University Press, 1993).

5. For a brief recounting of these efforts, see my article with Rachel Hare-Mustin, "A Short History of the Future: Feminism and Clinical Psychology," *Psychology of Women Quarterly* 15 (1991): 521–36.

6. See Sandra Harding, *The Science Question in Feminism* (Ithaca, N.Y.: Cornell University Press, 1986).

7. Kathy Grady, "Sex Bias in Research Design," *Psychology of Women Quarterly* 5 (1981): 628–38; Carol N. Jacklin, "Methodological Issues in the Study of Sex-Related Differences," *Developmental Review* 1 (1981): 266–73; Maureen D. McHugh, Randi D. Koeske, and Irene H. Frieze, "Issues to Consider in Conducting Nonsexist Psychological Research: A Guide for Researchers," American Psychologist 41 (1986): 879–90.

8. The *Diagnostic and Statistical Manual of Mental Disorders* (4th ed. [Washington, D.C.: American Psychiatric Association, 1994]) will be cited in the text hereinafter as *DSM-IV.*

9. For example, see Mary Crawford, *Talking Difference* (London: Sage, 1995).

10. See my "Psychology and Feminism: Can This Relationship Be Saved?", in *Feminisms in the Academy,* ed. Domna C. Stanton and Abigail J. Stewart (Ann Arbor: University of Michigan Press, 1995), 101–32.

11. Stephanie A. Shields, "The Role of Emotion Beliefs and Values in Gender Development," in *Review of Personality and Social Psychology,* vol. 15, ed. N. Eisenberg (Thousand Oaks, Calif.: Sage, 1995), 212–32.

12. See Wendy Hollway, *Subjectivity and Method in Psychology* (London: Sage Press, 1989); Jill Morawski, *Practicing Feminisms, Reconstructing Psychology: Notes on a Liminal Science* (Ann Arbor: University of Michigan Press, 1994); and Jill Morawski, ed., *The Rise of Experimentation in American Psychology* (New Haven, Conn.: Yale University Press, 1988).

13. For example, Michelle Fine, *Disruptive Voices* (Ann Arbor: University of Michigan Press, 1992).

14. See my article with Mary Crawford, "Psychology Reconstructs the Female: 1968–1988," *Psychology of Women Quarterly* 13 (1989): 147–65.

15. See Andrew Lock's discussion in Kenneth Gergen, Aydan Gulerce, Andrew Lock and Girishwar Misra's "Psychological Science in Cultural Context," *American Psychologist* 51, no. 5 (1996): 496–503.

16. See my forthcoming article with R. T. Hare-Mustin, "Clinical and Abnormal Psychology: The Politics of Madness," in *Handbook of Critical Psychology,* ed. Dennis Fox and Isaac Prilleltensky (London: Sage, forthcoming).

17. Hope Landrine, Elizabeth A. Klonoff, and Alice Brown-Collins, "Cultural Diversity and Methodology in Feminist Psychology," *Psychology of Women Quarterly* 16 (1992): 145–63; Aída Hurtado, "Relating to Privilege: Seduction and Rejection in the Subordination of White Women and Women of Color," *Signs: Journal of Women in Culture and Society* 14 (1989): 833–55; Oliva Espín, *Latina Realities: Essays on Healing, Migration, and Sexuality* (Boulder, Colo.: Westview Press, 1997).

18. Rachel T. Hare-Mustin and Jeanne Marecek, "Asking the Right Questions: Feminist Psychology and Sex Differences," *Feminism and Psychology* 4 (1994): 531–37.

19. Cf. Deborah Belle, "Attempting to Comprehend the Lives of Low-Income Women," in *Women Creating Lives,* ed. Carol Franz and Abigail J. Stewart (Boulder, Colo.: Westview Press, 1994), 37–50.

20. Sandra Graham, "Most of the Subjects Were White and Middle Class: Trends in Published Research on African Americans in Selected APA Journals, 1970–1989," *American Psychologist* 47 (1992): 629–39.

21. See my "Disappearances, Silences, and Anxious Rhetoric: Gender in Abnormal Psychology Texts," *Journal of Theoretical and Philosophical Psychology* 13 (1993): 114–23.

22. See Michelle Fine, "Reflections on a Feminist Psychology of Women: Prospects and Paradoxes," *Psychology of Women Quarterly* 9 (1985): 167–83; M. Brinton Lykes and Abigail J. Stewart, "Evaluating the Feminist Challenge to Research in Personality and Social Psychology: 1963–1983," *Psychology of Women Quarterly* 10, no. 4 (1986): 393–412; and Sharyl B. Peterson and Traci Kroner, "Gender Biases in Textbooks for Introductory Psychology and Human Development," *Psychology of Women Quarterly* 16 (1992): 17–36.

23. Sandra Bem, *The Lenses of Gender* (New Haven, Conn.: Yale University Press, 1994).

24. Alice H. Eagly, "The Science and Politics of Comparing Women and Men," *American Psychologist* 50 (1995): 145–58.

25. Herbert Harari and Jean M. Peters, "The Fragmentation of Psychology: Are APA Divisions Symptomatic?", *American Psychologist* 42 (1987): 822–24.

26. Crawford and Marecek, "Psychology Reconstructs the Female," 147.

27. Michelle Fine, "Working the Hyphens: Reinventing Self and Other in Qualitative Research," in *Handbook of Qualitative Research,* ed. by N. K. Denzin and Y. S. Lincoln (Thousand Oaks, Calif.: Sage, 1994).

28. Jane Roland Martin, "Aerial Distance, Esoterism, and Other Closely Related Traps," *Signs* 21, no. 3 (1996): 584–614.

Shifting Locations: Third World Feminists and Institutional Aporias

Mona Narain

If indeed we are "now involved in the construction of a new object of investigation — 'the third world,' 'the marginal' — for institutional validation and certification,"[1] then it is particularly urgent that the specific location and politics of the third world academic feminist within the institution be discussed and examined. If the third world feminist is not to find herself colluding with an institutional validation of the "third world" simply as an object of knowledge production that neutralizes politics of resistance to hegemonic tendencies within academia, then a process of self-examination and self-clarification must be a part of such a politics of resistance. Indeed, the practice of "self-consciousness," as Teresa de Lauretis terms it, is one of the hallmarks of feminist studies as a critical practice and political critique.[2]

My essay is a project about such a self-critique. The essay takes as a point of departure the notion that the discursive boundaries of feminism for each of us correspond with the subjective limits of our own histories. It uses personal experience, among other strategies, to facilitate the articulation of discursive and theoretical concerns. I begin with a contextualization of the intellectual genealogies of third world feminists. I then go on to describe some of the possible locations that a younger generation of third world feminists find themselves in, in academia and the ensuing challenges generated by such locations. I end with a discussion of Cheryl West's *Jar the Floor* as a text that exposes, delineates, and, finally, attempts to answer some of the crucial questions faced by different generations of women of color.

Different Histories and Different Trajectories

The intellectual and professional genealogies of most third world feminists are inevitably composites of an induction to the two, often conflicting, approaches espoused by dominant white feminism and the feminism of women of color. For precisely this reason the generational conflicts for and between third world feminists cannot be comprehended and theorized without accounting for the category of race. Lourdes Torres has explained how autobiographies have been sites of resistance and expression for women of color where their specific and different history (both public and private), myth, fiction, and fantasy are juxtaposed. Autobiographies also become discursive locations where women of color write to reclaim an identity and history that they have been taught to despise. As Torres puts it, "In order to do this, they must work through all the cultural and gender socialization and misinformation which has left them in a maze of contradictions.... No existing discourse is satisfactory because each necessitates the repression of different aspects of the self."[3]

A text such as *Getting Home Alive* by Aurora Levins Morales and Rosario Morales is a composite autobiography of a mother and daughter.[4] It crosses the conventional boundaries of genre by combining different genres such as short stories, poetry, and prose in a fragmentary yet narrative fashion. Mother and daughter often, but not necessarily, respond to each other's texts. The autobiography speaks of the problematic of the diasporic woman and her location at the crossroads of two cultures. It also allows the reader to participate in the process of the resistance of the mother and daughter to the essentializing demands of choosing one identity (Jewish or Puerto Rican) and their recognition at the end of the text of their multiply constituted and different selves. Such a subjectivity is novel and constructed partly through the reaffirmation of their relationship. In this text, generational difference is the basis for different knowledges. However, it is also the catalyst for the formation of a specific yet multiple subjectivity. *Getting Home Alive* writes a different history of the third-world feminist and documents indisputably her recognition that just like herself, her mother is different.

At the most basic level, such a realization also confirms for the third world feminist what she had always known instinctively—that she has different intellectual mothers from her white counterpart.[5] In another text, "Journeys: Reclaiming South Asian Feminism," coauthored by a mother, Sayantani Das Gupta, and her daughter, Shamita Das Gupta, the daughter describes just such a moment, in this instance especially about their feminisms:

On the wall above my desk where I sit to write this essay are pictures of the traditional feminist foremothers, including Susan B. Anthony, Elizabeth Cady Stanton, Alice Paul, Margaret Sanger. Although these women's eyes have peered down upon me throughout my conscious life, it was not until recently that I realized only one of the women looks anything like me.... Sojourner Truth.... Thus, despite my initial introduction to feminist consciousness through mainstream avenues, it becomes painfully clear that The Great White Foremothers on my wall never expected to look over a young woman of South Asian descent. They would probably roll over in their graves if they knew that their presence has instigated my critique of mainstream feminism in general.[6]

More recently, white feminists such as Jane Gallop have confessed in print that "race only posed itself as an urgent issue to me in the last couple of years."[7] Implicit in such statements by established white feminists is the belief that feminism is a politics and ideology "natural" to the West. Two decades of extensive feminist writing produced by women of color have worked to displace two widely held beliefs among feminists. One is the claim that whiteness is natural, normative, and unproblematic, and the other is the attitude that accounting for the category of race should only be the concern of nonwhites. Yet many white feminist discourses still perpetuate the notion that the history of feminism is a phenomenon and product of white Western society. Essays such as Chela Sandoval's "The Theory and Method of Oppositional Consciousness in the Postmodern World" stress the importance of delineating the history of feminist writing by women of color produced from the very beginning of the second wave of white mainstream feminism. She points to the texts of Paula Gunn Allen, Velia Hancock, Angela Davis, and Audre Lorde, among others, and later to the writing of Cherríe Moraga, Maxine Hong Kingston, Amy Ling, Alice Walker, Barbara Christian, and many more as examples. Sandoval clarifies that U.S. third world feminists "have long understood that one's race, culture, or class often denies comfortable and easy access to either category, that the interactions between social categories produce other genders within the social hierarchy."[8]

In her 1986 book *Feminism and Nationalism in the Third World*, Kumari Jayawardena further contests the appropriation of feminism as a specifically Western phenomenon. She argues that feminism, in fact, was not imposed on the third world by the West. The rise of feminism, while partially attributable to Western imperialism, was a

process influenced by many complex historical circumstances producing material and ideological changes that affected the position of
women. As Jayawardena argues, "Debates on women's rights and
education were held in 18th-century China and there were movements
for women's social emancipation in early 19th-century India; the other
country studies show that feminist struggles originated between 60
and 80 years ago in many countries of Asia."⁹ Jayawardena's book
does the important task of historicizing feminist struggles in the third
world as well as discussing their link to the material circumstances of
colonialism. She explains that these movements arose and gained
ground in the process of the formulation and consolidation of national identities that mobilized independence struggles in third world
countries. Such movements were also a part of the reconstruction of
precapitalist structures in an attempt to "modernize" third world societies. These insights provide us with a context to understand the
historical legacies of contemporary struggles of postcolonial women
and women of color against neoimperialism and global capitalism.

Charting the Journey, published in 1988, is a text that uses the legacy
of colonialism as a "common context of struggle" for British third
world women.¹⁰ The editors write that the book was about the idea
of "blackness" in contemporary Britain. Perhaps the most valuable
aspect of this book is its acceptance and declaration of the contradictory and conflictual positions of various third world women in Britain
and yet its hope that the "idea" of the coalition of black women in
Britain may be preserved despite these differences.

These are some of the texts that have shaped the intellectual genealogy of the younger generation of third world feminists. For example, their introduction to French feminist theory is inevitably accompanied by reading Gayatri Chakravorty Spivak's critique of it in
an international context.¹¹ As much as the third world feminist's location is as a "mestiza," the domain of her knowledge, its construction and production, is part of being a "mestiza" as well. This differentiates her from white feminists of her own generation, and it
differentiates her from her intellectual mothers as well—that is,
from the previous generation of third world feminists. The initial
challenge for women of color in academia ten to fifteen years ago
was to create a consciousness that rebelled against the overt and
covert racialization integral to hegemonic institutions and to formu-

late feminist methodologies that were informed by a consideration of the categories of gender as well as race.

One of the challenges that a younger generation of third world feminists faces now is to devise a way of integrating the knowledge produced by third world feminists in prior years with the knowledge they have from mainstream white feminisms and charting their own individual path. Furthermore, there remains the challenge of taking the production of feminist knowledge in new and different directions that are germane to the present historical moment while using the invaluable groundwork done by the previous generation. Part of this task involves a continual resistance to complacency against subsumption and appropriation by institutional structures. This task also demands that younger third world feminists situate themselves in the context of current conflicts between second-wave white Western feminists and second-wave third world feminists.

Yet another challenge is recognizing differences and conflicts among women of color themselves, with a growing body of feminist theory and literature written by women of color and their participation in academia. Chandra Mohanty writes that "the practice of scholarship is also a form of rule and of resistance, and constitutes an increasingly important arena of third world feminisms."[12] It is important for third world feminists now to practice scholarship that continues to take into account one of the basic tenets of third world feminism, which is precisely a recognition of the contradictions and conflicts among third world women and their insistence on accounting for the historical specificity of their differences in the production of knowledge.

As the proponents of neocolonialism gain parlance outside the institution under the cover of global capitalism, the effects of ecopolitical transformations trickle down into the institution in curious ways. In the first half of the '90s, the rhetoric of global capitalism was metamorphosed in academia into an unexamined and celebratory rhetoric of "multicultural curricula" and "global feminism." Riding on the waves of multiculturalism, global feminism subsumes the unease produced by the presence of alterity into a repressive tolerance of the marginal. As a product of global capitalism, global feminism keeps the practice of tokenism alive and well by allocating space to different voices, variable and fragmented subjectivities. Tokenism carries out the task that overt assimilation was unable to do, that is, find a space for the dissonantly marginal while maintaining the hegemonic structure of the institution. In the classrooms, tokenism takes the shape of syllabi that compete with tourist brochures in order to give the student a "taste and flavor" of other cultures. One has to only look at "third-world-ist" job descriptions to see how tokenism encroaches on hiring practices. In feminist literary discourse, a form of tokenism occurs when analytical categories such as "woman" are "naturalized," effacing their cross-cultural validity that ends in a simple mystification of difference.[13] Caren Kaplan has argued that "the discourses of 'global feminism' have naturalized and totalized categories such as 'third world women' *and* 'first world women.' "[14]

As a graduate student from India in the late eighties and early nineties in a large state research university in the United States, I found myself gravitating toward seminars on postcolonial theory and literature and third world feminism. On a personal level, the experience was disorienting and exhilarating at the same time. Finding an academic vocabulary that articulated my position as part of the diasporic milieu was exhilarating. Reading Aída Hurtado brought the realization that the political consciousness of women of color stems from an awareness that "the public is *personally* political."[15] It was disorienting to have texts articulate the material circumstances of being a foreign student from the third world, of my racial Otherness being a visible reality after having lived most of my life in a fairly racially homogeneous India and having no material conception of being a "minority." I understood, then, that my location as a third world student on a scholarship, if tangentially, was a product of, and was mediated by, the flow of global capitalism. At the time, refusing an allocated subjectivity of the exoticized Other became important as a politics of resistance. This translated into my professional trajectory through my decision not write a dissertation in the field broadly construed as postcolonial cultural studies. In a somewhat pretentious moment of high-mindedness, I decided to resist what I perceived as a future of being potentially ghettoized as a third world feminist in my profession. I wrote my dissertation in British eighteenth-century studies, the other area of literary studies that had attracted me in my years at graduate school. It seemed to me that I was successfully resisting the allocation of a prescribed identity.

My wake-up call occurred when I was presenting a paper on Aphra Behn's *Oroonoko* at a prominent women's studies conference.[16] In hindsight, the internal dynamics of the panel were inevitably conflictual, with two final-year graduate students who were "about-to-be" assistant professors presenting papers that questioned the notion of a "feminist literary tradition." The chair and respondent were two well-established feminist scholars, and at least two other well-known senior scholars were present in the audience. The panel played out all the classic conflicts that this anthology seeks to problematize and address. Of interest to my essay is how the interchange became indisputably encoded, not only in terms of a generational gap but in terms of race as well. Among the various objections to my paper (some of which were admittedly quite valid) was one about my assertion that the character of the black princess-turned-slave, Imoinda, in *Oroonoko* was doubly marginalized in the text by both the black male protagonist and the white female narrator. The feminist scholar chairing the panel disagreed strongly with me, pointing out that the decisive moment in the narrative occurs when the black male protagonist, Oroonoko, leads a slave rebellion at the behest of Imoinda. In her reading of the text, this clearly allocated a great degree of power to Imoinda, eventually more so in the dynamics of the text than to the white female narrator, as opposed to my claim of the complete disempowerment of Imoinda by the end of the book. As this was a rather crucial point for my argument, I did not have an adequate answer at the time. On this issue, at least, my argument appeared weak.

On my return from the conference, having read the text several times again, I realized that one important aspect of the narrative had not been discussed in our interchange. In the narrative, Imoinda convinces Oroonoko to rebel against his enslavement by the white colonizers for the future and freedom of their unborn child. Imoinda's ascendancy despite being a black woman in the gendered power hierarchy between her and the white female narrator is only through the *patriarchally* sanctioned power of motherhood. Imoinda is granted agency only through the traditional domestic influence incurred as the mother of Oroonoko's future heir — not through the freedom of her own subjectivity. Moreover, even this is finally negated by the appropriation of Oroonoko, and the preservation of his memory for posterity by the white female narrator's pen. Imoinda is subsumed and consecrated in the same fashion. The reader knows Imoinda's history only as the white female narrator delineates it.

This rather textual argument illustrates not only some of the points made in the first section of this essay; it has further metatheoretical importance. It illuminates the reception of knowledge contaminated by racist hierarchies within an academia largely dominated by white feminists, some of whom are still reluctant to examine their complicity in the production and dissemination of such hierarchies. It reminds us that produced knowledge continues to be reinscribed when it is received. Taking into account the category of race in the construction of feminist readings and critiques is not enough; one has to be cognizant of how one receives it as well. Furthermore, if one is in a position of power, how and when one sanctions or condemns these particular productions of knowledge become crucial. I do not argue that the woman of color be continually ascribed the position of victim within power hierarchies (both as the subject of investigation as well as the investigating subject). Clearly, she has a subjectivity that *has* agency in either scenario. What I would argue for is a more minute analysis of the context of this agency. Is it self-generated and empowered? Or is "granted" by other sources? And who or what sanctions its empowerment? As Gayatri Spivak notes, "the long-established but supple, heterogeneous, and hierarchical power-lines of the institutional 'dissemination of knowledge' continue to determine and overdetermine its conditions of representability."[17]

Spivak also observes that when the third world feminist is within the institution of academia, names such as "Asian" or "African" have "histories that are not anchored in identities but rather secure them."[18] My experience at the conference brought me a simple yet crucial realization: that my location in academia was one of a third world feminist, whether my chosen area of discourse was eighteenth-century studies, or postcolonial studies, or any other. Without embracing an essentialist identity, I produced knowledge (and discourse) that *was* informed by my own specific history and intellectual genealogy as a third world feminist. It was not a coincidence that I was discussing texts like *Oroonoko* and questions of marginality within Aphra Behn's feminist discourse in a particular way. While my argument before the panel discussion had been mainly a textual critique of the position of the woman of color, it was only when I realized my own location as a reader of the text with a specific history that I was able to contextualize the text and the discourse surrounding its reception and the reception of my paper. It is not that my location as an academic is rooted in a unidimensional identity as a woman of color. Rather, it is multiple in the sense that it is gendered and racial. Within the institution, I speak from various positions as a woman, as an Asian, as a teacher, as well as often as a student. These multiple locations are inscribed with different degrees of power. Hence, my discourse is informed by the location or locations that I speak from at that specific moment. One's practice, as Spivak argues, is very dependent on one's positionality, one's situation.[19] It seems to me that my recognition was crucial to having a valid identity as a third world feminist in the current historical moment.

By acknowledging these shifting and multiple boundaries of the position of being a third world feminist, the third world feminist can not only bring a "self-consciousness" to her own feminist practice but also be able to resist being allocated a fixed position of marginality by subsuming tendencies within the institution and consequently being tokenized. Michel Foucault has cautioned that "if 'marginality' is being constituted as an area of investigation, this is only because relations of power have established it as a possible object; and conversely, if power is able to take it as a target, this is because techniques of knowledge were capable of switching it on."[20] In order not to be appropriated by discourses like multiculturalism and global feminism, which are controlled by the techniques of global capitalism, third world feminist practice must be aware that its own position in the hierarchy of power can also be one of sanction and hence is in danger of being commandeered by the disciplinary support for "the conviction of authentic marginality by the (aspiring) elite."[21]

This is particularly germane for a younger generation of third world feminists in ways that it was not for the prior generation. With official and state endorsement of the policy of multiculturalism in the past few years (for example, financial support extended by the National Endowment for Humanities to liberal arts institutions with curricula and hiring practices that toe the multiculturalist line), more and more nonwhite or diasporic academics are visible in the institutional environment. As all departmental hiring committees are aware, hiring a woman of color is the ultimate success to achieve a "politically correct" visibility for a school. With the increased presence of third world academics in the profession, especially for women, the danger of becoming "double tokens"—being women and being of color and/or being from the geographical location of the third world—is high. In this context, the formulation of a strategy to resist tokenism and institutional appropriation is a necessity for a younger generation of third world feminists in order to remain politically viable. Therefore, a future third world feminist politics that is active in academia must keep the issue of tokenism as one of its central concerns while constructing forms of resistance.

Among such forms of resistance has to be a denial of the demands of producing an "authentic" discourse of the marginalized by hegemonic forces visited on academics perceived as possible tokens. Such demands from hegemonically propelled institutional arenas are fairly recognizable, and most third world feminists expect it as an occupational hazard and prepare for it. Unfortunately, younger third world feminists also have to be aware (and an increasing number are) of the dangers of celebrating marginality among their own ranks. Such a rhetoric is often predicated on a desire and call to return to an "authentic" epistemology that is indigenous and uncontaminated by Western concepts. I believe that there are very few among us, even those who are from geographically distant third world locations, who can claim that their intellectual genealogy has not been influenced by epistemologies of the West. There is no such thing as a "purely" indigenous theory. It seems to me that one has to take into account at some level the role of Western epistemologies, without making it central, and the role of capital in the production of gendered subjectivities, whether the site of knowledge production is in the first world and at the center of neocolonial institutions or elsewhere. Thus, calls for indigenously pure theory are needlessly perpetuating the binarism of center/margin again when more challenging issues await the energies of this generation of third world feminists.

Jar the Floor

One of the currently interesting ongoing debates in academia now is about the role of third world postcolonial and diasporic intellectuals. Sara Suleri's 1992 article "Woman Skin Deep: Feminism and the Postcolonial Condition" has partially spearheaded the debate on feminist intellectuals.[22] She castigates several established third world feminists for becoming compromised in their politics by institutional demands, the rhetoric of postmodernism, simple binarisms, and ethnic differences. While the merits, demerits, and validity of the specific critiques launched by Suleri on other second-wave third world feminists are much discussed, two issues that arise from such discussions are of interest to this essay. The primary issue is that the area of third world feminist studies is in a crisis with serious public rifts among third world feminists. Furthermore, members of the next generation of third world feminists need to situate themselves with regard to these issues and to examine their own positions on them. More so now than ever, the need to form alliances and communities of resistance that take into account such conflictual issues has become urgent.

Cheryl West's play *Jar the Floor* delineates and even anticipates some of the generational differences and other conflicts among women of color.[23] West's note to the readers in her introduction about the characters in the play is worth quoting here at some length:

> The harder these women try not to be like each other, the more like they become. It is often said by children that when they have children they're going to behave differently as parents. They will be better. I submit that we're doing good if we're one step above our parents. To attempt more produces extremes. The women in *Jar* all think they're better than the generation before them and spend a lot of time convincing themselves of that fact. And in their zeal to be better, they lose sight of their own failings, their own contribution to each other's failings. And yes, their actions are humorous, but to them it is not about fun, it is about jarring the floor in the midst of the very people who have the power to hurt them the most.[24]

These four generations of women of color are each very much the products of the historical moments in which they achieved consciousness of the materiality of being women and of color in the United States. As the differences in their ideological beliefs become apparent to the audience, so does the fact that their subjectivities have been indisputably shaped by each other. Yet at the beginning of the play they themselves do not have this realization, and, indeed, this is one of the recognitions that they have to arrive at in order to resolve their conflicts toward the end of the play. West portrays the classic generational conflict in the following conversation between mother and daughter, Maydee and Vennie, respectively:

MAYDEE: You're right. I don't like you.
VENNIE: And? What am I supposed to do, cry? Tell me something I don't already know. . . .

MAYDEE: You are selfish, arrogant and spoiled rotten. . . . And I don't like it. I don't like that I had anything to do with creating what you are at this moment. . . . If I could do it over again I probably wouldn't have bothered.
VENNIE: I wish you hadn't. Would've saved us both some trouble.[25]

The mother's desire to shape the daughter in her image comes out strongly as does the daughter's repudiation of this desire. Shutting themselves off from each other, the pair do not acknowledge that while they are separate people and are different from each other in their ideas, beliefs, and politics, their consciousness of themselves is shaped in some way or the other by each other. Toward the end of the play, each of these women realizes that her own identity changes as she responds to the changes the other members of the family undergo in their intellectual and material lives. The dynamic nature of their core-lation with each other becomes the crucial catalyst in their ability to jar the floor together.

The issue of acceptance of the "different" is subtly taken up by West through the character of Raisa, a white woman who is the outsider to their familial group. Raisa is not only the outsider who has to become the sister; her acceptance to the family circle is crucial to the family accepting themselves. Raisa has had breast cancer, and when she first enters the stage as Vennie's lover, the youngest member of the family, she noticeably has only one breast. Lacking a breast makes Raisa "less of a woman" and forms a bridge of pain between her and the other four women. Raisa's scars are visible whereas the other four women are struggling to keep their scars on the inside, hidden, and aided by silence to remain hidden. West emphasizes that until this silence is broken there can be no move toward any resolution of the conflicts and pain. Maydee's pain is attenuated only when she breaks her silence of forty years finally to confront her mother, Lola, about her complicity in the abuse she suffered as a child at the hands of her stepfather. Vennie verbalizes her anger at being made to live in the image of Maydee, of being denied an independent identity from her mother. Lola and Madear, mother and daughter, each express their own frustration and resentment toward the other about the other's lack of communication and perceived lack of care.

It is only through this dialogue, as Madear tells Raisa, and by accepting one's own scars of pain that these women reconcile the materiality of being women, who while being marginalized in the outside world on account of their race, gender, and lack of conventional feminine attributes are also marginalized in each others' lives through the silence that had reigned between them. Audre Lorde has written that women of color must deal not only with "the external manifestations of racism and sexism," but also "with the results of those distortions internalized within our own consciousness of ourselves and one another."[26] These are the distortions, along with individual differences, that are resolved to a certain extent at the end of the play when the women break their silences and establish a dialogue with each other. This resolution is not a static one, and the audience knows that there will be other conflicts; yet with the renewed understanding that the women have of each other they are able to jar the floor loudly in a communal dance together.

The play functions as an apt allegory for the conflicts and dissonances among third world feminists that often, or could, represent issues facing different generations. Yet such a crisis is a productive one because the discussion of these conflicts establishes a space for dialogue among feminists and an opportunity to break their silence. There may be no quick and long-lasting solutions, but we can still jar the floor together within and across generations.

Notes

This essay is dedicated to Mohini Narayan.

1. Gayatri Chakravorty Spivak, *Outside in the Teaching Machine* (New York: Routledge, 1993), 56. My usage of the term *third world* is descriptive of economic *and* geographic location. It does not include economically disadvantaged groups in first and second world locations.

2. Teresa de Lauretis, ed., *Feminist Studies/Critical Studies* (Bloomington: Indiana University Press, 1986), 7.

3. Lourdes Torres, "The Construction of the Self in U.S. Latina Autobiographies," in *Third World Women and the Politics of Feminism*, ed. Chandra Talpade Mohanty, Ann Russo, and Lourdes Torres (Bloomington: Indiana University Press, 1991), 275.

4. Aurora Levins Morales and Rosales Morales, *Getting Home Alive* (New York: Firebrand Books, 1986).

5. I thank Patricia Sakurai for sharing this insight with me.

6. Sayantani Das Gupta and Shamita Das Gupta, "Journeys: Reclaiming South Asian Feminism," in *Our Feet Walk the Sky*, ed. Women of the South Asian Descent Collective (San Francisco: Aunt Lute Books, 1993), 213.

7. Jane Gallop, "Criticizing Feminist Criticism," in *Conflicts in Feminism*, ed. Marianne Hirsch and Evelyn Fox Keller (New York: Routledge, 1993), 363.

8. See Chela Sandoval, "The Theory and Method of Oppositional Consciousness in the Postmodern World," *Genders* 10 (Spring 1991): 4–5.

9. Kumari Jayawardena, *Feminism and Nationalism in the Third World* (London: Zed Books, 1986), 8.

10. Shabnam Grewal et al., eds., *Charting the Journey: Writing by Black and Third World Women* (London: Sheba Feminist Press, 1988), 1–2.

11. Gayatri Chakravorty Spivak, "French Feminism in an International Frame," in *In Other Worlds: Essays in Cultural Politics* (New York: Methuen, 1987), 134–53.

12. See Chandra Talpade Mohanty, "Feminist Encounters: Locating the Politics of Experience," *Copyright* 1 (Fall 1987), 31.

13. Ibid.

14. Caren Kaplan provides an incisive critique of what she terms "the politics of location as the politics of relativism" in her "The Politics of Location as Transnational Feminist Critical Practice," in *Scattered Hegemonies*, ed. Inderpal Grewal and Caren Kaplan (Minneapolis: University of Minnesota Press, 1994), 137, 144.

15. Aída Hurtado, "Relating to Privilege: Seduction and Rejection in the Subordination of White Women and Women of Color," *Signs: Journal of Women in Culture and Society* 14, no. 4 (1989), 849.

16. Aphra Behn, *Oroonoko* (New York: Norton, 1989).

17. Spivak, *Outside in the Teaching Machine*, 56.

18. Ibid., 53.

19. Gayatri Chakravorty Spivak, *The Post-Colonial Critic*, ed. Sarah Harasym (New York: Routledge, 1990), 57.

20. Foucault's phrase "techniques of knowledge" encompasses disciplinary regulations as well, in his *The History of Sexuality*, trans. Robert Hurley, vol. 1 (New York: Vintage, 1980), 98.

21. Spivak, *Outside in the Teaching Machine*, 57. Also see Arif Dirlik's "The Post-Colonial Aura: Third World Capitalism in the Age of Global Capitalism," *Critical Inquiry* 20 (Winter 1994). Although I do not agree completely with Dirlik's critique of postcolonial intellectuals, his point that postcolonialism is a discourse born out of the conditions of global capitalism and thus is privy to appropriation by neocolonialism as any other first world discourses is an important one.

22. Sara Suleri, "Woman Skin Deep: Feminism and the Postcolonial Condition," *Critical Inquiry* 18 (Summer 1992).

23. Cheryl West, *Jar the Floor*, anthologized in *Women Playwrights: The Best Plays of 1992*, ed. Robyn Goodman and Marisa Smith (Newbury, Vt.: Smith and Kraus, 1992).

24. Ibid., 54–55.

25. Ibid., 89–90.

26. Audre Lorde, "Eye to Eye," in her *Sister Outsider* (Bloomington: Indiana University Press, 1984), 147.

Jason Dreams, Victoria Works Out

Nancy K. Miller

In the spring of 1994 Sandra Gilbert and Susan Gubar proposed a Modern Language Association (MLA) forum called "Feminist Old Girls; or, What Have We Wrought?" The forum and related workshops were designed to provide a "retrospective on the achievements of feminist literary criticism over the past twenty-odd years" as well as an "assessment of our current situation." The title, Gilbert and Gubar explained, was meant to indicate "a certain degree of confusion" (as in FOG: Feminist Old Girls in a fog, but no one was amused) about a variety of issues, notably, "some keen concerns about current generational competitions, theoretical divides, methodological and political differences of opinion, and backlashes in the culture at large." Although the question of generational differences was not the only focus of these events, the proposal highlighted that aspect of "conflicts in feminism." (It was Gilbert and Gubar, after all, who in *Madwoman in the Attic* had made us understand the creative anxiety among women writers as less one of influence, killing the father, than one of authority, thinking back—hopefully—through the mothers.)[1]

What happens when generations in feminism must coexist? This was a problem that '70s old girls were not asked to confront. We had a literature but no teachers—of our own. Unlike '90s feminists, we could take ourselves for...Athena: proudly unmothered. "Sometimes to canonize its foremothers, sometimes to castigate them," a younger generation, they wrote, "has begun to look back two decades in order to examine how and with what methodological programs as well as what ideological goals feminist criticism came into being." By December 1994, the forum had changed its name—"Feminist Criticism Revisited: Where Are We Going? Where Have We Been?" (a riff on the title of a Joyce Carol Oates story)—which lost the reference to age and hierarchy in the title.

Asked to reflect on a collective history after more than twenty years of working personally as a feminist academic, I found myself think- ing more generally about the fate of academic feminism as a prob- lem, above all as a crisis, in representation. How is feminism repre- sented both in the academy and in what we call "the media"? Who represents feminism—again, both in academia and in the media? And finally, what might the answers to these questions mean to the youngest feminists in the academy: the students who think of themselves as going somewhere (or wanting to) in—even, through—feminism and its representations. How do they see us—us old girls?

The pages that follow were written for this panel, whose speakers included Barbara Christian, Jane Gallop, Florence Howe, and Elaine Showalter.

At a meeting of the Northeast MLA many years ago, in an obscure town in southern Massachusetts, a colleague who had been serving out a term as a dean regaled a table of academics in French with tales of the strange doings of academics in other fields. We thought French departments were bad in their factional infighting. At his university, he insisted, the philosophers were so split along ideological lines that every document bore the mark of the division. He had been particu- larly impressed by one c.v. in which a candidate had created, under the rubric of papers given at conferences, an entirely separate cate- gory titled "Conferences Attended." That was meant to indicate what side he was on: analytic or continental. Between wine at lunch and the fanciful bricolage inspired by this example, we were far gone in hilarity when the dean sent us over the top with the delayed punch line: not only had the candidate listed "conferences attended," but he had also included "conferences *not* attended"! We were off and run- ning as we maniacally reworked our c.v.'s to include everything we hadn't gotten around to doing: books not written, articles not pub- lished, grants not received, courses not offered, and so on. Tenure for being flops: the thought was immensely comforting.

The essay that follows has not been published twice. Let me ex- plain. Oh, I intended to publish it; I got tons of feedback; wasted end- less amounts of lots of people's time, not to mention money in xe- roxes, faxes, and e-mail. I could easily have finished my languishing book manuscript in the time it took to finish revising what had been commissioned as an op-ed piece. In both instances, I had a feminist panic attack (FPA) when I thought the piece would actually see the light of day—and, on the advice of friends, withdrew. I'm not usually this cowardly. I tend to write things because I want them to be read; I'm always happy—sometimes thrilled—when someone wants to publish something I write. So what went wrong here? So wrong that I'm not going to publish it today either! But rather than succumb to a case of terminal coyness, I will tell you what I had on my mind: feminists and faux feminists bashing other feminists in print.

Because Susan Gubar has already written brilliantly on the subject, I won't rehearse the annals of this practice, a time-honored tradition. In "Feminist Misogyny: Mary Wollstonecraft and the Paradox of 'It Takes One To Know One' " Gubar shows the long history of women bemoaning the thoughts and actions of their less fortunate sisters and marking themselves out as different (read: better). She describes the territory of contemporary academic feminism as one marked by "internecine schisms in women's studies, divisions widened by feminists faulting each other as politically retrograde or even misogynist."[2] And she worries about how, in the current climate, we run the risk of self-defeat—destroying ourselves and saving our true opponents the trouble. In the editing process, however, a sentence that goes to the heart of the matter was deleted: commenting on the work of a famous feminist basher of recent memory, Gubar wondered ruefully, "With friends like these, does feminism need enemies?" I was disappointed to learn that Gubar's barb was considered too pointed for the pages of *Feminist Studies* (too unsisterly?). So I'm happy to rescue the offending sentence from oblivion here. "Feminist misogyny" is, alas, the order of the day. With friends like these...

Who owns feminism? That question is the opening line of the op-ed piece about feminist bashing I didn't publish in *The Chronicle of Higher Education*. In it I tried to connect the scene of trashing within academic feminism that Gubar describes to the national media attention lavished on books by women bashing academic feminism across the board—notably Christina Hoff Sommers's *Who Stole Feminism? How Women Have Betrayed Women*—to see whether there was a common explanation.[3] The editors, however, deleted my discussion of Sommers's book because they felt that it "sidetracked" my argument; they also felt (in the summer of 1994) that she was becoming old news. The result of these editorial interventions left me with a very short and heavily edited reflection on the failure of feminist debate in the academy in which I wind up doing precisely what I both rail against and do now: attack other feminist critics for attacking other feminists critics in an ever receding horizon of institutionalized postmodern complaint. Although I consoled myself by thinking that I at least took the high road (I didn't name names and I didn't vent my own hurt feelings), I decided in the end that little I believed in would be served by publishing what was left on the page (including whole sentences not written by me)—lamenting the tyranny of insider "feminist misogyny" within the walls of academe.

What is to be done about what we do to each other? Who benefits from the spectacle of our disarray? More than a year ago, Shirley Lim, a participant in my first (1987) NEH Seminar on feminist literary criticism and now, among other things, an editor at *Feminist Studies,* told me (protectively) about a paper given at a conference in which a "younger feminist" (unfairly, in her view) attacked me (that is, the politics of *Getting Personal*). Some time later, a friend, philosopher Rosi Braidotti, faxed me from Utrecht, urging me to read the book in which the paper had just appeared, and hoping—for the sake of "feminist dialogue"—that I would want to respond. Finally, a French colleague of a colleague (the by now ex-dean) asked on e-mail from California whether I had seen the frontal assault (which she described as "une suite de conneries"—the English doesn't quite render the flavor of the French) on my recent work. Dismayed by these overlapping accounts, but curious, I wrote to the author, saying I had heard she had criticized me harshly in public, and asking to see a copy of her remarks. She replied by saying that she always treated the work of other feminists with respect and that my letter sounded like intimidation. Chastened, I waited for publication. I thought, naively, that she might send me the "critique" when it appeared. I'm still waiting. If I haven't tracked down the volume myself, does that make me a bad "old girl"?

One of the problems I've always had in feminism is also an issue currently debated on a variety of academic and social fronts. To what extent is one's individual experience representative? Are you your category, or a category mistake? If I—a "senior" academic feminist who began writing in the 1970s—am harshly criticized by a "younger," or as my students ironically refer to themselves, "Generation X feminist," does this mean that "Feminism" is being "trashed"? Maybe it only means that the feminism of *some* seventies, middle-aged, Jewish, white, middle-class, hetero-feminists is under attack. Maybe it's only me. But has there ever been an "only me" in feminism? "We" who have prided ourselves on our collective identity. But which "we"? It was in part the fear that beneath my lofty rhetoric I might be defending "only myself" that led me to withdraw my piece. I've had to wonder whether my indignation about others being trashed is merely a displacement of personal injury. Is my desire to trash the trashers just a cover for my desire to get even?

In the context of a symposium organized this past fall at CUNY's Graduate School by Michele Wallace for the women's studies program under the rubric "Women's Studies for the Year 2000," Carolyn Heilbrun was asked to comment on a presentation by Ella Shohat. Speaking from her new book *Unthinking Eurocentrism,* which deals primarily with film and visual media, Shohat maintained that feminist positions today must be articulated within the context of a multicultural worldview; generalizing about women's difference from the standpoint of white feminism (as feminists did in the seventies) would no longer do.[4] Heilbrun tried to make the point that we need to emphasize commonalities and alliances among women, what joined women rather than what separated them. The strained exchange between Shohat and Heilbrun, however polite, was an exemplary instance of contemporary misunderstandings in feminism; the two speakers did not seem to be speaking the same language. I asked the students in my seminar on "Feminism and Autobiography" to comment on the event, which for many of them was summarized by this moment of tension. Here is part of one student's reaction, Victoria Rosner's, a meditation on trashing:

> Monday afternoon I went to the gym. I took with me Kate Bornstein's *Gender Outlaw* to read on the bicycle. When I got to the weight room, I left the book on the floor with my towel. The gym was pretty empty, but there was a well-muscled guy there lifting free weights, and he tried to chat me up between sets. Seeing the book on the floor, he asked me what I was reading. Not wishing to prolong our conversation, I said, "Oh, it's nothing," and kept lifting. He picked it up, glanced at the cover with its picture of the newly female Kate, and commented cheerily, "Well, as my father says, 'If it's by a woman, it must be trash.'"
>
> I walked out of the gym thinking about fathers who subordinate women by linking them with trash, and about feminist trashing.

Carolyn Heilbrun's response at "Women's Studies for the Year 2000" worried whether feminists, by using each other oppositionally, were trashing each other and making feminism vulnerable. Shohat's reply to Heilbrun seemed to suggest that rather than seeking to discard previous feminists, she was just taking out the trash by getting the patriarchal Eurocentrism out of feminist theory. Listening to Heilbrun and Shohat, I started to wish they could stop apologizing to each other for any possible offense and just have it out, trashing each other's ideas as necessary, as people who respect each other's intelligence but disagree. There's a real difference between trashing a person and trashing her ideas: one's childish and the other's essential to lively, uncensored debate. Frankly, I'm more concerned with protecting the debate than censoring those who argue on personal lines. . . .

These ideas are, I recognize, reductive, but after my little conversation at the gym, I had to think that if the fathers are going to assume women are trash anyway, then fuck it, let's valorize trash if necessary. Presenting a united, albeit self-censoring front to the fathers won't help feminism's image if we're being judged by our gender-bent covers.[5]

Victoria's mature view (as distinct from my childish one) seems to emerge from a different generational ethos. This point is also the conclusion of Ann duCille's "The Occult of the True Black Womanhood: Critical Demeanor and Black Feminist Studies." DuCille's critique of white feminism ends on a pessimistic note, tempered solely by the counterexample of her students who seem, she writes, to "grapple less with each other and more with issues, to disagree without being disagreeable, and to learn from and with each other."[6] Between this generation — X — and seventies feminists, however, is a vast published text of violence in which "the discourse of trashing," as narratologist Mieke Bal puts it in her essay on the subject, has become "a genre," not to say an industry.[7]

If we are doing something wrong in print, though, we may be doing something right in the classroom, a rethinking of feminist dissidence that works through the violence. What follows is a dream in which another student, Jason Tougaw (the only man in "Feminism and Autobiography"), by way of reacting to "Women's Studies for the Year 2000" comments autobiographically on a set of readings we had done by and about Sylvia Plath:

About two weeks ago I had a dream about the class. In my dream the grad center was on a real campus with benches, trees, old buildings, undergraduates, etc. We were having class in an office. The door to the office had a plaque on it, made from some shiny precious metal, with

"Nancy Miller" engraved on it. Then, along came this incredibly sexy undergraduate named Carlos, and I remember thinking that I had dreamed him before. His clothes were too big, hanging off a sturdy frame and there was a knife in a leather case prominently displayed on his hip, bouncing when he walked. Anyway, for some reason he wanted to kill me — or at least hurt me badly with his fists. I said, "Carlos, it's me!" and he started freaking out. "How do you know my name?" The implication was that I was some faggot who'd been stalking him, knew his name, all that. I wanted to say, but couldn't, "don't you remember, you've been in my dreams before." I still thought he was sexy, and he still wanted to rip my skin from my body. Then, along came Professor Miller, who turned out to be my savior. Carlos was a student of hers, and she stood between him and me, talking reasonably to him and he seemed to listen. I got to keep my skin, without any bruises. . . . Feminism can sometimes reveal what is threatening about things easily fetishized by gay men. Maybe it's because the same threatening gestures, for women, are more pronounced than they are for gay men — or maybe they're just more recognizable. At the same time, feminism has eased the burden of both gay politics and gay criticism. It has fought battles, staged debates, and mapped discourses that have paved the way for gay studies. But at the end of the dream, Carlos is still sexy, and there is no reason to think he won't become a threat yet again. I've had to think about him as both sexy and as a threat, and those are crucial in the constitution of my own sexual subjectivity and my relation to feminism. Jacqueline Rose would say that both those things are constituted by ambivalence. I guess I wouldn't want it any other way.[8]

I was surprised and moved to find myself in this dream not only because it casts me in a heroic role but because it figures precisely what I can't know: what I might mean (at least generically) to my students: the Feminist Professor. Jason's dream imagines the interesting coexistence of two things not thought to occupy the same space at the same time. A great deal of the violence that goes on within feminism emerges from this problem: the town just doesn't seem big enough for two of any of us. Feminists of different stripes or races.

Much feminist criticism in the '90s feels bent on an internal critique indistinguishable in its tactics from the standard masculinist model most of us were trained to emulate in graduate school. Feminist precursors are made to stand in for patriarchal law: it's Mom.[9] When a white feminist condescends to another white feminist for being insufficiently "transnational," when a black feminist excoriates another black feminist for her "essentialism," when a lesbian theorist chastises another lesbian theorist for a "naive" coming-out story, when a younger feminist derides an older feminist for "regulating" her freedom of sexual expression, it's not always easy to tell a friend from an enemy. ("One doesn't stir without the other," we used to say. But that was in another lifetime.)

In the front pages of *The New Yorker,* a small item captioned "More Than Friends" described the use of a Hollywood neologism, "frenemies." It seems appropriate that in an MLA conference held in California, we heed the local maxims: "Frenemies are the people you like the least but one day might need the most."[10] If, as feminists, we no longer like each other, or, as Jane Gallop's *Around 1981* argued, maybe never did,[11] we still may need each other in the perverse turns of this fin de siècle, where Rush Limbaugh, promoting *Who Stole Feminism?* on talk radio, calls some of our bravest colleagues "feminazis."

If feminist criticism fails to make it into the year 2000, it won't be because someone stole it; it will be, girls, because we'll have lost it. You'll find it on your c.v. under "sessions not attended."

I sent a draft of my essay to Peggy Waller, who, in her inimitably tactful way, sent me back to the drawing board. Wanting to acknowledge her acumen and her friendship, I found myself thinking about a powerful bond between generations in feminism that has been insufficiently recognized: the bond *between* old girls. By this I mean the relationship that continues after our students have students of their own. I'm not alone in my discovery that one's former—and sometimes current—students are one's best readers. We may give the grades and write the letters of recommendation, but they know things about us that they alone can know, the blindness of our insights—worked out *with them*—that they are uniquely trained to see; they are, in this sense, our best readers.

This is not just the chain of knowledge transmission that is the goal of any pedagogy, but the possibility of a new reciprocity—beyond symmetry and beyond possession. Does one ever have students of *one's own?*

Notes

1. Sandra Gilbert and Susan Gubar, *Madwoman in the Attic: The Woman Writer and the Nineteenth-Century Literary Imagination* (New Haven, Conn.: Yale University Press, 1979).

2. Susan Gubar, "Feminist Misogyny: Mary Wollstonecraft and the Paradox of 'It Takes One to Know One,'" *Feminist Studies* 20, no. 3 (Fall 1994): 453–73; reprinted in *Feminism beside Itself*, ed. Diane Elam and Robyn Wiegman (New York: Routledge, 1995).

3. Christine Hoff Sommers, *Who Stole Feminism? How Women Have Betrayed Women* (New York: Simon and Schuster, 1994).

4. Ella Shohat and Robert Stam, *Unthinking Eurocentrism: Multiculturalism and the Media* (New York: Routledge, 1995).

5. Victoria Rosner, unpublished manuscript.

6. Ann duCille, "The Occult of the True Black Womanhood: Critical Demeanor and Black Feminist Studies," *Signs: Journal of Women in Culture and Society* 19, no. 3 (Spring 1994): 624.

7. Mieke Bal, "Narratology and the Rhetoric of Trashing," *Comparative Literature* 44, no. 3 (Summer 1992): 293–306.

8. Jason Tougaw, unpublished manuscript.

9. The sharpest analysis of the "symbolic mother" in feminist generational struggles is Julia Creet's "The Daughter of the Movement: The Psychodynamics of Lesbian S/M Fantasy," *differences: A Journal of Feminist Cultural Studies* 3, no. 2 (Summer 1991): 135–59. I've been over this territory myself in a variety of places, with students and colleagues. See "Conference Call" (an exchange in which I participated with Barbara Christian, Ann duCille, Sharon Marcus, Elaine Marks, Joan Scott, and Sylvia Shafer), in *differences* 3:2 (Fall 1990): 52–108; "Criticizing Feminist Criticism" (a conversation with me, Jane Gallop, and Marianne Hirsch), in *Conflicts in Feminism*, ed. Marianne Hirsch and Evelyn Fox Keller (New York and London: Routledge, 1990), 349–69; and "Gender and Generations: Postmodernism and Its Discontents" (interview with Rosi Braidotti, Margaret George, Elizabeth Hollow, Rebecca Dakin Quinn, Nancy K. Miller, and Adriana Velez), *Found Object Six* (Fall 1995): 33–86.

10. *The New Yorker*, November 28, 1994, 51.

11. Jane Gallop, *Around 1981: Academic Feminist Literary Theory* (New York: Routledge, 1992).

An Open Letter to Institutional Mothers

Rebecca Dakin Quinn

The first thing good daughters should acknowledge is the debt they owe their mothers. This is no less true in the metaphorical mother-daughter relationship that obtains within academic feminism. So first I would like to say thank-you to all the generations of women who came before me, particularly the so-called 1970s feminists, who helped to create the intellectual space I now inhabit. Your labors gave me life, made it easier for me to claim a voice than it was for you. Those of you in the university especially have earned the gratitude of subsequent generations for establishing the women's studies departments, the feminist journals and conferences, and the programs and curricula that today's students take for granted as ordinary academic freedoms. We should not forget that these crucial supports did not exist for you, that you literally had to forge them from the void amid the forces of a powerful and intransigent opposition.

We should also remember that these same forces against which you fought so untiringly have not simply retired into history; it's just that one doesn't see them as often if one travels in certain circles. For example, the Friday Forum lecture series at the City University of New York (CUNY), when it sponsors a feminist speaker or symposium, fills the roomy Third Floor Studio to capacity. But if you look around, the faces you see are those of the women, students and faculty, who take a strong interest in feminist issues and scholarship. Other Fridays, the room is not as full, and the faces are predominantly those of the male critical establishment. Aside from the impression this gives one of continually being in the position of talking to oneself, this phenomenon should also be grounds for concern on an economic basis. After all, the institutional purse strings are in large part controlled precisely by those individuals who make dinner plans out of town on the Friday evenings slated to feature feminist speakers and topics. We should not imagine that the already scanty resources that fund our existence are irrevocable, lest we wake one morning to find ourselves in an academic world with an eerie resemblance to that of the 1950s.

But I want to return to this sense in the feminist community of always talking to oneself, preaching to the converted, because I think this idea functions to mask a larger reality: that we seldom really listen to each other. We are talking to ourselves in the most literal and narcissistic sense, and we endanger our collective identity when we forget that, despite our differences, the spirit of coalition has always been the most powerful fuel for women's advances, both within and outside the academy. For me, as a member of the next generation of feminist scholars, the problem is exacerbated by the impression I often have that you, the previous generation, the generation of my mother, are not listening to me, to us, your daughters.

For example, in the fall of 1994 CUNY held a symposium titled "Women's Studies for the Year 2000," at which a painful and protracted exchange between Ella Shohat and Carolyn Heilbrun demonstrated the extent to which feminists of different generations have been trained to speak completely different languages. Shohat spoke the language of high theory, while Heilbrun spoke the concrete language of political activism, and, to the discomfort and distress of their audience, the two appeared utterly unable to understand each other — or, perhaps, which amounts to the same thing, they were simply unwilling to recognize the linguistic terms of each other's argument. It was finally unclear whether they were actually listening to each other, in the sense of trying to hear each other's meanings, or whether the commitment to a certain rhetorical mode of discourse foreclosed this possibility from the outset. At any rate, the result of these ripostes was that nobody in the room, least of all Heilbrun and Shohat, felt that the substance of the disagreement had been addressed, and everybody was left feeling some degree of dismay, frustration, and even anger. An opportunity for meaningful debate between two intelligent and committed feminists had been lost, and blame, although some hastened to assign it, seemed to most of us to be beside the point.

Further, although moderator Nancy K. Miller made a point of quoting Carolyn Heilbrun's assertion that the future of feminism rests with the students, there were in fact no students participating on the panel. So it was not surprising that, after a student involved in the effort to resuscitate the languishing Feminist Students' Organization at CUNY voiced a desire that we begin in earnest to conduct transgenerational conversations, the following dramatized dialogue took place during cocktails:

[*A cosponsor of the symposium approaches the female student who spoke and introduces herself.*]

COSPONSOR: You know, feminism must be constantly re-created, so you shouldn't see it as such a negative thing that you've had to start the Feminist Students' Organization over again. I mean, you should look at it as an opportunity.

STUDENT: Oh, I didn't mean that the group shouldn't change and grow with the student population, but that it would be nice to have a sense of continuity, not to be always starting from scratch. Perhaps if faculty members got involved in our meetings and discussion groups—

[*At this point a bystander, clearly a friend and colleague of the cosponsor, literally steps into the middle of the conversation, although she does not address the student.*]

BYSTANDER: You know, this question of intergenerational communication is really interesting. We should try to work it into the calendar of events.

COSPONSOR: Yes, we really should arrange to do a symposium which would stage that kind of dialogue. You know, actually have a panel of feminist faculty interacting with a panel of students.

STUDENT: Yes, that would be interesting. But I was really imagining something more ongoing, less staged than this kind of an event. For example, if—

BYSTANDER: I can already think of several people, just off the top of my head, who would probably be interested in participating in such an event.

COSPONSOR: Yes, if we start planning this now, we could probably put something together for the late spring.

BYSTANDER: Of course, we'd need to see what the budget looks like. There's always *that* problem, but we could probably get away with....

In the midst of the mothers' monologues, the daughter's voice is silenced. The student walks away to sign up new members of the Feminist Students' Organization.

In the elevator, the student runs into an older woman who reminisces to her about how feminist faculty and students used to meet and study together.

OLDER WOMAN: It's not like that anymore. [*She says this wistfully, as the elevator doors open and she disappears into the crowd.*]

When the student returns to the Third Floor Studio, she sees that everyone is still talking to themselves. She is not surprised, only saddened].

So, one might reasonably ask, what is the point of this anecdotal record of experience and observation in one particular academic feminist community? Do I mean to charge the institutional mothers with neglect? No. Am I playing out some private Oedipal psychodrama through a process of pedagogical transference? Perhaps, unconsciously, I am. But consciously I mean to say only, crucially, this: if the institutionalization of academic feminism continues to reproduce the same adversarial mode that has characterized other critical movements, if the next generation of feminist scholars is trained to either worship or defile the powerful Word of the Mother, if we are unable to listen to each other transgenerationally, it won't be long before our short-lived success within the university is destroyed. Needless to say, this would have dire ramifications for feminist projects across the social spectrum, and we (ironically and briefly reestablished as a collective "we") would be compelled not only to ascribe but also to accept the blame.

The direction I would like to gesture toward is one in which we all, mothers and daughters, begin to recognize our responsibilities to each other. I would suggest that women in positions of relative power have a responsibility to include the younger generation in their projects and dialogues, and to listen to what we have to say about our experiences and perceptions. In our awe of your brilliance and power, we often suffer from the same kind of silencing you probably endured when you were expected to be the (lesser) disciples of your brilliant and powerful male professors during graduate school. Related to this, and equally important, is the responsibility of the younger generation to find our voices, to take the risks involved in standing up to be heard, and to help to redefine our critical activities so that we are no longer simply killing our mothers and committing violence against our sisters in the name of institutional recognition, advancement, and power.

Feminism has been quite successful in exposing the ways in which patriarchal systems operate to normalize and oppress their cultural Others. Thus far, however, in looking within our own ranks, we have only been able to imagine either a utopia of female solidarity or a hopelessly divided universe of proliferating differences. And in the academy, competition, compartmentalization, and commodification appear to have carried the day, for want of an alternative model of doing business. Mothers and daughters stand divided; how long until we are conquered?

Postscript

A year and a half have passed since I first wrote this epistle, quickly, in heated response to a recent event that had frustrated and angered me and many other students who had been at the symposium in question. Several of us vented our feelings in Nancy Miller's seminar the following week, voicing our grievances in response papers that were a regular part of the classroom agenda. I remember reading this piece aloud eagerly, though nervously, for it constituted a challenge in its very language right from the beginning; nobody could take a class with Nancy Miller and fail to recognize the extent to which she deplores the use of maternal metaphors in discussions of student-teacher relationships. But I wanted a response, something more than I had received at the symposium, and from the moment I read the title of my paper, I knew that this, at least, was assured.

In fact, following the outpouring of student discontent at our exclusion from the panel that took place in her class that day, Nancy took a leading role in arranging for student participation in an event scheduled for the following semester, adapting a conference on postmodernism to the theme "Gender and Generations: Postmodernism and Its Discontents." In March 1995, four students delivered response papers following talks given by Rosi Braidotti and Alice Jardine, and after the conference we participated in an hour-long roundtable discussion, transcripts of which were published in the journal *Found Object.* We even got to have dinner with these real-life feminist icons! Who could stay angry? Later, when the editors of this anthology expressed an interest in publishing the "Letter," I was filled with excitement and pleasure, not only at my own inclusion, but also at the prospect of a book that would address the generational challenges of a movement that has become a tradition in its own right.

That's when I began to wonder: Are things really as bad as I thought they were when I wrote the "Letter"? Maybe we, the students, had overreacted, blaming the faculty for not including us before we had even expressed an interest in participation. And was that maternal metaphor really useful? Didn't it reduce the special nature of the pedagogical relationship to a watered-down version of the Family Romance? Did I want *my* students thinking of me as "Mom"? The answer was a resounding "No!" That was way too much pressure for anyone, especially a twentysomething graduate student! I began fretting about the *matrophor,* a word I coined to express the persistent nature of maternal metaphors in feminism, and, although I had committed the "Letter" to publication, I began to feel terribly anxious about the idea of its ever seeing print. Didn't I just sound like a whiny graduate student with what pop psychologists would call "adult-child" issues?

Just as I was coming to the conclusion that my grievances about the student-teacher feminist divide had been overstated, if not imaginary, and that the matriarchal paradigm was material for the trash heap, something happened that forced me to resume consideration of these questions. Again, the catalyst was a set of talks sponsored by several CUNY Graduate School programs, this time an event titled "Embodied Visions: A Symposium on Feminist Cultural Studies." Following talks by Susan Gubar, Michele Wallace, and Christine Froula, Jane Marcus introduced a panel of her graduate students to discuss their work in modernism as it had evolved out of a seminar she had taught the previous semester. Nancy Miller again served as moderator on this occasion, and the first sign of semantic difficulty arose when Jane Marcus revised Nancy's introduction of her panel as "junior modernists," preferring instead to characterize them as "the next generation." Hardly a matter of heated dispute, this disagreement over diction nevertheless struck me as a telling example of the ongoing discomfort in the feminist community with the language we use to talk about our differences in age and/or professional status.

Beyond that, I had a difficult time distinguishing any real difference between the two labels. *Junior,* of course, comes from the Latin root *juvenis* meaning "young," but it has served in general usage to differentiate fathers from sons in the patriarchal name game. In other contexts, the word *junior* is used as device to rank the members of a hierarchy, as in a "junior partner." Leaving aside the practices of department stores that label women's clothing sizes with such euphemisms as "juniors," "petites," and "misses," it seems to me that to refer to feminist students as "junior" circumvents the maternal metaphor, the matrophor, only by reasserting a consummately patriarchal metaphor to stand in its place. Further, to replace this term with the construction *the next generation,* whose keyword hails from the Latin *generare,* "to beget, procreate" (and, according to my Latin dictionary, specifically "to father"), seems only to reinscribe this same patriarchal heritage in different (or not-so-different) language.

Obviously, the language we speak is saturated with meanings accrued over centuries, and women have only relatively recently begun consciously to contribute to the shaping of language. Only in a utopia could we speak a language free of the residue of its origins within variously oppressive systems. The point I'm trying to make, however, is that no matter how we choose to articulate our connections to and differences from each other, we are inextricably located, not to say trapped, in the language we have inherited. While this fact should not discourage or prevent us from exercising vigilance in our choice of language, it should also alert us to the reality that our entire lexicon is saturated by the aura of the Family Romance. It seems nearly impossible to express the basic idea of relationship without reference to a familial metaphor, however disguised by its familiarity and apparent distance from its origins. Admittedly, the mother-daughter metaphor is vexed by associations that don't occur within the father-son model; but then, feminism itself is fraught with similarly troubling tensions. Until we are able to explore these issues explicitly and productively enough to move beyond them, the matrophor, disturbing as it can be, may finally turn out to be a more honest and useful trope for thinking through the feminist generation gap.

I didn't come to these conclusions, however, until the final segment of the symposium, when Jane Marcus's students took the stage and began to speak. It had been a long day, the conference had started a little late, and the audience had been sitting, with one coffee break, for more than three hours. After the three longer papers had been delivered, most of the faculty members dispersed, and the audience for the graduate students' panel consisted mostly of other graduate students. I looked around and noted the large numbers of recently vacated chairs in the auditorium, thinking that it was unfortunate, although not unusual, that the student panel had to play to such an empty house. After the first student had given her talk, which lasted about eight or ten minutes, and the second speaker was being introduced, a hand suddenly began waving in the front of the room and a woman, a faculty member, called out loudly to Jane Marcus, "We talked about this the last time! Five minutes means *five minutes*! It's not fair to those of us who want to hear all the speakers if they don't adhere to the time limit!"

Now, I certainly don't know what happened "last time," although it was clear from the woman's tone and Jane Marcus's expression that the time-limit dispute had been a source of animosity in the recent past. It was also clear to me, by her own admission and by the fact that she was one of the few faculty members still voluntarily in the room, that the woman really was interested in hearing the students speak; otherwise, she might just as well have left quietly without hearing the other four students speak. Yet it seemed incredible to me that anyone should interrupt a panel of speakers, particularly academic speakers, a group famous for ignoring time limits, in order to insist that the talks be rushed or abbreviated to adhere to the original schedule. It probably would have struck me as humorous, I must confess, had the same scene taken place in one of the hotel conference rooms at the Modern Language Association in the midst of a protracted discourse on the status of the footnote in medieval hagiographies. But it would have been funny because it would have been completely unexpected; in fact, I can imagine it as funny only because I can't imagine its ever really happening. It seems to me that such an interruption was authorized solely by the gap, the generation gap, between the speakers and the faculty member.

The effect of this disruption on the students was obvious. Some prefaced their talks with the disclaimer that they "really would take only five minutes"; one finished by observing that she had only used three of her minutes and would yield the other two to the next speaker; and all but one rushed through their presentations at breakneck speed, barely pausing for breath between sentences. Anyone who has had any experience with public speaking knows how anxiety-provoking it can be, particularly the first few times, and especially when members of the audience are more experienced or knowledgeable in the field. Sitting in the back of the room, I winced as I listened to these students spew forth the results of their semester's work like ticker-tape machines ornamenting a parade. And I said a little prayer of thanks that I wasn't up there with them. But in a way I was.

So I'll conclude this letter inconclusively. I don't know if the students on that panel felt as though they had been silenced by a "mother figure," a "senior" scholar, a member of the "previous generation," or simply an impatient member of the audience who had been sitting in the same chair for too long. In my conversations with other students about what had transpired, the only point of agreement was that the exchange had been about power: one person had it, and five others didn't. Still, they hadn't finally been silenced; they had secured their five minutes of speech, had made themselves heard—which is all any of us really wants in the end: to know that somebody is listening.

Dancing through the Mother Field: On Aggression, Making Nice, and Reading Symptoms

Lynda Zwinger

Access to the object is only ever possible through an act of (self)identification. At the same time this relation of the libidinal object-tie to identification reveals perhaps at its clearest the paradox that the subject finds or recognises itself through an image which simultaneously alienates it, and hence, potentially, *confronts* it. This is the basis of the close relationship between narcissism and aggressivity. JACQUELINE ROSE, *Sexuality in the Field of Vision*

I'm realizing that one of the reasons I can't undercut my authority with students by being shockingly informal is that my authority is based on an authorial persona or a theoretical persona that is itself shockingly informal—that's part of its authority.... The sexual innuendo that functioned ten years ago to mark me as one of the girls with my students now marks me as one of the guys.
JANE GALLOP, in Margaret Talbot's
"A Most Dangerous Method," Lingua Franca

I don't know about you, but when someone says to me, "Not to get personal or anything, but..," I pretty much know I'm not about to have a Hallmark moment. Whatever is coming, I'm not going to like it—and it's also pretty certain that I'm going to reject whatever diagnosis is about to be offered as incorrect, inaccurate, or as simply not the real me. By the same token, when I've made whatever pitch I might be making, and my interlocutor leans back and says, "Well, *personally,* I'm all for it, but..," I know that the person in front of me is nevertheless about to turn me down. On the other hand, when smarting from some particularly apt criticism, I retort, "You don't have to get *personal* about it..," my antagonist knows that a direct hit has indeed been scored.

But when we say "personal criticism," we are supposed to mean criticism written by brave souls willing to lay out their vulnerabilities and insecurities for the cause. And that is what Nancy K. Miller's *Getting Personal: Feminist Occasions and Other Autobiographical Acts* means to do.[1] The book is a collection of conference and symposia papers that the back cover promises will examine the "rhetorical strategies of a feminism traversed by internal debates over its own self-representations." Miller declares that "representativity is a problem *within* feminism itself: a matter of self-representation and as such the subject of this book" (x).

For several years now, I have been investigating the stories we tell about fathers and daughters and the ways in which those stories dramatize—and dictate—the process by which girls learn to be good daughters.[2] Briefly, what I have seen over and over and in many guises is a basic plot. Janice Radway summarizes it well in "Women Read the Romance":

> A good romance involves an unusually bright and determined woman and a man who is spectacularly masculine, but at the same time capable of remarkable empathy and tenderness. Although they enjoy the usual chronicle of misunderstandings and mistakes which inevitably leads to the heroine's belief that the hero intends to harm her, the Smithton readers prefer stories that combine a much-understated version of this continuing antagonism with a picture of a gradually developing love.[3]

The heroine of the romance learns to overcome her initial hostility, learns to admit her initially mistaken reading of the hero's intentions (he wants her to change, not to hurt her), and learns to take instruction in how to win his approval. The heroine does all this for the sake of the rewards he has to offer: love, and *earned* approval. The erotic dynamic between the true romance hero and heroine is pedagogic: the hero occupies the position of mastery, the one who knows what the heroine should know and be—for her own good.

This also summarizes the father-daughter dynamic in the U.S.-English novel, from Samuel Richardson's *Clarissa* to Louisa May Alcott's *Little Women* to the pseudonymous *Story of O*. Despite great differences between them, these books share a basic plot: the father (or father figure) is the source of approval for the daughter; his approval is conditional; the daughter has to figure out what he wants and to learn to want that too. When she succeeds, she gets fatherly approval—which always means love and validation.

This familial learning process uncannily resembles my own experience as a graduate student. I was supposed to figure out—with more or less overt instruction, depending on any given master's pedagogical style—how a professor-in-training was supposed to act. If I did it right, I got approval. Love, approval, mastery: elements of the father-son story, too, of course. But the father-son story is one of overt struggle, even when it is couched in great reverence and respect. Eventually, the son is supposed to take over, to become the (next) master. The father-daughter story suggests that the daughter is to be *mastered*. The point is that the teacher-student relation as institutionalized, for women students at least, approximates the familial—or the culture's version of the familial—gender-power dynamic. I wanted to please my "daddies." They wanted me to please them. Once I figured out how to do it, I just repeated as necessary.

My women professors and I were more befuddled, due no doubt to the kinds of issues pointed out by, among many others, Susan Stanford Friedman in an essay in *Gendered Subjects: The Dynamics of Feminist Teaching*:

> The sociologist Norma Wikler... found students accepting high standards, discipline and toughness from their male teachers and deeply resenting any such behavior from their women teachers, especially in Women's Studies classrooms.... Both our students and ourselves have been socialized to believe (frequently at a non-conscious level) that any kind of authority is incompatible with the feminine.... A man stepping into the role of professor has a certain authority granted to him by his students that operates immediately. Women, on the other hand, must earn that authority and respect, which is in any event often granted with great resentment, even hostility. Some women become "100 percenters" to achieve authority, often taking pride in being tougher and less personal than many male colleagues. And as Wikler argued, students may pressure any woman-teacher to fulfill the role of the all-forgiving, nurturing mother whose approval is unconditional.[4]

Now, I don't want to suggest that a male teacher does not have his share of fear and insecurity when he approaches the classroom in his Professorial hat. Only that it is, for him and his students, a familiar, culturally fitted hat. His female colleague, in addition to all the usual stage-fright butterflies, has to figure out what to wear that will go with a top hat or a derby...and nothing in her closet works. And behind that, we can see lurking the whole question of where we learned to dress like that anyway: feminine apparel (indeed, femininity itself) is already an assumed ensemble, designed to produce a certain kind of persona—it is, in short, a masquerade.[5]

A female teacher faces a double bind: the positions of knower and known, knowing and not-knowing, are essentially gendered ones in our culture—as Luce Irigaray, Sherry Ortner, Catharine MacKinnon, and many others have demonstrated. The subject positions are coded as masculine, the object ones as feminine. The pedagogical relation mimes the (familially coded) relation of desire. Women aren't supposed to tell what they want—they're supposed to be what's wanted. For a woman teacher, then, a double masquerade seems called for: the masquerade of mastery, the masquerade of femininity.

Pedagogy, gender, and mastery all have the same plot, the plot of desire. Desire is that process wherein satisfaction is always impossible—what you get is never enough, never what you *really* wanted. If I want to avoid the plots of mastery, of gender, of pedagogy, if I want my students to want to avoid them, where do I begin? Or what begins me? By now, academic feminism is grown-up enough to have a classic answer: my mother/my self.[6]

I want to consider here the connections between our notions of the "personal" and the symptomatic appearance of tropes of and anecdotes about mother(s) that appear as suturing devices therein: as ways, that is, not to see the connections between the messy, gothic, monstrous dimensions of our various rhetorical enterprises and what we hope, wish, and desire to be doing, being, saying.[7] Personal criticism rarely opens easily to, well, personal criticism; we are interested in how this works and what it functions to help us overlook. What follows, then, is meant to be read as a performance of my own readerly (professional, generational, familial) *symptoms*. It is not, that is, about Nancy K. Miller (or "Nancy K. Miller"). It's about me. It's personal. It's me working the mother text that works me into—whatever monstrously sutured entity you see herein.

In her first chapter, Nancy K. Miller turns her attention to an exploration of self-representation that has been particularly meaningful to her: a Jane Tompkins essay titled "Me and My Shadow." She describes herself as having been "electrified" by Tompkins's piece when it first appeared and announces that the criticism it has received "makes me want to defend it" (*Getting Personal,* 4). Miller quotes what she takes to be two key moments where we find Tompkins referring to herself as "myself as a person" writing the essay we are reading and "thinking about going to the bathroom":

> When I read the passages I have just quoted, I was ... "hooked." I loved it. But not so much because I felt I had entered a personal relationship with the author — a person in fact I know — but because this inscription of physical detail, this "bit of story" produced for me the portrait of a writer — like me: and in that sense, "just myself as a person." (6)

She loves it, but Miller is willing to go so far as to admit that she finds Tompkins's insistence on the phrase itself disquieting. (At least I think that's what Miller says: "I'm moving her off the insistence on the signifiers of her phrase that I have identified — 'myself as a person' — because it's making me uncomfortable: as a person" [6]. This convoluted syntax does seem to point to some embarrassment somewhere.) And she attributes it to an identical "embarrassment" on their part when she searches for an explanation why her students, "especially the women," "were unhappy — uncomfortable," "put off" by the piece. Why would they react so differently from her? She disarmingly confesses that she was not successful in countering the students' objections and indicates that their resistance to the essay's charms was rooted in their embarrassment about "going" — or in their embarrassment at being parties to Tompkins's "going" (and Miller's own embarrassed enthusiasm for it?).

Well, I wasn't there, but I can tell you that *I* am not embarrassed by Tompkins and her bathroom business — I can even say "peeing" in public. I can also tell you that I am rather pissed off to be addressed as though I am critically impeded by such delicacies. Am I living proof of the problem within that Miller was talking about? The self that Miller's "I" inscribes is an other who I don't want to be.

Miller remarks in her preface, titled "Feminist Confessions," that the "current proliferation in literary studies of autobiographical or personal criticism" (ix) "may be interpreted, no doubt, as one of the many symptoms of literary theory's mid-life crisis" (ix–x). But this isn't always its function, evidently, as Miller later asserts: "The autobiographical act — however self-fictional, can like the detail of one's [note the impersonal pronoun] (aging) body, produce [a] sense of limit" (xiii).

Four more references to age and aging occur in the eight pages of the introduction: these refer to Miller but are not, apparently, to be taken as referring to a *personal* midlife critical crisis. To the contrary, it would appear that this book represents a kind of celebration: "I've become middle-aged along with the coming of age (the so-called institutionalization) of feminist criticism. . . . I confess to feeling a good deal more sanguine about feminism than about me: after all, this wave of the movement—as well, of course, as the new generations moving within it—is a lot younger than I am and better prepared to work for change" (xv). This despite the "other development" coincident with the turn toward the personal, described a few pages earlier as "a kind of critical misogyny practiced by women as well as men . . . published violence against feminist ideology in general and individual critics in particular (ad feminam)" (x).

OK. So, what is my job here as the intended audience of this book (the back of the book says this is women studies-slash-criticism)? I already figured out that "personal" criticism might not be personal—sometimes it's just the red sports car or trophy wife of an aging critic. But I'm supposed to approve of personal criticism when it's *really* personal because then it's a tonic for just such critical self-indulgences—it establishes a limit. But again, there is a limit there, too: some people get too personal—which is to say political—attacking (sometimes this is called "trashing") not only "feminist ideology" but also "individual critics in particular," and this is called "ad feminam" and is not cricket.

Plus I actually want to be fair here. That Miller is taken by the apparatus of academic publishing to be representative of a certain feminism is not her fault, and she certainly has produced important and valuable work from which I have learned a great deal. I have been a longtime admirer of Nancy Miller's work . . . do you hear a "nothing personal, but . . ." coming here? Well here it is: nothing personal but all this mandatory niceness is boring.

This kind of readerly restraint is solicited and policed by the "personal" anecdotes and details throughout the volume that overlay the image of Nancy Miller, famous-established-feminist, with Nancy Miller, nervous assistant professor facing a scary graduate class that involves slides, and she's machine-anxious to boot; Nancy Miller, eager but foredoomed cherisher of an ambition to become a perfect (nonna-

tive) speaker of the French language who covers herself with shame
ingloriously with a false friend at an important bigwig dinner; Nancy
Miller, who can't get along with her own mother, although she waxes
sentimental at written portraits of someone else's difficult mother; and
so many more Nancy Millers insistently offering themselves as just
like me. And despite superficial differences (of mere fame and glory!),
we are more alike than not.

This same gesture is noticeable in another representation of Nancy
Miller, one-of-our-critical-foremothers. Marianne Hirsch and Evelyn
Fox Keller, editors of *Conflicts in Feminism*, staged a conversation
(which they then edited by compromise from a transcription of a
recording of the original discussion) among three erstwhile "rivals"
who have crossed the border into "friendship"—Jane Gallop and
Marianne Hirsch were the other two participants.[8] Echoes of past
struggles among them are quite audible; the louder they get, it seems,
the more strenuous the efforts to identify with one another on the
basis of a common sensitivity. They are clearly more interested in dis-
playing, discussing, and acknowledging their own and one another's
vulnerability (at least in the version they agreed to publish) than they
are in their positions as representative and established feminists. In
their references to younger "generations" of feminists, they scrupu-
lously avoid placing themselves in any but the most benign positions
apropos of the students they are "training." The conversation also
takes up the vexed and vexing question of feminists "trashing" (as
opposed to "criticizing," another continuing and vexing distinction)
other feminists—seen as an intra- and intergenerational practice:

NANCY [they are designated by their first names in the text]: Yes, there's
been a change in our status but I don't think what that means is so simple.
There is always a way in which as a tenured, published, feminist one
necessarily becomes fair game. . . . When I give a lecture I feel not that *it's*
being criticized but that *I'm* being attacked.

MARIANNE: . . . we never really *feel* in power. It is important for tenured
feminists to articulate that, as difficult as it may be for younger feminists to
hear.

JANE [who is characteristically aslant]: I got up and said I want to speak
here as somebody who has an endowed chair, as somebody who is not
marginal but centrally in the academy. I want to talk about how difficult it
is as a feminist even to say that. Not that it is easier to be marginal, but it is
easier to speak in a feminist context as from the margins. After I spoke,
people got up and started to attack me.[9]

All of these women understand that they have relatively more "power" than much of their audience and that this matters in a practical and real sense. Yet they also want, and even expect, their younger feminist audiences to *identify* with them—with their feelings, their reactions, with them as "personal" entities. Which is what Miller wants of me, as a person, when she tells me stories that she thinks make her like me. And that will make me—I am technically one of those "younger" feminists I suppose—"like" her.

What is dropping out of the equation here is that identification—the process by which we see ourselves in another or another in ourselves—is not an entirely pretty business. The kind of mirroring relation that Miller and critics like her try to set up—the kind Miller described herself as having with the Jane Tompkins of "Me and My Shadow," based on the "bit of story" that Miller said "produced for me the portrait of a writer—like me" (6)—is not finally a matter of simple reflection, of uncomplicated or even mutual admiration societies.

Teresa Brennan remarks in her introduction to *Between Feminism and Psychoanalysis* that the "four stagnant issues" discussed in the collection are deadlocked because "their specific political *or* psychoanalytic contexts have been neglected":[10]

> It should be stressed that identifications are not coterminous with identity. Because identification forges a unity with another, it also poses an imaginary threat. To maintain a separate identity, one has to define oneself against the other: this is the origin, for Lacan, of that aggression towards the other who threatens separateness, and thereby threatens identity. That one is not what the other is, is critical in defining who one is. Thus the truism, that one is most likely to define oneself against who or what one is most like.[11]

Many of my churlish reactions to Miller's book—maybe even especially the ones that I consider based on aesthetic grounds—are undoubtedly produced in and by an analogous process. Jane Gallop puts it this way: "For Lacan, aggression is produced in response to the mirror image. There is a rivalry over which is the self and which the other, which the ego and which the replica."[12] Personal criticism, with its foundational first-person gesture, inscribes these relations: it raises the problem of who is "I," and what "I" am I as a result. The vanilla police of feminist criticism—embodied in the omnipresent injunction to play nice and don't be trashy—state and imply that we can skip all the ugly parts and be one, if not in methodology, status, and politics, then anyway, and more important, in purpose and feminist identity.

A similar proposition was once dominant in film theory and criticism. The idea was that the spectator in the darkened room replays some version of an uncomplicated mirroring. Mary Ann Doane describes it thus:

> The spectator sitting in a darkened auditorium repeats the scenario of the infant before the mirror, corroborating his identity through an alienating image. Because the imaginary order is frequently defined in terms of the plenitude of the image, the cinema would seem to provide the perfect theater for its operations. Yet, as Jacqueline Rose has demonstrated, this description neglects the fact that aggressivity is a necessary corollary of the imaginary.[13]

Doane goes on to locate the aggressivity left out of account by the earlier formulation, in the structure of the shot/reverse shot as well as "displaced, incorporated within the diegesis."[14]

Without such a theoretical armature, a close critical reading of Miller's text isn't possible. Without some kind of psychoanalytic edge, I'm reduced to whining — about the commodification of "stars" in the academy, about the "narcissism" of publishing unrevised talks, about my refusal of some of the explicitly named readerly reactions prescribed for me by the "I." But thinking psychoanalytically about it enables me to posit that some of my anger is provoked by the untheorized and unadmitted aggression in the relation itself — the relation, that is, that the text wants to establish or discover between Miller and me. If that is the case, then there may also be something analogous to the displacement and circulation of the aggressivity component Doane locates in the cinematic text.

There are moments in *Getting Personal* when the text more or less takes a break from its strenuous insistence on getting personal and actually just does it. Those moments give me something to do, something to read, something to work with and through (which is to say, perhaps, I am no longer an infantilized/festishized mirror audience). Two of these occur in "Coda: Loehmann's, Or, Shopping with My Mother" — a coda interestingly provoked by Miller's invocation of a mother-daughter relation that mirrors her own that she has found in Vivian Gornick's *Fierce Attachments*.[15] It is a book, Miller says, that she has "come to think of as 'my' autobiography — its 'I' is New York,

Jewish, middle-aged, intellectual, difficult, etc." (136). She is quick to point out differences between herself and this "I," differences important to "the checkpoints of locational identity," but nevertheless

> I felt written by this book. The place of identification for me, or rather the point of entry into the deepest rhythms of the text, was in the particular intensity of the relationship to the mother, a long, violent, and ongoing war, though perhaps evolving at the end into a more complex and productive antagonism. (136)

I should add too that the triggering phrase connecting the academic problem of autobiography and the "personal" connections Miller wants to excavate is a question put by Gornick's mother figure and repeated by Miller: "Why don't you go already?" (138). (Is it necessary to remind ourselves of the admonition made to us—by our mothers no doubt—to get the bathroom stuff done before leaving the house?)

Miller then goes—to Loehmann's, and without her mother, despite the title. It is "a pilgrimage to the site of archaic female bonding rituals." Miller and her mother had shopped there often, in the early 1970s. She was hoping, she says, "to have a Proustian experience" and also to score a bargain. The bargain she got was a coat, and it seems to be more than a mere coat:

> The coat even had that original detail—an attached shawl—that always satisfied my mother's rigorous shopping standards: not for her the "Fords," the coat (or dress) everyone else wore (and that I cravenly desired when I was young). (140)

After this setup, we find Miller concluding, "nothing magical happened." But she says that where her trip to Loehmann's failed, Gornick's book succeeded. A scene in a diner evokes instant recognition, the triggering phrase, "Because I'm your mother." The identification Miller makes has to do with a memory of sitting with her mother in a coffee shop:

> Hunched into the far corner of the booth, rigid with embarrassment (or was it merely resentment?), I would ostentatiously light a cigarette when my mother, like Gornick's, made the waiter come back to our table with a fresh pot of steaming coffee until it satisfied her requirement for "hot" (in which the "t" always carried an extra charge—almost a dentalization, normally repressed, to make the point). (141)

I am tempted to linger over some of the delicious textual details here: the daughter's resentful refusal to ingest, her solidarity with the male server, the ghost of the vagina dentata, the counterphobic response of rigidity so familiar to us from Freud's reassuring analysis of male responses to the Medusa's head—but time waits for no woman. The main point for me here is that Miller has reduced/repressed her mother into occasional cameo appearances inserted for purposes of female bonding (e.g., "Yeah, my mother was a real bitch too"), has reduced her to a detail of style (while her father gets a chapter and a Major Theoretical Issue of his own). Despite that textual indirection, here is where we will find our missing aggressivity—which is much more than a matter of mere female adolescent leftovers. This is a story about becoming (NOT!) her mother. And not finding it becoming—despite the coat with the original (which is to say conforming to rigorous maternal standards) detail. And Miller's anger at finding that she can't altogether deny that mirroring:

> Remembering those scenes between mother and me through the memory of another's mother, it suddenly became clear that what pained me now was not what mattered then: the recourse to maternal entitlement—particularly unfair, I thought, since it looked more and more unlikely that I would be trading roles [?] with a child of my own ("You'll see when you have children"). What I saw now through Gornick's then was my mother's imperious, personal determination to get what she wanted. At least within this circumscribed realm of daily life, she got her hot coffee. And I? (141)

Miller needs here an extra mirror to begin to excavate the inextricable narcissistic/aggressive facets of this identification. Notice the anger that seems to attend on the idea that a mother (no—not a mother, *my* mother) has *personal* determination that effects a fulfillment of a personal demand; all the while her daughter sits rigid with "embarrassment" unhelped in her need to trade places with her mother in the literal biological sense. If it is a mark of difference that "I" have access to the personal—"I" am not a mother, "I" can write personal books—then it is a return of the same to have had the epitome of the personal, style, usurped by that woman who isn't me and isn't not. The mirror stops here and it's not a pretty picture. This is a textbook illustration of the theoretical problem of the mirror: there are two of us here; we are alike; therefore, what she gets, I don't.

What about the concluding sentence: "And I?" It points to Miller's sorrow about her own inability to have a child; does it also point elsewhere?

Reproductive anxiety does occur at other moments in *Getting Personal*, notably surrounding Miller's pedagogical insecurities (admission of which is another of those engaging, like-me gestures). Asking the question of what an appropriate feminist pedagogy might be, and noting the political and economic difficulties currently facing academic job candidates, Miller continues:

> What is it, I ask myself, I think I am doing by encouraging these women to continue (or begin) working for a degree that will theoretically entitle them to bear the title of professor? Am I not encouraging them to "imitate" me—under conditions far less favorable to their success? Perhaps this peculiar form of female narcissism—a term more apt, I think, than the cooler and sociological notion of "role modeling" to describe the psychic miming at the heart of this doubling—is not only irresponsible but wrong. (39)

There is absolutely no question in my mind that Miller means this sincerely, completely, utterly. She clearly has her students' welfare, their personal welfare, very much at heart. What is curious here is the amount of aggression that is occulted by a dip into another field's rhetoric, a field whose "cooler" mothering language (e.g., "bonding") also often helps us suture the ugly stuff of life and careers and necessity (see Ruthe Thompson's essay, which follows, for a discussion of this issue). Thus, it might be wrong for me to encourage my students to try for the kind of life I have, or for some version of it—that would make it okay and even nice of me to try to keep them out of it, to make them stop trying to be a better me than I am (compare the coat coup above). That the question of pedagogical reproduction is uncomfortably close to maternal doubling is suggested by such gratuitous details as calling pedagogical narcissism "female," and referring to the pedagogical/mentoring project as "doubling." We do and do not want to be our students' mothers; we do and do not want to know why we do and do not.

The rest of the piece abandons the problem of responsibility to focus instead on Miller's belief that it is important to train these students to have a mastery of phallocratic mysteries and to be able to imitate her in her own willingness to retain it by ostensibly letting it go. (Typically engaging, she doesn't so much as take credit for the gesture: "What I am claiming is that this particular teaching situation—in which I was forced to let go of my own fragile claims to mastery by virtue of taking on the visual—allowed me to bring out into the open the stakes of theorization itself" (41). What is not allowed here—any more than it is in the three-way conversation about intergenerational feminist trashing—is an acknowledgment of the aggressivity involved in that narcissistic, transferential, scandalous, personal, "maternal" enterprise, teaching. The Bad Stuff is Out There—in hierarchy, in the times, in the economy, in the phallocratic theory—not in here, where the mirror is.

But the mirror stops here and it's not a pretty picture. So let's really take a long look at it. Personal criticism is what our mothers did to us when we were touchy adolescents; it's also what we do now to be sure we aren't our mothers. But like a worried mother tremulously snooping in her rebellious daughter's diary, the maternal worms its way back into this discourse, by hook or by crook.

Thus, from a *Lingua Franca* piece that is also very much about feminisms and generations, on the Jane Gallop sexual harassment saga (an episode replete with more grist for this mother-mill, for that matter):

> "One of the things I have experienced is that our students tend to imagine that we have more power than we do," says Nancy K. Miller, a feminist literary critic at the City University of New York. "Our generation had no women ahead of us: We were rebelling against father figures, and that was simpler in some ways. Now I'm the same age as some of my students' mothers, and I stir some of those feelings of identification and repudiation you might expect."[16]

So. Are we done yet? No. Nervously and personally, I need to go just a bit more. Nancy Miller is here as "Nancy Miller." And as "Nancy Miller" she has also written some of the most important feminist theory and criticism we have in the archives. She is, though I have never physically been her student, my mother (one of two or maybe three) in the profession; I respect and even love her—"love" here being that odd mixture of transference, emulation, and, yes, identification I have been working through here—for her work and what it has enabled me to do.

I have, I think, hoisted myself by my own personal petard. Which is, finally, what I am arguing we must push the personal a bit harder in order to do—to and for ourselves, to and for our "mothers," to and for our project.

Notes

1. Nancy K. Miller, *Getting Personal: Feminist Occasions and Other Autobiographical Acts* (New York: Routledge, 1991). All subsequent references will be cited parenthetically in the text.

2. Lynda Zwinger, *Daughters, Fathers, and the Novel: The Sentimental Romance of Heterosexuality* (Madison: University of Wisconsin Press, 1991).

3. Janice Radway, "Women Read the Romance: The Interaction of Text and Context," *Feminist Studies* 9 (1983): 64. See also Radway's *Reading the Romance: Women, Patriarchy, and Popular Literature* (Chapel Hill and London: University of North Carolina Press, 1984).

4. Susan Stanford Friedman, "Authority in the Feminist Classroom: A Contradiction in Terms?", in *Gendered Subjects: The Dynamics of Feminist Teaching*, ed. Margo Culley and Catherine Portuges (Boston: Routledge & Kegan Paul, 1985), 205–6.

5. The classic text here is Joan Rivière, "Womanliness as Masquerade," *International Journal of Psycho-Analysis* 10 (1929). Reprinted in *Formations of Fantasy*, ed. Victor Burgin, James Donald, and Cora Kaplan (London: Methuen, 1986), 35–44.

6. Nancy Friday's *My Mother/My Self: The Daughter's Search for Identity* (New York: Delacorte Press, 1972) inspired countless riffs on its title.

7. For the theoretical ground I am basing this essay on, see Lynda Zwinger, "Blood Relations: Feminist Theory Meets the Uncanny Alien Bug Mother," *Hypatia* 7.2 (1992): 74.

8. Marianne Hirsch and Evelyn Fox Keller, eds., *Conflicts in Feminism* (New York: Routledge, 1990).

9. Ibid., 354, 355.

10. Teresa Brennan, *Between Feminism and Psychoanalysis* (New York: Routledge, 1989), 1.

11. Ibid., 11.

12. Jane Gallop, *Reading Lacan* (Ithaca, N.Y.: Cornell University Press, 1985), 62.

13. Mary Ann Doane, *Femmes Fatales: Feminism, Film Theory, Psychoanalysis* (New York: Routledge, 1991), 109–10.

14. Ibid., 110.

15. Vivian Gornick, *Fierce Attachments* (New York: Farrar, Straus, Giroux, 1987).

16. Quoted in Margaret Talbot, "A Most Dangerous Method," *Lingua Franca* 4.2 (1994): 30S.

Working Mother

Ruthe Thompson

If you worry about being a good mother, now or in the near future, forget it! There is not the remotest possibility these days (or in the years to come) of being a good mother. This is not just pessimism; things are destined to turn out this way — it's simply impossible. ANILÚ ELÍAS, "Mission Impossible: Mexico"[1]

With its clean, well-lighted photographs of attractive women and children; slick advertisements for Corningware, Rice-a-Roni, and designer cigarettes; and glossy articles with titles like "The Power of Puppy Love: Those Early Crushes Are Practice for the Important Relationships That Lie Ahead" and "Quick & Cool: Beat the Heat with These Summer Suppers," *Working Mother* could hardly be considered a "feminist" text.[2] Yet feminist politics and philosophies have surely helped to create an atmosphere in which a monthly magazine targeted toward mothers in the labor force could flourish as *Working Mother* has done. Introduced in 1979 by the same publishing firm that owned *McCall's, Sassy, Success, Working Woman,* and *Ms.* magazines, *Working Mother* established a circulation rate base of 925,000 readers[3] by 1995 and boasted in 1996 a proven ability to reach a target audience of "nearly 3 million" "career-committed working mothers" across the nation.[4] With 24.2 million women reported by the U.S. Census Bureau to be working at full-time employment while living with children under age eighteen in their homes,[5] *Working Mother* has managed to sell a magazine a month to one of every twenty-five women in its potential audience, a publishing coup by anyone's standards. And while public approval is no particular gauge of merit (a statement perhaps particularly true for feminists), the fact that so many people read this magazine regularly indicates a powerful need for a popular literature that addresses the issues faced by women endeavoring to be the "good" mother that Anilú Elías finds "simply impossible" in the epigraph above.

Before you protest that *Working Mother* is an odd thing to cite in an essay that purports to treat feminist generations, that the magazine is produced for the primary purpose of selling advertisements and not for promoting female equality in the labor force or in the home, or even for discussing women's social and political roles in any depth; before you complain that the magazine's yuppified slickness is more likely to reify existing constructions of motherhood than to challenge them, and that *Working Mother* has nothing to do with the serious work of feminist scholarship on motherhood in any case, let me explain. I am proposing here that feminists, academic and otherwise, have failed to deal adequately with the problem of motherhood in patriarchy despite a proliferation of published articles, books, talks, and conferences on the subject. And I am arguing that we perform this failure using many of the same gestures found in *Working Mother,* the columns of which do manage to offer readers a chance to discuss the stressful nature of their lives and to let off steam, but which perform this function by tucking the untidy threads of guilt, worry, and overwork that stray out of reader letters and the mouths of interviewees[6] into tidy articles about responsible parenting or the "relaxed" family, and columns that offer "humorous" admonitions like the following passage from a feature called "Wit's End":

> If you're thinking of having a baby, don't go into it blindly, as we did. Be cynical and suspicious. The first question you should ask yourself is: Why are there so many lullabies? . . . Actually, there are lots of things people aren't telling you. Here's a helpful list: "Crying happens. . . . Poop has a name. . . . Colds and flu are forever. . . . You'll be late. . . . Who is this man I married?" The good stuff. Of course this is the part that absolutely nobody tells you about. How can anyone explain why the baby saying her first full sentence can make you bawl? How can anyone describe the unmitigated joy when the baby generously tries feeding her bottle to you? . . . This is a category of events that no researcher of any country can possibly interpret. However, there is an expression in Iceland for this phenomenon. It goes "Yada it, yada yada it." Which, loosely translated, means "Try it, you'll like it."[7]

"Try it, you'll like it" is a singular way to consider the years-long project of raising a child. Yet similar suggestions about the joys of motherhood crop up with predictable frequency in the pages of academic feminist texts: the tender prefatory gratitude for a family set aside or cared for by others while mother finished her book, the familiar dichotomy that targets mother for either idealization or censure in early critiques of the maternal role such as Jane Lazarre's *The Mother Knot*,[8] the suggestion in a questionnaire for graduate students with children that "your efforts as a parent conflict with your obligations as a graduate student,"[9] the footnoted sorrow that a successful academic career left no time for reproducing,[10] or Elías's recommendation, echoed in the passage from "Wit's End," that mothers ought "above all, [to] enjoy it now. Their infancy will pass soon enough and later you'll miss everything except the quarrels. And like fireworks, you'll forget why they drove you so crazy."[11]

Given the propensity of the popular press to stereotype mothers, lampoon feminists, and satirize the yearly conference proceedings of the MLA (Modern Language Association), it is surprising (or maybe not) that the academics have a good deal in common with the journalists when it comes to mother. Admittedly, the question of mother is a problematic one. All women have mothers, and all women have the potential (and sometimes the expectation) to become mothers in one form or another. Certainly the regularity with which women of a certain age are mistaken for mothers needs no explanation here. And perhaps a magazine like *Working Mother* performs a cultural function similar to that of the female/feminist academic mentor: both magazines that "care" about working mothers and female instructors or professors who "care" about students may occasionally tend to rely on, and will certainly become at one time or another the emotive stand-ins for, the sentimentalized version of mother that readers and students alike often seek. But there are some women who choose not to perform the roles constructed by the "enormous amount of cultural work in taming, binding, dividing mother,"[12] and who believe it may be possible to feed, clean, live with, and help to foster the emotional and intellectual lives of children without becoming the mother her daughter inevitably learns to hate. Up to this point, however, and with only a few exceptions,[13] feminist scholarship has invested itself primarily in trying to discuss motherhood without tarnishing the sanctity of the maternal position, unless of course the feminist critic in question is discussing her *own* mother, in which case mother becomes an enormous problem.

The preface to Michelle Fine's anthology *Disruptive Voices: The Possibilities of Feminist Research,* for example, introduces the collection with a story about the editor's upbringing and maternal ancestry. She begins with the sentence "I remember as a child watching my mother cry on the kitchen table" and states that her mother, Rose, "told me her secrets" while "I carried her silences."[14] Although the short essay aims primarily to introduce the essays in the collection and to dedicate the volume to four generations of women from Fine's family, it does so in part by singling her mother out for distancing and blame, particularly when Fine reveals a moment of dialogue between Rose and a therapist during a session also attended by Fine and her sister Sherry. "At one point in the hour," Fine writes, "the therapist asked my mother for her thoughts about our conversation. It was probably then that this book was first conceived " (xi).[7] Asked to "formulate an answer," Rose simply "couldn't," and in the "silence [that] echoed the countless, contradictory voices sedimented shut, nestled between the layers of Rose," Fine experiences a reproductive moment (xi–xii). She "conceives" an idea and labors thereafter to bring forth a book. Fine states earlier in the essay that "since adolescence I have voiced [my mother's] outrage," and she identifies the essay collection as such a statement (vii). Yet if Rose *had* given voice to rage, either in therapy or during her daughters' childhoods, would Fine have been able to write her conception/her mother? Or would Rose have become a species of the bad mother depicted in this (forgiving) statement from Hélène Cixous's "The Laugh of the Medusa"?

> What about she who is the hysterical offspring of a bad mother? Everything will be changed once woman gives woman to the other woman. There is hidden and always ready in woman the source; the locus for the other. The mother, too, is a metaphor. . . . I don't mean the overbearing, clutchy "mother" but, rather, what touches you, the equivoice that affects you, fills your breast with an urge to come to language and launches your force; the rhythm that laughs you; the intimate recipient who makes all metaphors possible and desirable; body. . . . In woman there is always more or less of the mother who makes everything all right, who nourishes, and who stands up against separation; a force that will not be cut off but will knock the wind out of the codes.[15]

The accidental pun in the title of *Working Mother* delineates the tendency I am trying to pinpoint here. I have no disagreement with the claim of editors Jean F. O'Barr, Deborah Pope, and Mary Wyatt in the introduction to *Ties That Bind: Essays on Mothering and Patriarchy* that "few have investigated the institution and experience of mothering with more care, urgency, and insight than feminist scholars."[16] Yet the feminist editors share with journalists, sentimental novelists, filmmakers, pop lyricists, and other purveyors of popular thought a startling willingness to "work" mother for all she's worth: intellectually, commercially, and most of all, sentimentally. Or if not sentimentalizing mother, we frequently take an alternative route to the same symbolic usage, and, like Fine, disavow her, rejecting mother as a model of adult womanhood that *we* would never emulate. The *Ties That Bind* editors seem to prefer the sentimental version of motherhood. Admittedly, their introduction and the essays that follow do participate in "the complex and nuanced remapping of this literal and psychic geography, seeking to trace not the one high road but the multiplicity of routes" (2). And, yes, the collection offers valuable insights into cultural constructs that "are not just the realities of mothers" but "exist as an inextricable manifestation of an ideology that fundamentally oppresses all women" because "no woman remains untouched by the coercive prescriptions for gender behavior.... And mother is the [a?] core of femininity" (3–4). But why, in the midst of this discussion, do the editors feel impelled to add too many lines of gooey *tendresse* to the mother they are writing? Why do they include a totalizing statement like "Motherhood is arguably the most profound life transit a woman undertakes, the deepest knowledge she can experience" (1), or a passage like the one quoted below, which makes redundant statements about mother's subject status while invoking the same sort of sentiment the editors have targeted for critique?

Often the essays are acts of retrievals, moments less of discovery than recovery, especially of the voice and subjectivity of those who actually mother. This reclaiming of voice is even more necessary where custom and discourse have suppressed it, as with women of color, lesbian mothers, and all whose identities lie outside the white, Western, nuclear model. Thus, while the material and rhetorical enforcement of patriarchal paradigms of motherhood is articulated in these pages, there are important, countering voices asserting their own claims of subjectivity and authority. This assertion proves to be historically deep and invariably culturally resistant; it is the insistent selfhood of those who actually mother: the travelers on this ordinary/extraordinary journey. (2)

Here's overkill in the touchy-feely department, if you ask me, a sister "traveler" on the long road to the adulthood of multiple children who finds the journey dismayingly "ordinary" on most days, and for whom it is difficult to understand why grown academics can't talk about mothers without dredging up a magnitude of emotional glop. Such emphasis on the mother's "insistent selfhood" seems to me ironic when it appears in a genre of critical writing that continually projects the maternal "self" against an idealized backdrop of mother paragons, often paired with the saintly mother's evil twin — the mother witch. The actual mother, toiling at her endless round of responsibilities, always seems to come up wanting in these scenes, both in her own eyes and in the reminiscences of her adult children, as this essay will attempt to demonstrate.

"It would seem that the concept of motherhood automatically throws into question ideas concerning the self, boundaries between self and other, identity," writes Mary Ann Doane in *The Desire to Desire*.[17] Doane's statement about the problem of identity helps to explain the insistence of many feminist scholars on distinguishing themselves from their own mothers in print — the disavowal tactic mentioned earlier — much as journalist Judith D. Schwartz does in *The Mother Puzzle: A New Generation Reckons with Motherhood*. Schwartz asserts that she is "completely different from my mother. How, then, could I become what she is — a mother? And would I *want* to?"[18] Similarly, Nancy K. Miller notes in an article about two decades of feminism in the academy that she remembers a consciousness-raising group in the early '70s where "we talk about how we don't want to be like our mothers, who, we believe, did not know what they wanted. Do we know what we want?"[19] And Patricia Meyer Spacks employs a subtly damning anecdote about her mother in the 1994 presidential address to the national convention of the MLA:

> My mother taught me that *So what?* was a rude question, but I can't get along without asking it. What my mother objected to, of course, was its rhetorical usage, as a contemptuous judgment — not a question at all, really, but a derogatory statement. I, however, use the expression for serious inquiry, in the classroom and in my head.[20]

When Spacks makes discursive use of her mother's homespun advice, distancing herself from the role of mother-teacher in the process, she pigeonholes the maternal position as a space in which, and by which, thinking is discouraged. She forgives mother, of course, with an explanation about what "mother really meant to say." But in ventrilo-quizing mother to serve her own rhetorical purpose of encouraging a national body of English professors to teach critical thinking to the masses, Spacks sharply distinguishes familial instruction in polite discourse—mother's work, after all—from the "serious inquiry, in the classroom and in my head" that she herself practices and that she wants her students to learn. The passage implies that Spacks's mother taught her *not* to think critically because thinking was somehow rude, and that Spacks has had to learn, on her own, to think and to speak the "So what?" that allowed her to evolve into the distinguished scholar she grew up to be.

As Lynda Zwinger points out in her contribution to this volume, "Dancing through the Mother Field," "What is dropping out of the equation here is that identification—the process by which we see ourselves in another or another in ourselves—is not an entirely pretty business." Effaced from these statements is any attention to the fact that their authors are endeavoring to foster identification with their points of view, and that this process of identification involves a large element of aggressivity. In his essay "The Mirror Stage," Jacques Lacan notes the "connection between the narcissistic libido and the alienating function of the *I*, the aggressivity it releases in any relation to the other, even in a relation involving the most Samaritan of aid."[21] Neither Spacks nor Fine, Schwartz nor O'Barr et al., Miller nor the friends she writes into "Decades," want to see themselves as their own mothers—or as anyone else's for that matter, as a survey of the years of feminist literature on mother will illustrate. We get around that problem, however, by "working" mother into our texts in the form of suture.[22]

Suture confers subjectivity through narrative. It "names the relation of the subject to the chain of its discourse" and figures within that discourse as "the element which is lacking, in the form of a stand-in."[23] In much feminist writing on motherhood, the aggressivity inherent in identification is displaced onto the figure of mother, that saint/devil we love to love almost as much as we love to hate. It is our fantasized ideal of mother as a paradoxical, impossible mixture of loving, generous nurturer and controlling, repressed bitch that fills the gap, or in cinematic terms, the "cut" in the "shot/reverse shot" sequence as discussed in Doane's analysis[24] and in Zwinger's argument. Mother provides a handy bit of representational thread to mend the psychic

wound caused when the reader absents herself from her "self" in order
to occupy/inhabit the perspective of the fictional speaking subject or
narrative voice, or to hover somewhere near these perspectives as a
judgmental Other in relation to the text.[25]

Kaja Silverman argues that suture "attempts to account for the
means by which subjects emerge through discourse."[26] Jane Gallop
defines it as "the supplementation of an absence, the joining of a gap
by representation."[27] A problematic category in fiction, film, and popular culture, mother — or representations of her — becomes the trope
of choice for writers, novelists, filmmakers, and critics who wish to
align their readers with a particular point of view — to encourage those
outside the text to identify with the subjects that speak it and the objects it portrays. Academic feminists, like the journalists who create
Working Mother, have relied on mother to suture, among other things,
the idealized story of motherhood and family that it seems we still
desire to believe.

For women who attempt to live a life in which they must work for
wages outside the home, while also raising children within it, electronic mail might serve as suture for relationships that could not otherwise exist because these women simply do not have time to be in
the same physical space in order to talk. The age of electronic discourses presents opportunities for interactive dialogue through e-mail,
newsgroups, or listservs without the physicial maneuvering understandable to anyone who has ever taken their small child(ren) to a seminar
(or movie, for that matter), hoisted a fifty-pound set of weights for a
workout, changed a tire on a busy road, hauled multiple sacks of groceries from store to kitchen, or jammed seventy-five student essays into
a backpack already filled with library books and carried it home —
only to ... (return to top of list and sing to the tune of "Row, Row,
Row Your Boat"). The politics and practices of mothering, motherhood, and the maternal will thus obviously undergo reinterpretation,
now in terms of the disembodied personal. But it hasn't happened
yet, and the texts on motherhood that I have highlighted, along with
a vast profusion of texts that I haven't room to cite, indicate that many
feminist scholars have continued to make mother do the textual/cul-
tural work of suture in the service of some rather worn-out stories.

Over the decades in which two generations of academic feminists
have become a force for change in universities and the culture at large,
these critics and writers have posited motherhood as a troubling and

contradictory, but ultimately transcendent, experience—especially on the subjective level that often finds its way into the prefaces, introductions, or acknowledgments of their texts and that employs the figure of hard-fought battles in motherhood to suture the reader into identifying with an often wholly unrelated exercise in scholarship. Similarly, feminists in academe frequently have valorized the maternal as a superlative, empowering state that, as Elías argues, will turn out just dandy if you "give your children that which comes from inside you, sincerely, and [that which is] true to yourself... [including] your doubts and contradictions."[28] Giving the children (the students?) our doubts and contradictions may seem a simple notion when it's a question of whether to let the kids eschew vegetables at dinner or have another round on the video game before bed, to study this author or that genre, to write a paper employing this theory or that; but how can our imaginary, suturing mother answer the questions that constantly plague the feminist scholars who have responsibility for children in my (virtual) neighborhood?

20-APR-1994 10:06
I have already had the worst day of my life. I can't wait for the rest of it. Here's a teeny weeny sample: I have not one second to my name, don't know where any of my clothes are, haven't writ one word of paper, have two guests from out of town coming in to stay tonight. coolers aren't working. toilet is broken and needs replacing. Cats peed on couch. Dog ate entire loaf of bread. I have to meet plane at 11:30. will not get worktime today. I smell. My teeth have a forest primeval on them. My hairs have needed grooming or sandblasting for days now. When I got back—have I mentioned that child won't take baths these days?—she had covered—I mean covered—herself with brilliant magic marker—fuschia and purple. all over legs, face, hands, even back. WHY I howled in anguish. There goes the 1.5 hrs I cadged this a.m. to work. It will take a long time to clean her up.—L[29]

21-APR-1994 14:10
I have had emergency call from sleeping baby despite babysitter presence. I am ax murderer. neglecting baby chile and STILL no essay. rotten me—five more years of therapy for her. *tant pis pour nous.*—L

Here, then, are the more important questions (well, some of them anyway): does mother work now and feel guilty about the children later? Or does she pay attention to children now and feel guilty tomorrow that she hasn't finished the work? And by the way, why is the work of child rearing not validated by anyone in this culture?

And is there any better way to do this? Have you thought of one? Because caring for children or caring physically and emotionally for anyone, really, who is relatively helpless in the world requires enormous amounts of uncompensated time. Moreover, there's little to no material profit in the process, although some clever people are able to wrangle whole books out of examining its angles, cornices, and sides. Sure, mothers get love, they experience tender moments, but try turning that love into a seminar or a conference presentation; try making those tender scenes count toward tenure or signify study for an advanced degree. And without the seminar and conference papers, and the tenure for which one first must get the degree, there will be fewer tender moments as mother struggles to glean some meaning and enough pay out of a job taken, possibly, because there was no way to sustain a concentrated intellectual life and take care of young children without hiring more help than she could afford. Even in the professional child-care industry, turnover is high and caregivers often suffer "burnout" or risk their emotional health by getting too involved, too "motherly," with the children in their charge.[30] Outside the industries of advertising and the popular press, outside sentimental movies and literature, and beyond a certain strain of feminist criticism, romanticizing mother won't get a mother very far.[31]

But instead of examining those questions, feminist scholars have suggested that while careers can interfere with having babies, there is always a way to keep babies from getting in the way of careers; they have researched the "autonomous agency" of mothers in the "playgroup" setting[32] and found that scientific analyses of mother-child "bonding theory" overlook what mothers "know" but "have never been given [a] chance" to prove;[33] they have written volumes of personal/critical information about whether or not to mother and the consequences of that decision, and they have collaborated on an issue of *Feminist Studies* that "start[s] to invent...a feminist theory of motherhood...with our hands on our pulses," but that does not, writes Rachel Blau DuPlessis in her introduction to the poetry, personal essays, photographs, and critical readings that comprise the text, "turn out to be a practical issue of the journal":

> Nothing here about child care, about parenting, about fathers, nothing about the choice not to parent, about the family as a unit. Somehow the questions raised here did not take on a problem-solving or

strategy-laden dimension but rather concern the mothers, mothering, motherhood. As we found them inside us.[34]

"Nothing here" but "mothers, mothering, motherhood." Nothing "practical." And yet the lives of people who care for children need to be grounded in the practical, in the minutiae of details that keep small bodies alive and undamaged. A mother's life, in this text, is "nothing." It is a gap, a wound, an empty place in which to plug the representations of mother that answer a certain "poetics of discovery and telling, exploring and naming."[35] We write mother with *her* hands on *our* pulses, or our temples, or wherever we expect our caretakers to lay cool palms whenever we have a sore head or a heartache. We require mother to perform the textual trick that sutures our identifications with something beyond (better than?) mother, to avoid or allay any potential for recognition of our own mothers in our own lives and stories. We work mother, as Spacks's presidential remarks illustrate, to avoid the possibility of having to identify with those who do "mother's work," a traditionally non- or ill-paid labor in Euro-American culture, and one that garners little respect from other professionals, with its necessary proximity to the necessities of the flesh. This use of the maternal image may help to explain why feminist critics have largely ignored the nasty orts that comprise many a mother's working day: the lack of adequate and affordable day care on or off campus,[36] the constant fragmentation of time that makes the possibility of sustained thinking excruciatingly slim, the hands-on dealings with the "abject" matter that children are forever emitting at inconvenient times and in unfortunate places.[37] And yet these contingencies are certainly more than half of what caring for children is all about.

4-OCT-1993 09:38
It's quite possible that said article reading made me sick, but it seems also to have made the girl sick too. We spent a very large portion of last night crying, walking the floor, and throwing up a truly astounding quantity of surprisingly smelly curdled milk puke. Not to mention the sponge bathing each of us required, and the bedding changing and the calming downing — her not me; I'm not yet. But you know all about this, so I won't blab on. It is uncanny, speaking of which, though, that this timing thing is always so perfect. How do they KNOW it's the night before class and you have everything to do? — L

19-OCT-1993 21:24
It's precisely the lack of distance the substance has traveled, metaphorically and otherwise, that makes it abject to me.

I can handle a good ol' smeary stinky diaper full of unimaginable end products (sic, sick) any time just fine.
The other stuff makes me unsteady on my pins. — L

3-AUG-1994 11:04
uh oh gots to change serious poop.
Can't expose bottom to sun also bec of mosquitoes. Big as airplanes. She looks like she fell in a cactus patch already po lil. And that WITH repellent. She's too busy scratching mosquito bites down to bloody nubs anyway. — L

In light of the physical realities of having children in the house, and the textual evidence that feminists don't want to talk about *that* (in public, anyway), nineteenth-century novelist Olive Schreiner's arguably autobiographical protagonist Lyndall, who has been called the "first wholly feminist heroine in the English novel,"[38] remains something of a revolutionary when she declares, "I am not in so great a hurry to put my neck beneath any man's foot; and I do not so greatly admire the crying of babies. . . . There are other women glad of such work,"[39] especially when this statement is considered against the foreground of representations of motherhood as "arguably the most profound life transit a woman undertakes, the deepest knowledge she can experience,"[40] or as an experience that most women "want," and at which they will ultimately be successful, however they ended up having it, as Nancy Chodorow claims in *The Reproduction of Mothering*. Chodorow states that her study is an attempt

> to provide a theoretical account of what has unquestionably been true — that women have had primary responsibility for child care in families and outside of them; that women by and large want to mother, and get gratification from their mothering; and finally, that, with all the conflicts and contradictions, women have succeeded at mothering.[41]

But I expect I could find a woman or two among the readers of this very essay who "by and large" do *not* "want to mother" and might even be persuaded to admit it, and I wonder how many of those who no longer have a "choice" about whether they are going to "mother" feel they are "succeeding" at the job?

11-AUG-1994 05:52
Well people don't seem to think that we make a conscious choice to be heterosexual (though the Bible belters do think that gay people choose or can choose not) so that is the angle I like the best and have been

trying to get on paper: that whatever we say about motherhood had
best not have an invisible grounding in "choice" at least not on
individual level, and that we can't really ("really") talk about REAL
motherhood but only narratives thereof. we being litcrits for sure and
prolly the rest of us too though maybe they don't know it. of course
the litcrits don't hardly know so either. — L

All of which leads me to ask not the question posed at the outset
of journalist Schwartz's *The Mother Puzzle* ("Why are so many educated women ambivalent about motherhood?")[42] nor the questions
in the "Wit's End" column, but to rephrase the problem identified
earlier in this paper: what does academic feminism's continued desire
either to sentimentalize or disavow motherhood mean when considered in light of Lyndall's claims (although Schreiner, too, uses mother
as suture in the statement "other women are glad of such work");
what does it mean when considered in light of our own — and maybe
I should say *my* own — objection to being constructed as entities who
"want" to mother, who have a fighting chance of succeeding at the
game if they find themselves playing it? Why do we continue to find
an apparent resistance to clear-eyed analytical investigation of motherhood in our own generation, and what does this resistance imply
for current and future generations of academic feminists, many of
whom will rear children alone, having discovered that most women
are single parents whether their domestic arrangements include partners or not?[43]

18-MAR-1994 21:25
Wouldn't it be nice to live a life in which you could immerse yourself
completely in your work and "know" that everything would still be
there when you resurfaced?? — R[44]

18-MAR-1994 21:27
Subj: the best lil def of male/patriarchal priv is this:
That is a very good formulation of male privilege — have you said it
before or should I extract it and send it back? — L

Like *Working Mother,* which claims to be invested in giving employed mothers a "voice" while simultaneously selling them the ex-
pensive products and stylish mother/child images on its pages,[45] academic feminists have continued to purvey a notion of motherhood as
an emotionally resplendent experience, either in their own reproductive and family lives and book prefaces, or in the feminist utopia
they imagine for a far-off future generation. They seem to interrupt

that portrayal only to despise its underside: the bad monster mama who was so often purportedly their own parent. Mary Ann Doane has more to say about the ticklish attempt to differentiate between self and Other, that question of identity: "Perhaps this is why a patriarchal society invests so heavily in the construction and maintenance of motherhood as an identity with very precise functions—comforting, nurturing, protecting."[46] And perhaps this is also why academic feminists work so hard at published assurances about the sanctity of their own motherhood, as prefaces to many feminist studies demonstrate.[47]

I-FEB-1994 22:27
It just occurred to me, prolly not for the first time but I dunno bec I am senile, that we try to keep mothers out of heterosexuality (as a culture I mean, per representation and blah blah) and in sentimentality, yes, but mebbe that is also a form of projection/denial/disavowal (like the mother wants to devour me thing)—what happens mebbe is that women's lives are hard hard hard but they can just barely be done until motherhood puts them over the can't stand it edge. that is, the added workload shoves our faces into the unfixability-unworkability-on-any-terms-but-theirs nature of the hetero contract.—L

2-FEB-1994 10:35
Did you mean that mothers are complicit in being excluded from heterosexuality because they are just too tired to resist or fight to get in or something? Which smells suspiciously of a double bind.—R

2-FEB-1994 11:11
No, I mean that heterosexuality as a set of cultural/gendering/familial-making practices doesn't really work very well if at all for girls, but there's lots o stories blurring that at our foundational sexual/gendered selve ("selves") level. We don't want to know it doesn't work very well either. But then when Motherhood, as cultural practice(s), with all its double binds and double blinds and gaslight crap gets added to being a hetero girl, it all falls apart real quick—the "all" here being the stories—but we don't know that it is the fault of the practices in question bec there are all these cover stories that make it our own individual faults.—L

2-FEB-1994 11:20
And the sentimental is supposed to make that all better?—R

2-FEB-1994 11:32
And the cultural cover story that makes motherhood all sentimental and no sex and no gothic is a cover/alibi for the fact that hetero practice doesn't work for ANY girls and esp not for mothers and since Mothering is what makes it show for the big lie that it all is we have lots o ways of tricking/wrapping/guilting Her out of knowing that it is a cultural fix not a indiwiddly problem.—L[48]

The suturing mother masks the fictive nature of our own sentimental stories — the ones we tell our readers, our students, our lovers, our children, and our selves — and she "jams" the fictional nature of the narratives that create us.[49] But of course, we didn't invent this mother unaided. It has been presented to us as a gift from a patriarchal culture in which the nuclear family has been for a good many years the primary, if not the only, model of "family," although that model does not seem to be working well for a lot of people in America and elsewhere at this particular historical moment, to be sure. The fact is that working mothers, and poor mothers, and mothers who work and are still poor, and mothers who aren't afraid to discuss their anger about the frustrations of their work or their poverty or their children, and apparently even mothers who *are* afraid to examine their rage (cf. Fine, *Disruptive Voices*) cause anxiety. Even among feminists. Even when these feminists are speaking, presumably, *as* mothers, academic or familial. Mothers are "supposed" to be good creatures, as Barbara Christian notes in an article about generations of feminisms published in *differences,* where she states that academic feminists "nurture, approve or disapprove of, desire (no matter what we say) to reproduce students much like ourselves; but our love *is not nearly as unconditional as a mother's is supposed to be* nor is our tenure with our students long enough to call ourselves parents."[50] Caring, nurturing, generous. We are invested in representing mother this way; we need her to be this "good" in order for us to tell our own "not-my-mother" stories. But while a small industry of feminist critics and theorists has presented ample evidence over the past twenty years that this cultural supposition about mother-as-saint is simply not true, we can't seem to hide our guilt about having hinted at the notion; we can't seem to admit, or even to see, the purposes that we expect that image of mother to serve.

3-AUG-1994 11:31
gots to go child requested [!] nap. bye

Notes

1. Anilú Elías, "Impossible ser buena madre," *fem.* (Mexican feminist monthly) (May 1991): 101, reprinted as "Mission Impossible: Mexico," *Connexions* 43 (1993): 8. All other references are to this reprint.

2. Susan Kleinman, "The Power of Puppy Love: Those Early Crushes Are Practice for the Important Relationships That Lie Ahead," *Working Mother* (August 1994);

and Helen Taylor-Jones and Carol Guthrie Dovell, "Quick & Cool: Beat the Heat with These Summer Suppers," *Working Mother* (August 1994). All subsequent references are to this issue of the magazine and will be cited hereafter as *WM*.

3. Telephone interviews with Roslyn Gillespie, sales assistant in the advertising department at *Working Mother*, August 17–18, 1994; with Bernice Savran, *WM* advertising coordinator and assistant to the publisher, July 31, 1996; with Danielle DiMatteo, *WM* customer service manager in the circulation department, July 30, 1996; and with Barbara Delfyett Hester, account manager at *WM*, July 31, 1996. Circulation had increased to 929,508 subscribers by December 1995. Advertising rates are based on the 925,000 figure. *WM*, *Ms.*, and *Working Woman* were purchased in June 1996 by MacDonald Communications Corporation, current owner and publisher of the magazines.

4. MacDonald Communications Corporation, "*Working Mother* Fact Sheet" (New York: MacDonald Communications, July 31, 1996), 1 (faxed to author). It should be noted that *WM* defines its main readership as "working mothers with a median age of 34 years, two young children (median age is 5.4 years old)" and "a median household income of $62,700."

5. U.S. Bureau of the Census, *Statistical Abstract of the United States: 1995; The National Data Book*, 115th ed., table 668, "Employment Status of Women, by Marital Status and Presence and Age of Children: 1960–1994" (Lanham, Md.: Bernan Press, 1995), 406.

6. Among these voices in this 1994 issue of *WM* is cover model "Cynthia Phelps, principal violist with the New York Philharmonic," who poses for the cover shot with her daughter Christina, age three. Dressed in similar outfits of soft pink fabric, mother and child stand in front of the lighted concert hall at dusk, heads bent together, bodies touching, Phelps's arm encircling her child. On an inside page, next to an article on eye makeup, a column called "On Our Cover" gives details. This text asserts that "no amount of practice could have prepared single mom Cynthia Phelps for the balancing act of caring for her three-year-old daughter and pursuing her career." Phelps states: "It's hard not to get overwhelmed by all I have to do. That's why I try to take care of things like bills and phone calls during my lunch hour so my time at home is reserved for Christina" (14). But lunch and "time at home" are apparently not enough to meet the exigencies of mothering a child and maintaining a professional life. The *WM* writer (no byline is given) notes that "motherhood has made Phelps adjust her practice regimen, as well" and again quotes the musician: "I've now learned to really focus my concentration, so I get as much out of practicing for twenty minutes as I used to get from a longer session" (14).

Readers have no way of knowing, of course, how much time a "longer session" might have contained. Thirty minutes? Sixty? Several hours? This question is left to the imagination, but a short article printed a few pages earlier helps to illuminate the problematic I am examining: the ways in which the trope of motherhood is *worked*— or employed, made use of, capitalized on—for the purposes of popular or scholarly text. This short article titled "Mother to Mother" asks readers to respond to the question "How do you usually spend your lunch hour?" (12). The published answers echo Phelps's description of the professional and domestic business she takes care of during her lunch break. In fact, the magazine editors remark that "because of the volume of letters we received from readers in response to our lunch-hour question, we're planning to run a feature article on this subject in the future.... We want to learn more about how moms spend that precious time at midday" (12).

This *WM* feature provides readers with a compendium of maternal images that invite readerly identification with the mother who "does it all" uncomplainingly. She handles work, family errands, and personal fitness on a diet of family leftovers and still finds time to write publishable statements for magazines in the wee hours. Yet the responses quoted below indicate that the metaphor of "balancing" (like the equally clichéd image of "juggling" that peppers the magazine's text and also finds its way into a feminist questionnaire about parenting; c.f. McNenny, "Graduate Students," note 9 below) is always inaccurate, and that nothing akin to balance exists in the lives of mothers who work in jobs outside the home—or even, I would argue, in the lives of mothers who don't work for wages, but who depend instead on the beneficence of a mate or lover, or on the increasingly tight-fisted federal or state government (which for many women is doubtless a safer bet) for food, and shelter, and cash. The juggling and balancing metaphors, however, like the images of tireless maternal dynamos presented here, persist as a way of encouraging readers to feel good about the status quo:

"When I sprint out of my office door at lunchtime, I'm like a marathon runner at the beginning of a race.... On a good day, I can pick up dry cleaning, gas up my car, go through a car wash, visit the card store, buy groceries, and order a birthday cake all in one hour. Doing as much as I can during lunch gives me precious time after work and on the weekends to spend with my family" (12—Jamie Block, Newton, Mass.).

"I use my lunch hour to go to a local gym and exercise. This is truly the only time of day that is *my* time. I'm not anyone's mother, wife, or co-worker, and the only demands facing me are the ones I put on myself" (12—Stephanee Everson, Proctor, Minn.).

"Working at a university, I am fortunate to always find a secluded study area, a library carrel or a quiet café where I can eat my lunch (usually dinner leftovers) and read, read, read. I enjoy reading very much, be it magazine or mystery novels, but rarely have time to read at home, when I'm spending time with my eight- and four-year-old daughters" (12—Sophie Luzecky, Cherry Hill, N.J.).

"I work, attend college, and get my exercise all on my lunch hour!" (12—Mary Sanders, Kettering, Ohio).

This reader mail illustrates nicely (or horribly, perhaps) the scant time and overwhelming guilt about spending any of it on oneself that weigh down the life spent performing what could easily be considered *three* full-time jobs: housekeeping, parenting, and wage earning. This is not to mention—and these stoic readers don't—the sheer fatigue such domestic and professional enterprises surely entail.

7. Lynne Bertrand, "Wit's End," *WM* (August 1994), 96.

8. Jane Lazarre, *The Mother Knot* (New York: McGraw-Hill, 1976). While Lazarre's autobiographical account of a biracial couple succeeds in expressing the unadulterated rage sometimes experienced by mothers, she contrasts that rage with a mother paragon image that her narrator both despises and holds up as an ideal. Lazarre places this familiar pairing within a traditional domestic story. The male parent, Lazarre's husband, focuses exclusively on career—Yale Law School and early legal practice, in this case—while the female parent struggles with child rearing alone. But by the end of the memoir, the angry and discouraged woman of its early pages has settled down to welcome a second pregnancy. There is brave disclosure in this early effort at critiquing the institution of motherhood, but Lazarre leavens her narrator's overweening frustration by describing tender moments that essentialize parenting as experienced by women: "Every year, before my son's birthday, I feel mild labor pains and the tingling of milk moving in my breasts. This dimension of our relationship is extremely difficult to overcome and it often threatens to edge us beyond the normal limits of identification" (ix); and "I...began one of those uncontrollable crying fits experienced by pregnant women" (20).

9. Gerry McNenny, "Graduate Students Who Are Also Parents," memo/question-naire circulated within the University of Arizona English department, July 1994, to gather information for a paper presented at the 1994 MLA panel session "Ties That Bind: Parenting in the Academy," sponsored by the Committee on the Status of Women in the Profession (1–2).

10. See Annette Kolodny, "I Dreamed Again That I Was Drowning," in *Women Writers in Exile,* ed. Mary Lynn Broe and Angela Ingram (Chapel Hill: University of North Carolina Press, 1989), 170–78, in which Kolodny writes of her 1975 sexual discrimination lawsuit against the University of New Hampshire, an unprecedented case that was eventually settled out of court in 1980 after "set[ting] important legal precedents from which Title VII complainants after [her] would benefit" (175). In what was to become for Kolodny a characteristic gesture of practical and political support for younger feminists, she used the settlement from this case to establish a legal defense fund for female scholars fighting similar discrimination suits. Yet at the close of this essay, when Kolodny describes her anger at the lack of support she received from female colleagues and at the toll the court proceedings took on her personal life, she deflects the aggressivity of her "rage" over her colleagues' refusal to imagine themselves in her position — to *identify* with her — onto the absent figure of the mother she argues the suit prevented her from becoming: "I have never forgiven those women their lack of courage. Even today I avoid seeing or speaking to them at professional conferences. I have never forgiven the University of New Hampshire for trying to exile me from its private 'club.' . . . And, finally, I will never be reconciled to the fact that the University of New Hampshire mired me in debt and emotional anguish during the last years in which I might reasonably have planned on pregnancy. Forced to concentrate all my energies on professional survival, I watched the biological time clock run out. I realize as I write these words that the rage I felt ten years ago is still with me" (177).

See also Nancy K. Miller's "Decades," *South Atlantic Quarterly* 91.1 (1992): 65–86, in which Miller states that "probably the most important piece of this fallout [that results from the "panic of my own aging" (81)] involves my not having had a child — not, as it turned out, entirely by choice. This had everything to do with feminism in the 1970s" (85, n. 26). Also see Barbara Christian, "Conference Call" (note 50 below).

11. Elías, "Mission Impossible," 8.

12. Lynda Zwinger, "Blood Relations: Feminist Theory Meets the Uncanny Alien Bug Mother" *Hypatia* 7.2 (1992): 74.

13. An important exception is Nancy Chodorow and Susan Contratto, "The Fantasy of the Perfect Mother," in *Rethinking the Family: Some Feminist Questions,* ed. Barrie Thorne with Marilyn Yalom (New York: Longman, 1982). The authors review a tendency in popular and critical feminist writing to hold up mothers to either idealization or blame and suggest that, in future work on motherhood, feminists "move beyond the myths and misconceptions embodied in the fantasy of the perfect mother" (71). Among the writings reviewed are Myra Dinnerstein's *The Mermaid and the Minotaur* (New York: Harper and Row, 1976), *Feminist Studies'* special issue on motherhood titled "Toward a Feminist Theory of Motherhood" (4, no. 2 [1978]), Nancy Friday's *My Mother/My Self* (New York: Delacorte, 1977), and Adrienne Rich's *Of Woman Born: Motherhood as Experience and Institution* (New York: Norton, 1976).

14. Michelle Fine, *Disruptive Voices: The Possibilities of Feminist Research* (Ann Arbor: University of Michigan Press, 1992), vii. All subsequent references will appear parenthetically in the text.

15. Hélène Cixous, "The Laugh of the Medusa," in *New French Feminisms,* ed. Elaine Marks and Isabelle de Courtivron, trans., Keith Cohen and Paula Cohen (Amherst: University of Massachusetts Press, 1980), 252.

16. Jean F. O'Barr, Deborah Pope, and Mary Wyatt, eds., "Introduction," in their *Ties That Bind: Essays on Mothering and Patriarchy* (Chicago: University of Chicago Press, 1990), p. 1. All subsequent references will appear parenthetically in the text.

17. Mary Ann Doane, *The Desire to Desire: The Woman's Film of the 1940s* (Bloomington: Indiana University Press, 1987), 83.

18. Judith D. Schwartz, *The Mother Puzzle: A New Generation Reckons with Motherhood* (New York: Simon and Schuster, 1993), 17.

19. Miller, "Decades," 70.

20. Patricia Meyer Spacks, "Presidential Address 1994: Reality — Our Subject and Discipline," PMLA 110.3 (1995), 350.

21. Jacques Lacan, "The Mirror Stage as Formative of the Function of the I as Revealed in Psychoanalytic Experience," in his *Ecrits,* trans. Alan Sheridan (New York: W. W. Norton, 1977), 6.

22. For a discussion of the origin of this term see Jacques-Alain Miller, "Suture (Elements of the Logic of the Signifier)," *Screen* 18.4 (1977/78): 25.

23. Stephen Heath, "Notes on Suture," *Screen* 18.4 (1977/78): 48–76.

24. Doane, *The Desire to Desire,* 110–11.

25. For development of this line of thinking, see my forthcoming dissertation "*Working* Mother: The Birth of the Subject in the Novel," University of Arizona.

26. Kaja Silverman, *The Subject of Semiotics* (New York: Oxford University Press, 1983), 199–120.

27. Jane Gallop, *The Daughter's Seduction: Feminism and Psychoanalysis* (Ithaca, N.Y.: Cornell University Press, 1982), 45.

28. Elías, "Mission Impossible," 8.

29. E-mail communication from Lynda Zwinger. Subsequent personal e-mail is from the same source and will be cited as authored by "L." For further development of much of this material, see Zwinger's forthcoming study "Violence and the Maternal."

30. Margaret K. Nelson, "Mothering Others' Children: The Experiences of Family Day Care Providers," in O'Barr et al., eds., *Ties That Bind,* 146–48. See also Susan Rubin Suleiman's "On Maternal Splitting: A Propos of Mary Gordon's *Men and Angels,*" *Signs: Journal of Women in Culture and Society* 14, no. 1 (1988): 25–41, for a discussion of the difficult relation between mothers and caregivers.

31. For an idea of what feminist scholars are up against when we attempt to reinterpret mother, see (and you really must) the Harry F. Harlow and CBS Television Network documentary titled *Mother Love,* directed by Harold Mayer and produced by Carousel Films, 1960. This film follows Harlow in his laboratory at the University of Wisconsin as he demonstrates his efforts to "measure and define" an infant rhesus monkey's love for its mother. The "mothers," of course, are man-made (pronoun used advisedly) objects of wire or cloth, some with baby bottles attached to their midsections, which provide the monkeys' nourishment and "affection" throughout their doubtless brief and experimental lives. Because the young monkeys prefer to sit on the "cloth" mother rather than the bare wire bars of their cages or the wire "mother" made from what appears to be the same material as their confinement, Harlow claims to have proved that the monkeys reared in cages with cloth mothers "love" these objects. "It seems to me [the cloth mother] is doing better than some live mothers," quips host Charles Collingwood of CBS, when the terrified monkeys cling to the cloth structure

after being frightened during the documentary. The film was first telecast on the CBS documentary *Conquest*.

32. See Christine Everingham, *Motherhood and Modernity: An Investigation into the Rational Dimension of Mothering* (Philadelphia: Open University Press, 1994).

33. William Ray Arney, "Maternal-Infant Bonding: The Politics of Falling in Love with Your Child," *Feminist Studies* 6.3 (1980): 568.

34. Rachel Blau DuPlessis, "Washing Blood," in *Feminist Studies* 4.2 (1978): 1.

35. Ibid., 1.

36. By *adequate and affordable day care*, I mean care from which the kids do not return crazy because they have been controlled by poorly paid, mostly bored "counselors" for the past three hours in an after-school program, or for preschool children for an entire day, and care that does not take an inappropriate bite out of the monthly income. I recognize that it's difficult to make "affordable" a thing that, I also argue, should not be "poorly paid." The lowly status of child care as occupation, vocation, or necessity is another of the cultural cues to mother's unfortunate position.

37. See Julia Kristeva, *Powers of Horror: An Essay on Abjection,* trans. Leon S. Roudiez (New York: Columbia University Press, 1982), esp. 70–86.

38. Elaine Showalter, *A Literature of Their Own* (Princeton, N.J.: Princeton University Press, 1977), 199.

39. Olive Schreiner, *The Story of an African Farm* (New York: Penguin, 1986), 184 (originally published in 1883).

40. O'Barr et al., eds., *Ties That Bind,* 1.

41. Nancy Chodorow, *The Reproduction of Mothering: Psychoanalysis and the Sociology of Gender* (Berkeley and Los Angeles: University of California Press, 1978), 7.

42. Schwartz, *The Mother Puzzle,* 20.

43. 20-NOV-1993 19:27 Subj: never get it
RE: our remark that they never get it. Absolutely yes. that's why my friend Amy [Doerr of SUNY Buffalo] says all mothers are single mothers. It's just that only some of us notice that.—L.

44. E-mail signed "R" is mine.

45. WM features a short announcement/column headlined "Write Us!" that asks readers to "share your thoughts with our staff and other readers by joining our reader panel" (24).

46. Doane, *The Desire to Desire,* 83.

47. For a few examples (and there are plenty more), see Susan Rubin Suleiman, "Writing and Motherhood," in *The (M)other Tongue: Essays in Feminist Psychoanalytic Interpretation,* ed. Shirley Nelson Garner, Clare Kahane, and Madelon Sprengnether (Ithaca, N.Y.: Cornell University Press, 1985), 352–77; Marianne Hirsch, *The Mother/Daughter Plot: Narrative, Psychoanalysis, Feminism* (Bloomington: Indiana University Press, 1989); Diana Basham, *The Trial of Woman: Feminism and the Occult Sciences in Victorian Literature and Society* (Basingstoke: Macmillan, 1992); Alison Booth, *Greatness Engendered: George Eliot and Virginia Woolf* (Ithaca, N.Y.: Cornell University Press, 1992); and Sara Ruddick, *Maternal Thinking: Toward a Politics of Peace* (Boston: Beacon, 1989), who write, respectively: "*At the present time,* any mother of young children (and I don't mean only infants, but children of school age and beyond) who wants to do serious creative work—with all that such work implies of the will to self-assertion, self-absorption, solitary grappling—must be prepared for the worst kind of struggle, which is the struggle against herself" (Suleiman, 363, italics hers).

"There are other kinds of help that make the work of writing possible: I would like to thank the day care workers at Hanover Day Care, Norwich Day Care, La Petite

Creche, and the Radcliffe Child Care Center for caring for my children so that I might have the time to write. I also wish to thank Peggy Kendall for her work in our household" (Hirsch, x); "in 1977, pregnancy and nursing afforded me the time to read 'for myself' " (Hirsch, 17). "This may seem paradoxical, but I was fortunate to have a three-months maternity leave from teaching, and like many women I know, I experienced this first pregnancy as a time of self-nurturing" (Hirsch, 203, n. 29).

"I would also like to express a debt of gratitude to my friends, and especially to my family, who have supported me throughout the trial of writing this book, and who have endured with fortitude the many bizarre and uncanny occurrences associated with its production.... Finally, I would like to acknowledge the help I received from my mother in providing child-care while I wrote this book, and to thank my daughter, Hester, for her enthusiastic acceptance of my work" (Basham, x).

"Like any authorship, mine is a kind of collaboration, and it might be best to thank these times of academic ferment and feminist inquiry. But it is more purposeful to thank my known collaborators [thanks colleagues and mentors].... My father's fine suggestions and example have generated much of the pleasure I have had in rewriting this work; he has been a demanding, dedicated, loving editor. Throughout, David Izakowitz has been my best and truest collaborator; though he has not been the wife who selflessly typed it all, we have managed both spheres, the home and careers, together, and to him and to our children I owe my happiness" (Booth, xii-xiii).

"As always, William Ruddick has listened to my most unformed ideas with attentive respect.... We have shared in a daily way philosophical and feminist questions and, for the whole of our children's lives, the tasks of mothering and the challenges of maternal thinking" (Ruddick, ix); "throughout my years of mothering I have lived a heterosexual life with one man who is the biological father of our children and who also is, after some conscious efforts on our part, their egalitarian co-mother" (54).

48. For development, see Zwinger's "Violence and the Maternal."

49. In the "*Encore* Encore" chapter of *The Daughter's Seduction*, Gallop makes the following comments about Stephen Heath's "Notes on Suture": "In French feminism [Heath] finds statements about a feminine writing, writing which although not necessarily by a woman 'jams the machinery of theory' (this is a quote from Luce Irigaray) or (this from Michèle Montrelay) 'ruins representation' " (46). Gallop says later in the essay that "surprise jams universalization, and a listening attention, an attentiveness to specification, guards against confidence, certainty of possession" — an attitude it would behoove us to take, I believe, as we continue to reconsider the representation and interpretation of mother (48–49).

50. Barbara Christian, "Conference Call," *differences* 2:3 (1990): 52–108 (my italics). In this piece, Christian discusses her fear about "whether I would have any [academic] children at all," but this ostensibly professional or philosophical "fear" evolves into a self-positioning symptomatic of the problems many feminist scholars seem to experience when discussing motherhood. As an established feminist scholar, Christian writes, "I find myself an academic mother to more children than I could have possibly imagined, and to types of children beyond my conjuring"; "I have become a mother overwhelmed by children at a time when many of my white counterparts are already academic grandmothers" (57). She states: "Perhaps because my 'sisterhood' was so precarious, perhaps because I have come so late to the role of academic mentor to graduate students, perhaps because I am a single mother in my other life, I question the familial metaphor as an accurate metaphor for feminist scholars" (58).

So far, so good, but Christian goes on to write in the sentence previously cited: "True, we nurture, approve or disapprove of, desire (no matter what we say) to reproduce students much like ourselves; but our love *is not nearly as unconditional as a mother's is supposed to be* nor is our tenure with our students long enough to call ourselves parents" (58, my italics). Here, Christian somewhat paradoxically employs the representation of her own motherhood ("perhaps because I am a single mother in my other life") as a possible disclaimer for her desire ("no matter what [sh]e say[s]") to "reproduce students much like ourselves" even though she can't give students the "unconditional love" a mother is "supposed" to feel for her child. She also notes that she is still "overwhelmed" by children when her white colleagues have passed their intense mentoring duties on to a second generation of academic feminists. Christian's cautious distancing of students, her careful positioning of white feminist scholars, and her deliberate traverse across the sticky terrain of the identifications that may take place among all of these positions are shot through a sequence of suturing devices that include class (her "'sisterhood'" was "precarious" because she was "a low-status mother" studying Afro-American women writers), age ("I have come so late to the role of academic mentor"), and personal experience as a single, working mother.

"Somewhere in Particular": Generations, Feminism, Class Conflict, and the Terms of Academic Success

Linda Frost

The life which men praise and regard as successful is but one kind.
Why should we exaggerate any one kind at the expense of the
others? HENRY DAVID THOREAU, *Walden*

What determines class identity? It's not sheer economics because I
earned substantially more on an oil refinery crew eight years ago
than I do now in academia. It's more than income; it also has to do
with the range of choices one has in life.
DONNA LANGSTON, "Who Am I Now?"

The only way to find a larger vision is to be somewhere in
particular. DONNA HARAWAY, "Situated Knowledges"

Reviewing our subjectivities and the politics of identity that comprise
those subjectivities has become a trend, if not a fad, in current feminist
writing. Yet, like other things popular, it isn't necessarily bad. Reviewing our positioning within the frameworks of our lives, our communities, and our nations is an essential part of understanding why we
do what we do and how we can do it better. Feminist writers therefore don't have to apologize for using personal narrative as a means
of analysis; the personal is, as we well know, political. So this is not
an apology. But it is an explanation of why I want to use my own
stories in order to talk about how the generational influences—familial, feminist, and academic—that have done their work on me continue to play a part in my work as a feminist working in the academy.
Joan E. Hartman uses Hayden White's term to explain that "we construct our selves as agents by piecing together our telling stories, by
emplotting the events of our lives"; more specifically, she explains

that "as we make our narratives our own, we apprehend ourselves as agents: we become conscious of ourselves as makers of our lives as well as makers of narratives about our lives."[1] It is the telling of the story that offers the beginning to empowerment, to recognizing our power and using it responsibly. At a time when intellectual activity is viewed as increasingly suspect, we need to learn to use our personal narratives to forge and strengthen our connections with our students and our communities. And at a time when academia is further threatened externally by rampant budget cuts and internally by an increasingly narrow ideology of success — a success that is available to only a very few — we need to remember not only the power of what we do, but the numerous scenarios and ways in which we enact that power. Feminism as a theoretical practice has opened conversations about power relations that extend far beyond itself, and feminism must continue to move into those conversations. This is what part of the generation of feminist scholars of which I am a part is, I think, attempting to do. I want to talk here about being indoctrinated into this profession, about moving through the generational gap bordered by the identities of student and teacher, and about what it means to be an academic when academia is a world far away from the one in which you grew up. My experiences are not unique and that is, I believe, their value.

The issue of generations arises in terms of the paradigms by and in which we function as scholars and teachers. I am of the generation of scholars contending with the assertions of postmodernists and poststructuralists who inform us of the multiple subject positions we each occupy. What Christina Crosby calls the triumvirate of "race/class/gender" is indeed the stuff of our generational positioning. Crosby contends that "in the academy we are confronted with a duopoly, a structure of 'simultaneous opposition' which seems agonistic but is remarkably stable. What is foreclosed is the possibility of thinking differently about differences."[2] She argues that we must reevaluate and reconceptualize our understandings of difference:

> Otherwise differences will remain as self-evident as identity once was, and just as women's studies once saw women everywhere, the academy will recognize differences everywhere, cheerfully acknowledging that since everyone is different, everyone is the same. Such is the beauty of pluralism. (140)

Crosby believes that by "reading how truths are produced, including the truths one holds most dear," we can begin to do this (140). Feminists need to address and are addressing the truths of feminism itself; for too long academic feminists have assumed that our sisterhood is all that is necessary to unite us. It seems clear, though, that much of what is produced as textualized feminism leaves unexamined the question of academic privilege and the class structure perpetuated, if not installed, within and by academia.

Just as it is no longer admissible to dismiss the issue of race when talking about feminism, it can no longer be admissible to dismiss the issues of class and regional background. How we individually enter, move in, and re-create the academy is partly defined by our class background and class positioning. Generations define us. We are part of the generation that follows our parents, and it is against those generations that we construct ourselves, that we react. Likewise, as a student I am part of the generation instructed by a particular group of scholars and teachers concerned with theoretical models that define and redefine textualized perceptions of reality and identity overall and our profession in particular. It is in part this focus that has led me to the questions I ask now about my own identity and place in the profession. Somehow, and in not easily defined ways, these generational influences intersect and configure one another, competing and jockeying for ideological space in my self-determination and my less controllable subjectivity. These generational forces work to shape me as I become literally the "next generation," part of the group that will then influence yet another generation of academic hopefuls. How well and how clearly I can understand these influences will obviously contribute to how I reflect and utilize them in my teaching of the generation that follows me.

The Path to Success; or, Submit, Early and Often

Sometime during the fall of 1992, I spent an afternoon at one of the cleaner laundromats in the economically depressed midwestern coal town where I lived and worked as an assistant professor of English. My job was, as the euphemism goes, "not a bad first job," but it was not what I had been instructed to recognize as a "dream job" either. I taught three courses a semester at a two-year regional campus in a large state university system. I was perhaps initially overburdened by committee work, but my classes stayed relatively small—rarely larger than thirty. I made a competitive if not remarkable salary, and my campus provided me with money to travel to the professional meetings and conferences I was expected to attend as a tenure-track faculty member. Our campus library holdings might not have merited a high school accreditation, but our fine librarian understood the value of reference texts and, as part of a university system that included a major research institution, we had a fairly comprehensive and efficient interlibrary loan program. Perhaps the most problematic aspect of the job was the dearth of same-age women companions and similar-interest colleagues; only five of us taught English full-time and only three of the five held Ph.D.'s, all in very different areas. We had one history professor, one economics professor, one sometimes-there-sometimes-not philosophy adjunct and no full-time foreign languages instructor. I'm not sure I'd say either the drawbacks or the benefits outweighed the other, but the job certainly had both.

Nevertheless, things were financially problematic in my not-quite-paradise, and I was preparing myself for the unhappy prospect of job hunting in a highly competitive job market. I had just loaded my clothes in the washers when I sat down to flip through an article in an MLA publication that dispensed career advice to the woman academic just starting out. It was liberally sprinkled with advice sound bites, things like "get a good mentor," "build your sense of yourself as a professional," "write to scholars whose work you like," "*submit* early and often."[3] There was no denying the wisdom of such advice, but for some reason the article made me angry. The essay seemed to emit a kind of single-mindedness in terms of achievement, a sense that *this* was the path to success, these steps the only sure ones to take, and if this wisdom were ignored, one could expect to miss the academic boat altogether. These usually oral lists of advice are reproduced and redistributed like chain letters among academics; if you ignore them and, worse, don't perpetuate their ideological stone-in-a-pond ripple effect, you can expect to meet a fated and early career end. "*Submit,*" as the article says, "early and often."

But the problem with such advice—like any other—is that it evolves out of a complex package of assumptions. These assumptions were what made me angry, what I responded to without fully understanding how it was that the piece made me feel so excluded. The article assumed, first, that success in an academic career was a standardized, monolithic entity—basically, a job at a major research institution such as the author had obtained, with all the subsequent privileges, publications, and prestige—and, second, that its reader would have a particular kind of knowledge about and relationship to the profession prior to actually entering it. This attention to professional success is perhaps yet another generational effect; the appearance of the literary theorist has made possible the latest advent of literary stars. Such figures were and are held up as models for graduate students in Ph.D. programs today (the fact that most Ph.D.'s don't attain such status was largely ignored in my doctoral program). The fact that I had a job was, by definition of the article, not in itself a success at all and, by having had a background that did not include a familial knowledge of professional life and pursuits, I was out of the game before it had even begun.

The article was directed at women working on their Ph.D.'s, women who had yet to actually enter the academic job force. The article traced its author through her first experience at a national conference during which she hoped to learn something about the profession from others who, like herself, were trying to "figure it out." But as I knew too well, even to anticipate a need to figure out the workings of an academic profession necessitates an understanding of the professional world prior to entering it. Donna Langston argues that "career consciousness is a skill learned in middle-class families. In working-class families people are more concerned with getting and keeping jobs. It never occurred to me when I won scholarships to attend institutions of higher learning, that it made a difference which school I went to. A B.A. was a B.A., right?"[4] While I knew when I started college that a degree from Harvard was certainly somehow different from one from the state university in Ohio where I had received a full-tuition scholarship and therefore decided to go, I believed that by working hard and keeping a high grade point average, I could prove my worth just as surely in the glacier-scraped flatlands of northwestern Ohio as anywhere else. And I did work hard, hard enough in high school to have earned that scholarship and to have won awards in a variety of intellectually and creatively weighted extracurricular activities. I worked hard in college as well, making A's in my courses, schooling myself in the craft of poetry, and actively participating in our university theater program. I also worked hard at our student union where I spent one year recording food purchases in a big black inventory register we called the Monster and two more making salads with Marilyn and Dorothy, two widowed farm women from the nearby town of Perrysburg. For extra money in the summers, I worked hard as a waitress with the university's catering company. And while I was certainly learning about the worlds of the theater, the university's creative writing program, and the student union, I wasn't learning what it meant to be a "professional." I hung out with Ph.D. students, but they were the actors and directors who shared the stage, green room, and smoke-filled student union with me, not the harried English-teaching graduate students with whom I had little interaction, if any.

In other words, I wasn't learning to think of graduate school as the place where people became "professional." There was nothing and no one in my nonprofessional background and family to prepare me for thinking about my career in professional terms. I was a believer in the faulty but lasting American assumption that if you worked hard, you would succeed, but I didn't then understand how success in my profession was defined. In fact, graduate school became an agreeable option for me not because it would usher me into a professional state of being but because I didn't want to leave the work of college for work behind a corporate desk (the "what else" you could do with an English degree, according to one adviser); I couldn't yet be the writer I imagined I wanted to be because I hadn't yet read enough "literature," which I could and would do in graduate school (it took a while to learn that there were books and "good" books, and most of my time as an undergraduate, particularly in the creative writing program, was devoted to this education); and I wanted desperately to move to the urban east, to get out of Ohio where I'd grown up. I knew that I could just as easily be accepted by a school in New York as I could by one in Ohio (this desire was constructed in part by my new artsy friends and in part by seductive images of the Big City — New York, Boston, San Francisco, and so on — that small-town midwesterners like me carried around like wallet photos of imaginary lovers). I also knew that if I pursued an advanced degree in English, I could conceivably convince my parents that *this* degree would do more than "enrich" me; it might find me a *job,* certainly my father's primary concern.

I understand now how different these reasons were from those of many of my colleagues and friends who, either because of their backgrounds or because they were at a different stage in their indoctrination to the profession, made their graduate school choices and decisions based on very different things, things like finding someone with whom they wanted to work, link their name, and consequently position themselves professionally right from the start. Some of them knew to choose a school that had a strong department in the area of their "interest"—again, something I discovered much, much later. None of these things played a part in my final decisions. I chose the graduate school that offered me the most money for an assistantship, the school that—based on recommendations from two of my favorite undergraduate professors—had the "best" reputation of those that had offered me funding, and the school nearest to my dream city, New York.

I even changed my degree plan—originally, to pursue a M.A.—because one university would only offer me an assistantship if I entered their doctoral program. One of my theater Ph.D. buddies advised me to go for the Ph.D. right away because the M.A. was "useless"; the school offering the Ph.D. assistantship likewise offered me the largest stipend. I took it. I now realize I used graduate school in much the same way my father used the Navy to escape his rural hometown of Flora, Ohio, where the total population equaled the number of his family members and their livestock. I wanted to become part of a world of culture I was just beginning to realize existed, a world that was far, far away from where I grew up and that I believed, of course, was much, much more important.

The Back Story

Entering graduate school, I was probably most excited about being in New York and only a train ride away from New York City. It was a breathtaking thought for a twenty-three-year-old whose father detested New York City enough to make sure our family vacations never extended in its direction. I was enchanted, thrilled, terrified. But I was *not* concerned about my ability to gain the cultural currency I needed to "make it" in the profession. I didn't realize I even needed that currency. I had spent my infant years in a rundown neighborhood in Akron, Ohio; when I turned four, my parents were able to swing the purchase of a $21,000 home in the so-called suburbs. I know now that terms like *suburbs* and *middle class* are hopelessly ill defined. Working farms bordered the "allotment" of houses in which I grew up that was itself several miles from the nearest store. The stench of manure that wafted seasonally over the houses inevitably provoked the neighborhood kids' chant—"Bossie's out! Bossie's out!" This "middle class" simply has nothing in common with the miles of several-hundred-thousand-dollar homes that Long Islanders casually call the suburbs. The township in which I grew up, Suffield, was too small even to have its own zip code. But rural, technically, Suffield wasn't either, and I remember the surprise my best friend from graduate school (who hailed from Cranston, Rhode Island, a stone's throw from Providence) registered when she came home with me during a term break. "Wow," she said, not unkindly, "I expected you to live out in the country, the way you talked about where you grew up." It's hard to describe yourself in general terms when regionally specific factors keep getting in the way.

My mother was a nurse who once dreamed of earning a college degree in engineering. She had opted for something more "practical" and immediate when her family was faced with the medical bills incurred as a result of her mother's prolonged death from cervical cancer. My mother was twelve when her mother died. It took years for her father (and eventually, his second wife) to pay off these debts, and my mother decided to spend her time in nurses' training before getting a job and working full time, which was what her older sister had done after high school. Both my aunt and my mother had helped their family out financially in high school by working as babysitters for local tire tycoons, Akron's being, as it was, the Rubber Capital of the World. To this day, the great regret in my mother's life is that she wasn't able to complete her college degree. Her parents were German immigrants for whom education was extremely important. One of the first things my eighteen-year-old grandfather did after coming to this country was complete his American high school degree. He and my grandmother left each of their grandchildren $1,000 for college; we called the gifts our "Ganzer Scholarships."

My father had worked in the Akron tire industry for years, and with the help of my mother's generous tutoring, received his B.A. in business administration from Akron University when I was a toddler; he attended night school for ten years. My father's background differed significantly from my mother's. I have photographs of my two grandfathers that symbolize the contrast between my maternal and paternal lines. In one, my mother's father, Martin Ganzer, stands by a German tractor with a group of other German men; all are dressed in suits, and several have watch chains dangling from their pockets. These are the farmers with whom my mother's father had worked during a stint at an experimental agricultural center in Bavaria before coming to America. The other photograph shows my father's father, Kermit Hall Frost, as a ten- or eleven-year-old boy on a camping trip; he holds a long rifle in one hand and a tall bottle of beer in the other. His father, Windsor Eugene, who taught history in a one-room school-house, sits next to him and his head falls forward in a drunken droop. The other men in the photo have tossed their hats onto the sloping tarp extending from the Model T behind them, and one rifle-bearing camper sports a grizzled white beard more than two feet long. These pictures symbolize what I see as the contrary nature of my class background; "cultured" German immigrant/Meigs County hick.

The Game of Choice

In an article that looks at the role class plays for women in the academy, Angelika Bammer writes:

> Awareness of class as a factor in our professional actions and interactions is rare. It is perhaps experienced, briefly and fleetingly, as a touch of scorn, a flush of embarrassment, a feeling of unease or estrangement in relation to someone of a different class, but rarely does this feeling surface to become conscious thought. Thus we talk about class as an abstract concept; as an experience, it remains intangible.[5]

Other voices, however, contradict Bammer. Rather than the subconscious experience of class consciousness Bammer describes here, Pam Annas illustrates quite clearly the *constant* feeling of awkwardness and inadequacy that one who comes from a working-class background feels in the academic environment:

> As a graduate student, once I stopped working and started hanging out in the library cafeteria like everyone else, I found that I often didn't know how to talk to people who had had Shakespeare or T. S. Eliot read to them when they were children, who spent their winter vacation in New York seeing the latest plays (I hadn't even seen a play until I was twenty-two), and whose parents were paying for their education.[6]

The struggle to force white feminists to acknowledge our own racism has clearly illustrated that even feminists, committed to the work of empowering the marginalized, can themselves perpetuate a universalizing and exclusive vision. The feeling of identity and belonging of which one is not aware is the feeling of the privileged, of inclusion. It is the marginalized who, in order to survive and succeed, need to know the language, behaviors, and manners of the dominant group, not the other way around. Those of us who do not come from a staunchly middle-class, professional, probably northeastern, possibly West Coast, certainly urban culture do *not* find that "awareness of class as a factor in our professional actions and interactions is rare." We may take years learning how to articulate this feeling, but aware of it we undoubtedly are. I certainly have felt and continue to feel the kind of awkwardness Annas describes here, and I have watched my family feel it because of the situations in which my career choice has placed us all.

My father was continually confused about that choice, not understanding the allure of a degree that couldn't firmly pop me into a solid and respectable job. When I finished my Ph.D., I convinced my parents to skip the graduation ceremony (few of my friends attended) and instead attend my dissertation defense, which, as I explained it to them, was really the important event. As the day approached, I recall feeling embarrassed that my family was coming all the way from Ohio to New York, when most students didn't invite anyone to come from "outside," other than readers from the philosophy, comparative literature, or history departments. Nevertheless, my family wanted to support and celebrate with me, so come they did. During my defense, my father leaned over and whispered to my mother that it was scary, hearing me talk like that; he couldn't understand what I was saying. He told her it was as if I had become someone he didn't know. At the time I think I felt that this was some kind of accomplishment, a clear indication of how far I had come. Now, it is the pain of the distance between myself and my family, which was what my father was expressing, that I feel.

After the defense, we went out for a traditional lunch with several fellow graduate students, my parents and sister, and my dissertation director, the Marxist theorist of the department—a smart, arrogant, confrontational man. The conversation at lunch turned for a moment to racquetball, a game in which my father had recently developed an interest and that he played in a fitness group for potential cardiac patients that my mother had somehow convinced him to join. My dissertation director, always the argumentative critic, began his impassioned "critique" of the game, claiming that it had no art to it, no grace, no "class" next to squash, which was, of course, his game of choice. My father let the argument go—a rare event—and I realized that he was embarrassed. Later, he registered this feeling as anger, which consoled me somewhat; his embarrassment was also mine. A similar incident had occurred on another New York visit when my father had argued with a friend of mine who denounced Louis L'Amour's novels as trash after my father announced that L'Amour was his favorite writer.

Despite his discomfort in these situations, my father always bragged to his friends, relatives, and acquaintances about my academic progress and achievements. But I could never tell him how hard I had to work to appear culturally competent in these supposedly "informal" academic settings or how important it seemed to be to feel that way. And I could never explain to him, or anyone else in my family for that matter, how divided I always felt between my home, where I had developed the artistic interests that would later lead me into the academic world, and that world itself in which, after almost ten years, I am still struck dumb by the sight of foreign words that mock my pronunciation, in which I avoid serving dinner to colleagues for fear of their disapproving and undoubtedly more refined palates, and with which I am now beginning to realize I don't really need to make peace.

Integration and Maintenance

Suzanne Sowinska explains that at twelve she was transformed from an innocent reader of gothic novels to the class-informed consumer of classics; this process continued as she moved along in the academic world:

> More and more I began to live in two very separate worlds, the one that I was born into and the one I was constructing out of various fictions of what I thought normal, intelligent, educated people were really like. Today, I've learned to label these self-limiting activities as attempting to "pass" for middle class, but for a long time, including all of my undergraduate years, I lived in a confused state of preconsciousness where I often, although not always, felt an urgent need to mask my working-class origins.[7]

As I began to understand that this "profession" into which I was headed and in which I was determined to "succeed" meant a kind of class acculturation and cultural complicity as well as the hard scholarly work I was used to, I felt more and more alienated from my family and my own background. I fought with my parents and my sister about how they spent their leisure time, the books they read, the TV shows they watched, the political stances they maintained. And as I professed to them this thing that I was myself only just beginning to claim, they felt an anger and disappointment I'm sure all of us believed I felt toward them. Actually, it was a disappointment I felt about myself because I couldn't comfortably fit into the urban, urbane academic community into which I was desperately trying to move. While I had always explained my career choice to my parents in terms I thought would gain their approval—as a *job*—I was learning that being in this profession meant much more than that. Being an academic in part meant a continual performance of and pretense to a class that Langston claims can be absurdly mocked: "It never fails to amaze me," she says, "how just acting with dominating, elitist classist attitudes is described as being 'brilliant.' "[8] As a graduate student working to become a "scholar" in a doctoral program at a school sixty miles east of New York City, and in one of the most wealthy counties in the United States, I clearly knew I didn't fit in.

In fact, many (if not most) of my academic colleagues and cohorts who come from a background somehow marginalized by academic culture may not articulate this dilemma of class division as a dilemma at all. While someone like Langston indicates her concern that she may lose her working-class identity by being absorbed into academia, many I know are more than happy to lose it and have struggled valiantly to discard or minimize the presence of their backgrounds in their daily academic lives. They have "outgrown" their friends from childhood and don't have much in common with their parents or siblings anymore, and given how radically altered their values have become from those fostered in their childhood homes, this must only be true. They go back to where they grew up infrequently or, for some, almost never at all. They have left their pasts behind them and moved into the middle-class culture of academe. This is of course often not only unavoidable but necessary for many people attempting to divorce themselves from destructive family situations. Working-class families are at least as dysfunctional as any other class's. I'm not interested in romanticizing the working class here, although I understand how easily the painful separation I am describing may be read that way. But, as bell hooks notes, you can no more ignore the developing academic culture of your life than you can that of the place and people with which you grew up; the two must somehow be recognized and, hopefully, equally celebrated.[9]

Sowinska claims that it has taken her a long time, but she has reached a point where she has "not needed to discard my family or cultural values."[10] Instead, she says she lives "in a strangely ambiguous middle ground, insisting on the validity of my working-class roots and experiences yet also feeling outside of them, transported by means of education and political awareness to another place I can't quite call home" (160). Along with my family, I have also been learning to live in this space. Like my father, my mother often didn't understand how it was exactly that I spent my time, and we, too, waged a long, now mutually won war over the value of the "historical sex novels" (as I called them) that she insisted on reading. She has demanded a copy of every poetry and scholarly publication that bears my name, and she keeps them all stacked on her dresser, on top of a copy of my dissertation. The gift my mother has given me is her understanding of my need to explore the kinds of self-expression of which poetry, research, and teaching are all forms. Because of our more carefully tended communication and because many of the values I have adopted from academia are middle-class values that she, too, esteems, my mother and I have been able to explore these issues together. But it has been a long and difficult process.

bell hooks confirms the need for the working-class academic to embrace all parts of her experience and identity. She argues that

> maintaining connections with family and community across class
> boundaries demands more than just summary recall of where one's
> roots are, where one comes from. It requires knowing, naming, and
> being ever-mindful of those aspects of one's past that have enabled and
> do enable one's self-development in the present, that sustain and
> support, that enrich.[11]

Feminist discourse made it possible for me to begin this articulation, this naming of the particles of my past that place me today. The move to affirm one's position in critical prose and reattach the experiential to the theoretical has allowed me to validate and reclaim much of what academic and so-called high cultures have dismissed, if not belittled. As hooks says,

> Often I tell students from poor and working-class backgrounds that if
> you believe what you have learned and are learning in schools and

universities separates you from your past, this is precisely what will happen.... It was my responsibility [as an undergraduate at Stanford with a Black working-class background] to formulate a way of being that would allow me to participate fully in my new environment while integrating and maintaining aspects of the old. (106–7)

For me, the problem was not how to leave my family behind but how to bring them along. I internalized the voices of the dominant middle class and, like Linda Blair's inhabitants in *The Exorcist*, they spoke through me. I tried desperately, for a long time, to bridge the gap by shaming my family into adopting my new values. I don't do this anymore. Now, I see myself reaching back home through my research. When I immerse myself in popular magazines published during the years of and surrounding the Civil War, I think of my father's abiding passion for Civil War battle sites, memorials, and cemeteries. It is reassuring, and I feel connected rather than fragmented. My interest in nineteenth-century popular women's fiction, a gift of '70s and '80s feminist criticism in American literary studies, reflects my mother's passion for popular romances and historical fictions. Through the work of feminist scholars from the generation that precedes me — E. Ann Kaplan, Janice Radway, and Jane Tompkins, for example — I am finding a way to reclaim my own, still somewhat guilty desire for popular texts. The institutionalized practices of this generation of feminism — anthology production, literary criticism, theory, canon reformation, and so on — have allowed these paths to be opened to me, and I am grateful to them. Rather than lose myself in my work, I more and more *find* myself in it.

Professing the Partial Self

Recognizing and understanding the way not only gender, sexual orientation, and race, but socioeconomic and geographic factors affect our positioning in the academy and acknowledging that they may even dictate how and what we relate to our students indicate that we should rethink our notions of self-understanding, self-vision. In her discussion of what she calls "situated knowledges," Donna Haraway argues vehemently against a transcendental objectivity for feminist theory, the assumption of which she calls "the god-trick."[12] By imagining the vision of her dogs, Haraway explains that she has learned to rethink objectivity and see that it necessitates not a vaporized sense of self but, rather, "particular and specific embodiment" (190). Noting that "all eyes, including our own organic ones, are active perceptual systems, building in translations and specific *ways* of seeing, that is, ways of life," Haraway shows that there is no "unmediated photograph" — all vision is distinct, different — "there are only highly specific visual possibilities" (190). She holds that there is "good reason to believe vision is better from below the brilliant space platforms of the powerful" and that such subjugated knowledges are particularly useful for feminism because "they seem to promise more adequate, sustained, objective, transforming accounts of the world" (191). But such knowledges and the standpoints from which they stem must be carefully critiqued as well. These "situated and embodied knowledges" are responsible in a way that "unlocatable, and so irresponsible knowledge claims" are not: being irresponsible means being "unable to be called into account" (191).

While Haraway calls for an accountable knowledge and objectivity, she also argues for a "mobile positioning and...passionate detachment" that is predicated "on the impossibility of innocent 'identity' politics and epistemologies as strategies for seeing from the standpoints of the subjugated in order to see well" (192). For Haraway, we see best when we're on the move:

> The split and contradictory self is the one who can interrogate positionings and be accountable, the one who can construct and join rational conversations and fantastic imaginings that change history. Splitting, not being, is the privileged image for feminist epistemologies of scientific knowledges.... The knowing self is partial in all its guises, never finished, whole, simply there and original; it is always constructed and stitched together imperfectly, and *therefore* able to join with another, to see together without claiming to be another. (193)

What Haraway calls for, then, is a vision that is at once embodied and contradictory, an understanding of the impossibility of speaking from any "one" position and the willingness to record the journey from one way of being, knowing, and seeing into another.

As an academic feminist with a Ph.D. and a working knowledge of words like *discourse, subjugation,* and *hegemony* as well as a woman with a nonprofessional and, by some definitions, working-class background, I clearly have access to two different worlds. What has felt like a doubly denied citizenship may in fact be the "split and contradictory" positioning that Haraway offers as a means to a new and feminist objectivity. It is this multiple access that I find myself claiming in the classroom. It is as a teacher who understands the hostility of a student working forty hours a week, attending two classes a week, and expecting to complete his or her undergraduate degree in possibly seven or eight years that I am best able to draw on this multiple vision. The resistance I have often encountered in the classroom from my state university students is at least as much a resistance to what they perceive as my class positioning as it is a resistance to me as a woman with authority. Rather than assume that most of the power relations in my classroom are configured along gender lines, I now understand—because of my personal experience, the acknowledgment of that experience as a kind of knowledge by feminism, and the questions my generation of literary theorists and critics ask about identity and subjectivity—that class and regional affiliation play a huge role in how those relations are established and maintained. My students certainly perceive me not only as a woman, but a woman with a Ph.D. who certainly has middle-class or even upper-middle-class pretensions because I talk about literature all day long.

I know as a graduate student, I felt less alienated as a woman from academia as I was then experiencing it than I did as a working-class or lower-middle-class state university product fresh from the netherlands of Ohio. Unable to feel comfortable with the upper-middle-class feminists in our department, I chose a man to direct my feminist dissertation who was not particularly interested in or supportive of the feminist project at all. What mattered most to me in that situation was that I felt somehow safe with him, less likely to embarrass myself or commit a class blunder than I did with the feminist professors who were available. While it was feminism that gave me the language I needed to talk about issues like these, that allowed me to consider my personal response to academic work and life as valid and in some way important, the feminist presence during my graduate years was— at least at the level of professor—intimidating and ill matched to the kinds of experiences I'd had as a girl and young woman in the world. The anti-intellectualism of American undergraduates is probably often a similar defense mechanism prompted by just such a perception of class inequity, protecting them from revealing their class identities when discussing ideas they've never before encountered, which will possibly—this time—seal their sense of their own inadequacy.

Every class I teach, I am forced to explain why it is important for my students to read, to question, to analyze, and to learn, and I engage in this explanation because I grew up with many of the values they now present to me. I engage with them over these questions because this is one of the areas in which my experience has uniquely trained me. To refuse to engage students in a dialogue regarding the importance and relevance of the humanities to them is to reinforce class divisions that many students too clearly understand work to marginalize them, particularly in the realm of the traditionally "genteel" arts taught in the humanities. It frightens me when I hear overworked, frustrated, insecure, elitist professors exclaim, in voices staccatoed with disgust, that "these kids shouldn't be in college; it's that simple." What's simple is that we cannot use our power and our educationally granted privilege to clarify and redraw the lines of class stratification; as a scholar with my background, it is for me imperative to continue to open up the foundationally democratic, if flawed, system of American higher education to whomever is willing to move within it. The elitism and classism that is often perpetuated by academia is precisely what threatens us today as government officials supposedly representing the interests of all classes decide what is valuable to them about higher education. More basically, such a dialogue of accountability allows my students the same kind of self-expression my mother encouraged me to explore and that gave me the impetus to enter this profession in the first place.

My father used to joke with my sister and me whenever we would complain about something we were working on: "Plan your work and work your plan," he would say in a voice he emphasized was not to be taken in total seriousness. But his joking proverb slinging (the phrase has its origin in the military) had a point nevertheless; it was, for the most part, up to us to decide what it was we had to do and how we would go about doing it. For me, that path has always been a necessarily unique one, and I thank both of my parents for allowing me that. It is unfortunate that our profession doesn't typically encourage the same kind of multiple vision despite the very different circumstances that surround and define each of us in our work. Bell hooks reminds us that "if the terms of success as defined by the standards of ruling groups within white-supremacist, capitalist patriarchy are the only standards that exist, then assimilation is necessary. But they are not."[13] We can set the terms for much of what is considered successful in our profession, and we don't have to defer endlessly to a model that excludes who we are. Success for me could not have appeared in a form of a high-profile job at an Ivy League institution for a multiplicity of reasons, both self- and institutionally determined. The work I'm planning now in a regionally marginalized part of the country with an urban, mostly older, mostly working student population is not much different from what it was when I started teaching as a graduate student at a large state university, although I don't think I could then see the plan I was following. It was and is mostly this: to help my students see different things in different ways and to encourage them to feel safe in trying out these new and tricky angles. It is what I continue to try to do in my own work and my own life; it is what I hope those of us in academia continue to do about the positions and powers each of us hold in it.

Notes

I would like to thank Devoney Looser and the anonymous reviewers of this volume from whose remarks I benefited significantly. Thanks also go to Michalle Barnett whose commentary and support helped get the article off the ground. And finally, I'd like to thank my mother for her guidance while writing this essay and to dedicate it to both of my parents, without whose support I would never have been able to figure most of this out.

1. Hartman, "Telling Stories: The Construction of Women's Agency," in *(En)Gendering Knowledge: Feminists in Academe,* ed. Joan E. Hartman and Ellen Messer-Davidow (Knoxville: University of Tennessee Press, 1991), 12.

2. Crosby, "Dealing with Differences," in *Feminists Theorize the Political,* ed. Judith Butler and Joan W. Scott (New York: Routledge, 1991), 140.

3. Dana D. Nelson, "Being a Woman Academic; or, The Importance of 'Me-Mates,' " *Concerns* 22.3 (Fall 1992): 34–35.

4. Donna Langston, "Who Am I Now? The Politics of Class Identity," in *Working-Class Women in the Academy: Laborers in the Knowledge Factor,* ed. Michelle M. Tokarczyk and Elizabeth A. Fay (Amherst: University of Massachusetts Press, 1993), 68.

5. Bammer, "Mastery," in *(En)Gendering Knowledge: Feminists in Academe,* 242.

6. Annas, "Pass the Cake: The Politics of Gender, Class, and Text in the Academic Workplace," in *Working-Class Women in the Academy,* 168.

7. Sowinska, "Yer Own Motha Wouldna Reckanized Ya: Surviving an Apprenticeship in the 'Knowledge Factory,' " in *Working-Class Women in the Academy,* 160.

8. Langston, "Who Am I Now?", 70.

9. bell hooks, "Keeping Close to Home: Class and Education," in *Working-Class Women in the Academy.*

10. Sowinska, "Yer Own Motha," 160.

11. hooks, "Keeping Close to Home," 106–7.

12. Donna Haraway, "Situated Knowledges: The Science Question in Feminism and the Privilege of Partial Perspective," in her *Simians, Cyborgs, and Women: The Reinvention of Nature* (New York: Routledge, 1991), 189.

13. hooks, "Keeping Close to Home," 108.

The Objectification of *Julia:* Texts, Textures, and Contexts of Black Women in American Television Situation Comedies

Angela M. S. Nelson

African Americans became involved with experimental and full-scale television network programming as actors and entertainers in 1939 with *The Ethel Waters Show* on NBC. Over the past fifty years of American commercial television, African Americans have appeared in various forms of action-adventure and melodrama including medical, family, and detective dramas as well as Westerns, made-for-television movies, anthologies, soap operas, miniseries, and comedy variety shows. However, blacks have appeared in the situation-comedy genre more than in any other television formula. American broadcast and cable television has aired approximately 800 situation comedies since 1947, and since 1948 there have been 165 situation comedies that have featured African Americans in either starring, costarring, supporting, or transient roles. Of this number, sixty-six are black sitcoms.[1]

The first prime-time dramatic television series to star an African American was the sitcom *The Laytons* (DuMont, August 11-October 13, 1948). This domestic sitcom (domcom) starred Amanda Randolph and white actress Vera Tatum.[2] Although very little is known about this series, the only roles available to African American women, outside of *Amos 'n' Andy* (CBS, 1951–1953), were as domestics. Therefore, it is probably safe to assume that Randolph was a domestic in this domcom. Including *The Laytons,* there have been twenty dramatic series (all situation comedies) that have simultaneously featured African American women, adolescents, or girls in starring roles, were created specifically for black actresses with or without nuclear family units, and featured plotlines that sometimes focused on their lives as females in general and as black females in particular. Seven of these series, *The Beulah Show* (ABC, 1950–1953), *Julia* (NBC, 1968–

1971), *Good Times* (CBS, 1974–1979), *Gimme a Break* (NBC, 1981–1988), *A Different World* (NBC, 1987–1993), *Living Single* (Fox, 1993-present), and *Moesha* (UPN, 1996), are especially useful as viable historical sources for gaining insight into the role of women, African Americans, and African American women in American popular culture because they aired (or air) within significant moments of American social and cultural history and have broken new thematic ground in American television.[3]

In this essay, I will review the portrayal of "Julia Baker" in *Julia* by specifically investigating the series and its relationship to the sitcom formula, to the American television industry, and to American culture as a whole.[4] I have chosen *Julia* because it is important to American television history as the first major black sitcom since 1948: as the first black sitcom to break from the domestic mold of sitcoms of the late '40s and early '50s as seen in *The Laytons* and *The Beulah Show*, it represented for the first time in television history a new type of black woman, and it is especially useful for illustrating and comparing the ways in which black women have been objectified on television since 1950. I will attempt to place *Julia* as such within its appropriate context by briefly comparing it to *The Beulah Show* and *Living Single* where appropriate.

The Texts of *Julia*

As "Julia Baker" in a national weekly television series, Diahann Carroll portrayed a black woman who had traditionally never been seen before on television and film. She was articulate, slim, sexually attractive, glamorous, and trained as a registered nurse. Being the first sitcom to star a black woman since *Beulah*, *Julia* was a drastic change. Nineteen years earlier, film and Broadway star Ethel Waters, as Beulah, was large, hardly glamorous, and employed as a maid for a white suburban family. This Beulah had no husband, no last name, and no family to mention, while Julia Baker was the mother of a six-year-old son Corey and the widow of an Air Force captain who was shot down fighting for his country during the Vietnam War. After her husband's death, Julia migrated to Los Angeles from Kansas, moved into a racially integrated apartment building, and obtained a position as a registered nurse at the Astrospace Industries Company Clinic. As compared to Beulah, Julia's life was perfect indeed. Beulah had one friend (Oriole) who was also a maid, a boyfriend (Bill Jackson) who would not commit to marriage, and a family who was never mentioned on the radio (where the show began) or in the television series. Julia Baker, on the other hand, often talked about her relatives (they came to visit), and her boyfriends were willing to commit to a long-term relationship, even marriage.[5]

The sitcom formula in American prime-time commercial television consists of a recurring cast of characters dealing with a problem that can be resolved within twenty-two to twenty-four minutes. There are three types of situation comedies: actcoms, domcoms, and dramedies.[6] The actcom, or action comedy, focuses on physical and/or verbal actions of the sitcom characters. *The George Burns and Gracie Allen Show* (CBS, 1950–1958), *I Love Lucy* (CBS, 1951–1957), and *Seinfeld* (NBC, 1990–present) are examples of this type of sitcom. The domestic comedy has been the most common of all sitcoms heard on radio and seen on television. This sitcom focuses on the moral and ethical development of child and/or adult characters. *Father Knows Best* (CBS, 1954–1955; NBC, 1955–1958; CBS, 1958–1960), *The Cosby Show* (NBC, 1984–1992), *Living Single,* and *Friends* (NBC, 1994–present) are examples of domcoms. The third type of sitcom, dramatic comedies or dramedies, focus on the social development of its characters. Hence, sitcoms of this type will revolve around a social theme such as war, bigotry, racism, and crime. The dramedy format is very rare. The best examples of this type of sitcom have been *Julia, All in the Family* (CBS, 1971–1979), M*A*S*H (CBS, 1972–1983), *Maude* (CBS, 1972–1978), *Barney Miller* (ABC, 1975–1982), and *Frank's Place* (CBS, 1987–1988).[7]

Julia is a dramedy because it thematized an African American's experiences with racism and discrimination. For example, in the pilot episode, "Mama's Man," Julia is confronted with a racist personnel manager at Astrospace Industries who suggests (though not explicitly) that she is not qualified for the position because she is black. On the insistence of Dr. Chegley, Julia's soon-to-be supervisor, Julia is granted an interview. However, in the second episode, "The Interview," Julia walks out of the interview with Dr. Chegley and his nurse Hannah Yarby because Julia perceives that they, too, are racist. In fact, Julia viewed the adversarial relationship of Dr. Chegley and Nurse Yarby as an assault against *her* because of her race. Predictably, there is a happy ending. By the close of the episode, Hannah visits Julia at home, explains her sometimes aggressive relationship with Dr. Chegley, presents Julia with a uniform, and entreats her to accept the position—which Julia promptly does.[8]

While *Julia* can be categorized as a dramedy because of its thematization of racism and discrimination toward blacks, it is also a domestic comedy because of the maturation experiences of Julia Baker's son Corey, including his desire to have a "new daddy." For example, in "Mama's Man" there is an emphasis on Corey's meeting his new neighbor Earl Waggedorn and his creating an opportunity for his mother to meet a prospective husband under the guise of a broken television (there was no problem—Corey simply unplugged the set). Even then, Corey's development often involved his experiences with racial prejudice. For example, in "Paint Your Waggedorn," Corey and Earl meet Pamela, the white granddaughter of one of the residents. The grandmother, Bernice Bennett, disapproves of Corey and does not want Pamela to play with him because he is "one of those people." Therefore, Corey, too, was dealing with the effects of racism and discrimination. In fact, the ways in which racism and discrimination were thematized and the execution of plotlines unlike those of traditional sitcoms of the 1950s and 1960s make it somewhat difficult for me to describe *Julia*. What can be said, however, is that *Julia* made a serious attempt to address real social issues that had not been thematized in a dramatic comedy program—and this occurred before Hawkeye and Archie Bunker were even introduced to the television-viewing audience.

The Textures of *Julia*

Julia was called a "new experience in television" no doubt because a "new black woman" was cast as its star.[9] The changes in the representation of black women on television as seen on *Julia* (and as compared to *Beulah*) provided a vehicle for a different kind of objectification. Julia Baker became a woman-on-display. In fact, when Hal Kanter, the white creator and executive producer of the show, spoke to Carroll about the part, he told her that Julia Baker was to be "a very simple middle-class woman." He said that he wanted her to be "attractive but not glamorous" because the television audience would have to be able to "relate to her."[10] Actually, from the beginning of the series, Julia Baker was glamorous.[11] However, Kanter's insistence on a "simple middle-class woman" who was also "Negro" set the tone for a different type of objectification. Julia had to become a person (object) to whom (which) all female viewers could relate. Henceforth, Julia Baker was not going to be another Beulah. At least, not the Beulah that Kanter knew so well since he wrote for the radio series back in the late forties. Julia Baker had to be showcased in ways very much like white women in film and television before her to entertain the "largest possible audience."[12]

The textures of *Julia* offer pertinent information about the uniqueness of the program. The timbre or singular personality of *Julia* is clearly seen in its production techniques. These techniques also highlighted the objectified figure of Julia Baker. This was evident in three ways. First, Julia was objectified through camera shots of her face and body including her clothes, hair, and makeup. Close-up and medium shots were frequent. While the Norman Lear comedies of the early 1970s are noted for the use of close shots,[13] the *Julia* series predated them by a few years with close-ups of Julia's face and medium shots of her body. The close shots were indeed compelling. In the first episodes, Julia's face seems to fill the entire screen. Surely, Kanter's intent was to emphasize Julia/Diahann's beauty. Furthermore, in episodes where Julia prepared for dates, she was presented emanating from her bedroom as if on a fashion modeling ramp. Here, camera shots of her entire body were emphasized. Richard Warren Lewis in *TV Guide* stated that fashion designers and photographers "had long been attracted to Diahann's almond eyes, high cheek bones, full lips, swanlike neck, and lithe torso."[14] And, to make this point even clearer, at the end of the March 14, 1970, *TV Guide* article about Carroll and the *Julia* series, readers were told to "turn [the] page for a view of Miss Carroll in some California fashions."[15]

Not only was Julia Baker an objectified television character, like all television characters, but she also became a fashion model. This peculiar conflation of television character Julia Baker and actress-entertainer Diahann Carroll could only occur as a result of the lifestyle and stage experiences of Carroll. Based on Carroll's interviews with *Ebony, Ladies' Home Journal,* and *TV Guide,* indeed, at times it seemed difficult to separate Diahann Carroll from Julia Baker.[16]

Another way that Julia was objectified was through the manner in which men looked at her or responded to her presence. Responses included mouths dropped open, uttered expressions like "wow," and ear-to-ear smiles.[17] Even Julia's boss Dr. Chegley did this at times. This should not, however, be a surprising occurrence. Julia Baker was the perfect middle-class woman. She embodied all of the characteristics that men would want in a woman: she was caring as a mother, attractive, fashion-conscious, yet, in a curious way, somewhat ordinary. Julia Baker was *the* woman-on-display of the late '60s.

In addition to the camera outside of the program objectifying Julia and the men within the text of the show objectifying Julia, the camera shots of Julia's apartment and surroundings were also objectified. Characteristic of both *Julia* and *The Bill Cosby Show* (NBC, 1969–1971) were the long shots of their apartments and the environment of Los Angeles. This strategy of showcasing material success for the American viewing audience has long been a part of the television sitcom formula. *The Bill Cosby Show* and *Julia* demonstrated what was to become a predominant theme in prime-time drama programs of the seventies and early '80s: the exhibition of numerous material objects as seen in *Columbo* (NBC, 1971–1977), *McMillan and Wife* (NBC, 1971–1977), and *Banacek* (NBC, 1972–1974). Furthermore, episodes of *Julia* featured overhead shots of the apartment interior that illuminated the spaciousness of her residence.[18]

One key to understanding the role of *Julia* in American popular culture lies in examining the textures of the series. These textures, or production techniques that included carefully crafted camera shots, set designs, and wardrobe collections, illustrate how this "new black woman" was objectified. In film, it is generally accepted by feminist critics that women (in particular white women) are objectified by a male gaze.[19] *Julia* was different, however, in that it was a television situation comedy with a premise that featured a black woman's life and work in late-1960s America. The (white) male gaze was now on an African American woman on television. It would thus be neglectful to overlook the notion of the exciting, the fashionable, the exotic, and the "glamour of blackness" when discussing *Julia*.[20] Julia Baker *was* different. She was fashionable, exciting, and glamorous. She was a woman objectified in order to be consumed by both men and women. Julia Baker's type (black and beautiful) had not really been seen anywhere in American popular culture before. With the exception of most of the films of Dorothy Dandridge,[21] it was not until the soon-to-be avalanche of blaxploitation films of the 1970s that both black men and women became glamorized.[22] The manner in which this new woman was objectified, however, came at a time when black and white Americans were not entirely ready for it.

The Contexts of Julia

The broad social context of *Julia* was marked by the civil rights and Black Power movements of the late '60s. By the time *Julia* debuted, Martin Luther King Jr. and Robert F. Kennedy had been assassinated. African Americans in such urban cities as Los Angeles, where Julia Baker lived, were horrified by the assassinations and by the social conditions of most blacks in America. The criticisms mounted against *Julia* were unlike the criticisms heard earlier. During the radio programs of the '30s and '40s and the television shows of the early '50s, middle-class blacks complained about the stereotypical portrayals of their particular social class. They disliked the sambo-type male characters, the hen-pecked husbands, the bossy, loud-mouthed wives, and they disapproved of blacks in such subservient and menial roles as maids and handymen.

In the late '60s, the criticism continued to include positive versus negative black images. Now, however, blacks *and* whites were accusing such characters as Julia Baker and Bill Cosby's Alexander Scott in the spy drama *I Spy* (NBC, 1965–1968) of not being "real" for newer reasons. The fact that Julia and Alexander were not portraying sambo and servants' roles was overlooked and not celebrated. Critics complained that these characters were unreal because they were too assimilated and, for the most part, too completely integrated into America's white mainstream culture. To illustrate this concern, in a letter to Hal Kanter, one black woman from Los Angeles wrote:

> Your show is geared to the white audience with no knowledge of the realness of normal Negro people. Your work is good for an all white program—but something is much missing from your character—Julia is unreal. To repeat again—Julia is no Negro woman I know & I'm Negro with many friends in situations such as hers.[23]

Simply put, many television critics and audience members—black and white—did not accept a black middle-class woman living as Julia Baker lived. For example, another viewer said this:

> The show does not portray the life of the typical probing Black woman[;] it is rather a story of a white widow with a Black face. Even though she does possess the physical appearance of a Black woman (minus expensive clothing, plush apartment, etc.) she lacks that certain touch of reality. (158–59)

Furthermore, critics and viewers complained of the absence of a father figure in *Julia*. By the late '60s, single parents were popular television characters. A black woman in this role, however, was not received well by all viewers. One viewer wrote:

> After viewing the season premiere of "Julia," I, as a black woman find myself outraged. Is this program what you call a portrayal of a typical Negro family (which is, incidentally, fatherless)? If so, you are only using another means to brainwash the black people who, unfortunately, may view your program weekly. (160)

Saturday Review's television critic Robert Lewis Shayon devoted three separate columns to reviews of *Julia*. Diahann Carroll became concerned about Shayon's first attack against the show when he opined that there was no permanent, adult black male role model for Corey:

> What curious irony that this well-meaning TV program should contribute to the castration theme in the history of the American Negro male. The Negro female accommodates to the white power structure; the Negro male is aggressive in his demands for responsibility, and such aggression would hardly be welcome in a TV series.
> Attention to Negro males should be high on any list of priorities. Corey Baker needs a role model to adjust his self-image upward.... Such a role model, linking with the boy, would encourage the Negro youths among TV viewers; he would also sensitize white viewers to the truer dimensions of life for the Negro male.[24]

Kanter's response to Carroll's concerns was framed by the constraints of the television industry and by the formula of situation comedy. He told Carroll that the fact that there was no man in the family had nothing to do with race. He said that single parents were a "proven format" and that since the format worked, there was no need to argue with success.[25]

Taken together, these criticisms from professional television critics and viewers represented a confusing aspect of criticisms directed toward African Americans in general and African American women in particular on television. On the one hand, Julia Baker was an assimilated black middle-class woman fully integrated into white mainstream culture in Los Angeles in 1968. On the other hand, she was a black single parent. Persons critical of the program disapproved of both characterizations. They objected to her middle-class lifestyle because it was unreal. They also disapproved of her single parenthood because it was real. In *The Cosby Show* in the mid-1980s, a father figure was present, but blacks and whites still criticized it because of the family's upper-class lifestyles.[26] This ambiguity with regard to *Julia* only demonstrates the confusion of the sixties in general and the uncertainty in particular over what African Americans wanted from a medium as pervasive, persuasive, and powerful as television was then and is now.

Interestingly, both arguments against *Julia* stem from the same foundation: the expectation that television must correspond to the real world.[27] The only problem here in *Julia* is that it did project some aspects of the real world of blacks (single parenthood) while omitting other aspects (the nuclear family). Underlying the unintentional (and intentional) agendas of African Americans critical of the program seemed to be a desire to have more (or total) control of deciding which black images get to the television screen and under what circumstances. Regardless, this reflectionist, or realist, argument is misleading and ineffective within the context of American commercial television and within the context of American television situation comedy. For one thing, the only real world that television has ever attempted to create has been one in which audience members are conditioned to purchase objects, relying on commercials as behavior modifiers, even when they have no need for these objects: the structure of television in America has always sought to create a world that invites audience members to become consumers.

Another problem with this line of reasoning has to do with the politics of the sitcom. It, too, is not concerned with the real world. Stereotypes are the mainstay of American popular culture, especially in situation comedies. It is the formula, or standardization, of people (representing groups of people) in dramatized art forms that provides the audience and creator/author with a common language. Julia Baker was a stereotype (the all-knowing mother) who was very familiar in many ways, yet innovative in other ways (she was a beautiful African American mother). In hindsight, perhaps, the broad social contexts of *Julia* would not have conflicted as much with critics' and viewers' expectations had the textures of *Julia* not objectified Julia Baker as a woman-on-display. In other words, if Julia Baker had not been placed on such a high pedestal of perfection where all women, black or otherwise, would want *to be* her and where all men, black or otherwise, would want *to have* her, perhaps criticisms would have taken another direction. One thing, however, is certain: *Julia* was a "new experience in television."

Overall, *Julia* was bound by the reality of black social unrest in America, bound by the American television industry, and bound by the situation-comedy formula. The context of American commercial television and the American television situation comedy has changed very little since the golden age of television (1945 to 1955). Demonstrative of this is the sitcom *Living Single*. *Living Single* debuted on the Fox network during the 1993 fall season, twenty-two years following the cancellation of *Julia*, and it focuses on the lives of four black twentysomething women. Its debut marked the fact that the pendulum of stereotyping arguments had swung back to the rhetoric of the 1950s. However, *Living Single* was not criticized for portraying such superassimilated blacks as Sidney Poitier's film characters, Bill Cosby's Alexander Scott, and Diahann Carroll's Julia Baker. Rather, they were criticized for behaving like "man-crazed Fly Girls."[28] As such, the criticism has become more gender-oriented. In other words, Beulah and other servants at the time were criticized because of the stereotyping of their race and occupation. Kingfish and Andy were criticized primarily because of their race. Julia was criticized because of her class. The female characters of *Living Single* are criticized because of their gendered behaviors, which include desiring male companionship and objectifying male bodies.

The Beulah Show, Julia, and *Living Single* appeared in diverse periods of black images in American television situation comedy. The hybrid minstrelsy period (1948–1961), of which *The Beulah Show* is a part, is marked by blacks shown in subservient positions to whites and portrayed as domineering mammies, loyal Aunt Jemimas, philosophical Uncle Toms, lazy coons, and "unprofessional professionals." *Julia* debuted in the assimilationism period (1961–1971) that included black characterizations that did not inscribe any of the race, class, and gender conflicts that actually existed in America in the 1960s. These black images appeared for the most part to have been fully assimilated into mainstream America with very little reference to black culture, and they did not appear to be "real." Overtaking the assimilated hybrid minstrelsy period (1972–1983), mostly characterized by Norman Lear's and Bud Yorkin's (re-)creation of black buffoonish characters, *Living Single* appeared during the simultaneity and appropriation period (1984–present) that commenced with Bill Cosby's *The Cosby Show* (NBC, 1984–1992). *Living Single* has none of the aural and visual qualities representative of *The Beulah Show* and other black domestic or comic types of the early '50s. While all of the black women in *Living Single* are basically "new black women" like Julia

Baker, they are visually and aurally more rooted in African American culture and life. For example, the characters of *Living Single* lead successful careers and for the most part exhibit the kind of humor that is easily traced to black folk and popular culture. No doubt, this is due to the fact that the creator and executive producer of *Living Single* is an African American female (Yvette Lee Bowser) who began her career with Cosby's *A Different World.*

African Americans in general and black women in particular have always been criticized in television sitcoms. *The Beulah Show, Julia,* and *Living Single,* singularly and combined, represent the different ways in which black women have been objectified on television. They also confirm certain observations made by J. Fred MacDonald concerning black performance in American popular culture and criticisms directed toward *Julia.*[29] Essentially, he observed that each appearance by an African American in radio, film, and television takes on "added weight" and is "vulnerable to special criticism." Scholars of American popular culture will only be able to unpack the burden of this added weight, or this burden of representation, when they begin to carefully examine the texts of these actors' specific television programs within the contexts of the values of American culture *and* African American culture. Cultural studies scholars in particular will need to examine closely the values and assumptions of the people who unnecessarily place such tremendous responsibility on a television series of a particular formula in order to understand the role of the black entertainer in American popular culture. That is what this essay attempted to do. It was written in order to help me to begin my own journey of understanding what I gained from sitcoms, how I read them, and what they tell me about American people and black people. As I make this journey, unfortunately, I am finding that there is still much more work to be done.

Notes

1. I define *black situation comedies* (or *black sitcoms*) as open-ended series of thirty-minute self-contained episodes that revolve around a single umbrella plot or situation, a regular cast of core characters of African descent, stereotypical characterizations, ritualistic humor, and an irrational approach to reality. In addition, they are made for network television broadcasting; have a black producer, director, and writer, or black performers; speak to black or "American" audiences; and emerge from self-conscious intentions, whether artistic, economic, or political, to illuminate African American characters and/or black experiences. For a general discussion of the sitcom formula

see Arthur Hough, "Trials and Tribulations—Thirty Years of Sitcom," in *Understanding Television: Essays on Television as a Social and Cultural Force*, ed. Richard P. Adler (New York: Praeger, 1981), 201–23. For a discussion of black film genres see Thomas Cripps, *Black Film as Genre* (Bloomington: Indiana University Press, 1978).

2. See Tim Brooks, *The Complete Directory to Prime Time TV Stars, 1946–Present* (New York: Ballantine Books, 1987), 83; Tim Brooks and Earle Marsh, *The Complete Directory to Prime Time Network and Cable TV Shows, 1946–Present*, 6th ed. (New York: Ballantine, 1995), 585; and George Hill, Lorraine Raglin, and Chas. Floyd Johnson, *Black Women in Television: An Illustrated History and Bibliography* (New York: Garland, 1990), 5.

3. Therese Daniels and Jane Gerson, eds., *The Colour Black: Black Images in British Television* (London: British Film Institute, 1989), 10.

4. My analysis of *Julia* is based on seventeen episodes I viewed during the summer of 1995 at the Library of Congress in Washington, D.C.

5. See episodes "Cool Hand Bruce" and "Ready, Aim, Fired!"

6. See Richard Francis Taflinger's dissertation, "Sitcom: A Survey and Findings of Analysis of the Television Situation Comedy" (Ph.D. diss., Washington State University, 1980).

7. Recently, the Fox network attempted to resurrect the dramedy format in 1993 with *South Central,* a sitcom that focused on a black family headed by the mother, residing in the South Central section of Los Angeles. This series was short-lived.

8. Other episodes highlighting the theme of racism and discrimination included "Homework Isn't Housework," "Paint Your Waggedorn," "A Tale of Two Sitters," "Ready, Aim, Fired!", "Who's a Freud of Ginger Wolfe?", "Am I, Pardon the Expression, Blacklisted?", "Dancer in the Dark," and "Romeo and Julia."

9. Richard Warren Lewis, "The Importance of Being Julia," *TV Guide,* 14 December 1968, 27.

10. Diahann Carroll, *Diahann! An Autobiography* (Boston: Little, Brown, 1986), 137.

11. Carroll suggests this in her autobiography: "Two months later I returned to L.A. to shoot the pilot Hal needed to sell the show to the network. Because he had insisted that Julia should not be too glamorous, I was a little surprised by the opulent wardrobe and very attractive apartment. They were certainly beyond what could be afforded on a nurse's salary. But I reminded myself that even with the racial angle, *Julia* was still a fantasy like every other situation comedy on the air" (138).

12. Lewis, "Importance," 28.

13. Episodes from *All in the Family* are excellent examples. In the episodes of the first season particularly, Archie Bunker is the focus of most close-ups.

14. Lewis, "Importance," 25.

15. Ibid., 30.

16. Carroll told Kanter that she understood what he wanted in Julia Baker. "Over the years, the long fingernails and coiffed hair and designer clothes had become something of a personal trademark. But clearly such attire and attitude were not appropriate for Julia" (*Diahann!,* 137).

17. "The Unloneliest Night of the Week" is an excellent example of when this occurred.

18. This can be strikingly seen in the episode "Am I, Pardon the Expression, Blacklisted?" when Corey is pretending to fly around the apartment just as he imagines his father did in Vietnam.

19. For an overview of feminist criticism and its potential applications to television criticism, see E. Ann Kaplan's chapters "Feminist Criticism and Television," in *Chan-*

nels of Discourse: Television and Contemporary Criticism, ed. Robert C. Allen (Chapel Hill: University of North Carolina Press, 1987), 211–53, and "Feminist Criticism and Television," in *Channels of Discourse, Reassembled: Television and Contemporary Criticism,* 2nd ed., ed. Robert C. Allen (Chapel Hill: University of North Carolina Press, 1992), 247–83.

20. See Thomas Cripps's article "The Noble Black Savage: A Problem in the Politics of Television Art," *Journal of Popular Culture* 8.4 (Spring 1975): 687–95; also "Newest Faces in Hollywood," *Jet,* 5 June 1969, 58–61.

21. Between 1950 and 1955, Dorothy Dandridge appeared on the cover of *Ebony* three times. In a December 1955 *Ebony* article, the magazine editors wondered whether blacks had a future in Hollywood. They suggested that Dandridge's success with the all-black film version (*Carmen Jones*) of the opera *Carmen* had to do with Hollywood's changing attitude toward black actors and actresses. The biggest attitude change was toward giving a black performer a "big build-up" or "the glamor treatment," as was done with Dandridge. Not incidentally, the "sex appeal" of Dandridge was greatly emphasized.

22. See Donald Bogle's chapter in *Toms, Coons, Mulattoes, Mammies, and Bucks: An Interpretive History of Blacks in American Films,* 3rd ed. (New York: Continuum, 1995).

23. Aniko Bodroghkozy, " 'Is This What You Mean by Color TV?' Race, Gender, and Contested Meanings in NBC's *Julia,*" in *Private Screenings: Television and the Female Consumer,* ed. Lynn Spigel and Denise Mann (Minneapolis: University of Minnesota Press, 1992), 158–60.

24. Robert Lewis Shayon, " '*Julia*': Breakthrough or Letdown?" *Saturday Review,* 20 April 1968, 49.

25. Carroll, *Diahann!,* 144.

26. See Mark Reid's chapter on "African-American Comedy Film," in *Redefining Black Film* (Berkeley and Los Angeles: University of California Press, 1993).

27. Daniels and Gerson, *The Colour Black,* 10.

28. Harry F. Waters, "Black Is Bountiful," *Newsweek,* 6 December 1993, 59–61.

29. What MacDonald originally opined in 1983 is equally pertinent to black entertainers today: "Since few African Americans have as yet enjoyed the recurring exposure granted to the stars of hit TV series, when the black actor does achieve such success he or she is vulnerable to special criticism. If a role seems too accepting of white social dominance, the star as well as the character he or she is portraying may be attacked as too acquiescent. If the role is one of a middle-class suburban black, it may be assailed as too bourgeois and unsympathetic to inner-city 'brothers' and 'sisters.' If the role involves no racial politics, it may be censured as not 'black' enough. And if it is critical of social injustice, it may be assailed as hostile, radical, or heavy-handed. In effect, in the late 1960s, whenever a black entertainer appeared, he or she was expected to represent all African Americans, embodying the panorama of black from slum to suburb. Because of its patent failure to do this, no successful black series was more controversial than *Julia*" (MacDonald, *Blacks and White TV: Afro-Americans in Television since 1948* [Chicago: Nelson-Hall, 1983], 115).

When Feminism Met Postfeminism: The Rhetoric of a Relationship

Jane Kalbfleisch

It's on the couple that we have to work if we are to deconstruct
and transform culture.

HÉLÈNE CIXOUS, "Castration or Decapitation"

This essay sets out to work on a distinctly feminist couple: namely,
that produced by the relationship between feminism and postfeminism.
Although feminist-postfeminist coupling is undoubtedly informed by
other cultural relationships and identities, it requires analysis of and
on its own terms. Because the survival of (post)feminism[1] relies, perhaps above all, on our ability as women to relate to one another, it is
politically crucial to examine how we represent—and consequently
experience—the relationships among us. I hope that eventually such
reconsiderations of what feminism and postfeminism mean to each
other will prompt us to reconceive our-selves, which is to say, the very
terms *feminist* and *postfeminist*.

To begin, I focus on the two rhetorical positions that continue to
be the most prevalent today.[2] The first position, which has dominated
the debate since its inception in France in the midseventies, situates
feminism and postfeminism antithetically. The second position, which
emerged in the eighties as many academic feminists were seduced by
the rhetoric of poststructuralism, strives to escape the binary logic of
the first through a tolerance of difference. Dissatisfied with both of
these representations, I suggest an alternative based on insights from
other contemporary critical relationships. Specifically, I propose that
the relationship between feminism and postfeminism is, in the current
moment, better cloaked in the rhetoric of Jane Gallop, Jane Tompkins,
and Jean-François Lyotard in their respective discussions of feminism

and psychoanalysis, the personal and the critical, and modernism and postmodernism.

Audre Lorde has insisted that "survival is not an academic skill."[3] In this instance, when the survival in question involves relationship work, the academy does seem a particularly odd place to turn. There is no need to assume that the relationship between feminism and post-feminism—academic though it may be—will function best in exclusively academic terms: critical theory may prove less productive than mainstream tropes; the relationship between feminism and postfeminism may mean more when described as an (impassioned? sordid? tired?) affair than as a theoretical moment. Not accidentally, Tompkins and Gallop, two of the critics whose rhetoric will be here explored, characteristically infuse academic discourse with what we might call experiential discourses. Tompkins's governing metaphor in "Me and My Shadow" and Gallop's trademark rhetoric of desire prompt us to access other sites of knowledge, an effort that may also function, like Lorde's statement, to question the academic (post)feminist's valorization of her own privileged discursive forms.

The image I keep returning to, of a self perpetually made and re-made—like the girl preparing for a date, the women's studies scholar finding a voice within (post)feminism, or the mother and daughter negotiating their interdependence—captures for me the performativity involved in any attempt to re-represent and reexperience our relationships with women. Like the clothes in the girl's closet, the forms available for feminism and postfeminism to try on are limited and limiting. Yet there is choice among the forms that do exist, and as each one distinctly constrains meaning, it also distinctly generates meaning. In other words, each discursive form will inevitably foreground and facilitate some things but not others. The choice, then, is not whether our relationships will fall into some rhetorical pattern but which pattern, for how long, and to what ends.[4]

She's Only after One Thing: The Rhetoric of Opposition

For many contemporary feminists, postfeminism—along with its partner in crime, postmodernism—amounts to nothing more than a fashionable version of patriarchy. French feminist Christine Delphy, for example, argued as early as 1976 that postfeminism, "in the way it is put forward," is at the very least "suspect" but more likely an instance of "antifeminism."[5] More recently, Elizabeth Fox-Genovese in *Femi-*

nism without Illusions describes postfeminism as a "skewed, if not perverse, perspective."[6] Likewise, in *Feminism without Women*, Tania Modleski offers a "postmortem on postfeminism," cautioning her readers about texts that "in proclaiming or assuming the advent of postfeminism, are actually engaged in negating the critiques and undermining the goals of feminism—in effect, delivering us back into a prefeminist world."[7] Whether they reject postfeminist conceptions of identity, agency, history, or free play (to name a few of the more popular sites of resistance),[8] many contemporary feminists engage in a rhetoric of opposition that assumes feminism and postfeminism are fully distinguishable and, at least for the time being, distinct.

More surprisingly, those who advocate postfeminist positions often employ the same rhetoric. Julia Kristeva in "Women's Time," for example, erects a binary division in her analysis of the contemporary generations of feminist thought. Identifying three generations that Toril Moi later coins "liberal," "radical," and "post" feminism,[9] Kristeva states that the postfeminist generation exists because "it is now possible to gain some distance on these two preceding generations of women."[10] Reminiscent of the Cartesian subject, the new generation of postfeminists appears to speak from somewhere outside and above the body of feminist theory. Furthermore, as the prefix *post* suggests, this critical "distance" is also temporal. Speaking *after* liberal and radical feminists, postfeminists reap the benefits of a myth of linear progress by claiming some temporal edge over previous generations. Kristeva points out that the new generation does not replace the other two but allows for "the parallel existence of all three in the same historical time"; although all three generations are currently speaking, however, the postfeminist voice is the newest one, the latest trend, the one Kristeva herself "strongly advocate(s)" (33). Thus, as such rhetoric would have it, postfeminism poses not merely as the mind of feminism, but as its new and improved mind.

The following excerpt from Plato anticipates the present implications of the postfeminism-feminism split. Here I've taken the liberty to exchange Plato's term *body* with *feminism,* and *soul* with *postfeminism*:

> Surely postfeminism can best reflect when it is free of all distractions
> such as hearing or sight or pain or pleasure of any kind—that is, when
> it ignores feminism and becomes as far as possible independent,
> avoiding all physical contacts and associations as much as it can in its

search for reality. In despising feminism and avoiding it, and endeavoring to become independent, the postfeminist is ahead of all the rest.... Feminism provides us with innumerable distractions in the pursuit of our necessary sustenance.... Besides feminism fills us with loves and desires and fears and all sorts of fancies and a great deal of nonsense.... If we are ever to have pure knowledge of anything, we must get rid of feminism and contemplate things by themselves with postfeminism by itself.[11]

Asserting "I post, therefore I am," Kristeva's third generation claims to represent progress itself.

In response to this kind of Cartesian configuration, Delphy as well as Fox-Genovese and Modleski simply reverse its terms. Associating feminism with all that is "pure" and postfeminism with all that threatens to "distract" it, they maintain that "if we are ever to have pure knowledge of anything, we must get rid of postfeminism and contemplate things by themselves with feminism by itself." To preserve a myth of linear progress, they locate postfeminism with patriarchy as the latest version of the same old thing: once collapsed into patriarchy, even postfeminism's most immediate "perversions" can be located as that which feminism has long worked to move above and beyond, or — more to the point — to move past.

Undoubtedly, the postfeminist generation — *in the way it is put forward* — as the new mind equipped to master the entire body of feminist thought or as that perverse patriarchal body threatening, yet again, to contaminate feminist contemplation, is, as Delphy cautions, "suspect." Most suspect to my mind is the tendency of anti- and pro-postfeminists alike to represent the relationship between feminism and postfeminism through the very binary and linear thinking that (post)-feminism strives to displace. When situated oppositionally, feminism and postfeminism constitute a phallocentric pair that is engaged in the kind of coupling that Cixous describes as "a kind of war in which death is always at work."[12] The either/or exclusionary nature of the binary couple insists that One term can only exist by obliterating the Other: postfeminism can only exist to the exclusion of feminism, and feminism can only exist to the exclusion of postfeminism. While posed as opposites, both parties stifle the "great anxiety" that their difference would produce. As Jane Gallop explains, "difference produces great anxiety. Polarization, which is a theatrical representation of difference, tames and binds that anxiety."[13]

Two Hearts Beat as One: The Rhetoric of Inclusion

The second rhetorical current differs from the first by overtly con-
testing the binary logic of exclusion in favor of a rhetoric of inclusion. Although the second position explicitly strives to tolerate and
even celebrate difference, it persists in stifling anxiety by simply displacing polarizations from *within* (post)feminism to the relationship
between (post)feminism and some Other.

Toril Moi's move from the first rhetoric to the second, from her
1985 *Sexual/Textual Politics* to a 1988 article in *Cultural Critique*, enacts such a displacement. Throughout the former, Moi locates postfeminism and feminism in the same binary configuration as Kristeva.
In one fleeting moment in her introduction, however, Moi does take
issue with the exclusivity that configuration prescribes: "If the defense
of the third position implies a total rejection of stage two," she writes,
"this would be a grievous political error. For it still remains *politically* essential for feminists to defend women as women in order to
counteract the patriarchal oppression that precisely despises women
as women."[14] Despite this assertion, Moi's 1985 text does not pursue
the possibility of a nonbinary relationship between feminism and postfeminism. As readers of *Sexual/Textual Politics* are well aware, Moi
remains loyal to her apparent goal of critiquing (and occasionally hu-
miliating) liberal and radical feminists for their innumerable humanist
and essentialist distractions to the postfeminist pursuit of pure knowledge. Consequently, true to her postfeminist form, Moi proceeds here
(as she does in subsequent chapters) to argue that feminism's "undeconstructed" feminine wiles can only lead to postfeminism's fall: "an
'undeconstructed' form of 'stage two' feminism," she writes, "unaware of the metaphysical nature of gender identities, runs the risk
of becoming an inverted form of sexism" (13).

Three years later in "Feminism, Postmodernism, and Style: Recent
Feminist Criticism in the United States," Moi dramatically reconceives
the relationship between liberal, radical, and postfeminism. There she
writes:

> I believe that feminists today have to hold all three positions
> simultaneously. Simply to take up Kristeva's "third position" of
> deconstructed identities, as she herself advocates, is clearly
> impossible.... We must, then, at once live out the contradiction of all
> three feminisms and agonistically take sides: simply sitting on the fence

will never demolish patriarchy. As feminists we will have to make hard and often unpalatable political choices in the full knowledge of what we are giving up. Since every choice is an act of exclusion, to take up a political position means accepting the pain of loss, sacrifice, and closure, even if our choice entails following the free-wheeling paths of Derridean deconstruction.[15]

Here, Moi no longer situates the postfeminist generation as the new and improved mind of feminism but establishes it as just one of three diverse but united minds equipped to master the body of patriarchy. By situating all three feminist generations as politically essential to patriarchy's demise, Moi relies on a rhetoric of inclusion that appears to tolerate more difference not only between feminism and postfeminism, but within the (post)feminist subject.

I will return in a moment to the important contribution Moi makes here by locating all three generations within the individual (post)-feminist, but first I want to question her use of the term *patriarchy* to unify diverse positions. While we might generalize to say that liberal feminists take patriarchy to be their opponent, and that radical feminists perceive phallogocentrism — a kind of symbolic patriarchy — to be theirs, postfeminists perceive a decidedly *post*patriarchal problem.[16] Relentlessly uncomfortable with totalizing gestures that reduce contemporary culture to a series of binary pairs, postfeminists strive to dephallicize the couple — whether patriarchy/feminism, phallogocentric discourse/*écriture féminine,* or problem/solution. For Kristeva, such discomfort epitomizes the third generation of feminism, a generation she defines by its insistence that "the very dichotomy man/woman [or in this case, patriarchy/(post)feminism] as an opposition between two rival entities can be understood as belonging to metaphysics."[17] By displacing the oppositional logic within (post)feminism to the relationship between all feminisms and "patriarchy," Moi discounts the anxiety-provoking difference between the three generations in her very attempt to make that difference count.[18]

To take another example, Susan Rubin Suleiman also inscribes her position in *Subversive Intent* through a similar rhetoric of inclusion. Her preferred phrase, "feminist postmodern," implicitly establishes the parameters of the exchange: the *feminist,* while serving as an adjective, acts only to qualify the noun it depends on for its very existence; but the *postmodern,* a noun, a subject in its own right, exists independently. As Suleiman's syntax recalls the historical tendency in compulsory heterosexuality to define women only in relation to men, it takes as a starting point the impossibility of difference:

> I argue for the recognition of both differences and joint allegiances between male avant-gardes and contemporary feminists, as well as for the recognition of multiple differences between and among women.... In short, I argue for complication and fine distinctions over simple oppositions, for internal divisions and double allegiances, even at the expense of disorder and certain clutter.[19]

Once pronounced "feminist postmodern"—the philosophical equivalent of "man and wife"—Suleiman's marriage of "male avant-gardes and contemporary feminism" produces a couple that is not locked in a binary war but is decidedly content, troubled only by a little "disorder" and a "certain clutter" (he leaves the toilet seat up, and she squeezes the toothpaste from the top). Although Suleiman invokes the desirability of difference through the terms *multiple, distinctions,* and *complication,* her discursive practices simultaneously prevent its realization. And once again it is a new dichotomy, this time between the old guard and the avant-garde, which facilitates that rhetoric. The old guard smacks of Moi's monolithic patriarchy, while in the avant-garde we find a kind of Post-Prince Charming, a creature no more likely to please all feminists than his Post-Princess.

The move Moi makes from contemporary (post)feminism to the contemporary (post)femin*ist* suggests the extent to which Suleiman's rhetoric of inclusion functions, like Moi's, to preserve not only a specific vision of political movement but a particular notion of subjectivity. As long as we remain committed to the latter, it seems unlikely that we will ever genuinely challenge the former. Because we persist in understanding collective identity as a reenactment of individual identity, promoting unity within (post)feminism allows Moi and Suleiman to safeguard the unity of the (post)feminist subject. In short, the rhetoric informing Moi's (post)feminism and Suleiman's feminist postmodernism reinscribes the subject of traditional humanism. Moi herself has elaborated that

> at its centre is the seamlessly unified self—either individual or collective—which is commonly called "Man." As Luce Irigaray or Hélène Cixous would argue, this integrated self is in fact a phallic self, constructed on the model of the self-contained powerful phallus.

Gloriously autonomous, it banishes from itself all conflict, contradiction, and ambiguity.[20]

Following in Man's footsteps, the phallicized (or capital *F*) Feminist defines herself antithetically as not some Other. Unimplicated in the old guard and defined as that which patriarchy is not, the Feminist may vary her approach to the problem, perhaps even associate different approaches with different selves, but she will always know what and where the problem is—namely, in someOne outside her seamless self.

Sandra Harding neatly sums up her commitment to this Feminist subject position in *The Science Question in Feminism*: "I argue for the primacy of fragmented identities," she writes, "but only for those healthy ones constructed on a solid and non-defensive core identity, and only with a unified opposition, a solidarity against the culturally dominant forces of unitarianism."[21] By subordinating multiple and fragmented identities to a "core identity," Harding suggests that (post)feminism can happily preserve the phallic subject position of traditional humanism while, at the same time, apparently embracing postmodernism's direct assault on it.[22] As they solidify fragmentation, unify opposition, and prevent dis-ease, those committed to a rhetoric of inclusion safeguard (post)feminism and (post)feminists from the anxiety of difference.

A Thin Line between Love and Hate: The Rhetoric of Anxiety

As we have seen, both the rhetoric of opposition and the rhetoric of inclusion rely on polarizations that eradicate the anxiety-producing difference between feminism and postfeminism and within feminists and postfeminists. To borrow a contemporary rhetorician's use of the term, neither rhetorical practice creates "presence" for the contradictions within (post)feminism.[23] Every rhetor necessarily foregrounds something at the expense of something else so that "what is present is foremost in our minds and important to us. Curiously, what loses in importance becomes abstract, almost nonexistent."[24] By polarizing feminism and postfeminism, the rhetoric of opposition gives presence to division, always reduced to binary terms, between some version of us and them. What becomes "abstract, almost nonexistent" is the potential for overlap and ambiguity between the two groups and the possibility of conflict within each one. The rhetoric of inclusion, on the other hand, in pitting (post)feminism against some Other, creates presence for the presumed commonalities among feminists and postfeminists while effectively erasing their potential differences. In both rhetorical approaches, the identification of a common enemy functions to promote a sense of unity among those who identify with the dominant term, thereby facilitating a sense of sisterhood for the group as a whole. As Kenneth Burke puts it, those "who can unite on nothing else can unite on the basis of a foe shared by all."[25]

Less obviously, the foe also facilitates a sense of unity within the self. By perpetuating the phallic subject position of the Feminist, the identification of a common enemy prevents us from creating presence for difference within each individual member of the group. Through what Burke describes as "the curative process that comes with the ability to hand over one's ills to a scapegoat,"[26] the (post)feminist discursively projects outside her-self and onto some Other everything a unified identity cannot tolerate.[27] Consequently, Modleski views herself as untainted (if not unscathed) by those "[post]feminis[ts] without women"; Kristeva claims to have resisted any liberal or radical feminist contamination; and Moi locates all patriarchal impulses outside the (post)feminist subject. Of course, this process of handing over one's ills is "curative" only if self-contradiction and ambiguity are presumed sick. Given the naturalization of phallic subjectivity, particularly in academic discourse (a place where contradiction, conflict, and ambiguity signify weakness), it is not surprising that the unity ascribed to the Feminist has, to date, received far less attention than that ascribed to feminism.

Although these rhetorical approaches have, in some ways, served the movement well,[28] they have also functioned to perpetuate a familiar (and, no doubt, familial) construction of and experience with difference. Lorde explains that "as women, we have been taught to either ignore our differences or to view them as cause for separation and suspicion rather than as forces for change."[29] My analysis of the way we represent the relationship between feminism and postfeminism suggests that (post)feminist discursive practices, in erasing and taming our differences through some binary configuration, perpetuate those teachings. The relationships between us would be better cloaked, it seems to me, in a rhetoric of anxiety. By creating presence for difference, the alternate rhetorical practices I'm proposing would foreground the conflict, contradiction, and ambiguity both between and within us. It would urge us to identify both collectively and individually around the site of difference itself while playing up the paradoxical impossibility of any such identification. When reinscribed and reexperienced through a rhetoric of anxiety, the relationship between feminism and postfeminism would allow our differences to function as Lorde advocates, as "forces for change."

We find such a rhetoric of anxiety in the work of Jane Gallop. Unlike the other two rhetorics we've considered, Gallop's practice in *The Daughter's Seduction* self-consciously resists any simple opposition between feminism and some monolithic enemy lurking outside feminism—be it postfeminism, patriarchy, or, in Gallop's case, psychoanalysis. "The repeated gesture of this book," she states in the introduction, "is to set up what appears to be an opposition between two thinkers or terms, and then to move beyond the belligerence of opposition to an exchange between the terms."[30] Located in the anxious space between feminism and psychoanalysis, Gallop strives to sustain "the continual working of a dialectical tension" between them:

> The book claims to be psychoanalytic and feminist. Yet I am not a psychoanalyst and others have questioned my right to the label "feminist." I would not endorse most of the traditional practices of either, but hope that the encounter of the two can bring each to its most radical potential.... The radical potential in their marriage is not a mystical fusion obliterating all difference and conflict, but a provocative contact which opens each to what is not encompassed by the limits of its identity. (xii)

As Gallop relentlessly succumbs to and betrays feminism, psychoanalysis, and any mystical fusion between them, she facilitates and replicates the anxiety between French feminist theory and psychoanalytic theory more than a decade ago. Gallop's position differs from the other two rhetorical positions because it resists erecting the dichotomies (or stroking those already in place) that could offer some kind of easy reconciliation. Committed to dis-easing representation, Gallop assumes and abandons multiple identities to play up anxiety-producing difference.

Through that very commitment, however, Gallop's rhetorical practice runs up against what she would call "the difficulty of keeping infidelity from becoming fidelity to a system of infidelity"—a fidelity that would ultimately function to annihilate difference by being so (un)dyingly loyal to keeping it alive (51). Gallop's conviction that her rhetoric of anxiety exclusively constitutes a "strength" limits her potential for anxiety about anxiety itself (xi). In a sense, then, she does in *The Daughter's Seduction* precisely what I have begun to do in this section: to polarize a rhetoric of anxiety with anOther. As Gallop and I pit some rhetoric *against* anxiety (which I've delineated as the rhetoric of opposition and the rhetoric of inclusion) against some rhetoric *for* anxiety, we produce another phallocentric couple. Like all such pairs, the rhetoric for anxiety/rhetoric against anxiety binary cannot facilitate the anxiety of difference.

Jane Tompkins's rhetoric in "Me and My Shadow" does not produce such certain uncertainty or comfortable discomfort. In that article, Tompkins find herself in the anxiety-producing gap between the critical and the personal, but she is undeniably anxious about being there:

> There are two voices inside me answering, answering to, Ellen [Messer-Davidow]'s essay. One is the voice of a critic who wants to correct a mistake in the essay's view of epistemology. The other is the voice of a person who wants to write about her feelings. This person feels it is wrong to criticize the essay philosophically, and even beside the point: because a critique of the kind the critic has in mind only insulates academic discourse further from the issues that make feminism matter. That make *her* matter. The critic, meanwhile, believes such feelings, and the attitudes that inform them, are soft-minded, self-indulgent, and unprofessional.[31]

As Tompkins proceeds to speak as both critic and person, each voice is perpetually contaminated by the sarcastic asides, sustained monologues, and innumerable disruptions of the Other. For example, at the very moment we are all most impressed with Tompkins's critique of Messer-Davidow's theoretical "mistake," the personal intrudes to mock Tompkins's critical impulse (and our complicity with it) with the words "Here endeth the epistle" (126). As the critic strives to enlighten us about Western epistemology, feminist criticism, and the politics of the father tongue, the person tells us that she has to go to the bathroom, that she is intellectually dependent on her husband, that her father is ill. Like Gallop, Tompkins's discursive practice moves "beyond the belligerence of opposition to an exchange between the terms," yet unlike Gallop, Tompkins's practice cannot entirely reassure us or her-selves that the conflict taking place is good for her or for feminism.

Significantly, in their moments of relative solitude, both voices in "Me and My Shadow" dream of erecting the polarization that would shut out the voice of the Other: the critic longs to return to business as usual—namely, literary criticism without the interjection of the "soft-minded, self-indulgent, and unprofessional"—while the person fantasizes that she can reduce the critical to a mere "game I enjoy playing but which I no longer need or want to play" (130). Despite these dreams of autonomy, their exchange reveals that each identity is quite "alien and constraining," qualities that Gallop attributes to each and every identity.[32] The personal is no better equipped to handle Tompkins's desire "to correct a mistake in the essay's view of epistemology" than the critical is "to write about feelings." The inextricability of the One from the Other points to the extent to which Tompkins's dominant desire as critic *generates* her Other desire. Judith Butler proposes that "repression may be understood to produce the object that it comes to deny."[33] That is, the Other is not some original identity waiting to be either embraced or repressed, but is precisely that which is created (even as it is paradoxically erased) through the act of repression. Thus, in the same way that Tompkins's upbringing as "an only child who caved in to authority very early on" produced in her the anger that she claims "is now a source of identity for me," her complicity with the critical may be understood, in part, as producing (her identification with) the personal.[34]

Representing feminism and postfeminism with such a rhetoric of anxiety would play up their inextricability as well. Perhaps feminism creates postfeminism in the same way spending time with Jane Gallop makes me miss Jane Tompkins (or is it the other way around?). By the same logic, perhaps the third generation's desire to repress the first and second generations of feminism functions to perpetually (re)-produce the very liberalism and essentialism it strives to eliminate. Appropriately, then, it is precisely while professing the evils of phallic subjectivity that Moi herself assumes and advances a phallic Feminist subject position. Likewise, Kristeva can only embrace the postfeminist suspicion of binary logic by naturalizing new binaries: her characterization of the third generation, for example, as the insistence that "the very dichotomy man/woman as an opposition between two rival entities can be understood as belonging to metaphysics" relies on a split between the metaphysical and the physical, which, in turn, facilitates a split between postfeminism and its predecessors. In short, the louder the One proclaims its autonomy, the larger the Other will loom.

If this doesn't seem to fit (or even if it does), we could try on Jean-François Lyotard's notion of the future anterior. In a discussion of the relationship between modernism and postmodernism in *The Postmodern Condition,* Lyotard introduces the future anterior to posit that "a work can be modern only if it is first postmodern. Postmodernism thus understood is not modernism at its end but in the nascent state and this state is constant. . . . *Post modern* would have to be understood according to the paradox of the future (*post*) anterior (*modo*)."[35] Borrowing Lyotard's framework, we might propose that "A woman can be feminist only if she is first postfeminist. Postfeminism thus understood is not feminism at its end but in the nascent state and this state is constant. Postfeminism would have to be understood according to the paradox of the future anterior." Like Lyotard, I should say that I am uncomfortable with his "slightly mechanistic meaning" (79), but I am intrigued by the way this formulation problematizes Modleski's call for a "postmortem on postfeminism" while simultaneously returning us to her link between postfeminism and prefeminism.

Besides upsetting the myth of linear progress that governs so many contemporary representations of and experiences with the relationship between feminism and postfeminism, Lyotard's formulation also serves us well through the ambiguity of the term *nascent.* If postfeminism is feminism in its nascent state, then contrary to its self-professed sophistication, it is an infantile feminism—immature, underdeveloped, naive; simultaneously, despite the postfeminist contempt for the likes of origin, purity, and nature, it is feminism in its originary moment, in its purest and most natural state. The postfeminist preoccupation with representation, for example, which is so often celebrated or rejected for its alleged departure from feminism, offers a case in point. The insistence on the way *representation* functions as *reality* and on the ultimate indistinguishability of the two terms does not take us away from feminism. Feminists have always known that to change the reality of women's lives, we must change the way our potential, our bodies, our work, our writings, and our relationships are represented. This purportedly new postfeminist emphasis on representation is nothing new to feminism, but arguably the very premise of feminist critique. Postfeminists have not invented the deconstruction of the representation/reality binary (or the related oppositions of language/action, appearance/reality, form/content, gender/sex)—they have merely seized it, dwelled on it, pushed it to its limits. And because the nascent state is constant, we can expect them to continue to do so. No doubt, Gallop, Tompkins, and Lyotard are only a few of the critics whose relationships will have been addressing the relationship between feminism and postfeminism in ways that allow for the anxiety of difference. Although no rhetorical practice will serve (post)-feminism across all contexts, it seems to me that in this cultural moment—in the academic contexts in which the debates I've been describing are taking place—practices that allow us to facilitate and finally experience the differences between and among will best ensure (post)feminism's survival. Paradoxically, giving up on the possibility and desirability of the unity produced by a movement without contradiction, a self without ambiguity, or a relationship without conflict may be precisely what will function to unify us. In other words, our work on this feminist couple and others may allow us to strive not in spite of our differences but because of them.

Notes

I want to thank the editors, Devoney Looser and E. Ann Kaplan, as well as Maria R. Bevacqua, Martine Watson Brownley, Rebecca Kalbfleisch, and Jennifer Thomas for their comments and suggestions. I am also grateful for the generous funding I received as a recipient of Social Sciences and Humanities Research Council of Canada Doctoral Fellowships and the American Association of University Women International Fellowship during various stages of this project.

1. For lack of an alternative, I use the term *(post)feminism* throughout this paper to refer simultaneously to feminism and postfeminism. I also use *(post)feminist* to refer to the self that is at once feminist and postfeminist. The awkwardness of these terms is, I think, appropriate.

2. With Kenneth Burke, I define an act as "rhetorical" if it involves "the use of words [or symbols] by human agents to form attitudes or to induce actions in other human agents [or the self]" (Burke, *A Rhetoric of Motives* [Berkeley and Los Angeles: University of California Press, 1969], 41). For New Rhetoricians like Burke and Chaim Perelman, the term *rhetoric* loses its pejorative sense as every symbolic act is a rhetorical act.

3. Audre Lorde, "The Master's Tools Will Never Dismantle the Master's House," in *Sister Outsider* (Freedom, Calif.: Crossing Press, 1984), 112.

4. I find myself echoing Judith Butler here: "To enter into the repetitive practices of this terrain of signification is not a choice, for the 'I' that might enter is always already inside: there is no possibility of agency or reality outside of the discursive practices that give the terms the intelligibility that they have. The task is not whether to repeat but how to repeat" (Butler, *Gender Trouble: Feminism and the Subversion of Identity* [New York: Routledge, 1990], 148). My notion of rhetorical performance, like Butler's notion of gender performance, neither reinscribes the autonomous humanist sub-

ject nor precludes the possibility of agency. For Butler's discussion of this point, see *Bodies That Matter* (New York: Routledge, 1993), x–xii, 1–22.

5. Christine Delphy, "Protofeminism and Antifeminism," in *French Feminist Thought: A Reader,* ed. Toril Moi (Cambridge: Basil Blackwell, 1987), 107.

6. Elizabeth Fox-Genovese, *Feminism without Illusions: A Critique of Individualism* (Chapel Hill: University of North Carolina Press, 1991), 153.

7. Tania Modleski, *Feminism without Women: Culture and Criticism in a "Post-feminist" Age* (New York: Routledge, 1991), 3.

8. Patricia Waugh, for example, insists in *Feminine Fictions: Revisiting the Postmodern* (New York: Routledge, 1989) that the postmodern deconstruction of identity directly undermines woman's necessary pursuit of subjectivity and her capacity for agency. Fox-Genovese emphasizes questions of history, arguing that postmodernism's "wholesale rejection of our history and traditions risks the substitution of dialectic for rhetoric and an attendant divorce from the most pressing problems of our time" (*Feminism without Illusions,* 203). Modleski claims that "the postmodern play with gender in which differences are elided can easily lead us back to our 'pregendered' past where there was only one universal subject — man" (*Feminism without Women,* 163).

9. Moi labels the first generation "liberal feminism" and the second generation "radical feminism" in *Sexual/Textual Politics: Feminist Literary Theory* (New York: Methuen, 1985), 12. In "Feminism, Postmodernism, and Style: Recent Feminist Criticism in the United States," she introduces the term *postfeminism* to refer to the third generation (in *Cultural Critique* 9 [1988], 5).

10. Julia Kristeva, "Women's Time," trans. Alice Jardine and Harry Blake, *Signs: Journal of Women in Culture and Society* 7:1 (1981): 33.

11. Plato, *Phaedo,* II.65c–67d, cited in Sara Ruddick, *Maternal Thinking: Toward a Politics of Peace* (New York: Ballantine Books, 1989), 188.

12. Hélène Cixous, "Castration or Decapitation?", trans. Annette Kuhn, *Signs* 7:1 (1981): 44.

13. Jane Gallop, *The Daughter's Seduction: Feminism and Psychoanalysis* (Ithaca, N.Y.: Cornell University Press, 1982), 93.

14. Moi, *Sexual/Textual Politics,* 13, her italics.

15. Toril Moi, "Feminism, Postmodernism, and Style," 6-7. In an interview published in 1990, Moi reasserts her clarification of (if not departure from) Kristeva: "There can be no question of taking up the stage three position in isolation from the two other ones. I think that Julia Kristeva herself in "Women's Time" is somewhat unclear on this point. In her text there is perhaps a tension between the claim on the one hand [that] these stages are always already informing each other, and on the other hand that the third position is preferable" (Moi, *Feminist Theory and Simone de Beauvoir* [Cambridge: Basil Blackwell, 1990], 101). As I explain in my discussion of Kristeva, I don't perceive the same tension. Kristeva seems to me to be quite decided.

16. Outside the academy and in a few contexts within it, these terms circulate in ways that would not allow for the generalization I make here. Following Kristeva and Moi, my use of the terms *liberal, radical,* and *post* privileges women's relationship to the Symbolic Order, a specifically literary and particularly poststructuralist preoccupation. In those contexts, liberal feminism can be defined as the pursuit of equality for women within the Symbolic Order; radical feminism as the rejection of the Symbolic Order on the grounds of some essential or constructed female difference; and postfeminism as the insistence that that Order produces the very premises of liberal and radical feminism.

17. Kristeva, "Women's Time," 209. The metaphysical/physical dichotomy that Kristeva invokes in this passage also deserves closer scrutiny. Although, as Butler has argued, Kristeva preserves a sense of the physical in her work on the maternal, the postfeminist would typically maintain that the physical does not exist. Without it, what can it mean to locate anything in "metaphysics"? For Butler's reading of Kristeva's essentialism, see *Gender Trouble*, 79–93.

18. In her introduction to *French Feminist Thought*, Moi further discounts the possibility of (post)feminist difference by advising her readers that a genuinely different third generation of feminism cannot truly exist because postpatriarchy does not exist: "The point to remember," she writes, "is that true post-feminism is impossible without post-patriarchy" (12).

19. Susan Rubin Suleiman, *Subversive Intent: Gender, Politics, and the Avant-Garde* (Cambridge: Harvard University Press, 1990), xvii.

20. Moi, *Sexual/Textual Politics*, 8.

21. Sandra Harding, *The Science Question in Feminism* (Ithaca, N.Y.: Cornell University Press, 1986), 247.

22. Christine Di Stefano makes the same observation, noting that Harding attempts to "have her cake and eat it too." As Di Stefano elaborates, Harding maintains that "the critical deconstructive insights of postmodernism can be explicitly, defensibly, and plausibly harnessed to a progressive and substantive feminist politics." Christine Di Stefano, "Dilemmas of Difference: Feminism, Modernity, and Postmodernism," in *Feminism/Postmodernism*, ed. Linda J. Nicholson (New York: Routledge, 1990), 77.

23. For a discussion of "presence," see Chaim Perelman and L. Olbrechts-Tyteca, *The New Rhetoric: A Treatise on Argumentation*, trans. John Wilkinson and Purcell Weaver (London: University of Notre Dame Press, 1969), 115–42; also see Chaim Perelman, *The Realm of Rhetoric*, trans. William Kluback (London: University of Notre Dame Press, 1982), 33–40.

24. Perelman, *The Realm of Rhetoric*, 36.

25. Kenneth Burke, *The Philosophy of Literary Form: Studies in Symbolic Action* (Berkeley and Los Angeles: University of California Press, 1973), 193.

26. Ibid., 202.

27. The scapegoat may also be located within the self. Distinguishing in the same binary terms between a false self and real self, the Feminist may attribute the former to her enemy's contamination and the latter to some authentic or liberated state.

28. The institutionalization of feminist literary criticism in the American academy, for example, which Gallop dates back to "around 1981," simultaneously relied on (and reinforced) the construction of a shared identity and sense of purpose: the feminist literary critic intent on doing feminist literary criticism. Academic women situated themselves as not nonfeminist, a distinction facilitated by locating the enemy outside feminism; and also as not unacademic, a distinction facilitated by locating the enemy within feminism but outside the academy, or within the academy but outside the legitimizing reach of poststructuralism. In doing so, literary academic women could do what they needed to do—namely, project a collective ethos and construct a relatively cohesive field of study. For a discussion of the institutionalization of feminist literary theory, see Jane Gallop, *Around 1981: Academic Feminist Literary Theory* (New York: Routledge, 1992).

29. Lorde, "The Master's Tools Will Never Dismantle the Master's House," 99.

30. Gallop, *The Daughter's Seduction*, xi.

31. Jane Tompkins, "Me and My Shadow," in *Gender and Theory: Dialogues on Feminist Criticism*, ed. Linda Kauffman (New York: Basil Blackwell, 1989), 122.

32. Gallop, *The Daughter's Seduction*, xii.

33. Butler, *Gender Trouble*, 93.

34. Tompkins, "Me and My Shadow," 136–37.

35. Jean-François Lyotard, *The Postmodern Condition: A Report on Knowledge*, trans. Geoff Bennington and Brian Massumi (Minneapolis: University of Minnesota Press, 1984), 79–81.

Feminist Misogyny; or, What Kind of a Woman Are You?

Theresa Ann Sears

Introduction

When I began to write this article, my mother was dying, although no one knew it. A working-class woman of Eastern European peasant stock, she had begun to die in her own mind much earlier, when she was in her forties. If she had remained in her mother's land, she probably would have died that young, since she gave birth only with great difficulty. Granted a reprieve by better medical care, my mother never found a use for the extra nearly forty years; once she had pushed her daughters out of the nest (and she did so resolutely and completely), she had complied with her duty and could find nothing else compelling to fill her time and mind. By the time I presented a version of these musings at the 1993 Modern Language Association convention, Christmas photographs of family gatherings show my mother for the last time among her children and grandchildren. The confusion that had been dimming her mind for some time shows in her eyes, as if the hectic holiday atmosphere generated by five children and their gifts caused her more fear than pleasure. In the last photograph taken of her, on Mother's Day in a nursing home, she confronts the intrusive camera with the gaze of a wild animal, trapped and bewildered by suffering. It is a painful picture, one that my sisters and I cannot bring ourselves to look at for long. My mother died soon after.

I preface my remarks with my mother's story because I believe it tells us something of the cost of social change for the individual. Transplants to new worlds — an Eastern European peasant to suburban America, her daughter to academe — remain in some sense incapable of assimilating the world they have joined. Their stories are always different, and they maintain a critical distance from that new world.

Institutional Feminism and a Woman's Life in Academe

"She's from an older generation of feminism," my would-be mentor explained to me. "She believes a woman never opposes another woman."

"That's stupid feminism," I replied, not believing, in my (now obvious) political innocence that anyone would actually make a case for such an illogical method of proceeding.

It is therefore not difficult to imagine my profound surprise, not only at the argument as it was presented to me in a Boston hotel room, but at the seriousness with which it is regarded in feminist criticism. Pronouncements such as "Professional sisters perceive the workplace as a place where women are at a disadvantage, and therefore they realize that women need to support each other"[1] abound, and many, if not most, imply that such support should be unconditional. Rare, indeed, in the feminist critical canon is the recognition at which Evelyn Fox Keller and Helene Moglen arrive: "Not only have feminists inherited a mythology of sisterhood that fits poorly into a world of scarce material and emotional resources, we have found that sisterhood itself—real or mythic—is often inappropriate to our circumstances."[2] Even in the extraordinarily clear-eyed analysis of the latter critics, who are willing to admit that "the doors to the ivory tower have swung open" (22) for women, many issues remain unexamined, obscured perhaps by the very "myth of sisterhood" that Keller and Moglen disavow.

Although feminism is gingerly beginning to confront the divisions within its own ranks, as the titles of such fairly recent books as *Competition: A Feminist Taboo?* (ed. Valerie Miner and Helen E. Longino, 1987), *Conflicts in Feminism* (ed. Marianne Hirsch and Evelyn Fox Keller, 1990),[3] and *The Secret between Us: Competition among Women* (Laura Tracy, 1991) indicate, the conditions under which feminists are willing to undertake such study often limit the scope of what they reveal. The two books that announce that their subject is competition, for example, leave out conflicts that do not involve head-to-head striving for what are frequently defined as scarce rewards. In this context, what Keller and Moglen call "the romance of woman's culture" (35) decrees that competition is an institutionally constructed evil[4] that women experience as a "dark, silent suffering room"[5] because it is foreign to their nature as women.[6] *Conflicts in Feminism* applies theory to a number of political divisions (radical/liberal, Anglo/women of color, feminist/postmodern, etc.) but betrays its underlying ideology in the implicit assumption that these differences are threatening aberrations, and that the ultimate goal is to bring all women together into a unified, supportive group. The viability or even desirability of such a plan is rarely questioned.

I would nevertheless contend that the premise of a unified womanhood begs to be questioned, and impetus for that process lies in the little dialogue with which I began: an older feminist declares a younger an "improper" woman, one whom the older "will not have" because of the younger woman's lack of solidarity. First of all, such a definition of fellow feeling ignores a vital distinction between principled opposition and professional or political competition. There is (or ought to be) such a thing as an honest judgment of an individual's performance in a given role. When the doctrine of universal support insists that we pass over individual qualifications and actions, it becomes psychologically naive, intellectually dishonest, and professionally unethical. Each of these charges must be dealt with in turn, as components of an academic institutional feminism that is neoromantic at its core, and that confuses the goals and methods of three strands of feminism: the personal, the political, and the intellectual. Personal feminism is emotional, even therapeutic, and serves to establish and reinforce a positive view of the self as woman. Political feminism is activist and ideological and strives to position women favorably within society and its powers. Intellectual feminism is analytical; it concerns itself with "reading" the representations of women in culture and its texts and artifacts. Furthermore, it is bound to deal honestly with the evidence that it discovers, no matter how personally disconcerting or politically unhelpful it may be. Attempting to formulate a philosophy that is at once therapeutic, ideological, and analytical ignores the inherent contradictions between the methods that each implies and blinds its believers to the limitations of the proposed mode of thought.

The psychological naïveté of the conflation of the modes of feminism implied in the doctrine of universal support of women reveals itself in most treatments of competition among women, which usually rely on personal anecdotes that detail the pain caused by such competition. The stories always have a protagonist who competed for some prize, often a professional position, and lost out unfairly. The heroines always act in good faith, apply rigorously honest, open, and trusting methods, and are always qualified. In these narratives, one never reads of a committee of well-meaning, competent professionals who, after careful consideration of all relevant documentation, conclude that a woman lacks the qualifications required. Nor do the anecdotes ever refer to a woman who receives a reward for political, as opposed to professional, reasons, or who manipulates the process, or who employs any of the other less than appropriate means that both men and women have used to achieve their goals. Instead, the women always fail because the system is flawed (no one should ever fail) and/or because competition itself is unjust (no one should have to be judged in comparison to anyone else).

This seems to be what María Cristina Lugones and Elizabeth V. Spelman mean when they argue: "One of the things wrong with competition is that it requires that there be fewer slots than people who need or desire to fill them; it requires that one's own success and well-being are impossible without someone else's failure and/or misery."[7] This assertion is problematic in several ways, all of which hinge on the verb *require*. The verb establishes competition as a self-creating effective force rather than the result of those very conditions here construed as competition's own creations. It implies that the number of university positions, let us say, is kept deliberately low so that many people will be unable to find one and so will be made miserable. The actual situation is precisely the reverse: there are far too many colleges and universities in the United States, and far too many producing graduate students with little hope of gainful employment in academe. Feminists would be little inclined to support sharp reductions in graduate programs, however, since many women would be excluded, and newer programs such as women's studies would no doubt suffer.

The intellectual dishonesty of the universally supportive argument is equally obvious, and it operates at several levels. At the most functional, unquestioning support of a woman because she is a woman renders meaningless the elaborate processes of evaluation and documentation that have evolved in academe in order to attempt to guarantee that candidates receive fair and equal consideration. At its most extreme, it may mean that the very procedures designed to reveal worth are used to conceal the fact that worthiness is being judged according to criteria other than competence. If the purpose of evaluating competence is to create a body (a department, college, or university, for example) that excels at teaching and scholarship, then supporting those who may not be competent "is inappropriate. Compassion is too passive, easy, disrespectful."[8] At yet another level, unconditional support, far from proving a woman's competence, announces her lack of it, for it suggests that she would not measure up if the usual standards of comparison were applied. In fact, it may mean that the woman can only compete as a victim, "burdened by need or suffering," where "her attempt to distinguish herself is in terms of degrees of suffering."[9]

At the institutional level, the charge of intellectual dishonesty is even more serious, especially when women are in positions of authority, as they more frequently are. Then it is only the most obvious irony of the situation that institutional feminists have acquired and maintained those positions at the very center of the academic profession by a consistent elaboration of the outsider's stance. There is thus a kind of slippage at the heart of institutional feminism, for having criticized the academic from the margins and for marginalizing, feminists now find themselves at the pinnacle of the same hierarchy. What is more, the "feminist sisterhood" in the academy is a perfect double, politically speaking, of the old boy network, when it is not simply part and parcel of it. Hierarchy and hegemony have not been eliminated; they have been renewed, albeit with their terms of value transposed. Hierarchy, it turns out, is not essentially patriarchal, although patriarchy is certainly hierarchical. One never hears of a feminist academic administrator who has abandoned her positioning title or refused the power to which it seems to entitle her, or the perquisites with which it rewards her.

More critically for feminist credibility with regards to ethics, decisions are made no more collectively or openly than under other regimes, and in many instances, the process may become even more closed, in order to avoid oversight. Substituting the "name-of-the-mother" for the "name-of-the-father," a feminist hierarchy for a masculine one, does not automatically result in a more just or moral institution. As Keller and Moglen rightly point out, "With the advent of conventional rewards (money, grants, publication, reputation, prestigious jobs) came the realization that collectivity may have had more to do with our status as outsiders than it did with feminism."[10] Reality bites, indeed, and bites with particular force when such feminism is confronted with women who do not subscribe to the doctrine of unquestioning support. To such women, the all-encompassing embrace is not offered.

Whereas the women who accept the idea are advanced regardless of incompetence, those who oppose it are rejected, and with particular virulence, regardless of competence.

Finally, universal support of any group as a group can be construed as professionally unethical, since it may mean that people with questionable skills are placed in classrooms and published, thereby undermining the purpose of an educational institution. Academe, in spite of recent arguments to the contrary, is not the same as the business world. It claims a higher purpose, as the forum in which both old knowledge is preserved and new knowledge produced, as well as (more crucially) the guarantor of the quality of the future in the form of the people who make up the student body. Academe announces, in other words, a more fundamental connection to the truth, however relative and contingent it may be. Universal support, in contrast, inevitably subverts that connection, for it posits an untenable link between group identification and individual competence.

Universal support of women qua women is ultimately a neoromantic, sentimental stance that lends itself to precisely the kind of oppression that grows out of a willingness to judge according to group, rather than individual, identity. To insist that "women...are at a real disadvantage in a workplace constructed to support and foster individual effort and competitive striving, since we value affiliation" overgeneralizes in an offensive way and rationalizes, even sentimentalizes, a regime of mediocrity.[11] Competition, after all, is the motor that drives improvement at all levels, from the individual to the corporate. I suspect that many women, especially younger women, would disagree with the assertion that "feminism is something to be lived,"[12] especially if it means that "to all, competition feels like loss. For all, competition with each other implies failure."[13] Many women rejoice in the full range of their individual talents, qualities, and achievements and do not wish to be once again, still, delimited by their sex and by what someone, male or female, believes is appropriate behavior for a proper woman.

Epilogue

My grandmother no doubt had an idea of what a proper woman was. I know my mother did, and I was not one. I read too much, became too educated, forged ahead in a difficult and incomprehensible profession, chose to remain childless, and moved too far away from home (odd, this last objection, in the daughter of an immigrant). From peasant swineherd to suburban housewife to college professor, we are joined by our sex but divided by experiences more fundamental and decisions more crucial than what can be encompassed by mere biology. I wear my mother's silver bracelet, but I have surrounded it with others that remind me of the places I have gone that have taken me far from her life. The same critical distance that sets me apart from mother, grandmother, and sisters and that makes it possible for me to choose to live in this new world makes it impossible for me to accept the values of institutional feminism. How could it be otherwise?

Notes

1. Laura Tracy, *The Secret between Us: Competition among Women* (Boston: Little, Brown, 1991), 173.

2. Evelyn Fox Keller and Helene Moglen, "Competition: A Problem for Academic Women," in *Competition: A Feminist Taboo?*, ed. Valerie Miner and Helen E. Longino (New York: Feminist Press at CUNY, 1987), 23.

3. Marianne Hirsch and Evelyn Fox Keller, eds., *Conflicts in Feminism* (New York: Routledge, 1990).

4. "Feminists frequently claim that academic resources are organized and distributed in ways that discourage cooperation and guarantee competition, and that competition among women in the academy is caused by institutional structures that are designed to foster it" (Keller and Moglen, "Competition," 35).

5. Helen E. Longino and Valerie Miner, "A Feminist Taboo?", in *Competition: A Feminist Taboo?*, 2.

6. Tracy, for example, claims that successful women "lose themselves" because "they've given up the female virtues of nurturance, compassion, and empathy" (*Secret,* 166).

7. María Cristina Lugones and Elizabeth V. Spelman, "Competition, Compassion, and Community: Models for a Feminist Ethos," in *Competition: A Feminist Taboo?*, 241.

8. Ibid., 246.

9. Ibid., 237.

10. Keller and Moglen, "Competition," 30.

11. Tracy, *Secret,* 142.

12. Lugones and Spelman, "Models," 234.

13. Tracy, *Secret,* 138.

Three Feminist Mother-Daughter Pairs in the Nineteenth- and Early-Twentieth-Century United States

Barbara A. White

Generational conflict has often taken the form of struggle between a feminist daughter and conventional mother, as in the case of Florence Nightingale, who defied her mother to become a nurse. Or sometimes the path of a feminist mother, like Charlotte Perkins Gilman, has been firmly rejected by her daughter. In this essay, however, I consider historical mother-daughter pairs in which both women identified themselves as feminists. The principal question is what kinds of generational tensions, if any, appear in the lives and writings of these feminist mothers and daughters?

I have looked at three mother-daughter pairs: Elizabeth Cady Stanton and Harriot Stanton Blatch, Lucy Stone and Alice Stone Blackwell, and Ida B. Wells-Barnett and Alfreda M. Duster.[1] Elizabeth Cady Stanton (1815–1902) was the major philosopher of the nineteenth-century women's movement; her daughter Harriot Stanton Blatch (1856–1940) introduced militant English methods to the U.S. suffrage cause. Lucy Stone (1818–1893), feminist orator and leader of the American Woman Suffrage Association, bequeathed to her daughter, Alice Stone Blackwell (1857–1950), the editorship of the movement paper, the *Woman's Journal*. Ida B. Wells-Barnett (1862–1931), the journalist who crusaded against lynching and founded suffrage clubs for African American women, was succeeded by her daughter, Alfreda M. Duster (1904–1983); Duster became a community activist in Chicago, frequently working with girls and through women's clubs.

With the exception of Stone, these women were also writers, and each engaged in some form of life writing. Stanton and Wells-Barnett wrote autobiographies, while Blackwell became her mother's biographer. Duster edited her mother's autobiography and outlined her own life in an oral history interview; Blatch edited her mother's writings and wrote an autobiography herself.

Although I have used all these sources, along with letters, diaries, and secondary works, it should be noted that the sources are not necessarily reliable. The autobiographical recollections come filtered through memory, and even the more immediate forms, like letters and diaries, may be shaped by cultural expectations of mother-daughter relations. In the nineteenth century these forms were also less "private" than now. For instance, the extended Blackwell family regularly passed letters from household to household, and Alice's adolescent diary was read by her mother, who sometimes blacked out comments she didn't like. Such editing was amply repaid by the younger generation. In the worst case Harriot Stanton Blatch tampered with her mother's letters and diary after her death and even revised her autobiography for reissue, deleting the chapter on the *Woman's Bible* and cutting references to Susan B. Anthony, whom Harriot resented.[2]

But even while maintaining a healthy suspicion of the sources, it is hard not to be struck by the common themes that emerge. Of course, there are numerous individual differences in the mother-daughter relationships and strong differences based on class and race,[3] but there are also striking similarities in the experiences of the three mothers, on the one hand, and the three daughters, on the other. The mothers' struggle to educate themselves and retain their identity in marriage, their idealization of motherhood at the same time they experienced doubled duties, led them to expect great things from the younger generations and be disappointed at their relative conservatism. Yet the mothers maintained very close, positive relationships with their own daughters. The daughters, far from rebelling against their mothers, identified with them so strongly that they carried on their work.

The Mothers

All the mothers wrote positively about their own mothers yet defined themselves in opposition to their mothers' fixed domestic roles. They struggled to educate themselves far beyond their mothers, Stanton insisting on reading the classics at her private schools, Stone becoming one of the first female graduates of Oberlin, and Wells-Barnett attending Shaw University in Mississippi, although she did not graduate because she had to support her younger siblings after her parents' death. The mothers of Stone and Wells-Barnett had barely been literate — Stone's mother was embarrassed to write a letter, and Wells-Barnett's, a former slave, learned to read the Bible after the Civil War. Interestingly, Stanton, Stone, and Wells-Barnett, however they surpassed their mothers academically, all felt their educations had not been good enough and would push their daughters beyond themselves: Blatch received a master's from Vassar, Blackwell attended top schools before graduating from Boston University, and Duster earned her bachelor's degree at the University of Chicago.

As the mothers prepared themselves for work beyond the domestic sphere, they hesitated to give up marriage and motherhood altogether. All were ambivalent about marriage, Stanton mildly (she broke her engagement several times), and Stone and Wells-Barnett more definitely so. Stone was pursued by Henry Blackwell for three years before she would agree to marry, and Wells-Barnett, before succumbing at age thirty-three, insisted on a year to devote solely to "the cause"; she says in her autobiography that unlike Susan B. Anthony, who criticized her (and the other two women) for marrying and having children, she could not get the support she needed to carry on alone.[4] But if they were ambivalent about marriage, all three women embraced motherhood with fervor. Stanton apologized to Anthony after every child but ended up with seven; Wells-Barnett made up for lost time with four quick children to add to her husband's two by a previous marriage; Stone had one child at age thirty-seven but adopted others and was called by a friend "a devoted, almost too self-sacrificing mother."[5]

All the mothers experienced what Anthony called a "divided duty" (quoted in Wells, 255). When Lucy Stone left her baby with a neighbor in order to lecture in New York, she couldn't sleep at night; the baby caught cold and Stone was chastised by her husband (who himself was seldom around during Alice's babyhood). Stanton excused herself to Anthony from attending a women's rights convention in Rochester with the following: "Yesterday one of the boys shot an arrow into my baby's eye. The eye is safe, but oh! my fright when I saw the blood come . . . and witnessed her suffering! What an escape! Imagine if I had been in Rochester when this happened!"[6] Wells-Barnett took her first baby with her on the road, employing nurses and claiming to be "the only woman in the U.S. who ever traveled throughout the country with a nursing baby to make political speeches" (Wells, 244). But with her second child she decided "it was hopeless to expect to carry on public work" (Wells, 249) and post-poned working full time outside the home until Alfreda was eight, the same age as Alice Stone Blackwell when Stone resumed her career. Elizabeth Cady Stanton did not start lecturing extensively until her children were grown and even when Harriot was sixteen felt called on to justify her trips, writing her daughters that she was "rousing women" and "making the path smoother for you...and all the other dear girls" (Griffith, 163).

At the same time that the mothers chafed against the restrictions of motherhood, they idealized it. Wells-Barnett moves straight from her "it was hopeless" comment to a glorification of motherhood as one of the greatest "professions." She confesses that her "mother instinct" (all three women believed in a maternal instinct) may have been smothered by her early responsibility for her siblings, but once she became a mother she "revelled" in this "glorious advantage" of being a woman (Wells, 251).[7] Stanton, who also saw motherhood as a profession (and no doubt influenced Wells-Barnett's formulation), connected motherhood with strength—"That function gives women such wisdom and power as no male ever can possess" (*Elizabeth*, 2:270). She presented herself as a kind of supermother, stressing the ease with which she bore children. The autobiography is full of maternal advice and anecdotes about her curing sick babies on trains; clearly Stanton made use of a maternal image to soften and legitimize her radical social philosophy. Lucy Stone cultivated the same image in a gentler mode. Her daughter Alice passed it on, describing her mother for posterity as "different as possible from the imaginary picture of an equal rights advocate, a round, rosy little woman, whose very aspect suggested a husband and a baby."[8]

The mothers tended to be especially romantic about the mother-daughter relationship, seeing their daughters and the cause as intertwined, as in Stanton's "making the path smoother" comment.[9] Stone could write Stanton sentimentally of their work for the "little girls," even after their estrangement and the split of the women's movement into two groups (Kerr, 146). By the time the girls had grown up, Stanton's most popular lecture was "Our Girls," an address to the next generation, and Harriot and Alice had become "suffrage daughters," a phenomenon much celebrated by the late nineteenth-century movement; in the early 1900s Harriot Stanton Blatch would even organize a mother-daughter event at Seneca Falls.

Passing their feminism on to their daughters seems to have been relatively easy for the mothers. In this regard Ida Wells-Barnett's explanation of her motive for staying home while her children were young may be relevant: "I fully agreed with the Catholic priest who declared that if he had the training of a child for the first seven years of its life, it would be a Catholic all the rest of its days" (Wells, 250). There were some minor rebellions—the Stanton children, for instance, resented *The History of Woman Suffrage,* the mammoth history Stanton and Anthony worked on for years, and Blackwell said she got tired as a child of hearing about the woman's movement. At age twelve, however, she came across an antisuffrage essay and found herself in a rage (Blackwell 1930, 271). By fifteen she was attending conventions and publishing in her parents' journal. Blatch as a young woman overcame her dislike of *The History of Woman Suffrage* enough to contribute to the second volume; after all, when she was only ten her mother had given her and her sister the manuscript of her 1848 Seneca Falls speech, inscribing it, "I give this manuscript to my precious daughters, in the hope that they will finish the work which I have begun."[10]

The mothers felt satisfied, by and large, that their daughters would finish the work; even Stanton's second daughter Margaret became a suffragist, if not a leader. The mothers had some criticisms of their offspring—Stone worried over Alice's lack of business sense, Stanton wanted Harriot to take a leadership role sooner than she did. But Stone made her daughter coeditor of the *Woman's Journal* as soon as she graduated from college, and Stanton felt that Harriot possessed the "true spirit of the reformer" (Griffith, 174). The only serious disappointment seems to have been Ida Wells-Barnett's, as expressed by her daughter in her oral history interview. Alfreda Duster says that when she was nineteen, "without my parents knowing it, I became interested in marrying Mr. Duster. My mother had wished that I'd go to law school. She had always wanted to be a lawyer. She had not been able to study law, so vicariously she wanted me to be a lawyer" (Wells, 6). But in marrying early and having children, Alfreda was fulfilling one part of Wells-Barnett's creed. When Alfreda was a child, her mother had organized a symposium on "What It Means to Be a Mother" because she felt that the joyful "experience I had gained as a mother should be passed on to the young women of our race who had the idea that they should not have children" (Wells, 282).

Wells-Barnett's symposium was not entirely successful, any more than her later attempts to dispense advice. Like Stone and Stanton, she wanted to be seen as a model for the younger generation, even addressing her autobiography to them. But that generation rejected her, as it did Stone and Stanton. One of the most striking similarities in the experiences of the three mothers is that all were in some sense repudiated by the very feminist organizations they had founded. Wells-Barnett discovered that not only was her antilynching crusade forgotten in the last two decades of her life, but also the National Association of Colored Women, which she had helped organize, excluded her from a convention and later dismissed her bid for president. Stone was not rejected in any direct way, but the desire of the younger women in the American Woman Suffrage Association to unite with the Stanton-Anthony branch in effect removed her from leadership because the united organization was certain to be run by the more powerful Anthony. Stone also felt at the end of her life that her role in founding the movement was being erased from history. Elizabeth Cady Stanton lived to see worse. Although she had been the first to demand the vote for women, and had been ridiculed for it, late nineteenth-century suffragists stopped reading her letters at conventions because they thought her too radical; the younger women of the combined National American Woman Suffrage Association (NAWSA) led the way in voting to disassociate the organization from Stanton's *Woman's Bible*. Stanton was furious at the "dainty ones," as she called the younger women, and loudly criticized their conservatism. "Our younger coadjutors," she wrote, "seem to be too satisfied with painting in the brightest colors the successes of the woman movement, while leaving in the background the long line of wrongs which we still deplore" (*Elizabeth*, 2:338).

In the situation where all the mothers feel betrayed by the younger generation in general but very positive toward their own particular daughters one might detect a bit of displacement — perhaps a reversal of the dynamics suggested by Madelon Sprengnether in her essay "Generational Differences." Sprengnether sees contemporary young feminists as projecting an image of "disappointing mother" onto their older feminist colleagues.[11] Perhaps the nineteenth-century mothers had to project "disappointing daughters" in order to maintain their romantic vision of mother-daughter relationships.

The Daughters

It was materially the case, however, that most of the younger generation in the women's organizations were far more conservative than
Blackwell, Blatch, and Duster. The actual daughters, in fact, practiced
the same brand of feminism as their mothers; although it could be
argued that they were more religious than their mothers,[12] they were
hardly more conservative. Blackwell became an equal rights feminist
like her mother and after suffrage supported liberal causes; Blatch
leaned to the radical and militant, attracted like her mother to socialism (after suffrage she joined the Socialist Party); Duster was a com-
munity-oriented feminist who followed her mother in combining work
with the men of her race with an awareness of gender (she lived to
see the second wave of U.S. feminism, which she heartily embraced).

The daughters not only followed their mothers ideologically but enjoyed strong positive relationships with them. Of course, there were some
conflicts—both Alice and Alfreda, for instance, found their discipline-
conscious mothers less fun than their fathers in childhood and chafed
at the amount of housework they had to do; Harriot's hostile remarks
about Susan B. Anthony seem to carry unacknowledged resentment
of her mother. But there is much more warmth expressed than resentment and hardly any major conflicts. The daughters' most serious difficulties were in dealing with their mothers' fame. Alice Stone Blackwell clearly felt jealous of her mother's position, of the ability to "have
big audiences rise up en mass [*sic*] and applaud greatly when you come
in, and to have women whom you don't know come and embrace
you with tears."[13] She was torn between feeling guilty at an inheritance she had not earned and exploiting that inheritance; her delightful adolescent diary makes coy references to "Posterity" as audience
(Blackwell 1990, 23, 132), and when she came to memorialize her
mother in a biography she had trouble keeping the focus on Stone
rather than herself.

Unlike Blackwell, Harriot Stanton Blatch faced a crisis of vocation
after she graduated from college. She had nothing so specific as a newspaper to take over, and her trip to Europe and quick marriage to an
Englishman separated her from her mother and allowed her to learn
English techniques from Emmeline Pankhurst and others. It is not
that there was personal distance, for mother and daughter continually made extended visits, but Blatch found it difficult to take a lead-

ership role in the United States until Stanton—and Anthony—died. Duster felt the effects of her mother's fame in another way. She saw that Wells-Barnett's work "caused a lot of ill feeling against her" (Duster, 61): "I've seen my mother shed tears after she'd come from some organization where she worked so hard to try to get change...and had met with just obstinate antagonism. All these things had an impact on my life. I was determined I would never have anything to do in public life, that I was going to marry and have six children and stay home" (Duster, 36). Duster's reaction is similar to that of many contemporary daughters of feminists. The majority of daughters interviewed in the early 1990s by Rose L. Glickman answered the question "Would you want your mother's life?" in the negative: "These daughters who so admire their mothers' achievements look on their mothers' lives as an unrelieved obstacle course." Almost all the daughters in Christina Looper Baker and Christina Baker Kline's recent *The Conversation Begins: Mothers and Daughters Talk about Living Feminism* think their feminist mothers work too hard.[14]

Ironically, although Duster at first glance seems to be the only daughter who did not take up her mother's public work, she ultimately did so. When she was forty, her husband died and she went to work full time for the Illinois Youth Commission, concentrating on community organization of youth and prevention of "juvenile delinquency." Her mother's first job after the children reached school age had also been as a social worker, and Wells-Barnett founded the Negro Fellowship League for black youth. The descriptions of Duster's career in reference books—civic leader, activist, social worker, youth worker, lecturer—apply just as well to her mother. Duster also had five children (she regretted that it wasn't six like her mother).

Blackwell and Blatch also duplicated the patterns of their mothers' lives with an almost uncanny exactness. Not only did they play similar roles in the movement and carry on their mothers' particular variety of feminism, but they also followed their mothers' preferences in the personal realm. Blatch married early, with her mother's strong encouragement, and had two children. Blackwell was oriented toward women from her early years and, although her father pushed her to flirt with men and attract a husband, her mother remained ambivalent about marriage and advised differently. According to the fifteen-year-old Alice, "Mamma told me all sorts of queer things about boys—how if you show them any attention they immediatly [*sic*] think you want to marry them and that they would like to marry you. How very inconvenient!" (Blackwell 1990, 178). The adult Blackwell lived for many years in a Boston marriage with her adolescent love, her aunt's adopted daughter.

When asked if she planned to write an autobiography, Duster said she intended "to pick up in 1931 when my mother passed...and to bring it up—because I continued the same line of things that she did—to bring it up from 1931 to the present" (Duster, 2). It is interesting to consider what "it" means—a joint life? Although Duster never wrote her autobiography, Blatch did, and one of its most salient characteristics is the extent to which it imitates Stanton's in structure and choice of content.[15] There are also verbal echoes throughout, from the title (*Challenging Years* versus *Eighty Years and More*) to the statement that she was "eager to finish the work my mother had begun" (Blatch, 92)—an unattributed and probably unconscious quotation from her mother's Seneca Falls speech inscription.

Each daughter had this sense of continuing her mother's work, and each took on the responsibility of preserving her role in history. Blackwell pressed Stone, who never kept diaries or wrote an autobiography, for reminiscences when she was still alive and later used them for a biography. Duster edited her mother's unfinished autobiography and struggled for forty years to get it published, finally succeeding before she died. Blatch, as noted earlier, revised for publication her mother's autobiography, diaries, and letters. This tampering was not a deliberately hostile act, however, but an attempt to establish her mother's preeminence in the history of the women's movement; the playing down of the *Woman's Bible* was to make her more palatable to religious feminists, and the excision of Susan B. Anthony removed a rival. Blatch and her brother Theodore, who coedited Stanton's papers, fumed at the omission of their mother's name from the Equal Rights Amendment (ERA), the so-called Susan B. Anthony Amendment.

The daughters identified so completely with their mothers and their mothers' versions of feminism as to perpetuate their mothers' quarrels. At the beginning of my research, I hypothesized that the daughters might have taken on a harmonizer role, attempting to soften their uncompromising mothers' rough edges and smooth antagonisms with their associates. I was influenced in this formulation by secondary sources and comments by Blackwell and Blatch crediting themselves with bringing about the union of the rival suffrage associations (Blackwell 1930, 229; Blatch, 62). Duster fit in because she clearly thought her mother's style too abrasive. But the evidence does not really support the harmonizer interpretation. Duster, for example, criticizes the Church Terrell family (Duster, 30), reviving her mother's quarrel with Mary Church Terrell, the women's club organizer she saw as a rival. Blackwell and Blatch, although they played a part in uniting the suffrage associations, did so reluctantly and solely for political reasons; as Stone noted in a letter to a friend, "Alice dreads these people even more than I do" (Stone, 255). When it came to portraying their mothers for history, the daughters insisted on their mothers' side of the story to the point of extreme bias. Blatch claims that subsequent events proved Stanton and Anthony correct in their dispute with Stone (*Elizabeth*, 2:124); Blackwell argues that Seneca Falls was just a "small local meeting," whereas the Worcester convention, organized by Stone two years later, was national and "really launched the women's rights cause" (Blackwell 1930, 99). Blatch took championship of the mother a step further when she tried to separate Stanton from Anthony. Perhaps she was acting on her mother's unexpressed feelings of hurt or hostility; after all, Susan B. mentored the younger women in NAWSA and it was her "suffrage nieces" who had repudiated Stanton.[16]

Conflict or Concord?

In general, I discovered greater closeness and less mother-daughter conflict in the feminist pairs I studied than I had initially expected to find. I originally asked the question "What kinds of generational conflict appear in the lives and writings of these feminist mothers and daughters?" It never occurred to me to say "conflict and concord," to expect so much of the positive. This finding accords with the conclusions of Linda W. Rosenzweig in her study of ordinary (nonfamous) middle-class mothers and daughters from 1880 to 1920.[17] Although the prescriptive literature suggests an emerging female generation gap in the late nineteenth and early twentieth centuries, Rosenzweig did not find evidence of that gap in women's life writings; instead, she found a preponderance of warm, supportive mother-daughter relationships. (Of course, Rosenzweig's sources are subject to the same limitations as mine, and she relies heavily on mother-daughter letters, which might be presumed to be less honest than diaries.)

The clearest generational conflict seems to have been between the mothers and the young women of their daughters' generation, whom the mothers saw as ungrateful and conservative, and the daughters and other women of the mothers' generation, whom the daughters saw as—what? Perhaps too radical or too feminist—it is also tempting to say "unmotherly" or not maternal enough, for I think it significant that Susan B. Anthony was single. Not only Blatch but also Blackwell and Duster attack Anthony in their memoirs. Blackwell calls her "tall, sharp, dictatorial, conceited, pugnacious & selfish" (Blackwell 1990, 216), while Duster deprecates her advice against marriage and motherhood and labels her focus on suffrage "naive."[18] Perhaps the criticism of Anthony is the daughters' version of the mothers' deflections and projections discussed earlier. Ironically, the daughters seem to have rejected anything but the most traditional mothering, which they received in full from their radical mothers. A feminist like Charlotte Perkins Gilman, who tried to reform the institution of motherhood, had difficult relations with her daughter and failed to bring her to feminism.

Two of the three daughters went on to be mothers of daughters themselves, and the granddaughters also tended to repeat the basic patterns of their mothers' lives. Harriot Stanton Blatch had a daughter, Nora, named after the Henrik Ibsen character, who was the first woman in the United States to graduate with a civil engineering degree and later became an architect and builder; she married twice and had two daughters. Nora's unpublished autobiography reveals some hostility toward her mother, mainly in what she does *not* say about her. In the midst of lavish praise of her father and grandmother, she represents her mother as the person who had another daughter when Nora was nine (this daughter died in childhood) and sent Nora away to boarding school. Nora Stanton Barney credits her grandmother, whom she called Queenmother, with making her a feminist: "Queenmother was my guide and philosopher and it was she who explained the facts of life to me and told me of the history of woman and her long subjection."[19] Nevertheless, Nora shared her mother's left-wing feminist philosophy and worked smoothly with her mother in the suffrage movement, becoming Harriot Stanton Blatch's chief assistant in the New York state campaign. After suffrage she chose the same variety of feminism as her mother, supporting the ERA and opposing protective legislation for working women.

Alfreda M. Duster had children early in life, as we have already seen, and took very seriously her role as mother. When she went to work after her husband's death, she supported all five children, four sons and a daughter, through graduate school. Duster received a twentieth-century honor unavailable to Ida Wells-Barnett and the other mothers — she was twice named Chicago's "Mother of the Year." I have little information about her daughter, Alfreda Duster Ferrell, but she became a well-educated professional, concentrating like her mother and grandmother on youth work. Duster, always aware of family patterns, notes approvingly in her oral history interview that her daughter pursued a career *but* "stayed home with her children the first seven years" (45).

Notes

1. I use the form of name that each woman herself preferred; after her marriage Wells-Barnett chose to use a hyphenated name.

2. Harriot and her brother Theodore claimed that Stanton revised the autobiography before her death, but the evidence indicates they made the changes themselves. For discussion of the revisions, see Elisabeth Griffith, *In Her Own Right: The Life of Elizabeth Cady Stanton* (New York: Oxford University Press, 1984), xvi. Subsequent references will be cited parenthetically in the text as Griffith. See also Ann D. Gordon's afterword to *Eighty Years and More: Reminiscences, 1815–1897* by Elizabeth Cady Stanton (Boston: Northeastern University Press, 1993), 480–83. By my count Harriot and Theodore reduced the discussion of Susan B. Anthony from about thirty pages to seven. As for Stanton's diary, the original is lost and her children's version is "highly suspect as a text" (Gordon, 483).

3. Racism created the conditions whereby Wells-Barnett, although about the same age as the Stone and Stanton daughters, lacked their privileges and became a pioneer more like Stone and Stanton themselves. Also, in her autobiography Wells-Barnett contrasts her own position with Susan B. Anthony's and notes that race and sex prejudice combined to deny her financial support for her work; thus she needed to marry and did not have Anthony's choice of remaining single. Class differences affected mother-daughter relationships, too. The greater distance between mother and daughter in the generations of the Stanton family, even when the relationship seems to have been basically positive, can probably be attributed to class; there is more talk about nurses and servants in the autobiographies of Stanton, Blatch, and her daughter Nora Stanton Barney than there is about parents; the mothers appear as highly admired, larger-than-life figures who were not as available as the daughters would have liked. On the other hand, Stone and Wells-Barnett came from poverty and rose, primarily through marriage, to the middle class; they had close relationships with their mothers, which they replicated with their daughters. Stone and Wells-Barnett never felt secure in "society," but Duster reported that when she first became a social worker it was difficult to "really empathize with people who had come from nothing" (Alfreda M. Duster, interview by Marcia Greenlee, 8 March 1973, Black Women Oral History Project, Arthur and Elizabeth Schlesinger Library, Radcliffe College). Quoted by permission of Reed Reference Publishing, New Providence, N.J. Subsequent references to this interview are cited parenthetically in the text as Duster.

4. Ida B. Wells, *Crusade for Justice: The Autobiography of Ida B. Wells*, ed. Alfreda M. Duster (Chicago: University of Chicago Press, 1970), 238, 255. Subsequent references are cited parenthetically in the text as Wells.

5. Lucy Stone and Antoinette Brown Blackwell, *Friends and Sisters: Letters between Lucy Stone and Antoinette Brown Blackwell, 1846–93*, ed. Carol Lasser and Marlene Deahl Merrill (Urbana: University of Illinois Press, 1987), 93. Subsequent references are cited parenthetically in the text as Stone.

6. *Elizabeth Cady Stanton: As Revealed in Her Letters, Diary and Reminiscences*, ed. Theodore Stanton and Harriot Stanton Blatch (New York: Harper & Brothers, 1922), 2:56. Subsequent references are cited parenthetically in the text as *Elizabeth*. Other nineteenth-century mothers experienced problems with "divided duty," including Lucy Stone's sister-in-law Antoinette Brown Blackwell (see Stone, 94) and her friend Abby Kelley Foster, the abolitionist lecturer. Foster had also experienced a similar ambivalence about marriage. For a discussion of the early nineteenth-century "motherhood script" that helped foster this ambivalence, see Nancy M. Theriot, *The Biosocial Construction of Femininity: Mothers and Daughters in Nineteenth-Century America* (Westport, Conn.: Greenwood Press, 1988), 45–47, 77–90; in Theriot's scheme, Stanton, Stone, and Wells-Barnett belong with the daughters who revised the script.

7. Wells-Barnett wrote her daughters that "I have had many troubles and much disappointment in life, but I felt that in you I had an abiding joy. I feel that whatever others may do, my girls are now and will be shining examples of noble true womanhood." Quoted in Emilie M. Townes, *Womanist Justice, Womanist Hope* (Atlanta: Scholars Press, 1993), 124.

8. Alice Stone Blackwell, *Lucy Stone: Pioneer of Woman's Rights* ([Boston]: Alice Stone Blackwell Committee, 1930), 258. Subsequent references are cited parenthetically in the text as Blackwell 1930.

9. Stanton and Stone continually use language in which child and cause are interchangeable. See especially *Elizabeth*, 1:275 and 2:329, and Andrea Moore Kerr, *Lucy Stone: Speaking Out for Equality* (New Brunswick, N.J.: Rutgers University Press, 1992), 128, 122, 167. Subsequent references are cited parenthetically in the text as Kerr.

10. *The Elizabeth Cady Stanton-Susan B. Anthony Reader*, ed. Ellen Carol DuBois (Boston: Northeastern University Press, 1992), 27. Subsequent references are cited parenthetically as *Reader*.

11. Madelon Sprengnether, "Generational Differences: Reliving Mother-Daughter Conflicts," in *Changing Subjects: The Making of Feminist Literary Criticism*, ed. Gayle Greene and Coppelia Kahn (London: Routledge, 1993), 205.

12. Blatch was less antireligious than her mother, probably out of policy. Duster relied on God and the church more than her mother, who seems to have approved religion principally as a source of morality and whose writings are notable for a nineteenth-century African American woman in their lack of religious allusion and imagery. Blackwell rejected her mother's "set spinning and let go" theory, attributing Stone's occasional depressions to her lack of religious belief—Alice Stone Blackwell, *Growing Up in Boston's Gilded Age: The Journal of Alice Stone Blackwell, 1872–1874*, ed. Marlene Deahl Merrill (New Haven, Conn.: Yale University Press, 1990), 103. Subsequent references are cited parenthetically in the text as Blackwell 1990.

13. Alice Stone Blackwell to Emily Blackwell, November 14, 1886, in Blackwell Family Papers, Arthur and Elizabeth Schlesinger Library, Radcliffe College.

14. Rose L. Glickman, *Daughters of Feminists* (New York: St. Martin's Press, 1993), 150; Christina Looper Baker and Christina Baker Kline, *The Conversation Begins: Mothers and Daughters Talk about Living Feminism* (New York: Bantam, 1996), 363.

15. Blatch begins, as her mother does, with an account of her reception as a female baby. She then relates her "first memory," where her father ordered her down from a tree and she asked him why he didn't require her younger brother to climb down also. Harriot Stanton Blatch and Alma Lutz, *Challenging Years: The Memoirs of Harriot Stanton Blatch* (New York: G. P. Putnam's Sons, 1940), 4. Subsequent references are cited parenthetically in the text as Blatch. Griffith takes this incident literally, concluding that Blatch had feminist tendencies even as a child (174). But the story serves the same function as Stanton's account of learning to ride horseback and read Greek — it simultaneously announces her equality with boys and documents the discrimination she faced. Blatch goes on to discuss the family servants, the gloominess of her hometown, and her childhood fears, just as Stanton did.

16. Stanton generally deflected these hurt feelings onto the younger women in the movement. For instance, when she had failed to raise the money to publish a collection of her speeches, she wrote a friend in 1900 that if the younger women "had ever treated me with the boundless generosity they have my friend Susan, I could have scattered my writings abundantly. They have given Susan thousands of dollars, jewels, laces, silks and satins, and me criticisms for my radical ideas" (*Reader*, 197).

17. Linda W. Rosenzweig, *The Anchor of My Life: Middle-Class American Mothers and Daughters, 1880–1920* (New York: New York University Press, 1993), 134.

18. Duster, 11–12. It is probably also significant that Anthony was oriented toward women in her personal relationships. Although one of the disparaging daughters, Blackwell, was also lesbian (to use today's term), she made her criticism at age fifteen, when her father was pushing a script of compulsory heterosexuality.

19. Ellen Carol DuBois, "Spanning Two Centuries: The Autobiography of Nora Stanton Barney," *History Workshop Journal* 22 (Fall 1986): 145.

Fissuring Time, Suturing Space: Reading Bharati Mukherjee's *The Holder of the World*

Gita Rajan

For at least the past century, time and history have occupied a privileged position in the practical and theoretical consciousness of Western Marxism and critical social science. Understanding how history is made has been the primary source of emancipatory insight and practical political consciousness, the great variable container for a critical interpretation of social life and practice. Today, however, it must be space more than time that hides the consequences from us, the "making of geography" more than "the making of history" that provides the most revealing tactical and theoretical world. This is the insistent premise and promise of postmodern geographies.

EDWARD SOJA, *Postmodern Geographies*

Space was treated as the dead, the fixed, the undialectical, the immobile. Time, on the contrary, was richness, fecundity, life, dialectic. MICHEL FOUCAULT, "Of Other Spaces"

Just as the phenomenon of orientalism does not disappear simply because some of us have now attained a critical awareness of it, similarly, a certain version of "Europe," reified and celebrated in the phenomenal world of everyday relationships of power as the scene of the birth of the modern, continues to dominate the discourse of history. Analysis does not make it go away.

DIPESH CHAKRABARTY, "Postcoloniality and the Artifice of History: Who Speaks for Indian Pasts?"

Preamble

Writing for an anthology that self-consciously examines the alteration in focus from the first wave of feminist ideology and the burgeoning role of women in culture to the multitudinously splintered oeuvre of feminism(s) that incorporates the authority and enunciation of feminine subjectivity is exciting from a historical and theoretical perspective. Further, to query the evolving problematics of race and gender through the metaphor of generations reiterates the unfolding intellectual and methodological paradigm shifts of female/feminine identity in narrativity. In other words, tracing the imprint of critical and creative work of feminist scholars over the past one hundred years or so allows us to glimpse the historiography of female/feminine identity in the realm of culture.

The first step, then, in my essay is to try interlocking feminisms and generations. Loosely defined (and at the risk of oversimplifying), first-wave feminism, launched in the early part of this century, focused the spotlight on women's fundamental rights to equality in social spheres. This, in turn, came on the heels of the suffrage movements, both in Britain and the United States. Generations here can be envisaged as a spatial metaphor that signaled a cultural moment of solidarity between mothers and daughters, without specifically invoking these terms in their present critical sense. The space between older and younger women was spanned by ties of fraternity. This kind of subject position, occasioned to women within a slowly enlarging public space, allowed the second wave of feminist consciousness to develop from the 1960s onward. Here, generations can be understood as gesturing away from space to time because there was a certain demanding immediacy in presenting solutions and making resolutions. Younger women focused their attention on issues of particularized sexuality and personalized politics rather than on broad social discrepancies. Resistance was more radically politicized; it was coded, analyzed, and contextualized in dyadic vocabularies of new versus old and now versus then. These vocabularies were structural, synchronic, and emerged from diverse disciplines, which ranged from literary criticism to medicine and law, and from various classes in society as activist programs. The work and worth of these feminists built on the advances of women who came a generation before them, giving generations itself a temporal edge. In the third wave, which is what we are seeing now (and again, at the risk of oversimplifying), feminists are grappling with ways to articulate explanations for sociocultural interactions in a changing world order, where issues of ethics and technology have a global significance vis-à-vis the everyday business of life and are commingled with the problematics of race, sexuality, and gender. At this stage, generations signal the legacies of intellectual ancestry that traverse both temporal and spatial lines. In other words, now the pioneering work of feminists from earlier generations becomes the complex bedrock on which our work is based, which means that we operate from both the intricate gains and losses of past policies and experiences. Now, generations suggest a spatial dimension even as we speak from a temporal one.

It is in this frame that Bharati Mukherjee's *The Holder of the World* poses an interesting challenge because it lays bare that moment when feminist scholarship began to shift from the second to the third wave.[1] Mukherjee's readers today are familiar with foundational premises in feminist debates that center on voice for the female subject in culture, her essentialized, constructed identity in society, and a speaking subject position in any dialogue. These three quick markers call to mind a trajectory that numerous feminist scholars have traversed in charting identity politics and in discussing gender and race relations in cultural landscapes. Whatever nomenclature we choose at the end of the twentieth century, we concur that female/feminine voice (which shapes identity) must be given the option to speak against and be resistant to colonization in racial and/or gendered contexts. In short, questions of identity politics are now inherent in reading narratives.

In this essay, I examine Hannah, the central character in Mukherjee's novel, and explore her loss of voice/agency, the erasure of her female subjectivity (and of feminine sexuality), and the lack of her sovereign identity. By analyzing the heroine's voicelessness and lack of identity, I will show that Mukherjee is able to uncover her heroine's body by entombing her agency. Taking my cue from Mukherjee, I use history (time) and place (space) as my analytical tropes and begin by addressing postmodernity, the very subtext that she herself toys with. Appropriately enough, postmodernity focuses upon the fault line of time/space so that disorienting reality becomes the logical way to make meaning in a text. A precondition for postmodernity in the novel is the passing of time—from modernity to the next phase (whatever that may be) or from our reality into cyberspace (however we conceive of these spaces). Her novel examines the colony (America) as a *postcolony* (the United States) by foregrounding the fact that Hannah (and Mukherjee) can be grasped in purely generational terms: telling Hannah's story through the genealogy of the narrator so that colonial history guarantees the viscerality of the postmodern narrator. Mukherjee glosses over the play in the actual space of the colony (mapped through geography) and the relationships spanning that space (fraternal ties of women) by spotlighting, quite sharply, the temporal angle in her novel.

My defining impulse in foregrounding place as space/geography over time/history is, on the one hand, to extend the boundaries of postcolonial debates, which have consistently excavated the narratives of history to explicate exploitation, and, on the other hand, to show the radical possibilities of utilizing space to reimagine subjectivity, specifically, of the disenfranchised. I suggest that Mukherjee's novel, both in terms of its publication date (1993) and theme and content, should have reflected the generational shift in postcolonial fiction and moved the genre forward to provide a deferred reading of space, a different logic for feminisms, and a differing sensibility to the postmodern text.[2] In other words, Mukherjee is still anchored in that mind-set of second-generation feminist authors who addressed the diasporic/exilic experiences of women of color and implants in the minds of her readers the figure of the valiant yet pathetic heroine. Mukherjee has not been able to move past the history of colonization to articulate contemporary metaphors of surreal borders and global locations that show the pioneering work of postcolonial scholars/critics who are beginning to tease out the implications of *emplacing a body* and the theoretical shift from time to space. Further, Mukherjee misses the opportunity to capitalize on her opportune arrival at this moment in postcolonial studies and grasp the critical importance of remapping colonial memories by seizing transnational spaces.

The genre of contextualizing an imaginative break (a spacing out, if you will) within the discourse of history has a history (if you will): it has been done with exciting and radical results by Fanny Penny in *Diamonds* (1922), by Gita Mehta in *Raj* (1989), by Simon Schama in *Dead Certainties: Unwarranted Speculations* (1991), by Maryse Condé in *I, Tituba, Black Witch of Salem* (1992), by Carol Hill in *Henry James' Midnight Song* (1993), and others.[3] These writers move in an overtly fictional realm to problematize the subject (race and/or gender and nationality) to reveal the inextricable coupling of these terms with the history of colonization. For example, Schama creates a story around Benjamin West, who painted General Thomas Wolfe at his hour of death in Quebec in the battle between France and Britain (painting exhibited at the Royal Academy, 1771). In Schama's scheme,

West's genius lies in spatializing a moment in the formation of the American nation. He is able to *intervene in that space* in American history that sutures the battleground to nascent American nationalism. He incorporates the Native American iconographically as a noble savage but an essential citizen of the New World. Schama designs an identity for West and blazons it onto his disenfranchised entourage. Similarly, Gita Mehta's Princess Jaya *enters into that space* of preindependence India and consolidates a strong, feminist identity for herself as a courteous yet insurgent wife, as an obligatory colonial subject yet radically political strategist. This is another instance of an author creating a speaking subject position for the disenfranchised. And Condé *invades the impenetrable space* of white, colonial, Puritan America to fashion a black slave (witch) who explodes every stereotype of race, gender, and power. It is therefore regrettable that Mukherjee's work (chronologically, one of the latest examples in this kind of experimentation) has a narrator who swings from one extreme of postmodern cyberspace into the other extreme of nineteenth-century stereotypical orientalism with no ingenious outcome.

The Holder of the World reveals, at least partially, the logic of a writer who cannot move easily between sites. Mukherjee categorically rejects the Indian prefix to her name while emphasizing the American. Just as the author overlooks her nation/color in her stated preference (and rigidity) of citizenship, the narrator of the novel ignores racial specificities in the work. The tone of the first few pages signals the coming of a new cultural epoch, a new generation of writers, but her constructions of Hannah's racialized body are clichéd. Published as recently as 1993 (and reviewed quite favorably by leading critic Henry Louis Gates Jr.), the novel becomes part of an emerging canon of multicultural literatures of the United States by speaking of the "colony" (both America and India) as a textual reality. As mentioned earlier, this work is also eminently marketable because Mukherjee's colonies are worlded and exhibited with a certain polished aestheticism practiced in her earlier novel *Jasmine,* which was clearly well received in academia. Consequently, she has elided criticism of Hannah by presenting a charming, illusory world where a woman tells a woman's story. Herein lies the double bind—the narrator very carefully merchandises (the heroine) Hannah, so that the retrograde presentation of race and gender either gets erased or submerged in the excessively exoticized details supplied by the (female) narrator. For instance, Hannah's body is dematerialized in the theatricalizations of time travel, is fragmented and stored in the cultured halls of museums as "oriental" memorabilia, which can only be reconstructed by the enlightened, twentieth-century narrator through "information retrieval" (91).[4] The narrator deftly grafts America and India, as former colonies, onto Britain by making the sutures of history and geography run seamlessly over Hannah's body.

The narrator's yarn stretches from the historical spaces of America and India to the fictional spaces of high-tech computer modems and the supercharged stratosphere of intellectual elitism at the Massachusetts Institute of Technology laboratories. Yet for all this elaborately plotted novelty, the story is a familiar one. Mukherjee fabricates a narrator who tells us about a fictional/historical character called Hannah Easton born in the New World to a poor, Puritan family. The narrator begins Hannah's story in seventeenth-century Salem, tracks her to England, then to India, and back to Salem again. She reveals her encounters with outlandish Nipmuc Indians, obsessive New England Puritans, ruthless British buccaneers, freakish East India Company potentates, and exotic Indian rajas and Mughal emperors. The adjectives used here to describe the stereotypical characters form the sum total experience of the novel. If Madras is the locus of East India, then Salem is the (misnamed) site of West India within Britain's (and the narrator's) firm embrace. One factor in the narrator's tight grip on Hannah's body and her destiny is that Hannah has no originary privilege, that is, Hannah's father died of a bee sting in the outhouse on their farm and her mother was abducted by Nipmuc Indians. Thus, the novel places Hannah awkwardly—she is entangled within the discourse of history and buoyed on the borders of two cultures and, according to the narrator, can only be grasped by following a strict timeline of events.

But the narrator structures such a glimpsing and grasping of Hannah by inviting us into the text with a rare, postmodern tone. Mukherjee banks on the reader's understanding of the postmodern text as its ability to jar us loose from our moorings in narrativity, elude textual control, and rejoice in fragmentation by invoking a multiplicity that is limitless. This is but one understanding of postmodernity, and the first few pages of Mukherjee's *The Holder of the World* promise just this. The narrator focuses on fragments, space (locus) and time (narrative), and sudden destabilizations to pull the reader into the novel:

> I live in three times zones simultaneously, and I don't mean Eastern, Central and Pacific. I mean the past, present and the future.
> The television news is on, Venn's at his lab, and I'm reading *Auctions and Acquisitions*. . . . People and their property often get separated. . . . Nothing is ever lost, but continents [space] and centuries [time] get in the way. . . .
> Anything having to do with Mughal India gets my attention. Anything about the Salem Bibi, Precious-as-Pearl, feeds me.
> Eventually, Venn says, he'll be able to write a program to help me, but the technology is still a little crude. . . . He animates information. He's out there beyond virtual reality, re-creating the universe, one nanosecond, one minute at a time. He comes from India. (5)

The immediacy of time as an experiential reality fused randomly to the narrator, the Salem Bibi, and Venn (the narrator's lover) in the span of one paragraph grips our attention. Further, the speed of confronting differently dense media such as print (past), television (present), and virtual reality (future), again in that short paragraph, promises a postmodern frame to the novel.[5] Similarly, the last page leaves us gasping in colonial Salem, with a sense of nostalgia of having moved too quickly through the imaginative possibilities laid out in the initial pages:

> Joseph Hathorn, a boy of ten . . . son of the witchcraft judge, John Hathorn, was only nine years old when Pearl returned. . . . He went out to sea, driven from the taint of Salem, drawn by the stories of the China and India trade that White Pearl related as she sewed [duplicating Hannah's sojourn]. His great-grandson, Nathaniel Hawthorne, was born in Salem in 1804. (285)

Hannah's actual lived-in spaces and the narrator's socially inhabited sites (Boston, Salem, London, Madras) and their jaunt through history begin to fascinate the reader, who now embarks on this journey with them—part real and part simulated—to track Hannah, the Salem Bibi, through her own *Memoirs* and the records of history. The subtle detail that *Memoirs* (a legacy of memories) is often a reinscription and not merely recording of events gets glossed over. Instead, the narrator confides in the reader that this journey is mysterious and mystifying because even though she focuses on "Hannah through the lens of history," it is

> (a love song to [Venn], his "inputting" and virtual reality, his own uncommunicable Indian childhood, the parts of him that I cannot reach and the parts of me that he is afraid to ask about) . . . [it] is like

watching the birth of a nebula through the Hubble Space Telescope—
a chance encounter that ties up a thousand loose ends, that confirms
theories, upsets them. (59–60)

Here it is again, past, present and future, with the narrator hinting at
impossible experiences along the way. But gestures to the chimera-like
quality of time (as past/present/future) in this intergalactic, intercultural
journey quickly become facile components to make us jump through
the hoops of history.

More important, the reader's reliance on a knowledge of history
(even though it is selectively revealed by the narrator) as it interlocks
with power (the facticity of colonialization) begins to unfold as the
narrator continues to speak and fuse two epistemological units: America and India. These lands are colonies with their cultural particular-
ities, have genealogies (people in history), span terrain (space in geography), disclose a record of their haphazard smelting of races and
peoples—all of which in turn reveal the authority of the colonizer
(or the powerful narrator) writ large on the servile colonized (or the
fictional character). The intricate details of history mentioned here help
Mukherjee to dovetail these two epistemological systems and suture
them tightly with a grand, totalizing or universalizing scheme. The
overall effect of such evenly laid out polar systems (empire/colony or
powerful/powerless and narrator/character) anchors meaning in *The
Holder of the World* in an unyielding structural sense and stops it from
really being fragmentarily postmodern. What begins as a promise in
the first few pages of the novel as a postmodern project—challenging the sovereign or centered self by splintering narration and slash-
ing time, with a potential of moving into surreal, unimagined spaces—
is aborted in the systematic emplotting and emplacing of Hannah's
body within the narrator's vision of history. The story can only be
told when the narrator exhibits Hannah's body at every moment on
the tyrannical timeline of history. Mukherjee's heroine is forced to
face crisis after crisis and becomes progressively more *alienated* from
culture and society with no recourse. Within literary history such alienation is clearly indicative of modernity and not postmodernity. And,
within feminist literary history, this mode of objectifying the heroine
was challenged by the first generation of authors almost a century
ago. So one wonders why Mukherjee resorts to this retrograde treatment of gender and race within her latest novel.

Similarly, the end of the novel moves quickly from India to Salem, from Mukherjee's Hannah, the "Precious-as-Pearl," to Hawthorne's "Pearl" with a synchronized systematicity that does not take into account the liberatory possibility of playing with geography as a technique of re-presenting events. In *Subjects without Selves*, Gabriele Schwab discusses Michel Foucault's concept of the "end of representation," which requires more than a "mirroring" of "current epistemological configuration ... [so that] new literary forms actively take part in shaping a new episteme."[6] In narrative terms, the political capacity of the postmodern text works as a crucial heuristic device by allowing voice and identity to serve as the fertile ground for experimentation in the future of a subject. This anticipated, imagined dimension could have carried the story that our narrator began to tell with connotations of cyberspace to a new, exciting level, that is, to the next generation of postcolonial authors.[7] It would also have allowed Mukherjee to acknowledge the politics of race by shifting from a generalized, universal feminism to a particularized or culture-specific feminism. In other words, she could have shown Hannah's trajectory as the female subject moving from the first world to the (so-called) third world, moving between official or state history to enacting agency through subaltern womanhood.[8] This suggests but one direction in postcolonial and/or postmodern feminist scholarship, while other possibilities in the space-postmodernity paradigm remain to be explored.

Mukherjee, however, has another project in mind. Her narrator renders Hannah voiceless and identityless so that she herself can be the disembodying speaker. Hannah is placed in events and sites without her permission, and more importantly, the reader never escapes this overriding signifying power of the narrator's version of official history. John Berger's discussion in *The Look of Things* is important here. He says that contemporary works no "longer ... tell a straight story sequentially unfolding in time" because they have to "take into account the *simultaneity and extension of the events and possibilities. ... Prophesy now involves a geographical rather than historical projection; it is space not time that hides consequences from us.*"[9] Edward Soja also proposes space/geography as an epistemological model and says that using history as the only differential in the analysis of contemporary culture "induc[es] a myopia that sees only superficial materiality, concertized forms susceptible to little else but measurement and phenomenal description; fixed, dead, and undialectical: the Cartesian cartography of spatial science."[10] Therefore, within this context of methodological and theoretical debates in contemporary criticism, and in the tradition in which Mukherjee sets her novel, I raise the issue of the postmodern. As mentioned above, these theoretical debates have also been played out in the realm of fiction by Mehta, Condé, and Schama, for example, who allow their characters, Princess Jaya, Tituba, and Benjamin West, respectively, to delve into the very fissures of history, play in that unimaginable space of author-event-fiction, and produce texts that are pleasurably insurgent.

Regulating Hannah's Voice

Soja's comment that " 'life-stories' have a geography too . . . [with] provocative emplacements which affect thought and action" can be used to formulate a space/generations analysis of Hannah's lack of voice.[11] Even though the novel is Hannah's life story, the reader learns of Hannah's feelings, her emotions, her fears, and her anxieties from the narrator. We do not have a voice to match the carefully drawn character. Hannah is introduced as an object to be prized:

> The pendant is of spinel ruby, unpolished and uncut, etched with names in an arabized script. A fanciful translation of the names is squeezed underneath:
> *Jehangir, The World-Seizer*
> *Shah Jahan, The World-Ruler*
> *Aurengazeb, The World-Taker*
> *Precious-as-Pearl, The World-Healer.* (9; original emphasis)

And the leap from prized gem to prized figure is made a few pages later: "The tea-chest wood is nearly antique in itself, except for the Magic Markered notation: 'Salem Bibi's Stuffs.' The Salem Bibi — meaning the 'white wife from Salem' — Precious-as-Pearl! I have come to this obscure, user-hostile museum to track her down" (13). So intent is the narrator on her "find" that she remains oblivious to the domination in her own voice, which in turn silences Hannah's. Generations of feminists have consistently criticized such a strategy, and it is ironic that a so-called feminist narrator would resort to this technique. The narrator moves on, exclaiming over a set of Mughal miniature paintings also found in the "tea-chest":

> There is surely one moment in every life when hope surprises us like grace, and when love, or at least its promise, landscapes the jungle into Eden. The paintings, five in all, are small. . . . The corners are browned

by seawater or monsoon stains. . . . Here the Salem Bibi, a yellow
haired woman in diaphanous skirt and veil, posed on a stone parapet
instructing a parrot to sing, fulfills her visions in the lost, potent
language of miniature painting. She is always recognizable for the
necklace of bone. Later when the Indian imagination took her over, the
bone became skulls. (15)

The narrator reveals one detail after another in an attempt to paint
Hannah on a timeline whose "visions" and "language" are forever
lost. More pertinent than embellishing Hannah as the sensuous "Salem
Bibi" and priceless "Precious-as-Pearl" is the subtext of imminent danger in the passage.[12] The "skulls" evoke a femme fatale image (not to
mention collapsing the misnamed Indian with the figure of the "original" Indian) that Hannah wears like an obvious mark. Readers can
now recall Hawthorne's mark of a scarlet letter on Hester Prynne's
chest, which mirrors the bone/skull on Hannah's white bosom. The
narrator explicitly forges this link: "Rebecca was initiating her daughter into a whispered, subversive alphabet. '*A* is for Act my daughter.' . . . 'And *I*,' thought Hester [Manning], remembering the women
who wore it emblazoned on their sleeves, 'is for Indian lover.' . . . '*I* is
for Independence,' said Hannah" (54). Again, Hannah becomes the
chronometer to connect historical time in India (with Mughal emperor,
Aurengazeb) to literary time in America (with Hawthorne) with no
latitude to move anywhere but along the marked-out route. Even at
the level of a single literary allusion, this carefully constructed novel
holds rigidly to history, with no possibility in the gap of events between continents and cultures and no anomalies in signifying registers. One could perhaps argue that the above example is a clear instance of Hannah's voice or insurgence, but the narrator intervenes
by locking her, in the same passage, into a "to be feared" neurotic
stereotype with the remark, "Hannah babble[d] deliriously" (54).

Such narratorial control is further legitimized by recording that Hannah was "hysterical," which lost her a suitor.[13] The notation of hysterical—as uncontrollable excess—marks something problematic in
the connections between generations and feminism. In contemporary
critical terms, Mukherjee elides discourses of sexuality (or even race)
by resorting to a time in official history where it was *natural for women
to be incapable of articulating agency or desire and be cast off as hysterical.* The narrator presents the reader with a letter from the "Pyn-
chons . . . New England's upstanding families" (56). The letter is re-

printed in the novel, the narrator writes, from an anthology called "Puritans Come A-Courting: Romantic Love in an Age of Severity" (56), which, she herself acknowledges, reveals the class-gender divide: "Evidence of social mobility in Puritan New England; [and one that] feminists" found offensive because of its "implied sexism" (57). Again, the narrator weights our reading of this historical document by adding the adjective *implied* to qualify *sexism,* as if to maintain the veracity of official history with an empirical/objective method while denying the authenticity of the female subject. Class inequality is a sociohistorical fact, but gender is another matter, the narrator suggests. In keeping with this critique, the narrator recounts next that Mr. Fitch, Hannah's adoptive father, declines Mr. Pynchon's offer because Hannah is the "Bride" of the "Angel of Death" who marks her "through the Disruption of the Humors, Infections of the very Soul" (58). She is stereotyped as a hysteric; consequently, her actions and moods are indecipherable. Hannah is without language to articulate her wayward thoughts, both in her century and in ours.[14] The spatial dimension of such narratorial control remains veiled because Hannah's actions are recorded in time. For instance, when she arrives in India, ten years after this event, Cephus Prynn, the Madras factor, felt that "curbing of her spirit would require diligence and planning" (107) because she strayed from the mold. Such a regulative function that was performed by the Fitches in New England is carried on in India by the demented factor and maintained by the narrator with deliberate regularity. Experiences and actions in the *space* of one colony move seamlessly to another colony encased in Hannah's hysteric body because the narrator both states and implies that "it is a question of time not motive" (70). She notes one more detail from the *Memoirs* that supposedly chronicled Hannah's life:

> Hannah shrieked, though she didn't know until she heard it herself. This is an incident chronicled in the *Memoirs.* The hand raised. The face twisted tight in anticipation of pain. The woman's tormented shriek. She is witnessing an unnatural vanishing of justice, an unspeakable new face of violence. (116)

The "unspeakable new face of violence" is not extrapolated in spatial reality to match the temporal dimension of colonization. So neither Hannah nor her *Memoirs* has any words to describe the horror of her husband's brutal treatment of the Indian worker on the Madras beach. Only the inarticulatable overpowering "shriek" remains as evidence of the (quasi-)historical notation of her initiation into colonial life. The terror of the lived-in space of wife-husband relations or female sexuality is erased. Similar to her entrance, her exit from Imperial "White Town" (Madras) is marked by a memory of "hysterical faces" (216). " 'Bhagmati' " she screams. 'You the Lucky One! Make me lucky!' " (216). Even though we hear Hannah, it is at a moment when she completely abnegates her subjectivity, her agency, and her authority over her very destiny. The shriek is the only testimony of Hannah's being. Mukherjee would perhaps object and claim that Hannah does indeed chronicle her life in Madras in her letters to America. But it is the mindless reporting of daily events, not any sentiment of anticipation of the days to come—neither sorrow nor joy. Thus, the writing is vacant and holds no sense of self. She exists as a *firangi* (a pejorative term for whites in India), a blank to be scripted on (187). Her *time* in India is related as evidence of the trail of a "Precious" gem that the narrator wishes to track down, but her *place* in that land is made to seem inconsequential. Hannah's presence (essentialized)—not her voice or agency—is essential to the story line. In generational/feminist terms the question of race or identity politics is never asked.

In the last section of the novel the narrator recounts Hannah's encounters with Raja Jadav Singh, wherein the reader sees India splintered by the Hindu-Muslim divide:

> English attitudes saw Islam as a shallow kind of sophistication;
> Hinduism a profound form of primitivism. Muslims might be cruel,
> but true obscenity attached itself to Hindus, whose superstitions and
> wanton disregard for their own kind—burning young widows,
> denying humanity to those they called untouchable—excited
> contempt. Muslims had restrictions which were noble and manly;
> Hindus had taboos, which were superstitious and cowardly. (219)

The style is delightfully seductive, the contrasts between Hindu and Muslim so hypnotically rhythmic, and the focus so systematic that the reader does not immediately recognize that these are Hannah's disembodied sentiments made audible by the narrator's voice. We are reminded of that when "Venn bristles at Hannah's misconception of Hinduism" (219). We too "bristle," but for a far more profound reason. This could have been a place in the novel for Hannah to be more like Mehta's Jaya or Condé's Tituba or Schama's West and to subvert colonization. Instead, the passage echoes the master narrative of Imperial history. This mode of stereotyping Hindu and Muslim peoples was actually a colonizing device in India; the old English adage—divide and conquer—was a political ploy that ultimately resulted in splintering India into India and Pakistan in 1947. This historical trivia aside, the passage narratively parrots India's first Governor General Warren Hastings's orientalist philosophies and Lord Macaulay's oft-cited "Minutes on Indian Education," which provided one set of materials for Britain's legislated domination over India. Mukherjee, in her re-creation of the first moments of Imperial aggression, could have given Hannah the voice to resist domination as Condé's Tituba does with the whites in general and the Salem witch-hunters in particular: "Hester [Prynne] taught me to prepare my testimony. Trust a minister's daughter to know a thing or two about Satan. Hadn't she eaten at his table since childhood?" (*Tituba*, 99).

There is, however, an incident, profoundly ironic (and disturbing), in the pages that describe Hannah's life in Madras. The narrator relates a Hindu myth told to Hannah by her servant Bhagmati, which describes Sita, the wife of Rama (an incarnation of Vishnu), as having to prove repeatedly her chaste love for her husband. Sita had to walk through fire after being abducted by a lustful demon and again after being separated from Rama through natural disasters. Imperative to Hindu faith is the wife's compliance with her husband's wishes. When asked a third time to prove, yet again, her pure love for Rama, Sita becomes incensed and "miraculously the Mother Earth that had given her birth now swallows her whole, leaving no trace of Sita the mortal" (177). The narrator ends this anecdote by swerving to the present and the comfort of her own authority over this fictive telling: "Where is Sita's version of her captivity? . . . I want to hear Sita tell me of her resistance" (177). The reader feels exhilarated by the narrator's cognizance of the vitality of voice and the urgency of insurgence—but is immediately horrified at the blind spot in the statement "I may not have Sita's words, but I have the Salem Bibi's" (177). What "words" could Hannah have if she is puppeted in and out of events? Has she not been "curbed" and guarded with "diligence" (54) lest she become "hysterical" (56) and "shriek" (116) and "scream" (216) her abhorrence at being colonized?

Fashioning Hannah's Identity

Mukherjee's narrator resorts to two kinds of devices to shape identities in the book. At one level, she names her characters in a strategic fashion so that the identity of her fictional characters is *situated* in the reader's knowledge of history and literary texts. Hannah, "Precious-as-Pearl," befriends Hester Manning in Salem, who dies surrounded by rumors of indiscretion. This sets the stage for a mnemonic device. Cephus Prynn in Madras, who attempts to rape Hannah, locks our memory and concertizes our connection between Hannah-Hester-Prynne and the threat of feminine sexuality. Finally, Hannah's aimless or harmless walking tours almost always lead to "forests," whether they are in pastoral Salem or in fecund Madras. To ensure that this background knowledge pervades the reader's sensibility, the narrator seals the book with "Joseph Hathorn... son of the witchcraft judge, John Hathorn... went out to sea, driven from the taint of Salem, drawn by the stories of the China and India trade that White Pearl related as she sewed [duplicating Hannah's sojourn]" (285). The narrator, quite systematically, welds official history and literary history on the last page of her novel to indict female agency and feminine sexuality: "Nathaniel Hawthorne... wrote his morbid introspection into guilt and repression" (285–86). Hawthorne, then, is but one heir to Hannah, the real heroine, and the narrator's records of Salem history.[15] But writers such as Jean Rhys in *Wide Sargasso Sea* have tackled history/time along a linear plane without naming the empire or re-recording history.[16] Rhys deterritorializes England and defamiliarizes empire by systematically avoiding to name the imperial agent. Her fiction attempts to reverse the horror of colonization by generating an iconoclastic, fictional identity within literary/official history. Numerous critics, most notably, Frantz Fanon (*The Wretched of the Earth*) and Edward Said (*The World, the Text, and the Critic*), have pointed out that the act of naming the other is the most oppressive tool in the hands of colonizers because they appropriate identity and subjectivity exactly as they conquer the land.[17] This naming function, then, works against Mukherjee in the reader's eyes both in race and gender contexts as an inexcusable act of aggrandizement, totally robbing Hannah Easton of her identity through the Hannah-Hester-Prynne interlock. This is but one more incidence where Mukherjee misses the opportunity to learn from authors and critics from earlier generations who have theorized the politics of identity formation of the disenfranchised subject.

A slightly different identity construction (and an even older one in generational terms) is her technique of superimposing one kind of "Indian" over another by allowing the narrator to seal the joint between the two Indians with elaborate stereotypes. The demonized "red Indian" mirrors the orientalized "East Indian" where both are othered to tell her/history. She tells the Maritime Museum curator while examining some objects, "Looks Indian...Indian-Indian, not wah-wah Indian," continuing that she "hate[s] to play stupid for anyone" (14). If that is so, one wonders what the function of the hyphen between the two Indians connotes here beyond the yoking of stereotypes and the affixing of names by the Enlightened subject! She also connects the two Indians or "aliens" through their rumored/imagined savage virility: "Like Rebecca, I had a lover. One who would seem alien to my family. A lover scornful of our habits of effacement and reasonableness.... Venn was born in India" (31). The "unrecognizable" father (57), the Nipmuc Indian is superimposed on the body of Venn Iyer, the other Indian, moving from seventeenth-century Salem to twentieth-century Boston, from one culture to another as if the homogenized and totalized *misrecognition* could still hold true, however fantastical the fiction. There are several instances that graft and suture ill-fitting identities of Indian on Hannah's body, the last example is perhaps worth quoting: "She began to believe that the only woman... who could understand these feelings was her mother. She, too, lifted her gray tunic to the Raja when he entered, even with Bhagmati in the room" (230). This particular image evokes the memory from the first part of the novel where Rebecca passionately embraces her Nipmuc lover in Hannah's presence. The small irritation of Bhagmati being equated with alien-child-innocent is but barely tolerable in the face of the greater problem of trivializing race, which is evident in the whole work. Etienne Balibar's comment seems pertinent here: "From this point of view, historiosophies of race and culture are *radically acritical*";[18] this is another example of Mukherjee's failure to explore fully her postmodern trope of futuristic tales in terms of generations and racial-gendered identity. The examples with the Indian stereotype show the narrator's obsession with the imperial mentality toward race. Joan Scott says in "The Evidence of Experience" that

> when experience is taken as the origin of knowledge, the vision of the individual subject (the person who had the experience or the historian who recounts it) becomes the bedrock of evidence on which explanation is built. Questions about the constructed nature of experience, about how subjects are constituted as different in the first

place, about how one's vision is structured — about language (or discourse) and history — are left aside.[19]

Resolution

My argument is not meant to detract from the prominence of history as an analytical tool; it is, instead, to do with Bharati Mukherjee's mode of telling/writing history. She uses metaphors of cultural imperialism to frame the novel, and her narrator links disparate regions like Salem and Madras through evidence of colonial expansion by relying on her lover's data-processing system "called X 2989, which translates to October 29, 1989" (5). Every one of the narrator's tropes ranging from towns in continents to museums and halls of historical records are simulations of space, but she is not attentive to this dimension of narrativity. Her language, rich in libidinal energy and imaginative insights, obsessively recalls representational/mimetic functions of signification and gets embroiled in elaborate stereotypes, which in turn serve to reiterate her desire to coat history with an aesthetic gloss. But this technique, though rich in texture, never quite breaks free of the power of signifying systems to suggest experiences and meanings that *could have been, would have been,* if she had followed space/geography as carefully as she has followed time/history as her narrative model. However, she acknowledges her privileging impulse in the telling early on when she says, "It is a question of time, not motive" (70), and "Time, O Time! Time to tincture the lurid colors, time for the local understudies to learn their foreign lines, time only to touch and briefly bring alive the first letter of an alphabet of hope and horror stretching out, and back to the uttermost shores" (286).

The Holder of the World is a carefully crafted and buttressed novel, yet the narrativizing of historical facticity is predictable and the time gap in the presentation of events between continents and cultures is clichéd. The space for anomalies in semantic and semiotic registers is never enunciated. Paradoxically, the evidence of the translucent body of the author (Indian woman, American citizen) stands as an alibi for the dated politics of the narrator who inscribes her will on Hannah. Hannah is shuttled from a savage Nipmuc Indian settlement to zealously Puritan Salem to flaccid British domesticity and to the fecund Coromandel Coast. She has no room to maneuver — her itinerary is totally controlled, her path rigidly drawn, her fate in the hands of an unrelenting narrator. Space could have provided the map to embark on a new episteme, tell a different tale in feminist, generational terms.[20] Angela Davis's preface to Maryse Condé's *I, Tituba, Black Witch of Salem* serves as a counterexample of how to play with history and maneuver the "geopolitics" of colonization:

> As an African-American feminist, I offer my profound gratitude to Maryse Condé for having pursued and developed a vision of Tituba, Caribbean woman of African descent. Should a Native American Tituba be recreated, in scholarly or fictional terms, this would be true to the spirit of Condé's Tituba and her revenge. For in the final analysis, Tituba's revenge consists in reminding us all that the door to our suppressed cultural histories is still ajar. (*Tituba*, xiii)

One of the real tragedies in Mukherjee's technique is that Hannah's world is peopled by women without fellowship: the narrator Beigh Masters, who could have been her liberator, overpowers her; her mother Rebecca, who does not build trust, instead abandons her; her friend Hester, who fails to pledge solidarity at a crucial moment, forsakes her; and Bhagmati, who could have breached race lines in the embrace of sisterhood, is unrecognized by Hannah. Hannah, motored by Mukherjee, relegates Bhagmati to a position of racialized other until that epiphanic moment when she acknowledges "My God, they're alive! ... They're humans" (223). And last of all, the reader, who wishes to reach into the novel to counsel Hannah to be more insurgent, cannot find the space to make this entry. The epigraph from E. M. Forster's *Howard's End* comes to mind to describe Hannah's sepulchral body/agency: if she could "only connect."

Notes

I wish to thank Gurudev, Marie-Agnés Sourieau, Marcia Landy, Jane Sutherland, and Marion White for guiding me and carefully critiquing my essay. I also thank Devoney Looser who encouraged me to write this piece and who propelled me to clarify my arguments. And I thank Thais E. Morgan, who insisted that I be rigorous in all my analyses.

1. Bharati Mukherjee, *The Holder of the World* (New York: Knopf, 1993). Subsequent references are cited parenthetically in the text.

2. Mukherjee's *The Middleman and Other Stories* (New York: Grove Press, 1988) and *Jasmine* (New York: Fawcet Crest, 1989) have proven eminently teachable to undergraduates in U.S. universities. *Jasmine* is especially effective for various reasons. Chief among them is Mukherjee's strategy of coupling the diaspora metaphor with that of the American dream. It tells the poignant tale of Jasmine, a young Indian widow who flees oppression and violence in her native land to fashion herself anew in the United States—the land of milk and honey, of hope and opportunity. In the beginning of the novel, the heroine desires to immolate herself in the Indian tradition of sati, and

this captures the imagination of the U.S. students who are mostly familiar with the popular press coverage of this practice through *60 Minutes* and are informed by most teachers of the theoretical debates formulated by Gayatri Spivak and Jenny Sharp. I cite this scenario to show how the "postcolonial" becomes a sensational, pedagogic tool in the hands of the author and willing instructors who are eager to teach the "multicultural" with some degree of theoretical sophistication. The novel is at best a postcolonial künstleroman, and at worst a penny dreadful, which parades a beautiful yet pathetic ingénue. However, *Jasmine* raises issues of third world femininity and feminine agency, location and dislocation (or nation and diaspora) and sparks classroom discussions of race, gender, and nationalism. In this context, Hannah's journey across the oceans or her diasporic subjectivity are but the jazzed-up revisions of *Jasmine*'s clichéd theme and content. However generous we wish to make our critique of Mukherjee's attempt to *spatialize* reality in *The Holder,* the radical components of such an experiment are lacking.

3. In a purely theoretical fashion, Donna Haraway in *Simians, Cyborgs and Women* (New York and London: Routledge, 1991) tackles major paradigm shifts in identity politics and futuristic timelines. Her kind of postmodern imagination, however, is vastly more interesting than and different from Mukherjee's. Similarly, Rebecca Walker's anthology *To Be Real: Telling the Truth and Changing the Face of Feminism* (New York: Doubleday, 1995) brings together ideas of the postmodern narrative, cyberspace fiction, and feminism, and has a sharp critical edge to it. See notes 6 and 7 for more details. See also Maryse Condé, *I, Tituba, Black Witch of Salem* (Charlottesville and London: University of Virginia Press, 1992); Simon Schama, *Dead Certainties: Unwarranted Speculations* (New York: Knopf, 1991); Gita Mehta, *Raj* (New York: Ballantine Books, 1989); Fanny Penny, *Diamonds* (London: Hodder and Stoughton, 1922); Carol Hill, *Henry James' Midnight Song* (New York: Poseidon Press, 1993).

4. In contrast to Mukherjee's (and Hannah's) hold over the narrator, Maryse Condé clearly writes at the beginning of *I, Tituba*: "Tituba and I lived for a year on the closest terms. During our endless conversations she told me things she had confided to nobody else." What is also vastly different in Condé's work is her acknowledged humor in constructing both the text and her subject. Condé mentions in her interview at the end of the book that her work can best be relished when read as a "parody."

5. After reading the whole novel, one becomes aware of the obvious way in which Mukherjee presents iconic moments of conspicuous consumption (television, museums, etc.), which in turn emphasize the author's method of commodifying Hannah. But it is too early in the novel here to catch her at it.

6. Gabriele Schwab, *Subjects without Selves: Transnational Texts in Modern Fiction* (Cambridge, Mass: Harvard University Press, 1994), 3. Schwab continues: "This speculation will complement, but never replace, *one's fascination with the fundamental otherness of transitional texts, the sense that they anticipate the future of a subjectivity* that has not been formulated discursively and perhaps even resists discursive formulation, but that, precisely because of this resistance, it presents such a profound challenge to our available models of poetic language and literary subjectivity" (21, emphasis added). And, she says, "the unnameable seems to mock literary fictions whose characters are built according to the conventions of literary realism by exposing them to the light of philosophical models of subjectivity. But the inverse is also applicable, for he forces the most basic philosophical assumptions to collapse by testing them within the correctness of a fictional life. The medium of fiction grants him a space for probing epistemologies and ontologies that would be unavailable either as empirical or philosophical subject" (22).

7. Rebecca Walker's anthology *To Be Real: Telling the Truth and Changing the Face of Feminism* showcases this precise angle of intersection of postmodern cyberspace, sexuality, and race. My essay had already gone to press when Walker's book came out, so I could not use examples to compare her to Mukherjee. Walker specifically makes the leap from the earlier generation of feminist writers (like her godmother, Gloria Steinem, and her mother, Alice Walker) to the contemporary scene of cyberspace lounges.

8. See Gayatri Spivak's essay "Can the Subaltern Speak? Speculations on Widow Sacrifice," in *Marxism and the Interpretation of Culture,* ed. Cary Nelson and Lawrence Grossberg (Urbana: University of Illinois Press, 1988), 271–313; Gita Rajan, "Subversive-Subaltern Identity: Indira Gandhi as Speaking Subject," in *Decolonizing the Subject: The Politics of Gender in Women's Autobiography,* ed. Sidonie Smith and Julia Watson (Minneapolis: University of Minnesota Press, 1992), 196–224; and *Subaltern Studies* 3 (1988). See also Chandra Talpade Mohanty's essay "Under Western Eyes: Feminist Scholarship and Colonial Discourse," *Boundary* 2 12 (1984): 333–58; Harveen Mann's "Women's Rights vs. Feminism? Postcolonial Perspectives," in *Postcolonial Discourse and Changing Cultural Contexts: Theory and Criticism,* ed. Gita Rajan and Radhika Mohanram (Westport, Conn.: Greenwood, 1995), 69–88; and Maggie Humm, ed., *Modern Feminisms: Literature, Politics, Culture* (New York: Columbia University Press, 1992).

9. John Berger, *The Look of Things* (New York: Viking, 1974), 40 (original emphasis). For more see 40–56. As Fredric Jameson noted a decade ago, the responsibility of the literary artist is to create a "new architecture . . . [that] stands as something like a new imperative to grow new organs, to expand our sensorium and our body to some new, as yet unimaginable, perhaps ultimately impossible dimensions" (80). He continues: "The last few years have been marked by an inverted millennialism, in which premonitions of the future, catastrophic or redemptive, have been replaced by senses of the end of this or that (the end of ideology, art, or social class; the crisis of Leninism, social democracy, or the welfare state, etc., etc.,): taken together, all of these constitute what is increasingly called postmodernism," Jameson, "Postmodernism, or the Logic of Late Capitalism," *New Left Review* 146 (1984): 53. Jean-François Lyotard says of postmodernist culture that it creates a new kind of experience, that it attempts the impossible by going beyond the traditional boundaries of representation that utilize language, gestures, and sign systems that rely on a mimetic/realistic mode. See "Beyond Representation," *The Human Context* 3 (1975): 495–502.

10. Edward Soja, *Postmodern Geographies: The Reassertion of Space* (London and New York: Verso, 1989), 7. Michel Foucault says, "The heterotopia is capable of juxtaposing in a single real place several spaces, several sites that are in themselves incompatible . . . [such that] they have a function in relation to all the spaces that remain. This function unfolds between two extreme poles. Either their role is to create a space of illusion that exposes every other real space, all the sites inside of which human life is partitioned, as still more illusory. . . . Or else . . . their role is to create a space that other, another real space, as perfect, as meticulous, as well arranged as ours is messy, ill constructed, and jumbled. The latter type would be heterotopia, not of illusion, but of compensation, and I wonder if certain colonies have not functioned somewhat in this manner" (Michel Foucault, "Of Other Spaces," *Diacritics* [1986]: 25, 27).

11. Soja, *Postmodern Geographies,* 14.

12. Another passage comes to mind in connection with embellishing images and silencing voices. The narrator remarks that "Hannah knew him [Nipmuc lover] as her inadmissible father, the only man she'd ever seen her mother with. . . . This is the night

that Hannah has willed herself not to remember. What happened survives only as Rebecca's neighbor's gossip, embellished with speculations of scholars" (28–29). The
narrator (and the author, by extension) are linked metonymically to the scholar category, but ironically, it relegates her only to be able to spread the "gossip." This is one
instance of following the time/history line slavishly, instead of playing with the space
created between official and unofficial history.

13. See E. Ann Kaplan's work over the past decade on the damaging effect of the
image of the hysteric on female subjectivity. Also, the second generation of continental
feminists such as Julia Kristeva, Hélène Cixous, Luce Irigaray, Jane Gallop, and others
has systematically critiqued Sigmund Freud and Jacques Lacan in relating hysterics to
female subjectivity by way of psychoanalytic interpretations as generations — hysterical — postfeminist.

14. In contrast, Condé's Tituba describes her christening by Yao, her adoptive father, who was also a slave: "It was he who gave me my name: Tituba. TI-TU-BA. It's
not an Ashanti name. Yao probably invented it to prove that I was the daughter of his
will and imagination. Daughter of his love" (Tituba, 6). Unlike Hannah, Tituba revels
in her difference and speaks of her witch status with pride.

15. Condé is quite direct in her connection between her character and Hawthorne,
and her more veiled allusion to Arthur Miller's The Crucible. Tituba meets Hester
Prynne in her Salem jail and we hear two versions of colonization — women subjugated by men and the Church, and blacks subjugated by whites and capitalism. When
Tituba asks Hester what crime she has committed, she replies unflinchingly, "Adul-
tery." Then, Hester scorns Tituba for taking the name her father gave her and says,
"You accepted a name a man gave you?" to which Tituba says, "Isn't it the same for
every woman? First her father's name, then her husband's?" To this, Hester replies
with sadness, "I was hoping that at least some societies were an exception to this law"
(96). In another instance, Hester tells Tituba, "I had the misfortune to belong to a
family that believed in sexual equality and at the age when you normally play with
dolls my father had me recite the classics" (97). I quote extensively from Condé to
show the authority with which these characters conduct a dialogue in an imagined
space in history. In other words, the timeline remains steady, but the circumstances,
actions, and reactions are situated in that space where anything could be imagined.

16. Jean Rhys, Wide Sargasso Sea (New York: Norton, 1966).

17. Frantz Fanon, The Wretched of the Earth, trans. Constance Farrington (New
York: Grove Press, 1968); Edward Said, The World, the Text, and the Critic (Cambridge, Mass.: Harvard University Press, 1983).

18. See Etienne Balibar and Immanuel Wallerstein, Race, Nation, and Class: Ambiguous Identities (London and New York: Verso, 1991), 55, emphasis added.

19. Joan W. Scott, "The Evidence of Experience," Critical Inquiry 17 (Summer 1991):
777. Scott continues: "How have categories of representations and analysis — such as
class, race, gender, relations of production, biology, identity, subjectivity, agency, experience, even culture — achieved their foundational status? What have been their effects of articulation? What does it mean for historians to study the past in terms of
these categories and for individuals to think of themselves in these terms? What is the
relationship between the silence of such categories in our own time and their existence
in the past?" (796).

20. Foucault writes that "a whole history remains to be written of spaces — which
would at the same time be the history of powers (both of these terms in the plural) —
from the great strategies of geopolitics to the little tactics of habitat" (Power/Knowledge
[New York: Random House, 1989], 149, original emphasis).

The Anxiety of Affluence: Movements, Markets, and Lesbian Feminist Generation(s)

Dana Heller

Originally, I intended this essay to be a critical rumination on the generational shift from 1970s lesbian feminist politics to 1980s queer politics and the anxieties this shift has produced in U.S. feminisms of the 1990s. I set to work in a tenor of gravity and good will, but somehow, somewhere my fancy turned—as fancies are wont to do—to shopping.

How did this happen? Well, my trouble began when I got sidetracked in an effort to position myself as a generational subject of feminism. To my mind, you see, the term *generation* implies a body of beings who occupy a common step in a line of descent, a body organized by a loose combination of experiences, material practices, and social relationships that animate a generational *geist,* a shared sense of history's ineluctable hold on us. But if my engagements with feminist, lesbian, and queer studies have taught me anything over the years, it's that no such coherent "bodies" exist, at least not independently of the interests that flesh them out and mobilize them for the construction of a generational identity. Perhaps one might argue, as Katie King has argued apropos of feminist origin stories, that feminism's generational anxieties are *interested* anxieties, all of them.[1]

King's intervention is worth noting here for its scrupulous insistence that feminist historiographers and practitioners, in their "contests for meaning," or their competing efforts to capture feminism's formative moments, remain politically accountable for the ideological displacements that their stories inevitably enact. Indeed, every new telling of feminism's originary past reconstructs a political position for feminism's present. By appearing to tell the "real" story of the women's movement, however, origin stories often obscure feminism's historical lack of ideological coherence. They often eclipse the fleeting, local, and contested nature of identity. King's argument is that feminism's political identity cannot be unified or reduced to any singular meaning by recourse to stories of origin. Rather, these stories reveal competing interests, ephemeral identities, and histories bound to specific political moments whose meanings remain contingent on the specific ideological and rhetorical strategies of the teller.

Similarly, I would argue that articulations of generational subjectivity inevitably construct political positions within the present moment. They accomplish this by reconstructing and celebrating the originary events, tropes, images, and figures out of which our understanding of a generational ethos is believed to have developed. The defining moments of feminism's generational identities, and the key debates associated with generational shifts in feminist thought, are themselves constantly shifting constructions that are reworked by feminists, nonfeminists, and antifeminists alike. Our anxieties about the various shapes these constructions take may be read as symptoms of ideological collision and/or ambiguity, flashpoints where contests about the meanings of feminism's past and the directions of its future are briefly illuminated.

If generational identities are all interested, some seem to earn more interest than others. For example, we might consider Beatles nostalgia as a product of the media industry's investment in reaffirming the popular cultural capital of a generation. Here, however, *generation* would denote an ostensibly large, albeit amorphous, target consumer group: middle-class baby boomers whose political identities were ostensibly formed in conflux with popular music innovations of the 1960s.[2] Efforts to remobilize the dynamic purchasing power of this maturing market group recently resulted in a three-part television documentary, *The Beatles Anthology,* which aired on ABC during Thanksgiving week of 1995.[3]

On one level, *The Beatles Anthology* sought to capture the "real" iconography of a generation through a spectacular procession of where-were-you-then images, exclusive interviews, and classic melodies. On another level, however, producers and sponsors of *The Beatles Anthology* seemed far more interested in resuscitating the myth of a generation's progress toward consumer affluence, its earned privilege to traffic in a certain kind of commodity identification. Lest this opportunity be missed, viewers of *The Beatles Anthology* were reminded nightly that generational allegiance could be exercised by purchasing *The Beatles Anthology* CD box set, a just-released collection of Beatles music including "new" Beatles songs based on tracks that John Lennon had recorded before his death. Individual cuts from the CD set were premiered at the close of each night's broadcast. The scheduling of the broadcast was equally strategic, airing right at the onset of a holiday shopping season that economists were predicting would be sluggish because of low consumer confidence. But *The Beatles Anthology* sought to allay consumer angst by harnessing the commodity desire of a market group to belief in a unifying and discoverable generational identity. What remains to be explored are the specific mechanisms through which generational identities, myths of generational origin, and the material practices that constitute and reinforce them are at least partially generated by the political economies of postwar culture industries.

That said, let's consider what angst and what interests generated the shift from lesbian feminist to queer. According to numerous observers, the lesbian movement away from feminism was decisively marked by sex radicalism.[4] In this spirit, Sue-Ellen Case targets 1981–82 as "the great divide," the years that saw the outbreak of the "sex wars," fervid debates motivated not only by s/m (sadomasochist) lesbians' frustration with antipornography feminists but by an increasingly urgent political crisis stemming from the threat of a resurgent activist right wing and government inattention to AIDS.[5] Segments of the lesbian activist community began establishing new political and social alliances with gay men, whose networks of cultural productivity seemed to affirm a wider range of nonnormative erotic and sexual expression. A spirit of cross-gender coalition that had waned with the dissolution of the 1960s homophile movement and the rise of the second wave of the women's movement, was revived, albeit in response to new health, education, and corporate policy issues understood to have serious life or death consequences.[6]

Case identifies the controversial Scholar and the Feminist IX Conference, "Towards a Politics of Sexuality," held at Barnard College on April 24, 1982, as a watershed cultural moment in this period of political reconfiguration. The new lesbian politics that emerged out of the Barnard conference challenged antipornography feminism's celebrated doctrine of "politically correct" sex, rejecting its overbearing maternal role in policing lesbian desires. One must tread cautiously, however, among tropes of maternal repression and filial revolt, Oedipal tropes that tend to foreground generational conflict to the detriment of commodity critique. For as Case observes, by the end of the 1980s queer "performativity" would effectively re-present lesbian feminism as essentialist and binary-happy, thus erasing feminism's anti-capitalist roots in consonance with the new global capitalism and changing political terminologies that worked to obscure worldwide material conditions.

While the New Left and dialectical materialism produced the theoretical and activist consciousness of a lesbian feminist generation that came of age in the '60s and '70s, a subsequent generation's political consciousness was produced by the sex wars, poststructuralism, performativism, agitprop, and Queer Nation, which, according to Case, produced a new "queer dyke" who identified more with gay men than with lesbians, and whose exit from feminism contributed to the widespread closing down of women-centered bars, bookstores, and cultural centers, many of them collectively owned and operated. Queer Nation's transfiguration into the Queer Shopping Network of New York marked a decisive shift from movement to market sector, a politics of celebratory commodification organized around individual market intervention. The socialist logic of 1970s lesbian feminism would seem to have been outflanked by the commodity logic of consumer capitalism; accordingly, lesbian feminist leftists would seem to have been displaced by postfeminist market strategists, queer activists for whom engagements with commercial capital, cultural merchandising, advertising, and shopping are—at least potentially—politically enabling.[7] Indeed, even buying a feminist anthology such as this one could be construed as a politically empowering act. Granted, such possibilities are by no means unique to feminism or queer activism but reflect more general ideological shifts within leftism. But shouldn't we consider at what cost and at whose expense an activist/cultural studies agenda based in a postmodern affirmation of the relations between popular pleasures, consumer goods, and queer cultural agency has unfolded?

From movement to market sector, from lesbian feminist collectives to queer constituencies, from the Lavender Menace to the Leather Menace, from flannel and denim to lipstick lesbians, public stagings of difference based on gender-specific versus sex-specific analysis, assimilationist versus antiassimilationist strategies, essentialist versus constructivist approaches have significantly shaped and reshaped U.S. feminism's generational imaginary.[8] Now that "queer" has lost its cutting-edge momentum, however, generational anxieties float freely throughout the divergent discourses of a sexual movement that, according to Lauren Berlant and Elizabeth Freeman, poses "as a countercorporation, a business with its own logo, corporate identity, and ubiquity."[9] Reading the letters in *The Advocate*, I come across a case in point from Yvetta Grim:

> Driving home from visiting my family over the holidays ... I was in a mood full of despair and reflection (my family is still struggling with my coming out). Somehow I was jolted by a passing black Mitsubishi with Texas plates displaying a pink triangle, rainbow flag, and Ann Richards bumper stickers. In that moment I realized that I wasn't alone. I have this wonderful chosen family, millions strong. I have made it my New Year's resolution to discard my fears and to purchase the same items for my car to help pass this solidarity along.[10]

As an "out" lesbian participant in the predominantly straight world of bourgeois academic social relations, I can relate to Grim's longing for a solidarity that can be purchased in the passing lane, no time-consuming rest-stop coalition building necessary. At the same time, I see the logic in Case's concern that the ascension of "queer" merchandising and corporate organizing strategies has brought with it the wholesale commodification of lesbian politics, so that however much queer interrogates the "normal," it seems to overlook its own complicity with the "normalizing operations of patriarchy, capital and nation."[11] The danger is that our investments in commodity solidarity will provide an end in itself, when in fact the queering of American capital is not simply about the acquisition and circulation of rainbow flags and other "pride" symbols, but the establishment of a new sort of consumer consciousness that operates as a form of camp, a performative critique of desexualized, depoliticized bourgeois materialism. Such camp consciousness is not strictly commercial, but resistant to dominant commercial narratives (for example, heterosexual romance, maternal melodrama, family romance) and capitalist ideologies. In this way, camp commodity consciousness promises to reconfigure social identity, economies of familial affect, and lesbian political presence in the national public sphere (in Grim's case, the hyperspace of Amer-

ican road culture). It achieves this reconfiguration by aligning commercial goods with lesbians' collective capacities for economic and
emotional survival.

My concern is that recent modes and representations of lesbian consumption are overinvested in narratives of generational competition
and underinvested in histories of shifting economic relations.¹² Reading Grim's letter in light of my own collection of glossy magazine sub-
scriptions and in-your-face T-shirts, I am reminded of a character from
David Leavitt's novel *The Lost Language of Cranes*. Jerene is a black
lesbian feminist Marxist who amplifies and embodies social "differences" otherwise unexplored in the narrative, specifically race, sex,
and class. Through Jerene, lesbian feminism is represented as primarily a matter of what clothing a woman wears and whether or not she
deems it appropriate to bleach the hair on her upper lip. Jerene's mother
had taught her to do this years ago, before her family disowned her
on account of her lesbianism. Six years later, Jerene secretly persists
in bleaching her mustache, even though "it was a gesture of political
as well as personal rebellion to mock the tastes of mothers."¹³ Much
to her chagrin, while shopping in Macy's Jerene finds herself gravitating toward her mother's taste in shirts. She is troubled by guilt, even
though she "cheats" lesbian feminism in other "small ways":

> [She] dressed every day for years in the jeans and lumber jack shirts
> that were the only wardrobe possible for a serious lesbian leftist, but
> anyone with an eye for detail would have noticed that there was
> embroidery on her sleeves. And things were changing. These days her
> friends were wearing pink, wearing maid's uniforms, wearing nose
> rings. (141)

As she recalls women marching bare breasted in the annual Gay
Pride Parade, Jerene considers that, unlike gay men who wear makeup,
the shirtless women expressed "a different kind of pride, one that had
more to do with denying sexual attraction than flaunting it" (141).
As she labors over her never-ending dissertation and cruises the predominantly white dyke bars of lower Manhattan, Jerene grows weary
of her mannish attire, the lackluster dress code of the sexually repressed PC lesbian feminist. On an inexplicable whim (but with her
mother in mind, once again), she ventures into the Laura Ashley store
to shop for something frilly and forbidden. Finding more than she
bargained for, Jerene gets a date with the salesgirl—a pale, blond,
ethereal woman who lives with her parents on Park Avenue and whose

name, by sheer coincidence, is also Laura. Jerene falls hard for Laura and shortly afterward discovers her inner femme, the lipstick lesbian she was always meant to be.

Regrettably, Leavitt's account of Jerene's liberation from lesbian feminism's downwardly mobile dogma is lacking in the elements of parody and camp that were so crucial to the dyke style wars of the 1980s. Also, given Laura Ashley's association with a white, upscale market—as well as the racialized meanings historically attached to maid's uniforms and other camp accoutrements—Jerene's fashion conversion implies social contradictions that one might reasonably expect a Marxist feminist in the throes of a doctoral dissertation to at least take cursory note of. But Leavitt portrays Jerene as the by-product of a lesbian feminist generation for which politics ultimately means no more than what Banana Republic offered in its "Chosen Family" ad campaign: a queer elite consumer base, a bit part in capitalism's romance with difference. Jerene buys in, her customer satisfaction indicating a shift in the lesbian styling of political participation from butch politico to femme commodity aesthetic. The latter category ostensibly frees her to "flaunt" her bourgeois femininity in an affirmative manner, a manner those topless, anticapitalist feminists would never tolerate. And her transformation appears organic, as natural as the impulse to shop. Say goodbye to Marx, sterile intellectualism, and flannel shirts. Say hello to Laura Ashley, Victorian romance, and a closet full of pretty summer dresses!

In other arenas of queer cultural production global capitalism's capacity to satisfy individualized lesbian desires is more thoughtfully explored. For example, in Rose Troche's film *Go Fish*—a film heralded in the lesbian press as "a new film for a new generation"—shopping for romance represents a complex strategy for rethinking identity, a strategy with pleasurable and subversive potential.[14] In this way, the film deploys the genre of romance in order simultaneously to recall and rearticulate historical structures of lesbian subjectivity.

Go Fish opens with a classroom scene and a history lesson. A women's studies instructor, Kia Kabrina, asks her students to compile a list of women throughout history who are known or thought to be lesbian. Amid the fairly predictable responses—Sappho, Marilyn Quayle, the entire cast of *Roseanne*—someone asks what the point of the exercise is. Kia explains: "Throughout lesbian history there has been a serious lack of evidence that will tell us what these women's lives are truly about. Lesbian lives and lesbian relationships barely exist on paper. And it's with that in mind, and understanding the meaning and power of history that we begin to want to change history."[15]

Indeed, *Go Fish* wants to change—or at least restyle—lesbian history in terms of recent debates over identity politics, fashion, and political correctness. Furthermore, the film playfully explores queer investments in a liberal discourse of choice that connects the desire for romance with the desire for commodities, and the process of searching for a girlfriend with the gendered consumer trope of "shopping around."[16] The narrative focuses on a diverse community of urban lesbians whose emotional lives and relationships intersect. Max West, a young, aspiring writer, longs for intimacy, companionship, and romance. She goes on the market for a girlfriend and solicits the advice of Kia, her roommate. In a coffee shop frequented by lesbians, Max asks Kia to fix her up—to pick someone she knows from among the patrons and introduce them. Kia directs Max's attention to a woman named Ely, who sits unaware in the background. Max observes Ely's appearance—long hair, meek demeanor, hippie attire—and is singularly unimpressed. "Clearly your attraction to the seventies is much deeper than I realized," she remarks.

All kidding aside, Kia's prominent role as feminist teacher and primary engineer of Max and Ely's unlikely romance positions her as an agent of personal and political transformation within the narrative. Moreover, as a black lesbian feminist and defender of pro-sex practices considered sluttish by some, Kia's character embodies historical changes in feminism's history, changes that helped produce a movement more attentive to issues of difference and systems of interlocking oppression. In this way, Kia may be said to represent lesbian feminism's moral voice—a voice resistant to forces of capital—in contrast to Max's queer dyke who wants a quick fix, an instant girlfriend à la mode.

Later in the film, Kia ridicules Max's unrealistic fashion requirements: "Her ideal girlfriend is hip-hop Barbie." Yet despite her consumer-based ideals and her conviction that Ely is suffering from "a bad case of hippieitis" (a condition emphasized by the fact that her kitchen cabinet is stocked with every conceivable variety of herbal tea), Max overcomes her ambivalence and decides to give Ely a chance. Meanwhile, Ely is struggling with ambivalence of her own, as Max learns through networks of gossip and hearsay. Although Ely takes an interest in Max, she seems shy, predisposed to inertia, and wedded to an obligatory long-distance relationship with a woman she rarely sees and no longer has sex with. Nevertheless, as Max and Ely consume movies, shop for comic books, and change hairstyles, they discover the unpredictable pleasures of queer romance.

Go Fish is about the insertion of the "lesbian" as a romantic consumer and consumer of romance. On their first date, Max and Ely take in a queer film. "That movie sucked!" Max complains afterward. "Why do queers always have to be so pathetic? I mean, I'm queer and I'm finding it relatively easy not to hate myself."

Ely admits she liked the film: "We expect queer filmmakers to take the responsibility to represent the entire community. I think that's really a lot to ask."

"I just don't feel that we can stand such negative representation within our own ranks," Max replies. From here they move to another subject. But later, while enumerating for Kia the reasons why a relationship with Ely would never work, Max says that "she is not interested in her own oppression."

This brief conversation underscores the current lack of agreement among queer consumers about the responsibility of queer products and cultural producers to affirm and consolidate their investments in identity politics. Queers, like all consumers, rely heavily on products to promote positive identifications with history. Given the fact that no essential queer history exists, however, queer consumers remain necessarily ambivalent about their investments, and their responses to cultural activity remain necessarily contradictory. Rather than portraying this situation as hopeless, the makers of *Go Fish* contend that ambivalence and contradiction are surprisingly pleasurable, although not necessarily constitutive of lesbian political solidarity and agency. And it is certainly possible that an emphasis on pleasure may be more personally sustaining in the current conservative political moment than an emphasis on oppression. Along these lines, Max and Ely's exchange provides a sort of metacommentary on the qualities that, for some viewers, distinguish *Go Fish* from a previous generation of lesbian films. As one lesbian viewer put it, "this is the first lesbian movie I've seen that didn't leave me feeling depressed."[17]

Describing the film's original contribution to the new queer cinema, director Troche claims that *Go Fish* undertakes the "despectacularization... of lesbian lives."[18] I take this to mean that characters in the film are not sensationalized by the mere fact of being lesbian. How-ever, what Max and Ely's improbable courtship rituals lack in sensa-tionalism they make up for in spectacle, as is evidenced by Ely's tran-sition from dowdy, lesbian feminist antistyle to queer style suggestive of nomadic gender identifications and mobile sexual desires. The elab-orate and extended montage of images depicting Ely's long-overdue haircut suggests that this is a spectacularly transformative act-event for Ely. She trades in her bland, long-haired hippie "look" and her long-dead, long-distance relationship for a buzz cut and an exciting new sexual currency. While cruising the comics rack, Max and Ely chance to meet in a bookstore where Max gets her first look at Ely's new haircut. "You think it looks butch, right?" Ely asks. "It is a gender-bender," Max admits, adding, presumably in reference to Ely's crossover from long hair to buzz cut, "the butch-femme thing's really impres-sive." Indeed, Max is so impressed by Ely's "butch-femme thing" that when she leaves the bookstore she forgets to pay for her comic.

Max's forgetfulness is telling: it suggests aspects of lesbian eroticism and countercultural style that cannot be absorbed within the day-to-day exchanges of mainstream capitalist enterprise. But the question remains: can lesbians "despectacularize" into a queer market sector and still retain the presence and visibility of the body as part of what animates romance, let alone politics? What does the already notori-ous fingernail clipping scene say about the undeniable materiality of the lesbian body and the specificity of lesbian sexual practice? What are the romantic pleasures that viewers of Go Fish are invited to con-sume, even while they are asked to question the ability of cultural com-modities to mobilize political communities and coalitions? Is Go Fish an elegy for lesbian feminism or an argument for its recuperation?

These questions are currently the focus of academic cultural produc-tion as well. In a presentation delivered at a session of the 1994 Mod-ern Language Association (MLA) convention, Teresa de Lauretis states that lesbian studies is in a "predicament . . . caught between an older generation of lesbian scholars whose lives, works and political for-mation intersected with 70s and 80s feminisms, and the pressing con-sumer demand for new and more sexy academic performances."[19] Here, de Lauretis turns to Robyn Wiegman's introduction to The Les-bian Postmodern, an anthology treated as "symptomatic" of current generational shifts in the discourse on sexuality. De Lauretis para-phrases Wiegman, describing her vision of the project as an "adventurous...leap into the unknown," a book that will replace an outmoded lesbian feminist imaginary and displace the commodification of the lesbian that circulates in the mass media and in academia.[20] At the same time, de Lauretis notes, Wiegman rightly recognizes her own contradictory complicity with the commodity aesthetic embodied in the book's title.[21]

Notwithstanding this allowance, de Lauretis focuses on lesbian pomo's tendency to speak in the "very lexicon of the feminist theory that I have been practicing for some twenty years...long-familiar terms like *unsettle, destabilize, test limits, undermine, heterosexual hegemony* and so forth." Same vocabulary, different generational imaginary. This leads de Lauretis to ask: "What is Pomo about the lesbian without quotation marks, besides her rightly postmodern lack of historical memory?" The answer, it seems, is to be found in this rising generation's wholesale repudiation of femininity and the female body. In its place we now find a semiotic fascination with cyborgs, female-to-male transsexuals, and Barbie.[22] The current fixation is on creatures "beyond gender...efficient, clean, indestructible, and sexless." Lesbian boomers have, it seems, mortgaged their dream houses and financed their fun cars with critical currency heedlessly appropriated from an earlier generation. The irony is that this older generation mobilized its currency largely in resistance to patriarchal capitalism, while their progeny invests in cosmetic and technological fashion accessories that efface the originary site of feminist theoretical engagements with *female* sexuality.

I would not argue, as de Lauretis does, that a new generation of lesbian scholars has abandoned femininity and the female body as productive sites of cultural analysis. For example, it seems to me that a rearticulation and assertion of femme identities, along with a reconsideration of the near-limitless modes of female embodiment, have accompanied and advanced the critical foregrounding of multiple and contradictory forms of lesbian existence. And while I agree with Wiegman that we can no longer afford to be politically naive about "the context of commodification in which [these forms] are embedded" (4), I want to focus more concretely on the question of how a less naive, more politically aware alliance of feminist, lesbian, and queer critical practitioners might proceed to actively negotiate the terrain of academic commodity production in which we are variously invested. For as the academic job market becomes, for the majority of job seekers, virtually nonexistent, and as the operating budgets of humanities departments shrink (with monies settling at the administrative top), commitments to thought—commitments that fuel the production and consumption of knowledge—become refiguringly entangled with institutional politics, curricular restructurings, and intensified faculty competition for scarce material rewards. These competitions, in turn, have contributed to the production and prevalence of a feminist/lesbian/queer "star system" organized around an insidious politics of glamour. The perceived authority of such hierarchies often obscures the class-inflected nature of academic self-commodification. It reinforces the capitalist illusion of an elite generational coterie's progress toward affluence and achievement.[23]

In this sense, for some, the lesbian postmodern signifies a bourgeois style of historical amnesia, a generational trademark that proffers professional and political survival for middle-class lesbian academics with fast-track careers and disposable income. Admittedly, I share this concern, although I remain sympathetic with both lesbian feminist calls for historical accountability *and* lesbian postmodern's strategic slips and shifts around the tricky question of fixity. I am not, however, inclined toward working out a compromise or locating a secure middle ground. No middle ground is necessary when there is no bipolarity at issue to begin with. Indeed, what may be at issue is a difference with respect to thinking history, or how to practice accountability. In Wiegman's words: "This difference—between history as a recounting of a sequence of events and history as the problematic of temporality and sequentiality—has crucial implications for thinking the postmodern as well as for articulating the relationship between the lesbian and a political project no longer unequivocally committed to modernist categories of social identity" (6). Rather than thinking lesbian feminist generation(s) in terms of sequential time, or in terms of a younger generation's revolt against an older generation, how might we (re)think the commodity problematic of history? More specifically, how might we advance discussion of the commodity problematic of social movements historically organized around (female) sexuality? For such a project, I believe a postmodern perspective is useful.[24]

I would not, however, want to equate postmodern and queer epistemological positions in the way that de Lauretis seems at times quite willing to do. These terms have developed along a number of distinct historical, political, and aesthetic trajectories, although they certainly may enable similar kinds of questions and elicit similar kinds of doubt. To wit, de Lauretis's critique of the lesbian postmodern echoes, in many respects, recent critiques of *queer theory*, a term that she herself coined and has since distanced herself from because of its deployment in contexts that neutralize rather than specify differences. On these grounds, lesbian pomo actually takes issue with queer theory as Wiegman demonstrates, speaking on behalf of those who believe, notwithstanding ambivalence, that there is value in retaining the specificity of lesbian existence.[25] For some, however, the neutralization of bipolarities implicit in the category "lesbian" is precisely what made queer politics, and its academic consort queer theory, viable. *Queer*'s inclusion of multiple subjectivities that produce discontinuities of sex and gender in socially and racially diverse historical contexts promises stronger coalitions among gay, lesbian, transgender, transsexual, and bisexual communities in their efforts to reform institutionalized heterosexism. Furthermore, *queer*'s inclusivity seems to address the need for coalitions among sex-based, race-based, gender-based, and class-based movements, although the confrontational style that became Queer Nation's hallmark understandably makes some organizations uncomfortable.

Nevertheless, coalitions are urgently needed, as is made evident by the class and antitransgender bias implicit in a *Village Voice* article by Donna Minkowitz on the brutal death of Brandon Teena.[26] Brandon Teena (formerly Teena Brandon) was a twenty-one-year-old female-to-male transgender who was multiply raped and beaten by two men, one of them a former boyfriend of a woman Brandon was dating, in a small town outside Lincoln, Nebraska, after the local newspaper reported on his preoperative status. The report was occasioned by Brandon's arrest on charges of check forgery. The men who raped Brandon were questioned by police and released. One week later, they shot and stabbed Brandon fatally. In Minkowitz's account of Brandon's story, she insists on using the pronoun *she* in defiance of his efforts to define himself. Moreover, Minkowitz ignores the economic conditions that, on the one hand, prompted Brandon to steal in the first place and, on the other hand, made it impossible for him to relocate (as Minkowitz suggests he might have) to Denver or San Francisco.

On this score, I must agree with Kathleen Chapman and Michael du Plessis who argue that Minkowitz's insistence on reclaiming Brandon's "true gender" and "her attribution of homophobia, internalized as well as externalized, to the trailer park milieu of Falls City Nebraska...

are sustained by a comfortable, indeed somewhat smug, middle-class lesbian identity."²⁷ They make the case that lesbian feminists such as Minkowitz, as well as queer theorists such as Judith Butler, remain attached to heterosexist presumptions that work to erase the reality of transgender existence. They note, moreover, that when we turn to Marjorie Garber, a critic whose work is associated with queer theory, we learn that transsexuals and transvestites are more than ever becoming "united around issues like the right to shop—access to dresses and nightgowns in large sizes and helpful, courteous sales personnel."²⁸ Certainly, clothes that fit are a legitimate concern, and I don't mean to dismiss the importance of it or of Garber's impressive work. What I want to do is emphasize that there are lives at stake here, lives threatened by institutional structures of impoverishment that cannot be sufficiently redressed by trolling the racks at Contempo Casuals or by activating credit with Uncommon Clout.

In conclusion, assembling this essay has convinced me that my place in a lesbian feminist line of descent is determined by an intersecting network of market sector identifications—lesbian, queer, baby boomer, feminist, academic, and so on—each one offering a mixed bag of pleasure, agency, apathy, anxiety, and risk. Given this precarious position, a position that may be shared by some of the producers and consumers of *Generations: Academic Feminists in Dialogue*, I would like to offer some final observations intended to serve as grist for further thought and discussion.

Throughout this essay, I have argued that "generations" must be viewed, largely although not exclusively, as products of capital. Similarly, academic "generations" are produced by and within the capital-building technologies of academic institutions. I believe that academic feminism's so-called generational shifts could be productively analyzed as the effects of institutional restructurings, downsizings, and entanglements with local economies and global capitalist projects. As privileged participants in what Cornel West calls "the academic 'professional managerial class,'" we are in a position to be particularly attentive to the rise of a lesbian feminist managerial class whose newly attained status as a visible "target market" works to displace class difference and camouflage the emergence of a divisive class politics within lesbian movements and communities. Whether we identify as queer, lesbian, lesbian feminist, or nonheterosexist feminist, now may be the time to reevaluate the ways in which class differences inform academic feminism's manner of producing and consuming sex.

A significant and ever-growing number of lesbian scholars identify neither with lesbian feminism nor queerness, believing that the latter retains gay men as its implicit referent while the former has become increasingly centrist, complacent, and removed from the material and political realities of most women's lives. While this is not a new concern, it is one that feminist cultural producers and political organizers can scarcely afford to ignore as congressional threats to women's welfare, housing, and health become enacted in punitive funding cutbacks, and as right-wing discourses bemoaning the "mainstream" liberal assault on traditional "family values" continue to co-opt and distort the histories and identities of women, queers, blacks, immigrants, the poor, and persons living with HIV or AIDS. Katie Hogan, for example, has argued eloquently for the need of feminists—academic feminists in particular—to recognize that HIV/AIDS is an urgent women's health issue. In trying to write about her sister's death from AIDS in a feminist context, Hogan realized the frightening extent to which an established generation of feminists regard HIV/AIDS as a gay male issue or a nonacademic social problem.[29] In fact, AIDS is now the number-one killer of Americans between the ages of twenty-five and forty-four, and the percentage of female victims continues to rise.

Fifteen years have passed since the Barnard conference opened up a series of difficult and necessary debates on feminism and sexuality; and yet, I wonder, where was the *active,* organized feminist response to the firing of former Surgeon General Joycelyn Elders as a result of her willingness—her outspoken willingness—to defend safe, nonreproductive sexual practice? Now is the time for feminism to take careful account of the emerging discourse on safe sex before another explosion of open conflict—a Latex Menace, perhaps—impedes the formation of necessary social coalitions that in the long run may prove far more valuable and life-enhancing than any sense of feminist generational identity that we can manufacture or buy. From movements to market sectors, let us consider at what price uncritical images of queer commodity trafficking have ascended over abject images of lesbian feminist leftism, retiring critiques of consumer capitalism and commodity fetishism that will be necessary for our political survival in the uncertain years ahead.

Notes

This essay was originally prepared for a roundtable discussion on "Feminism's Generational Anxieties," part of a conference held at Indiana University, Bloomington, March 23–25, 1995, which brought together many of the contributors to the anthology *Feminism beside Itself,* ed. Diane Elam and Robyn Wiegman (New York: Routledge, 1995). At the invitation of Devoney Looser and E. Ann Kaplan, I have revised the piece for this collection.

1. This is a rephrasing of King's introduction to "The Situation of Lesbianism as Feminism's Magical Sign: Contests For Meaning and the U.S. Women's Movement, 1968–1972," reprinted in King's *Theory in Its Feminist Travels: Conversations in U.S. Women's Movements* (Bloomington: Indiana University Press, 1994), 124–37.

2. I recognize that *The Beatles Anthology* is also aimed at a younger market sector for whom the Beatles are a "retro" pop phenomenon. Like Oliver Stone's film *JFK* and the more recent *Nixon, The Beatles Anthology* offers a reinscription of popular history aimed at an audience who didn't necessarily experience that history firsthand. In this way, the culture industry invests in the construction of the next "generation" of consumers, primarily by linking its patterns of cultural consumption with liberal capital, which reproduces itself through such spectacles of the historical imaginary as Stone is given to create.

3. I do not mean to suggest that *The Beatles Anthology,* or Beatles nostalgia in general, is a corporate conspiracy. What I want to suggest is that generational identities, like commodities, have a complex dual nature as expressions of corporate ideologies *and* as potential tools of autonomous cultural self-definition.

4. See, for example, the essays collected in *Pleasure and Danger: Exploring Female Sexuality,* ed. Carole S. Vance (Boston: Routledge & Kegan Paul, 1984); *Powers of Desire: The Politics of Sexuality,* ed. Ann Snitow, Christine Stansell, and Sharon Thompson (New York: Monthly Review Press, 1983); SAMOIS, *Coming to Power* (Boston: Alyson Publications, 1987).

5. Sue-Ellen Case, "Toward a Butch-Feminist Retro Future," in *Cross Purposes: Lesbian Studies, Feminist Studies, and the Limits of Alliance,* ed. Dana Heller (Bloomington: Indiana University Press, 1997).

6. For a comprehensive history of the shifting conflicts and alliances that have shaped the lesbian and gay liberation movement in the United States, see Margaret Cruikshank, *The Gay and Lesbian Movement* (London: Routledge, 1992).

7. Danae Clark's "Commodity Lesbianism" remains a tour de force essay on the complex and contradictory processes by which lesbians appropriate the media images of the mainstream fashion industry in order to construct notions of identity, politics, and community. In *The Lesbian and Gay Studies Reader,* ed. Henry Abelove, Michele Aina Barale, and David M. Halperin (New York: Routledge, 1993), 186–201.

8. For an interesting account of the "eruptions of difference" that have shaped feminism's identities as well as its political histories see chapter 6 of Alice Echols, *Daring To Be Bad: Radical Feminism in America, 1967–1975* (Minneapolis: University of Minnesota Press, 1989).

9. Lauren Berlant and Elizabeth Freeman, "Queer Nationality," in *Fear of a Queer Planet: Queer Politics and Social Theory,* ed. Michael Warner (Minneapolis: University of Minnesota Press, 1993), 213.

10. Yvetta Grim, "Lesbian on Board," *The Advocate* (7 March 1995).

11. Case, "Toward a Butch-Feminist Retro Future."

12. John D'Emilio addresses a similar concern in his essay "Capitalism and Gay Identity," in which he argues for a wider understanding of the historical conditions that made capitalism a requirement for the development of modern lesbian and gay identity in the United States. In *The Lesbian and Gay Studies Reader,* 467–78.

13. David Leavitt, *The Lost Language of Cranes* (Toronto: Bantam Books, 1986), 140.

14. Elizabeth Pincus, "Compliments for Fishing," *Deneuve: The Lesbian Magazine* 4.4 (August 1994): 17.

15. *Go Fish,* dir. Rose Troche (Can I Watch Pictures, 1994).

16. Although it generally overlooks lesbian consumers, Hilary Radner's *Shopping Around: Feminine Culture and the Pursuit of Pleasure* carefully examines the contradictory interplay of gender identification and practices of consumption (New York: Routledge, 1995).

17. I am grateful to all the women who shared their responses to the film with me, and particularly to Jackie Knighten for this one.

18. Quoted in Pincus, "Compliments," 17.

19. Teresa de Lauretis, "The Homosexual Imaginary of Feminism," presented at the Lesbian Studies, Feminist Studies, and the Limits of Alliance special session, MLA Convention, San Diego, 28 December 1994.

20. Ibid.

21. In Wiegman's own words: "As a contributor to the anthology, my relation to the commodification of the lesbian and the postmodern is unambiguously complicit, even if I plan to argue that through this conjunction, through this incipient terminological marriage, some of the founding assumptions of contemporary feminist theory can be challenged and, at least potentially, displaced" (2). "Introduction: Mapping the Lesbian Postmodern," in *The Lesbian Postmodern,* ed. Laura Doan (New York: Columbia University Press, 1994), 1–22.

22. Presumably, de Lauretis is referring to Erica Rand's essay "We Girls Can Do Anything, Right Barbie? Lesbian Consumption in Postmodern Circulation," in *The Lesbian Postmodern,* 189–209. However, there are numerous examples of "queer" Barbie scholarship. See also Rand's book *Barbie's Queer Accessories* (Durham: Duke University Press, 1995); and Jacqueline Urla and Alan C. Swedlund, "The Anthropometry of Barbie: Unsettling Ideals of the Feminine Body in Popular Culture," in *Deviant Bodies: Critical Perspectives on Difference in Science and Popular Culture,* ed. Jennifer Terry and Jacqueline Urla (Bloomington: Indiana University Press, 1995), 277–313.

23. Interestingly, it could be argued that the media commodification of "lesbian chic," illustrated by cover stories in *Newsweek, New York Magazine, Vanity Fair,* and other popular magazines needs to be read alongside academic feminism's and queer theory's glamour politics. K.d. lang, whose designer-clad body has been fashioned into the generational trademark of lesbian chic, has ideally replaced the shrill lesbian feminist ideologue whose image has been effectively demonized by the mainstream media. Similarly, there is understandable concern that the camp commodification of leading academic thinkers such as Judith Butler, as was demonstrated in the satirical fanzine *Judy!,* depoliticizes her critique of identity categories, rendering it stylish critical currency for a generation of (in the words of one journal editor) "Judy Butler wannabes," aspiring theorists more committed to the quest for academic celebrity than to social critique.

24. See Diane Elam, *Romancing the Postmodern* (London: Routledge, 1992) for a more developed discussion of this usefulness.

25. Robyn Wiegman, "Introduction: Mapping the Lesbian Postmodern."

26. Donna Minkowitz, "Love Hurts," *Village Voice*, 19 April 1994, 24–30.

27. Kathleen Chapman and Michael du Plessis, " 'Don't Call Me *Girl*': Lesbian Theory, Feminist Theory and Transsexual Identities," in *Cross Purposes: Lesbian Studies, Feminist Studies, and the Limits of Alliance.*

28. Quoted in ibid. Garber's remark originally appeared in her *Vested Interests: Cross-Dressing and Cultural Anxiety* (New York: HarperCollins, 1993), 4. Noting the frequent elision of transgenderism and transsexualism in the work of prominent feminist, lesbian, and queer theorists, Chapman and du Plessis suggest that " 'queer theory' is perhaps a testimony . . . that the more a theory of sex changes the more it stays the same."

29. Katie Hogan, "When Experience and Representation Collide: Lesbians, Feminists, and AIDS," in *Cross Purposes: Lesbian Studies, Feminist Studies, and the Limits of Alliance.*

Feminist Family Values; or, Growing Old—and Growing Up—with the Women's Movement

Judith Newton

Growing Old: Forgotten Brothers, Wounded Mothers, Ungrateful Daughters, and Erstwhile Sisters

Making my way through a crowded lobby at the Modern Language Association (MLA) convention in San Diego in December 1994, I failed at first to recognize a good friend, one whom I had known in graduate school, had always felt close to, and had seen from time to time, in just these settings, over the past twenty years. Had John gained weight, I asked myself, after he called my name and I had sheepishly recovered enough to give him a hug. Or was it my appalling memory again? Had my eyesight actually gotten worse? Later that evening, over dinner, as we talked rather ruefully about our age, reflected on what had come to seem most important to us in our lives, and marveled at how long ago graduate school in the sixties had actually been, John mused for a moment over my failure to recognize him right away. "We've reached that age," he said, "when this starts to happen." Then, catching himself, he chivalrously assured me, "*You*, of course, are still *quite* recognizable." But I noticed with a pang that he no longer said to me, "You look just the same."

The next day at noon, its being the twenty-fifth anniversary of the first panels in feminist literary criticism at MLA, I attended a forum on "Feminist Criticism Revisited: Where Are We Going? Where Have We Been?" The forum was presided over by two founding mothers of American feminist literary criticism, Sandra Gilbert and Susan Gubar, and it featured five "feminist old girls," four of whom were my age or older—Barbara Christian, Florence Howe, Nancy K. Miller, and Elaine Showalter. (The fifth panelist, Jane Gallop, seemed a kind of

bridge figure to the much-invoked younger generation.) The proceedings were held in a large double ballroom, which was already packed
when I arrived, and as I turned this way and that, scanning the crowd,
beginning to feel, again, some thrill at our collective history, I saw
many familiar and seemingly familiar faces. (More than one of us, I
surmised, did not look "just the same.")

Growing old with the women's movement was, in fact, an implicit
and explicit preoccupation of four of the five speakers, who touched
frequently on the theme of generations. There was celebration, of
course, most particularly from Florence Howe, who reflected on the
achievements of the past twenty-five years—the development of feminist literary criticism, the recovery of women writers, the founding of
feminist caucuses, publishing houses, journals, and women's studies
programs. But, more insistently, there was the thematization of wound
and loss, as one speaker after another touched on the current lapse
of historical memory, the rejection or loss of political heritage and
commitment, feminist careerism and competitiveness, and the ingratitude of the young.

Florence Howe, for example, named "amnesia," "complacency,"
and "competition" as three current feminist diseases. Nancy Miller
reflected on the new generational ethos of "trashing," a "genre if not
an industry," in a "town" that doesn't seem big enough for all of us
anymore. And Elaine Showalter concluded with a thumbnail history
of American feminist literary criticism, in which she noted the adoption,
in the mideighties, of a new "contentious charter" in which "sweet-
ness" was renounced and the critique of feminist criticism from within
became "the most important project" and the occasion, not incidentally, for a series of successful career moves. These themes were to be
reinvoked in an associated workshop later on that afternoon, in Ruth
Perry's observation that this was a less collective feminist age than
were the seventies and in Bonnie Zimmerman's reflections on the phenomenon of young feminists seeking to establish credibility by setting themselves against the older generation. Queer daughters, Zimmerman observed, have turned away from their lesbian mothers in
order to bond with queer dads. Implicitly and explicitly, the figure of
ungrateful daughters hovered over the anniversary proceedings.

This trope, I should note, only characterized the discourse of the
white feminist literary critics whose talks I attended. The experience
of being *de*centered, perhaps, belongs most characteristically to those

who have been securely *at* the center and is felt most profoundly in relation to those—young white feminists in this case—who have come to occupy, or who desire to occupy, a (differently constituted) center in some numbers. Barbara Christian, in contrast, who spoke first at the noon forum, mourned the fact that young Black women are not even going into literary criticism these days and that, overall, Black Ph.D.'s in 1991 were below the level they had been at in the seventies. She spoke, therefore, not of filial ingratitude but of the need for taking care, lest there be no more generations of Black feminist literary critics to come.

The first generation of second-wave white feminist literary critics,[1] of course, has been critically and theoretically decentered not only by young white feminists, on occasion, but by the critiques of mainstream feminism on the part of feminists of color our age and younger. The latter is a decentering with which few of us would argue. Still, the pain of ungrateful, white daughters, "wiping the floor with your work," as Showalter put it, and then "asking for a letter of recommendation," may evoke the experience of losing other familial ties as well, such as the (illusory) sisterhood of the seventies, which once promised loving bonds across racial and sexual divides and which failed utterly to prepare us for the very notion of feminist generations.[2]

Despite the fact, moreover, that many first-generation feminists, white feminists and feminists of color, have come to embrace more current models of political community that self-consciously renounce the stable "passion of community" implied by so many sixties and seventies political metaphors, "sisterhood" and "the beloved community" (though perhaps not "a band of brothers standing in a circle of love") still resonate at times with the seductive promise of commitment, shared joy in struggle, and what bell hooks calls "home."[3] For all their other virtues these are not the qualities promised by more current metaphors of impermanent alliance across shifting identities and moving sites.

Back (but Also Forward) to the Future: The Return of the Father and the Birth of New Collectivities

Growing old with the women's movement has to account not only for anniversary occasions, such as the one I have described, with its stories of celebration, wound, and loss, but, at least in part, for the revival of autobiographical criticism among some feminist literary critics and for the current proliferation of anthologies of academic lives.[4] There is, among feminist veterans of twenty-five years or so, an understandable desire to construct historical memory, to tell our stories from our own perspectives before less sympathetic accounts are generated from the Packard Bells of those who were barely "there" when we first wrote second-wave feminist scholarship on our Smith Coronas. This narration of the past, however, while it serves to give voice to our own versions of our histories and to press the claims of our historical significance, may have less defensive purposes as well. It may serve as an exercise in constructing the history not only of our achievements and our losses but also of our failings and our errors. It may serve not only as a means of rethinking the past but as a preparation for, and a means of entry into, a different future.

Unfortunately, for academic feminists these days the future doesn't often look that good. On the national front antifeminist/antipolitical-correctness rhetoric has been displaced by far more pointed assaults on feminism by spokespersons for conservative and centrist "family values." Feminists have become a threat, not just to the academy, but to "the family" and to the national community, which the family is made to stand for.[5] Centrists, for example, often implicitly blame feminism for the "selfishness" of adults (read: female adults) who put their career satisfactions ahead of the nation's children and so jeopardize both familial and national well-being. According to David Blankenhorn, "the goals of women (and of men too) in the workplace are primarily individualistic: social recognition, wages, opportunities for advancement and self-fulfillment. But the family is about collective goals."[6] Rightists blame feminism for the high divorce rate, which began, of course, before the second wave broke, and for the proliferation of single mothers who, along with the social programs of the sixties and the "pathology" of Black, lower-class families, are held responsible for the rise in poverty, juvenile delinquency, drugs, crime, and most other social ills.

One of the "solutions" offered for our social woes, by the center and the right, is the restoration of a strong, male authority. On the personal and individual level this takes the shape of newly responsible fathers for "fatherless families." David Blankenhorn, for example, names "fatherlessness" as "our most urgent social problem," and Jay Lefkovitz, citing Blankenhorn, notes "an epidemic of fatherless families" and warns that "more than 70% of juveniles in state reform institutions come from fatherless homes."[7] (William Safire, meanwhile, reminds us that responsible fatherhood has a price: "Fathers who make the family effort need recognition as 'head' of a household.")[8]

Nationally, strong male authority takes the ungainly form of Newtly aggressive Republican patriarchs bent on cutting benefits to poor women and children as a means of asserting "responsible" leadership in a weakly fathered state. (Doonesbury currently represents Clinton as a floating waffle and Newt Gringrich as a levitating time bomb with a short, and burning, fuse.) In California, meanwhile, our governor, Pete Wilson, having cut benefits to the poor children of his own locality, having campaigned for governor on the back of Proposition 187, which would deny public education to the children of illegal immigrants, and having helped decimate the University of California (UC) system for generations of students to come, prepares to cap his career of abusive, fatherly attention by running for president on an anti-affirmative-action platform. More locally, as the anti-affirmative-action waters rise (natural disasters aren't our only problem here in the Golden State) our campus at UC, Davis witnesses an emboldened resurgence of conservative patriarchy as a group of highly organized economics and agricultural economics professors work, night and day evidently (what has happened, one wonders, to their research?), to prevent the campus Committee on Academic Personnel from investigating the provocative indicators of gender inequity in our pay.[9]

While academic feminist communities, therefore, appear at times to resemble dysfunctional (female-headed) households or simply merge at others into masculinist academic cultures of competition and attack, the antifeminist Right duly cites fatherless families as the source of all our social problems and urges the restoration of a (kinder, gentler) paternal authority as the cure. The politics of this return to the father, of course, are as deeply rooted in the politics of class and race as in the politics of gender. The return to the father and to the family, for example, serves to focus national attention on the individual familial sphere while obscuring the operation of larger forces such as global capitalism and economic restructuring and the impact of such conservative social and economic policies as massive tax breaks for the rich and devastating cuts in welfare for the poor. By the same token, family values rhetoric, in targeting poor, "fatherless," Black families, in particular, manages to blame the structural inequities produced by these forces on the most powerless of their victims. The intersection of gender politics with the politics of class, race, and sexu-

ality (gays and lesbians are also viciously scapegoated for "family decline") has seldom been so transparent or so threatening. Seldom has
broad alliance across identities seemed so obvious a necessity.

The usual identities, moreover, once indicators at least of potential
lines of alliance and fighting back, have become increasingly empty
signifiers. A Black UC regent, Ward Connerly, leads the anti-affirmative-
action forces on the state level. (Blacks should forget the past two
hundred years of American history, he asserted, at a recent campus
conference on affirmative action, and "just start over.") A self-identified white feminist administrator presiding over the downsizing and
reorganization of our College of Letters and Sciences announces that
small, and once protected, programs like ethnic and women's studies
will henceforth be expected to compete with larger departments, and
with each other, to prove that they are strong and "productive" enough
to survive.[10]

The one hopeful development in this era of conservative, free-mar-
ket ideologies and shifting charters—once a planned economy, our
campus has been declared a "free" market zone—is that new alliances
have begun to solidify. On the Davis campus, for example, women's,
ethnic, and American studies, already partially bonded through years
of negotiating with the administration to secure joint appointments,
have thrown in their lot together and have proposed themselves as a
separate section in the newly created Division of Humanities and Arts.
We are to be called "cultural studies." Multiple and historical meetings have ensued as feminists, men of color, and white liberal men
take turns at being leaders and framers of this new political bloc. A
young white feminist proposes a federation between the newly designated cultural studies programs for the purpose of creating shared
lower-division courses and a graduate program. The faculty of women's
studies begins to discuss the pros and cons of remaining autonomous
or merging with a new cultural studies department. The potentially
federated programs agree to regular meetings and perhaps a retreat
for the purposes of sorting out their mutual political and academic
fortunes. They form voting blocs for the purpose of combating the
right-wing turn in campus politics.

In embattled, regressive, but also paradigm-shifting contexts such
as these the familiar tensions of ungrateful daughters and wounded
mothers and the imperative always to mistrust white brothers (as in
the, not unreasonable, fear that cultural studies might translate into

a new sphere of paternal influence for white, leftist men) lose some of their past meaning and significance. The relational tasks of building brave new collectivities begin to efface somewhat the family drama of feminist sisters and generations, which, while meaningful and often deeply felt, needs continually to be assessed within the context of that larger and more threatening set of "family values" now being multiply enacted in national and local scenes.

The Seventies Revisited: A Second Look at Brothers

The cross-race, cross-gender collectivities that have emerged momentarily or more permanently in study groups, conferences, and cultural studies programs in California often have about them an air of openness and good will, although I suspect the emotional work of forging ongoing alliances will be far from easy. Despite the openness and good cheer, for example, our experience at Davis has already demonstrated that old histories and antagonisms still lurk. If we are to pursue broader alliances in earnest, some of these histories and antagonisms may need to be encountered, revisited, and rethought. It was, in fact, three years prior to the emergence of the collectivities that I have described above that my collaborator, Judith Stacey, and I began, as part of a larger project, to reassess the history between white feminists and white, progressive men.[11] Our rethinking of this past took the form of an oral history project on the political and intellectual journeys of radical, academic men, who, like ourselves, had been actively involved in sixties politics and who had made some translation of their politics into their published work.

We undertook this project for many reasons—most of which we have detailed elsewhere[12]—but central to our interest and our motivations were several features of our "growing old." We felt the need, for example, to take stock of what feminist and antiracist political struggles over the past twenty-five years had meant—the meanings of such struggles being tied to their effects on the minds and hearts of those whom one has struggled with. Having survived the Reagan-Bush era, we were convinced that broad political alliances were overdue. We were heartened, moreover, by our positive interactions with some male feminists and by our consciousness of the support that even white, liberal men on our campus have often given to women's and ethnic studies. Finally, we felt a greater humility about ourselves than in the past, a humility induced by the long critique of mainstream feminism by women of color, by the backlash and regressions of the Reagan/Bush era, and by the mellowing in time of some earlier rigidities.

Like many studies of an "Other," our study of white, progressive men produced unlooked-for insights into ourselves. As we strained to attend to the stories of these br/others who seemed at once so familiar to us and so unknown, as we tried to "see" male counterparts anew, we came unexpectedly on the dimly familiar features of the white seventies feminists we no longer thought we were and, indeed, were unaware, in many ways, that we had ever been. Much of what we encountered there did not bode well for political alliance no matter what the era or the identity of the potential ally. I want to describe some of our observations here for the bearing that they have not just on potential crossgender alliances of the future but for their bearing on female, feminist relations of the past and present.

From the moment we began gathering oral histories from white, heterosexually identified, progressive, academic men we began to encounter what, in retrospect, I might call white, feminist, narcissistic assumption. We had assumed, for example, that we had a good idea of what the men we interviewed would say about their first encounters with the women's movement. We had expected to hear narratives about feminist "impact," about previously concealed shock, anxiety, outrage, and possibly liberatory excitement as well. What we encountered, much to our initial confusion and dismay, was a species of rather daunting fem-amnesia: "Could we have talked about it (feminism) and I not remembered?" "It's a blank, an interesting blank." (A dramatic contrast, this, to our own and other white, female feminist narratives of feminist revolutionary awakening: "The scales fell from my eyes.")[13] From the beginning of our entrance into "the field" the narratives we elicited directly challenged and ultimately rewrote our initial egocentric assumption about early feminist "impact." We were not so central to the lives of our white male br/others as we had assumed. Was it our whiteness, we began to wonder, as well as our gender naïveté that permitted us to assume, indeed to expect, that the news of our subordination, along with that of women differently raced and classed, would seem as revolutionary a cause as that of the raced and classed others that we and our white male peers had championed in the past?

Another of our tenaciously held assumptions was that any lack of feminist "impact," including the failure of many of our subjects to

incorporate feminist insights, before the late eighties, into their published work would have to be explained by male intransigence, an
intransigence most probably rooted in fear of women or in the egois-
tic pain of being decentered from the mother's gaze. Some of our interviews, to be sure, did suggest elements of all three in the histories
of our male peers. But male intransigence (while a familiar concept
in our personal and political histories with men!) began to seem an
overblown construction, a construction that, in fact, obscured many
things, like, for example, "difference," the different materialities and
discursive contexts of our subjects' lives. Many of the men we interviewed, for example, entered into their first jobs just as the political
movements in which they had been most involved—an integrated civil
rights movement, the student and antiwar movements—were ending
or winding down and as feminism was just beginning to take off. For
many of these men entering into the establishment functioned as a
moment of shifting gears. If they did not exactly leave their politics
behind, they organized their energies rather differently, focusing less
on challenging "the establishment" than on securing some stable position within it.

For progressive men, therefore, entering into the academy had a
different political valence from what it had for female feminists. For
the latter, entering into a male-dominated academy seemed itself a
revolutionary act, a mode of changing and radicalizing a mainstream
institution. Taking one's first job was less likely to signify leaving
politics behind than to offer the mixed blessing of making a career of
political struggle. Publishing, moreover, meant both less and more for
women than it did for men. Since publishing in respectable, established
discursive slots offered fewer rewards in the seventies to women than
it did to men, writing feminist work, being unrespectable as female
feminists, could seem worth the risk. In the world of academia for
white men the stakes were different. The rewards for publishing re-
spectably were potentially quite high, and although discursive slots
for antiracist, anti-imperialist, even anticapitalist positions on the part
of white men had some historical precedent and validation, gender dis-
loyalty seemed, for many of our subjects, beyond the discursive pale.

Feminisms in the seventies, moreover, offered a set of narratives
that were very different, in some respects, from those offered by the
political movements in which our subjects had variously engaged. The
narratives of the civil rights and the antiwar movements, for exam-

ple, had focused on issues associated with the "public" sphere—imperialism, legal rights, economics—had privileged public and large-scale forms of protest, and had assumed male leadership. Feminisms, in contrast, focused on the personal and domestic sphere as well. Indeed, sexual politics, the politics of the personal, was a major emphasis of white mainstream feminism in the early seventies. Protests, moreover, were smaller scale while consciousness-raising groups, rather than mass meetings, were the primary form of organizing. Finally, the narratives of mainstream feminism cast white men in particular as "the enemy." As one of interviewees was to put it, there seemed no place in feminism for a man to "put his body on the line." Indeed, male bodies were not especially welcomed in the 'hoods where white seventies feminists hung out, while male publication on feminist themes was highly vulnerable to the damned-if-you-do-and-damned-if-you-don't conundrum of much white feminist response.[14]

White, feminist, narcissistic assumption also operated in our assessment of male response to feminist critique. It was our initial inclination, that is, to see the work on colonization in which many of our subjects engaged and in which they took on issues of power and authority in white Westerners of the past (implicitly male, white Westerners), as a form of anti-imperialist critique, of course, but also as a displaced, and therefore *illegitimate,* way of dealing with feminist and domestic antiracist politics. As some of our interviewees were later to suggest, the displacement part of this formula was not merely a fiction of our imaginations. Several of our subjects were aware, in hindsight, that displacement had been at work.[15] *Displaced* response, however, is not lack of response, as we were initially tempted to conclude. It is, more accurately, partial, and, most important perhaps, *not the response that we were looking for.*

If our subjects' amnesia and their critical displacement of feminism appeared to us at first a case of male intransigence, suspiciously evocative of anxiety over women and their power, harking back perhaps to male anxieties over all-powerful pre-Oedipal mothers, our own implicit assumption—that if men were not responding on our terms, there was no response at all—began to seem suspiciously tied to infantile emotion as well. It is not only men but female feminists whose politics may be informed by the unconscious, by the desire, the demand, the expectation, in this case, that politically intimate others will become for them the perfectly responsive being that they wished for from the moment of their entry into this world of loss.[16] Something of the wounded child, we began to feel, had entered into feminist insistence that if men did not respond in the terms that we were looking for, then male feminism was illusory or that men were perpetually underdeveloped beings who could not ever "get it right." Never mind that our terms have been somewhat uncertain at times even to ourselves and that our own feminism, not to mention that of our errant sisters, might sometimes have failed our own tests.

These modes of desiring, which it must be argued, much early white feminist discourse validated and encouraged, are not the burden of our generation alone. Many feminists, young and old, seem at times to treat each other as we were wont to treat white, progressive men — if your terms are not ours, your feminism is illusory. How is it that the (perpetually underdeveloped) proponents of that theoretical position can never "get it right?" How much infant-like desire has entered into the family drama of our relation not only to intransigent brothers but to hostile daughters, wounded mothers, and mean-spirited sisters with sharp tongues? How much are the familial metaphors by which we have defined political community accountable?[17]

Political Community at the Millennium: Does Growing Up Mean Leaving Home?

Jane Gallop, the fifth member of the anniversary forum on "Feminist Criticism Revisited: Where Are We Going? Where Have We Been?" while noting her pleasure at having been selected for the panel and thereby designated a "feminist old girl," duly authorized to engage in the "new phenomenon of taking backward glances at feminism," spent most of her allotted time in a series of reflections on why she had decided not to deliver the paper she had written. She had intended, Gallop explained, to examine feminist debates over the past few years in the interest of capturing something generalizable about feminist literary criticism, but the topic, she concluded, was "boring," if not impossible. Issues that seemed pressing ten short years ago now raised for her Lillian Robinson's classic question, "So what?" The very enterprise of her paper, moreover, presupposed an entity called feminist literary criticism that, given the diverse nature of the practice today, no longer seemed viable. A focus on gender, Gallop argued, had made unifying generalizations about feminist literary criticism seem possible but the nineties emphasis on multiplicity and difference made wholeness, an organizing pattern, seem no longer feasible or appropriate.

Gallop's characterization of feminist literary criticism seems applicable, in many ways, to the current moment in feminist constructions of political community as well. As with feminist literary criticism, the '90s emphasis on multiplicity and difference seems to have rendered unifying metaphors like sister or mother/daughterhood, with their implication of stability and sameness, obsolete. Tropes of travel, borderlands, fluidity, and change have become more current figures for political alliance. Much is gained, moreover, in making this discursive shift. A discourse of multiplicity and change pushes us to attend to difference, tensions, and contradictions within and among ourselves; it encourages us to sever politics from unified identities, to entertain the notion of coalition across old borders, to embrace several forms of political alliance, and to forgo the expectation that political allies will always, or ever, meet us on our terms. There is much here to rectify the limitations and blind spots of the past.

Are these, however, precisely the metaphors and models for community that will serve us best in the political struggles of the present and the future? In a national culture newly mobilized against social fragmentation, the decline of community, the fragility of family, and the rise of quick divorce, and in our own academic subcultures, where we are frequently beset by isolation, competition, lack of solidarity, and overwork, how widely compelling are metaphors that so thoroughly forgo the "passion of community" and so coolly reassert the tentative nature of all relationships?

The metaphors by which we name and attempt to construct political alliance at least deserve more attention in this time of flux not just because the old metaphors have broken down and new ones are in the making, not just because political alliances in the future must be broader and the relations they entail even more complex, but also because the racist, antifeminist, pro-corporate politics of the Right owe much of their continuing (and rapidly increasing) success to a nationally compelling rhetoric of what Linda Kintz has called "free floating affectivity."[18] Drawing on the symbolic capital of unanalyzed familial feelings, the Right's evocation of fear over the "decline" of the never-divorced, heterosexual "family" and its emphasis on restoring family through the reinstallation of a tender but authoritative fatherhood, have acted quite successfully to defuse critical distance about politics; to displace anxiety over the economy and the inequities of gender, race, and class; to direct national attention away from the operations of global capitalism, economic restructuring, and conservative social policies; to promote a return to traditional gender and sexual politics; to perpetuate racist scapegoating; and to glorify self-help and the fluidity of capital while denigrating any commitment to national, collective care. These ideological initiatives, of course, are being widely promoted in popular books and journalism by rightist and sometimes centrist "public intellectuals," often supported by or ensconced in well-funded think tanks and institutes.[19]

Identification of conservative politics with "family," moreover, has succeeded not just in forging what threatens to become a new ideological consensus, but in mobilizing voters and organizing grassroots political activity as well. Laura Stoker, for example, argues that as fundamentalism has become more aligned with politics, and as religious belief has become increasingly tied to voting patterns, "family values issues" (women's roles, the women's movement, abortion, gays, fundamentalism, and moral tradition) have come to define political cleavage in the United States. New Deal issues, she argues, are not having anything like this effect.[20] Conservative appeals to family, affectivity, and belonging, moreover, are more than symbolic. The Christian Right, in particular, provides many forms of community activity and support to families, from rituals of virginity, prayer and Bible groups, Christian men's gatherings, activities for children, parent training, marriage encounters, to grassroots activism and many forms of national political mobilization. It's enough to make you wonder, these days, what, in the context of all this, progressive and feminist political communities have to offer.

Clearly, one of our responses in our ongoing construction of political communities must be to put national politics on academic feminist and progressive scholarly agendas and to become more serious about writing for audiences beyond the walls of academe. It is time, perhaps, to take the step of actually becoming those public, "organic," intellectuals who are often praised in prose utterly impenetrable to audiences beyond our own discursive circles. It is important, too, that in the discursive communities of our work we take "family" issues — issues of personal relation, children, parenting, community — seriously. Judith Stacey, for example, has argued that one of the central tasks of feminism at the moment is to correct its own (now highly inaccurate) antifamilial image, to broaden the notion of "family" to include a multitude of affectional ties, and to press for policy decisions that are truly "pro-family" in making such ties easier to sustain.[21]

Perhaps part of our "homework" should also include renewed attention to the way we construct and represent political community, since the quality of community, as early feminists argued, does in fact have bearing on the numbers and motivation of those who belong — a fact that the old Left (like the new Right) seemed to have understood. It is crucial to give thought to the quality of our communities, our written, discursive communities, and the communities in which we (also discursively) engage with each other face to face, not only for the sake of swelling their membership, but for the sake of nourishing and giving energy and purpose to those of us who already belong. To take two examples of us at our worst: is the discursive slide in feminist literary criticism into haughty putdown and harsh critique a community tradition we want to preserve? Is the scorn with which attention to relationship and concern for comfort are sometimes regarded in communities on the academic Left an effective strategy for building alliances?

Constructing new paradigms of community, of course, may not be easy, and those already at work on them do not agree. On the one hand, for example, bell hooks notes that the civil rights movement transformed society in the United States because it was fundamentally rooted in an ethic of love, and she argues for the creation of "life-sustaining" "communities of resistance" that offer intimacy and space for the renewal of the spirit. Communities such as these can "happen only if we address the needs of the spirit in progressive political theory and practice."[22] One of hooks's metaphors for the desired bonds of intimacy and solidarity, bonds that always include progressive men, is "a sense of home," but a transformed home without the traditional patterns of domination (213).

Home, however, is too laden a term for others. Iris Young, indeed, argues that the word *community* itself is problematic in that it "relies on the same desire for social wholeness and identification that underlies racism and ethnic chauvinism on the one hand and political sectarianism on the other."[23] Young also warns against making "mutual friendship" a group goal in that people "find themselves wanting as a group if they do not achieve such commonality." "Such a desire for community," she continues, "channels energy away from the political goals of the groups and also produces a clique atmosphere which keeps groups small and turns potential members away" (312). Nancie Caraway offers a middle position in which she calls for "a more solid solidarity" based on relations between feminists who "don't love each other."[24] For Caraway feminist alliance might take the form of a "mediated community of feminist strangers" marked by "openness to unassimilated otherness," "mutual respect," and conflict without "savagery" (199, 203). This "crossover politics" would entail "multicultural coalitions without domination in which persons live together in relations of mediation among feminists with whom they are not in sisterhood but solidarity" (199, 201). I myself might prefer what Sheila Rowbotham once called greater "cosiness" than this, something involving communal dining, socialist volleyball, a sense of humor, wine at twilight, and comforting food.[25] Indeed, I resonate most fully with hooks, with her metaphors of "home" and spirit, with her evocation of a newly made "beloved community," bound together by "commonality of feeling" such as "love of a more just society," yearning for change, and joy in struggle. But I am a woman of a certain age and a veteran of the sixties. My preferences are deeply marked by the discursive histories I have moved through. What is needed now is to think across the affective investments and discursive predilections of generations, as well as those of race and now gender, too. What kinds of community can meet the political challenges of the Right, with its frightening infrastructure of well-funded think tanks, training institutes, foundations, legal centers, and grassroots organizations and with its current discursive monopoly on community and affectivity? What can sustain and nourish us as we face the end, and also the beginning, of another century?

Notes

1. Alice Jardine outlines four generations of feminist scholars: those who received their doctorate before 1968, those who received it 1968–1978, 1978–1988, and 1988–1998. Cited in Darlene M. Hantzis and Devoney Looser, "Of Safe(r) Spaces and 'Right' Speech," in *PC Wars: Politics and Theory in the Academy*, ed. Jeffrey Williams (New York: Routledge, 1995), 226. I am using *first generation* to refer to the first two categories.

2. It is hard to assess the degree of cross-generational tension. My own experience and the experience of many colleagues with graduate students on our campus, for example, has been overwhelmingly positive. Our students seem like young colleagues much of the time, although there is a good deal of nurturing and support on the part of faculty, which we faculty sometimes construct as maternal.

3. This was a term applied to the Student Non-Violent Coordinating Committee. See Todd Gitlin, *The Sixties: Years of Hope, Days of Rage* (New York: Bantam, 1987), 107; bell hooks, *Yearning: Race, Gender, and Cultural Politics* (Boston: South End Press, 1990), 214.

4. See, for example, Nancy K. Miller, *Getting Personal: Feminist Occasions and Other Autobiographical Acts* (New York: Routledge, 1991); Gayle Greene and Coppelia Kahn, eds., *Changing Subjects: The Makings of Feminist Literary Criticism* (New York: Routledge, 1993); Patricia Bell Scott, *Life Notes: Personal Writings by Contemporary Black Women* (New York: W. W. Norton, 1994); Ann Goetting and Sarah Fenstermaker, eds., *Individual Voices, Collective Visions: Fifty Years of Women in Sociology* (Philadelphia: Temple University Press, 1995).

5. Cary Nelson and Michael Bérubé point out that the attack on political correctness has not gone away but that the terrain of debate has shifted. Rather than trying to convince a sufficient fraction of the American public that their children are being taught by radicals, "the University's critics are now trying to convince the American public that their children aren't being taught at all," Cary Nelson and Michael Bérubé, "Introduction," in their *Higher Education under Fire: Politics, Economics, and the Crisis of the Humanities* (New York: Routledge, 1995), 6.

6. David Blankenhorn, "American Family Dilemmas," in *Rebuilding the Nest: A New Commitment to the American Family,* ed. David Blankenhorn, Jean Bethke Elshtain, and Steven Bayme (Milwaukee: Family Service American, 1990), 91.

7. David Blankenhorn, *Fatherless America: Confronting Our Most Urgent Social Problem* (New York: Basic Books, 1995); Jay Lefkovitz, "Where Dad Belongs," *Wall Street Journal,* June 18, 1993.

8. William Safire, "What Fathers Want," *New York Times,* June 16, 1994, A17.

9. An initial commissioned study by a feminist statistician indicated disparities of $10,000 and more in the pay of male and female faculty. Members of the economics and agricultural economics departments challenged the study and demanded that a new study be completed before any investigations were conducted by the College Committee on Academic Personnel. Their efforts to block the committee's investigations have resulted in a yearlong series of skirmishes in the Faculty Senate.

10. For an account of higher education budget cuts and downsizing nationally see Paul Lauter, "Political Correctness," in Nelson and Bérubé, *Higher Education,* 73–90.

11. Our large project included men of color, gays, and men younger than forty-five.

12. See Judith Newton and Judith Stacey, "Learning Not to Curse or Feminist Predicaments in Cultural Criticism by Men: Our Movie Date with James Clifford and Stephen Greenblatt," *Cultural Critique* 23 (Winter 1993):51–82; "Ms. Representations: Reflections on Studying Academic Men," in *Women Writing Culture,* ed. Ruth Behar and Deborah Gordon (Berkeley and Los Angeles: University of California Press, forthcoming); "The Men We Left Behind Us, or Reading Our Br/others: Narratives around and about Feminism from the Works and Lives of Left Wing Academic Men," in *Sociology and Cultural Studies,* ed. Elizabeth Long (London: Blackwell, forthcoming). See also Judith Newton, "Family/Value: Reflections on a Long Revolution," *Victorian Studies* 37 (Summer 1994): 567–81.

13. This is from one of our narratives. See also Rachel Blau DuPlessis, "Reader I Married Me," in *Changing Subjects,* ed. Greene and Kahn, 101, who uses the same term.

14. I am far from wanting to deny or to underestimate the role of progressive men's intransigence, their fear of and rage at women, or their varying investments in unequal power, but I am conscious of feeling, too, that feminism cannot be a political movement for women only and that it is not male intransigence alone that must ac-

count for the fact that female feminists have had to write the founding narratives of critical gender analysis, sexual politics, and familial and social revolution in language and in terms almost entirely of their own.

15. Some spoke of fearing that the person you offended would be sitting across the table.

16. See Gitlin, *The Sixties,* on sixties politics and the "primitive fantasy of fusion with a symbolic, all-enfolding mother: the movement, the beloved community itself, where we might be able to find, in Kenneth Keniston's words, 'the qualities of warmth, communion, acceptedness, dependence and intimacy which existed in childhood" (107).

17. See on this point Evelyn Fox Keller and Helene Moglen, "Competition and Feminism: Conflicts for Academic Women," *Signs: Journal of Women in Culture and Society* 12 (1987): 495; Jane Gallop, Marianne Hirsch, and Nancy K. Miller, "Criticizing Feminist Criticism," in *Conflicts in Feminism,* ed. Marianne Hirsch and Evelyn Fox Keller (New York: Routledge, 1990), 366; Madelon Sprengnether, "Generational Differences: Reliving Mother-Daughter Conflicts," in *Changing Subjects,* ed. Greene and Kahn, 201; and Hantzis and Looser, "Of Safe(r) Spaces," 236.

18. Linda Kintz, "Between Jesus and the Market: or Looking Again at the Church Lady," unpublished paper, 1994.

19. For an account of this funding in the attack on PC, see Ellen Messer-Davidow, "Manufacturing the Attack on Liberalized Higher Education," *Social Text* 36 (1993): 40–80.

20. Stoker's remarks were made during a panel on welfare and family politics at UC, Davis, April 24, 1995.

21. See Judith Stacey, "Scents, Scholars, and Stigma: The Revisionist Campaign for Family Values," *Social Text* 40 (Fall 1994).

22. hooks, *Yearning,* 244.

23. Iris Marion Young, "The Ideal of Community and the Politics of Difference," in *Feminism/Postmodernism,* ed. Linda J. Nicholson (New York: Routledge), 302.

24. Nancie Caraway, *Segregated Sisterhood: Racism and the Politics of American Feminism* (Knoxville: University of Tennessee Press, 1991), 199.

25. Like hooks, Rowbotham argued for the importance of "personal care and love" in political community: "The fear seems to be that cosiness means people get cut off from the 'real' politics. I think this should be put the other way round. If a version of socialism is insisted upon which banishes cosiness, given the attachment of most people, working-class men and women included, to having a fair degree of it around in their lives, this socialism will not attract or keep most people. Why should the ruling class have a monopoly of cosiness?" "The Women's Movement and Organizing for Socialism," in *Beyond the Fragments: Feminism and the Making of Socialism,* ed. Sheila Rowbotham, Lynne Segal, and Hilary Wainwright (London: Merlin Press, 1979), 81, 67–68.

Contributors

Diane Elam is professor of English and critical and cultural theory at the University of Wales, Cardiff. She is the author of *Romancing the Postmodern* and *Feminism and Deconstruction: Ms. en Abyme*, as well as the coeditor with Robyn Wiegman of *Feminism beside Itself*.

Elizabeth Francis is visiting assistant professor in American civilization and women's studies at Brown University, where she teaches women's history and modernist studies. Her scholarship examines the relation between feminism and modernism in America.

Linda Frost is assistant professor of English at the University of Alabama at Birmingham. She publishes on eighteenth- and nineteenth-century American literary and popular cultures and is currently completing a manuscript on national identity in popular nineteenth-century American periodicals.

Jane Gallop teaches in modern studies, an interdisciplinary graduate program at the University of Wisconsin, Milwaukee. She has recently edited a collection titled *Pedagogy: The Question of Impersonation*. Her latest books are *Around 1981: Academic Feminist Literary Theory* and *Feminist Accused of Sexual Harassment*.

Dana Heller teaches American literature, literary theory, and gender studies at Old Dominion University. Her most recent book is *Family Plots: The De-Oedipalization of Popular Culture*. She is also the coeditor of *Cross Purposes: Lesbian Studies, Feminist Studies, and the Limits of Alliance*.

Jane Kalbfleisch teaches English and women's studies at Wilfrid Laurier University and the University of Waterloo in Ontario. Her dissertation, "Of Feminism Born: The Constitution of the Feminist Subject in the Second Wave," completed at Emory University in 1997, explores the inscription of several subject positions in contemporary feminist theory. Her article "See Jane Play, See Dick (Run)," an analysis of feminist and postmodern pedagogies, appeared in *Border/Lines* 22 (1991): 32–37.

E. Ann Kaplan is director of the Humanities Institute at the State University of New York at Stony Brook, where she is also professor of English and comparative literature. Kaplan has written widely on psychoanalysis, women in film, television, cultural studies, feminist theory, and postmodernism. Her books include *Women in Film: Both Sides of the Camera, Rocking around the Clock: Music Television, Postmodernism, and Consumer Culture,* and *Motherhood and Representation.* She is the editor of *Regarding Television, Postmodernism and Its Discontents,* and *Psychoanalysis and Cinema.* Her most recent book, *Looking for the Other: Feminism, Film and the Imperial Gaze,* appeared in the spring of 1997.

Devoney Looser is assistant professor of English and women's studies at Indiana State University. She is the editor of *Jane Austen and Discourses of Feminism* and the author of articles on feminist theories, British women's writings of the eighteenth century, and contemporary popular film.

Jeanne Marecek is professor of psychology and women's studies at Swarthmore College. Her work draws on feminist theory and postmodern thought to interrogate the constructs and practices of psychology to propose alternative ways of producing knowledge about gender. Trained as a clinical psychologist, she is currently studying the practices by which feminist therapists reconcile the person-centered ideology of psychotherapy with feminist ideals of social change. She has spent several years in Sri Lanka, studying the social meanings and public discourses connected to suicide. She is coauthor (with Rachel T. Hare-Mustin) of *Making a Difference: Psychology and the Construction of Gender* (1990).

Nancy K. Miller is Distinguished Professor of English at Lehman College and the City University of New York Graduate School. Her most recent book is *Bequest and Betrayal: Memoirs of a Parent's Death*.

Mona Narain is assistant professor of English literature at Otterbein College. Her current research is on British eighteenth-century studies and women's studies.

Angela M. S. Nelson is assistant professor in the Department of Popular Culture at Bowling Green State University, where she received her Ph.D. in American culture studies. She has taught popular culture, ethnic studies, music, and television and has contributed to *Popular Culture: An Introductory Text, Black Sacred Music: A Journal of Theomusicology,* and *Christian History*. She is the editor of the forthcoming book *This Is How We Flow: Rhythm in Black Cultures,* and she has work forthcoming in *Signature Songs and Rhythms: Cultural and Physiological Aspects of African-American Music*. She is currently studying the history of African Americans in television situation comedy during the civil rights era.

Judith Newton is professor and director of women's studies at the University of California, Davis. Author of *Starting Over: Feminism and the Politics of Cultural Critique,* she is working on men, masculinities, and change in the 1990s.

Rebecca Dakin Quinn received her M.A. in English literature from the University of New Hampshire in 1994. She teaches English at Baruch College in New York City. She is enrolled in the Ph.D. program in English at the City University of New York Graduate School, where she is also completing the certificate program in women's studies.

Gita Rajan, who is working on a project that examines the pleasure of play in Indian aesthetic traditions, was an Andrew Mellon Fellow in the Humanities at the University of Pennsylvania and had a fellowship at the Yale Center for British Art. She is the coeditor of *A Cultural Studies Reader: History, Theory, and Practice, Postcolonial Discourse and Changing Cultural Contexts,* and *English Postcoloniality: Literatures from around the World*. She has published in the areas of postcolonial theory and fiction, Victorian studies, and film studies. She teaches Victorian literature, cultural studies, and post-colonial discourse at Fairfield University in Connecticut.

Judith Roof teaches English and feminist critical studies at Indiana University, Bloomington. She is the author of *A Lure of Knowledge: Lesbian Sexuality and Theory, Come As You Are: Sexuality and Narrative,* and *Reproductions of Reproduction: Imaging Symbolic Change* and coeditor (with Robyn Wiegman) of *Who Can Speak? Authority and Critical Identity.*

Theresa Ann Sears is associate professor of Spanish language and literature in the Department of Foreign Languages and Literatures at the University of Missouri, St. Louis. She received her Ph.D. from Cornell University and is the author of *A Marriage of Convenience: Ideal and Ideology in the Novelas Ejemplares,* a study of Miguel de Cervantes's novellas. She has also written on medieval and Golden Age literature and is at work on a two-volume study of the sentimental mode of European fiction.

Ruthe Thompson is completing her dissertation on mothers, subjectivity, and the novel at the University of Arizona. Her work explores processes of subject production in and through the narrative in the novels of Henry Fielding, Jane Austen, Harriet Beecher Stowe, and Henry James, and the periodical press.

Michele Wallace is the author of *Black Macho and the Myth of the Superwoman* and *Invisibility Blues: From Pop to Theory.* She is associate professor of English, women's studies, and cinema studies at the City College of New York and the City University of New York Graduate School.

Barbara A. White has recently edited *Wharton's New England: Seven Stories and "Ethan Frome."* A literary historian, she is the author of several books on American women writers, and she teaches women's studies at the University of New Hampshire.

Lynda Zwinger considers herself a member of the Notch Generation of Feminist Academics. She is associate professor of English at the

University of Arizona, where she is also affiliated with women's studies and comparative cultural and literary studies. Her recent work includes essays on the queering of Henry James, the Tonya Harding-Nancy Kerrigan knee-bashing spectacle, and aliens and other mothers. Her current book project is titled "Violence and the Maternal: Locational Politics and Cultural Identities."

Index